FOREWORD

The *World Energy Outlook 1998*, based on a new world energy model, considers energy demand and supply for ten world regions over the period to 2020. Our aim is not to foretell the future - the uncertainties are too great for that. Instead, we see this publication as an opportunity to identify and discuss the main energy issues that could arise over this period. We use a business as usual projection as a basis for this discussion.

For the analysis of energy demand, we have used the concept of *energy-related services*. Four such services are identified: electricity, mobility, fossil fuel use in stationary energy services and power generation. For most world regions, energy consumption in these energy-related services has closely followed the pattern of economic activity. Throughout the book, we chart past data and our future projections to demonstrate their consistency in a simple and transparent manner.

Because the Outlook now projects twenty-five years ahead, we have paid particular attention to the relationship between cumulative oil production to date and estimates of oil reserves. Our analysis of the current evidence suggests that world oil production from conventional sources could peak during the period 2010 to 2020. There will be no shortage of liquid fuels if this happens because reserves of unconventional oil are large; but some instability and a possible rise in the world oil price could accompany this transfer from conventional to unconventional oil for additional supplies. This is a highly controversial subject among experts in the field. Most past forecasts of reserve limitations on oil production have proved wrong. We do not see our analysis as a forecast but, again, as a way of raising the subject for serious debate.

Our work on natural gas suggests no reserve limitations on production at world level before 2020, although increasing use of unconventional gas in North America is likely.

Analysis of the policies needed to meet the commitments entered into at the 1997 Kyoto Conference is being undertaken by many agencies around the world. In this Outlook, we include *illustrative* calculations of the scale of the task, using either regulatory or market mechanisms. This is a limited study that takes no account of the many flexibility mechanisms that have been proposed.

This work is published under my authority as Executive Director of the IEA and does not necessarily reflect the views or policies of the IEA Member countries.

Robert Priddle
Executive Director

HD9502 WOR

INTERNATIONAL

DATE DUE FOR RETURN

V
E
C

19

INTERNATIONAL ENERGY AGENCY
9, rue de la Fédération, 75739 Paris cedex 15, France

The International Energy Agency (IEA) is an autonomous body which was established in November 1974 within the framework of the Organisation for Economic Co-operation and Development (OECD) to implement an international energy programme.

It carries out a comprehensive programme of energy co-operation among twenty-four * of the OECD's twenty-nine Member countries. The basic aims of the IEA are:

i) co-operation among IEA participating countries to reduce excessive dependence on oil through energy conservation; development of alternative energy sources and energy research and development;

ii) an information system on the international oil market as well as consultation with oil companies;

iii) co-operation with oil producing and other oil consuming countries with a view to developing a stable international energy trade as well as the rational management and use of world energy resources in the interest of all countries;

iv) a plan to prepare participating countries against the risk of a major disruption of oil supplies and to share available oil in the event of an emergency.

IEA participating countries are: Australia, Austria, Belgium, Canada, Denmark, Finland, France, Germany, Greece, Hungary, Ireland, Italy, Japan, Luxembourg, the Netherlands, New Zealand, Norway (by special agreement), Portugal, Spain, Sweden, Switzerland, Turkey, the United Kingdom, the United States. The Commission of the European Communities takes part in the work of the IEA.

ORGANISATION FOR ECONOMIC CO-OPERATION AND DEVELOPMENT

Pursuant to Article 1 of the Convention signed in Paris on 14th December 1960, and which came into force on 30th September 1961, the Organisation for Economic Co-operation and Development (OECD) shall promote policies designed:

- to achieve the highest sustainable economic growth and employment and a rising standard of living in Member countries, while maintaining financial stability, and thus to contribute to the development of the world economy;

- to contribute to sound economic expansion in Member as well as non-member countries in the process of economic development; and

- to contribute to the expansion of world trade on a multilateral, non-discriminatory basis in accordance with international obligations.

The original Member countries of the OECD are Austria, Belgium, Canada, Denmark, France, Germany, Greece, Iceland, Ireland, Italy, Luxembourg, the Netherlands, Norway, Portugal, Spain, Sweden, Switzerland, Turkey, the United Kingdom and the United States. The following countries became Members subsequently through accession at the dates indicated hereafter: Japan (28th April 1964), Finland (28th January 1969), Australia (7th June 1971), New Zealand (29th May 1973), Mexico (18th May 1994), the Czech Republic (21st December 1995), Hungary (7th May 1996). Poland (22nd November 1996) and the Republic of Korea (12th December 1996). The Commission of the European Communities takes part in the work of the OECD (Article 13 of the OECD Convention).

ACKNOWLEDGEMENTS

This Outlook has been prepared by a team led by Ken Wigley, Head of the Economic Analysis Division of the IEA. The members of the team were Fatih Birol, Keith Miller, Atsuhito Kurozumi, Maria Argiri and Sylvie Lambert D'Apote. The manuscript was prepared by Faye Bouré and Anne Brady.

The team members have drawn on reports and discussions with a wide range of experts, especially our IEA colleagues in the following offices: Long Term Cooperation and Policy Analysis; Non-Member Countries; Energy Efficiency, Technology and Research and Development; Oil Markets and Emergency Preparedness; Energy Statistics and Information Systems. We have been guided and encouraged in our work by the Director of the Long-Term Office, Jean-Marie Bourdaire. We are grateful for discussions with the many experts who attended the three IEA Workshops on Demand Modelling, Power Generation Modelling and Oil Reserves in November 1997 and the two Workshops on Biomass Energy in February 1997 and March 1998. Of course, all errors and omissions remain our responsibility.

Comments and questions are welcome and should be addressed as follows:

On general topics and the regional chapters:

Fatih Birol   Telephone (33-1) 4057.6670
               E-mail   Fatih.Birol@IEA.ORG

On fossil fuel supply:

Keith Miller   Telephone (33-1) 4057.6671
               E-mail   Keith.Miller@IEA.ORG

On regional chapters:

Atsuhito Kurozumi   Telephone (33-1) 4057.6672
                     E-mail   Atsuhito.Kurozumi@IEA.ORG

On power generation:

Maria Argiri   Telephone (33-1) 4057.6675
               E-mail   Maria.Argiri@IEA.ORG

On biomass:

Sylvie Lambert D'Apote Telephone (33-1) 4057.6507
                       E-mail   Sylvie.Lambert@IEA.ORG

Address: International Energy Agency
               9, rue de la Fédération
               75739 Paris cedex 15 - France
               Fax: (33-1) 4057.6659

TABLE OF CONTENTS

Boxes   Page

Tables

Figures

EXECUTIVE SUMMARY

This Outlook aims to identify and discuss the main issues and uncertainties affecting world energy demand and supply over the period to 2020. It does so in the framework of a "business as usual" projection which assumes energy policies existing before the Kyoto Conference of December 1997 remain in place and that no new policies are adopted to reduce energy-related greenhouse gases.

The Outlook projects world energy demand to grow by 65% and CO_2 emissions by 70% between 1995 and 2020 unless such new policies are put in place. It assumes a rate of world economic growth of 3.1% p.a. (1990 US dollars and purchasing power parity), close to the actual rate since 1971. Two-thirds of the increase in energy demand over the period 1995-2020 comes from China and other developing countries.

Fossil fuels are expected to meet 95% of additional global energy demand from 1995 to 2020. Oil is used increasingly to fuel rapidly growing demands for road and air transport. Coal remains important in power generation because of its low cost, when used near to producing areas, in both developed and developing countries. Where pipelines exist, or can be put in place, natural gas is the preferred fuel for many applications, especially for new power stations. Restructuring and facilitating the international transit of natural gas will need to be extended to allow the further use of gas worldwide. Reserves of both oil and natural gas will need to be further developed worldwide. This is especially the case in Russia and the Caspian Basin, where major opportunities will arise to supply European and Asian markets.

The oil-importing countries dependence on supplies from the Middle East will increase until liquid fuels from unconventional sources (shale oil, tar sands and conversion from coal, biomass or gas) begin to play an increasingly important role as 2020 approaches. Oil prices could rise during the course of this shift. With increased reliance on Middle East oil and the expected transition to the use of non-conventional liquid fuels, the probability of supply disruptions and price shocks could rise.

The Outlook shows the substantial reductions in CO_2 emissions that will be necessary to meet the commitments made at the Kyoto Conference. The commitments adopted there will affect the future growth and pattern of world energy demand. The challenge now is to identify policies that will ensure that these commitments are in fact met.

New policies will be required if the use of nuclear power and renewable energy sources is to help reduce fossil fuel consumption and greenhouse gas emissions. These policies would encourage the development of new designs for less costly nuclear power plants and find acceptable long-term solutions for radioactive wastes. Unit costs of renewable energy must be reduced and, in some cases, environmental problems posed by the renewables must be solved.

Energy intensity (energy use per unit of economic activity) will continue to fall, as in the past, through the introduction of new technologies, economic and industrial restructuring and the substitution of commercial for non-commercial fuels. These processes have already been taken into account in the projection. In the past, energy trends have been remarkably stable and so major new policies will be required to reduce energy intensity in order to stop the growth in CO_2 emissions. Some of these policies will tap the no-regret potential for reducing CO_2 emissions. All of these policies will need to take account of economic, social and political constraints.

Rapidly growing electricity demand and the need for climate-friendly technologies in non-OECD countries will require foreign investment as well as financing from domestic sources. This, in turn, may require restructuring, privatisation and regulatory changes in the electricity industries in these countries. The Kyoto Protocol and its further developments will encourage sustainable development projects that seek out the lowest cost means of abating CO_2 emissions in developing countries.

PART I

SUMMARY

CHAPTER 1
INTRODUCTION

A great many uncertainties surround future energy projections, especially those that look ahead as far as twenty five years. The main sources of these uncertainties range widely and include:

Economic output and structure, population growth. Projections of economic growth and population vary considerably, especially for developing countries. In the transition economies of the former Soviet Union and East and Central Europe, the pace of economic restructuring and the adoption of market economies are uneven, especially for major industrial sectors, and their future is uncertain.

Technical change and capital stock turnover. The nature and pace of technical change are inevitably uncertain. Furthermore, once new types of energy-using equipment become available, the extent to which they affect energy use, depends on the rate at which they are actually adopted and deployed.

Human attitudes and behaviour. As incomes rise, the demand for electrical appliances and heavier, more powerful cars may continue, or it may slacken off. In high income countries, some saturation in home heating may appear in the near future, but that is unlikely to be the case for air-conditioning. The extent and timing of these possible changes are uncertain.

Fossil fuel supplies and extraction costs. The magnitudes of economically recoverable reserves of oil and natural gas remain a matter of discussion and debate. The careful assessments of experts become dated as new technologies enable additional resources to be discovered and economically exploited. Production costs have been cut over the last decade with the application of new technologies and competitive pressures. Many believe that technical change will continue to develop, yielding increasing reserves and low production costs for many decades to come. Others believe that greater attention should be paid to the likelihood of diminishing reserves.

Energy market developments. Electricity and gas markets in many countries are undergoing restructuring, privatisation and shifting to more competitive structures. Their regulatory systems are being changed accordingly. Far-reaching alterations have been made in the United States and the United Kingdom, and many other countries have made moves in this direction. The details differ from one country to another. How far these changes will lead to more efficient industries and lower gas and electricity prices will take some time to determine.

Energy subsidies. In many developing countries, energy prices are set at levels well below the full cost of supply. This is especially true for electricity and some petroleum products. In some transition economies, heat and electricity are sold very cheaply. Over time, prices are expected to rise to cover the full cost of supply, or the corresponding import price, whichever is the lowest. This change will be necessary to make the supply industries financially viable, permit the privatisation of state-owned utilities and encourage foreign investment in energy supplies. It will also assist in reducing CO_2 emissions. But the timing of these changes is unknown and their effects on energy consumption are difficult to estimate.

Changing environmental objectives and policies. Governments have rapidly extended the environmental policies that affect energy, covering particulates, heavy metals, acid gases and greenhouse gases. Perhaps the greatest uncertainty currently affecting energy projections is that surrounding the policy choices that governments will make to meet the commitments they entered into in Kyoto.

Energy projections must take all these uncertainties into account. To present the results of an energy projection exercise, numerical estimates must be offered for future energy demand and supply. At the same time, the importance of all the associated uncertainties must be conveyed.

Business As Usual Projection

The objective of this book is not to state what the IEA believes will happen to the energy system in future. The IEA holds no such single view. Rather, the aim is to discuss the most important factors and uncertainties likely to affect the energy system over the period to 2020. The framework chosen is a "business as usual" (BAU) projection. This can be described as an illustration of how energy demand, supply and prices are likely to develop if recent trends and current policies continue. It specifically excludes the effect of new policies that may be adopted in order to meet the commitments taken at Kyoto. The BAU projection is presented by world region, by fuel type, by energy-related service and, in some cases by consuming sector. This is necessary in order to discuss the impacts of the main uncertain factors.

In fact, the IEA expects that the future for world energy will be quite different from that described in the BAU projection. This is partly because economic growth, energy prices, technology and consumer behaviour will turn out to be different from those assumed for the BAU projection. The most striking difference will most likely occur because governments in developed countries will want to change things, i.e. to reduce greenhouse gas emissions, particularly for CO_2.

Approach

The methods employed in preparing the projections are described in the following chapters and appendices. Energy demand has been analysed for each world region. Careful attention has been paid to past and projected energy consumption to provide four principal energy-related services:

- electrical services (total consumption of electricity by final consumers);
- mobility (non-electricity fuels consumed in all forms of transport);
- stationary services (mainly fossil fuels used for heating in buildings and industrial processes);
- fuels used in power generation.

Energy consumed in the first three of these energy-related services adds up to total demand by final energy consumers.

Transparency is achieved by providing graphs of energy consumption in each of these energy services as compared to income (gross domestic product) for both past and future periods. The purpose is to demonstrate that the methods used to project energy demand do not result in unexplained divergencies from past experience. Within the framework of the energy-related services, the impact of changes in economic activity and energy prices on energy demand have been estimated in some detail. For some non-OECD regions, energy price data are not readily available, thus limiting the scope of the analysis of energy demand.

A power generation model built for each region identifies the major electricity generation technologies and fuels available. This model is used to estimate, on a least-cost basis, the fuels required to generate the projected demand for electricity. Energy inputs into the other transformation processes (oil refineries, gas works, solid-fuel preparation plants and heat-only plants) are estimated separately.

Total world demands for the three fossil fuels, oil, gas and coal, are obtained by adding up the demands of final consumers, of power generation, of the other transformation sectors and changes in fuel stocks. The implications for fossil fuel supply are then considered.

A detailed model for conventional oil supply has been prepared that takes account of the likely increase in recoverable reserves of conventional oil arising from the reduction in uncertainties over time as new information becomes available on the extent and nature of the reserves and from the application of new technologies. The limitations imposed by finite recoverable reserves on the production of conventional oil are assessed, together with the implications for the production of non-conventional oil (e.g. shale oils and tar sands) towards 2020. Gas and coal supplies are projected separately on a regional basis. The relationships between fossil fuel prices and supply availabilities are discussed in the text, but not formally modelled. A study of biomass use (wood, animal waste and other wastes) has been carried out for developing countries.

Using this approach, the BAU projection provides energy balances for ten world regions and eight fuels, based on assumptions for economic growth, future population and world fossil fuel prices. Some calculations are made to illustrate the possible effects of varying the assumptions on economic growth and on the recoverable reserves of conventional oil.

Kyoto Analysis

In the BAU projection, CO_2 emissions grow rapidly within the OECD and in the world at large. It is not possible to prepare a projection that meets the Kyoto target because the countries involved have not yet announced the policies they intend to use. Instead, two stylised analyses have been undertaken. The first indicates the scale of regulation that would be required by OECD countries to meet their Kyoto commitments. The second indicates the "carbon value" that would need to be built into fossil fuel prices to meet the Kyoto commitments.

These two stylised analyses are very different from the approach used in the last World Energy Outlook published in 1996[1]. In that Outlook, an "energy savings" case provided an estimate of reductions in energy use that could be achieved by the application of cost effective technologies for additional energy savings through implied changes in the way consumers

1. *World Energy Outlook 1996 Edition*, IEA/OECD Paris, 1996.

make choices in the consumption of energy and other goods. The policies needed to bring these changes about were not specified.

Since that publication, the IEA has conducted three major modelling seminars on climate change policies[2]:

- "Economic and energy market impacts of implementing quantified emission and reduction objectives under the Framework Convention on Climate Change (FCCC)";
- "Closing the efficiency gap in energy responses to climate change: potential for cost-effective energy and carbon efficiency improvements";
- "Uncertainty and energy policy choices to meet UNFCCC objectives".

One of the main conclusions of the second seminar was the political difficulty of capturing the no-regret potential for reducing energy demand and energy-related CO_2 emissions. This difficulty arises because existing barriers to the take-up of the no-regret potential, involving subsidies, monopoly practices, etc., are part of the broad social consensus and difficult to change.

The two stylised approaches presented in this Outlook attempt to quantify the scale of the task of achieving the Kyoto commitments by OECD countries. They include, but are not limited to, capturing the no-regret potential for reducing energy-related CO_2 emissions.

---

2. *Insights from Modelling for Climate Change Policy,* IEA/OECD Paris, forthcoming.

CHAPTER 2
ASSUMPTIONS

This chapter discusses the main assumptions for economic growth, population and energy prices for the period 1995 to 2020. Actual data have been used, where available, for the early years of the period.

Economic Growth

Economic growth is arguably the most important driver of energy demand. Table 2.1 provides average economic growth rates for the ten world regions used in this Outlook. It compares growth rates for the past 25 years with assumptions made for the BAU projection and for low and high economic growth variants. The BAU assumption broadly continues the past world rate of economic growth. All regions are expected to experience slower growth in the future, except for the transition economies which are assumed to recover rapidly from the economic turmoil of the 1990s. As the shares of the rapidly growing developing countries are rising, the world average growth rate remains close to its past level.

In this Outlook, the gross domestic products of different countries have been converted into the common currency of US dollars using purchasing power parities (PPP) rather than market exchange rates. Purchasing power parities compare the costs in different currencies of a fixed, wide-ranging basket of goods and services that includes items both traded and not traded in international markets, whereas market exchange rates are based on international trade and capital movements. For this reason, the gross domestic products of different countries or regions converted using purchasing power parities can provide a more widely based measure of standard of living. This is important when considering the principal driving force of energy demand and for the comparisons of energy intensities (energy consumption divided by GDP) between countries.

Table 2.1: **Alternative Paths for Economic Growth**
Average Annual Growth Rates % in Gross Domestic Product

		Low	BAU	High
	1971-1995		1995-2020	
OECD North America	2.7	1.6	2.1	2.3
OECD Europe	2.4	1.6	2.0	2.3
OECD Pacific	3.5	1.4	1.8	2.1
Transition Economies	-0.5	2.6	3.3	4.0
China	8.5	5.0	5.5	6.6
East Asia	6.9	3.7	4.5	5.2
South Asia	4.6	3.4	4.2	5.1
Latin America	3.4	2.7	3.3	4.1
Africa	2.6	2.0	2.5	3.5
Middle East	2.7	2.1	2.7	4.0
World	**3.2**	**2.6**	**3.1**	**3.8**

The BAU assumption is based on an OECD study[1]. That work analysed the main components of economic growth:
- future growth in the labour force and its skills;
- future investment and the rate of growth of capital stock;
- and improvements in productivity.

There are two main reasons why most regions are expected to grow more slowly in the future than they have in the past. OECD regions are expected to have falling birth rates and ageing populations. In developing countries, economic growth tends to decline as countries achieve higher living standards. The OECD study compared the BAU case of 3.1 per cent per annum economic growth with a "high case" of 4.8 per cent per annum. The high case represents a "New Global Age" in which the major developed and developing countries implement a combination of successful policies aimed at encouraging world trade, investment flows and competitive markets.

Figure 2.1 plots world economic growth from 1950 to 1995 and four alternative projections. The IEA high and low economic growth assumptions are compared with the OECD low case - adopted as the IEA BAU assumption - and the OECD high "New Global Age". The

1. *The World in 2020: Towards a New Global Age,* OECD Paris, 1997.

uncertainty surrounding the future rate of world economic growth is clearly substantial. Figure 2.1 shows that the world economy has continued to grow since 1950. It does not seem unreasonable to assume a continuation of this growth rate into the future. Countries will, no doubt, try to do better, and maybe they will succeed. But, current financial turmoil in Asia impels caution over future economic prospects. The IEA high and low economic cases capture the uncertainty over future world economic growth. Table 2.2 indicates the impact of this variation on world primary energy consumption and CO_2 emissions, calculated around the BAU projection. The 30% range in world Gross Domestic Product implies ranges of some 24% in primary energy consumption and 27% in energy-related CO_2 emissions.

Figure 2.1: **World GDP Growth**
Data and Alternative Projections ($ Billion at 1990 Prices & PPP)

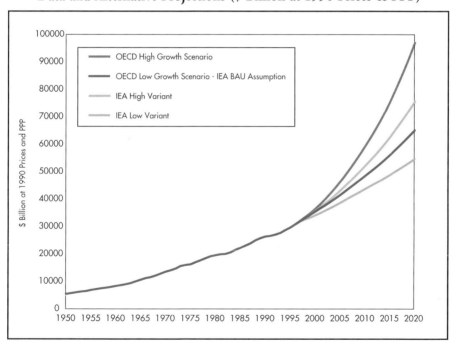

Future economic growth is particularly uncertain for China and the Transition Economies. For China, the issue is how to interpret past statistics in order to assess the past rate of economic growth. The main problem lies in the choice of prices used to convert past data for money incomes into real incomes. Until recently, many prices in China were determined administratively, not by the market. In this study, we use the official Chinese data on gross domestic product in terms of purchasing power parity. For the Transition Economies, current estimates of GDP are thought to under-record the level of economic activity. In addition, it is difficult to anticipate the future pace of economic reforms and their effects on economic growth and energy demand. As these cannot be estimated from past data, we have used our own judgments on these issues.

Table 2.2: **Effect of Changes in Economic Growth on World Energy Consumption and Energy-related CO_2 Emissions in 2020**

	Low Economic Growth Case	BAU Case	High Economic Growth Case
GDP	87	100	117
Total Primary Energy Supply	90	100	114
CO_2 Emissions	89	100	116

The Asian financial crisis is currently throwing a shadow over future economic prospects. The most visible effects are sharp falls in exchange rates and share prices in the Asian countries affected. The immediate concern is that the stability of the world economy could be affected by these events.

But the underlying problems, and their solutions, are much longer-term. Past investment projects in the crisis-affected Asian countries created employment and output so that the economies grew, but with little or no profit. Examples are commercial office blocks and factories for which there were no customers. In many cases, these projects were financed on short-term bank loans. When the interest on the loans could not be paid, the loans were called in. If the loans could not be repaid, borrowers went into receivership and the banks were in difficulties: investment projects were cancelled and share prices plummeted.

Long-term solutions will be difficult to achieve. They involve:
• clearer and stricter regulation of the banking and financial sectors;
• greater transparency of financial acounts;
• improved quality of accountability and risk management in institutions at all levels;
• cutting of links between government and commercial sectors;
• greater competition and control of monopoly practices in both product and financial markets.

As these measures are introduced, confidence will eventually return, bringing with it greater investment and higher economic growth. In the interim, economic output will be lower than previously expected.

Two themes can be drawn from our analysis of this situation:
• We are very uncertain about how long it will take for confidence in the Asian region to return, how low economic activity might fall during this period and what the economic growth rates will eventually be. Our conclusions are built into the BAU assumption for economic growth.
• The 50-year period since World Ward II saw many serious shocks to world economic activity, yet growth persisted over the period. We feel confident that our BAU assumptions are reasonable, provided that the uncertainties are kept in mind.

The energy projections described in this Outlook assume that the economic difficulties experienced in Russia during 1998 will not reduce the long-run economic potential of the Russian economy. These recent difficulties are therefore viewed as altering the short-term path of economic growth and energy demand, they are unlikely therefore to significantly alter the energy projections for 2020.

Population

Table 2.3: **Population Growth Assumptions**

Per cent per annum	1995-2020
OECD North America	0.79
OECD Europe	0.01
OECD Pacific	0.14
Transition Economies	0.01
China	0.79
East Asia	1.16
South Asia	1.54
Latin America	1.29
Africa	2.41
Middle East	2.47
World	**1.21**

The assumptions for future world population, set out in Table 2.3, are based on the latest United Nations medium population projection[2], in line with the OECD study, *The World in 2020*[3]. The population

2. *World Population Prospects, 1950-2050,* United Nations, *The 1996 Revision,* United Nations, Population Division, New-York, 1997.
3. *The World in 2020: Towards a New Global Age,* OECD Paris, 1997.

assumptions have been used mainly for the projection of biomass consumption in developing countries.

Energy Prices

World fossil fuel prices are not calculated explicitly in the Outlook. Instead, judgements are made on future prices based on the relationships between prospects for demand and supply and on the likely cost of marginal supplies.

Assumptions for the BAU projection are listed in Table 2.4 and plotted in Figure 2.2. Fossil fuel prices are held flat at their average 1991-1995 levels. The world oil price is increased between 2010 and 2015 to reflect the expected transition from conventional to unconventional oil as the source of marginal supply. The arguments are given in Chapter 7. The prices for natural gas in Europe and LNG in Japan (the price indicator used for the Asian-Pacific regions) are increased in the same proportion to reflect the close competition with oil products. The world price of coal is also increased to take account of the corresponding increase in transport costs.

The US natural gas wellhead price is increased over the period 2005 to 2015 to reflect a possible tightening of the North American gas market and increased use of unconventional gas. Chapter 8 discusses the reasons for this price increase.

Table 2.4: **Assumptions for Business-As-Usual World Fossil Fuel Prices**

	1995	**1996**	**1997**	**1998-2010**	**2015-2020**
IEA Crude oil import price in $ 1990 / bbl	15.0	17.5	16.1	17	25
OECD Steam coal import price in $ 1990 / tonne	40.3	39.3	37.2	42	46
US Natural gas wellhead price in $ 1990 / thousand cubic ft	1.35	1.92	1.96	1.7*	3.5
Natural gas import price into Europe in $ 1990 / toe	89.9	85.7	97.2	103	150
Japan LNG import price in $ 1990 / toe	125.6	130.1	133.4	141	210

* 1998-2005

Fossil fuel prices in international markets adjust to balance supply and demand. Where spot and futures markets exist, as for oil, prices adjust rapidly and are prone to volatility. In the case of the regional natural gas markets (Europe, North America and Asia-Pacific), long-term contracts are important and prices adjust more slowly. But these prices do fluctuate, as in all world commodity markets.

The price assumptions set out in Table 2.4 are meant to identify likely future movements of prices around which short-term fluctuations take place. For this reason, the fossil fuel price assumptions do not reflect current deviations from trend values, such as the currently low world oil prices.

Figure 2.2: **Business-As-Usual Assumptions**
Fossil Fuel Prices

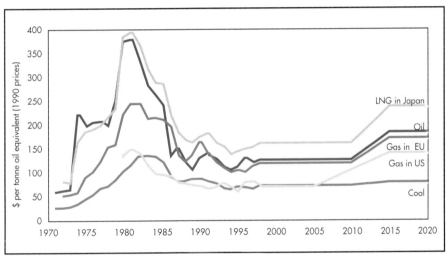

CHAPTER 3
PRINCIPAL RESULTS

This chapter presents the principal results of the Outlook. The highlights of the business as usual demand projection are presented first. These are discussed in more detail for each world region in Part III. The major implications for energy supply are then considered. These are more fully discussed in Part II. As explained in the Introduction, the aim is to identify and discuss the main uncertainties and issues affecting the energy outlook.

The Business As Usual Projection

Past and future paths for total primary energy supply, CO_2 emissions and energy intensity are presented in Figures 3.1, 3.2 and 3.3. Oil continues to dominate world energy consumption, with transport use increasing its share. Gas consumption rises to approach coal consumption

Figure 3.1: **World Primary Energy Supply and CO_2 Emissions 1971-2020**

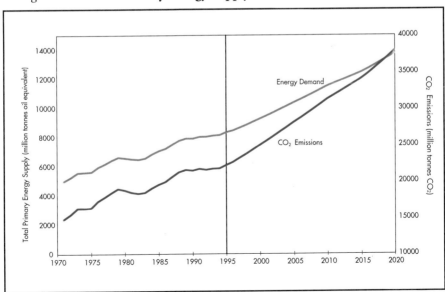

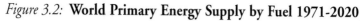

Figure 3.2: **World Primary Energy Supply by Fuel 1971-2020**

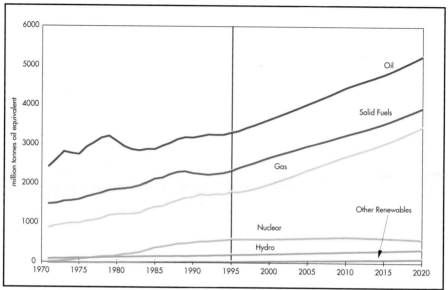

Figure 3.3: **Ratio of World Primary Energy Supply to GDP 1971-2020**

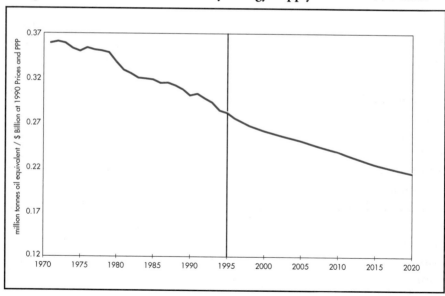

by the end of the period. Nuclear power stabilises. Hydro power and renewables increase steadily, but remain at low levels. Energy intensity falls for the world as a whole, at 1.1% per annum (total energy use rises

Figure 3.4: **World Primary Energy Supply by Fuel Type 1971-2020**

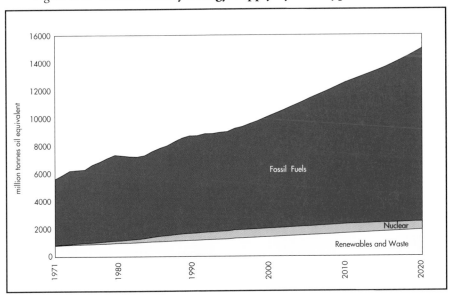

by 2% and economic activity by 3.1% p.a.). This continues the trend observed since 1982. CO_2 emissions rise with primary energy demand slightly faster than in the past. Contributing factors are the stabilisation of nuclear power generation and continued rapid growth in coal use in China and other Asian countries.

For the OECD regions, "solid fuels" contains not only coal and coke, but also combustible renewable and waste materials (e.g. biomass and industrial and urban waste). This is not the case for non-OECD regions. Figure 3.4 presents the information on world primary energy consumption in an alternative manner. In this Figure, solid combustible renewable and waste materials have been included for all regions. They are combined together with hydro power and other renewables under the single term "renewables and waste". They are shown together with fossil fuels and nuclear fuel in a stacked manner so that they add up to total world primary energy supply. Energy from renewables and waste rises from 1297 Mtoe in 1995 to 1883 Mtoe in 2020, an annual rate of growth of 1.5%.

Regional average annual growth rates for total primary energy supply, CO_2 emissions and energy intensity from 1995 to 2020 are given in bar chart form in Figure 3.5. China and the developing countries are projected to have major increases in their energy demands

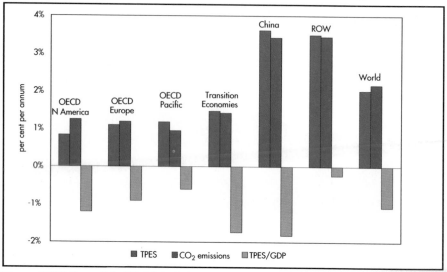

Figure 3.5: **Annual Rates of Growth 1995-2020 in Total Primary Energy Supply, CO_2 Emissions and Energy Intensity**

Note : ROW (Rest of the World) includes East Asia, South Asia, Latin America, Africa and the Middle East.

Figure 3.6: **World Primary Energy Supply**

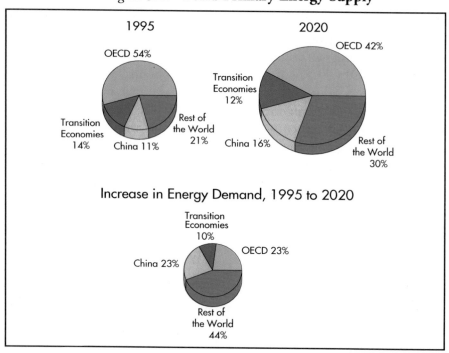

and CO_2 emissions. The large falls in energy intensity in the Transition Economies and in China reflect current opportunities in these areas for more efficient energy use, but are especially uncertain.

Figure 3.6 emphasises the important contribution made by developing countries to the growth in energy demand between 1995 and 2020. China and the other developing countries account for two-thirds of this increase. The implications for CO_2 emissions are discussed in Chapter 4.

Energy-Related Services

In order to present the main developments in energy demand, it is important to identify the principal purposes for which energy is used. Four major energy-related services[1] have been identified:
- electrical services (total consumption of electricity by final consumers);
- mobility (non-electricity fuels consumed in all forms of transport);
- stationary services (mainly fossil fuels used for heating in buildings and industrial processes);
- fuels used in power generation.

Figure 3.7: **World Energy-Related Services 1971-2020**

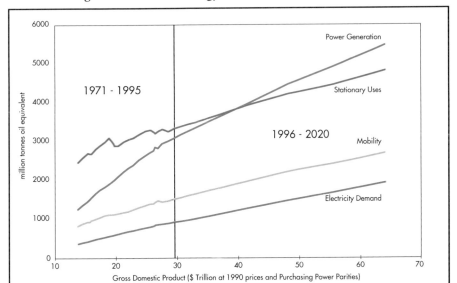

1. *The Energy Dimension of Climate Change and Energy and Climate Change,* IEA/OECD Paris, 1997, provides a discussion on this approach. A more detailed description of the energy-related services is provided in the definitions in Part IV.

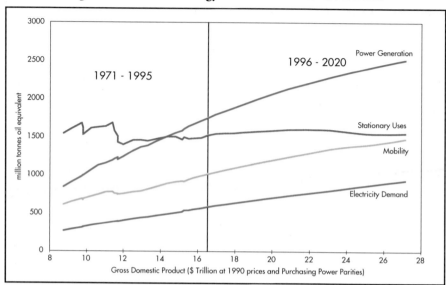

Figure 3.8: **OECD Energy-Related Services 1971-2020**

Historical data and future projections for energy used in these energy-related services are shown for the world in Figure 3.7, and for the OECD in Figure 3.8. These data are plotted against economic activity (Gross Domestic Product) to demonstrate the important relationships between energy demand and economic growth.

For the world and OECD regions, electricity consumption and energy use to meet mobility needs closely followed economic output up to 1995. They were largely unaffected by the 1973 and 1979 oil price shocks with the exception, for mobility, of North America in 1979-1982. This exception can be attributed in part to the introduction of Corporate Automobile Fuel Efficiency (CAFE) standards[2] in the US. Fossil fuel demand for stationary heat purposes, on the other hand, was strongly influenced by the two oil shocks. Successful energy efficiency policies, a shift towards service-oriented activities that require less energy to produce and the relocation of some industrial activities to developing countries, explain the stabilisation of heat-related fossil fuel demand in OECD countries as a whole. Since the late 1970s, most of the increase in the stationary use of fossil fuels for heat services has taken place outside the OECD. Economic development drives the demand for fossil fuel-based heat, especially for industrial activities, and also leads to the substitution

2. Green D.L., 1990, *CAFE or Price*, Energy Journal 11: 37-57.

of commercial fuels for non-marketed traditional fuels. Fossil fuel use for stationary services continues to rise with income in developing countries.

In the projection period to 2020, demands for electricity and mobility services continue their past upward trends. Fossil fuel demand for stationary services tends to flatten out in the OECD regions, but continues upward in China and other developing countries as industrialisation rapidly increases. Energy demand for power generation follows electricity demand, but growth slows as new generating plant is introduced with higher efficiency.

In the past, downward pressure on energy use from a steady stream of technological changes that raise energy efficiency has been offset by upward pressure on energy use from increased incomes and changing tastes to produce the persistently linear trends evident in Figures 3.7 and 3.8. Care has been taken to chart past data and projections in order to demonstrate that the results obtained from the energy demand projection methods used in this study do not produce unexplained deviations from past trends. The manner in which these two types of pressure will interact in the future contributes to the uncertainty of future energy projections.

Some energy uses will eventually become saturated as incomes increase. An example is the heating of residential, public and commercial buildings. In high-income countries, most buildings are already heated to normal comfort levels. A 50% increase in GDP in these countries will not mean that buildings will be heated to higher temperatures, although the number and size of such buildings may well increase. It is difficult to detect such tendencies in the data to date and their timing is highly uncertain.

For the Transition Economies, energy data and their relationships to GDP are difficult to interpret. Energy data collection was disrupted in the early 1990s and new forms of data collection have been introduced. Some data definitions have been changed from earlier systems, and inconsistencies remain. IEA staff are working with their counterparts in these countries to improve the quality of energy data. In addition, the transition to market systems, the restructuring of economies and the modernisation of industry and commerce mean that past statistics are unlikely to be a reliable guide for future energy developments. For all these reasons, projections of energy demand and supply in this region are based largely on judgement rather than analysis of the past, and they are especially uncertain.

Oil Supply Prospects

Prospects for oil production have been analysed by region, paying particular attention to the distinction between OPEC Middle East[3] and all other producers. Account has been taken of estimates of conventional oil reserves and the production profiles for oil in each region. A detailed discussion of this subject is provided in Chapter 7.

Oil reserve estimates are inevitably uncertain, and studies normally report them as ranges, rather than as point estimates. For example, the United States Geological Survey in 1993 reported a range of 2.1 to 2.8 trillion (10^{12}) barrels for worldwide recoverable reserves of conventional oil. Experts differ on these figures; some take a static view, emphasising geological and statistical issues that lead to a low reserve estimate, while others take a dynamic view, arguing that new information and the reduction of uncertainty will contribute to increases in identified reserves and that rapidly advancing technology will help discover more reserves and make a wider range of already known deposits economically recoverable. Experience in mature oil regions indicates that production builds to a peak when approximately half of the ultimately recoverable reserves has been produced, and then falls away. The application of new technologies, such as horizontal drilling and three-dimensional (3D) seismic analysis, determines the ultimate size of recoverable reserves. Technology can extend the peak and delay or slow the decline in production. But eventually production falls, given a fixed oil resource. This has been the experience, for example, in the United States.

This approach has been applied on a regional basis. It indicates that a peaking of conventional oil production could occur between the years 2010 and 2020, depending on assumptions for the level of reserves. Oil production outside OPEC Middle East would peak before OPEC Middle East production, producing a greater reliance on OPEC Middle East supply between the two peaks. A plateau in oil production for OPEC Middle East of 47.9 Mbd has been assumed, rather than a sharp peak.

BAU projections for oil production profiles for the world, OPEC Middle East and all other areas are shown in Figure 3.9. Ultimate recoverable reserves of conventional oil are assumed to be 2.3 trillion barrels, the modal value adopted by the United States Geological Survey in 1993. In this Figure, world demand for liquid fuels has been extended to 2030 at the average growth rate of 1995-2020 in order to illuminate the longer-term oil supply picture. Table 3.1 gives details of supplies for conventional and non-conventional oil. The use of non-conventional oil

3. Saudi Arabia, Kuwait, the United Arab Emirates, Iraq and Iran.

expands rapidly after 2015 to meet the increase in demand for liquid fuels. It compensates for the decline in conventional oil production.

The extent of any rise in the world oil price associated with these developments is in some doubt. To produce large and increasing volumes of oil from non-conventional sources will require many multi-billion dollar projects. Some unevenness in supply availability is possible

Table 3.1: **Oil Supply 1996-2020**
Conventional Oil Reserves of 2.3 trillion barrels

million barrels per day	1996	2010	2020
Total Demand for Liquid Fuels	72.0	94.8	111.5
Total Natural Gas Liquids, processing Gains and Identified Unconventional Oil	9.3	15.9	20.1
Conventional Crude Oil			
Middle East OPEC	17.2	40.9	45.2
World excluding Middle East OPEC	45.5	38.0	27.0
Total Crude Oil	**62.7**	**79.0**	**72.2**
World Liquids Supply excluding Unidentified Unconventional Oil	72.0	94.8	92.3
Balancing Item - Unidentified Unconventional Oil	0.0	0.0	19.1

Figure 3.9: **Oil Supply Profiles 1996-2030**

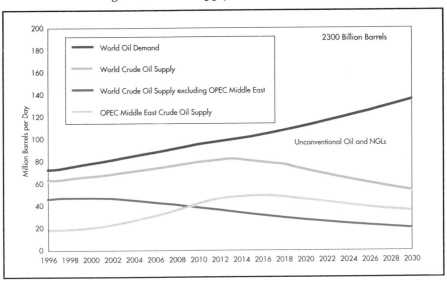

because of the long lead times required for these big projects and the difficulties in matching supply to demand in what promises to be a highly competitive market. But it is necessary to distinguish fluctuations in the world oil price from its longer-term average level. Some short-term price movements could well arise from supply-demand mismatches, as non-conventional oil sources take over the marginal supplier role. But opinion on the effect of this changeover on the longer-run oil price is mixed. Some observers expect long-run supply costs from major non-conventional oil production projects to be higher than current long-run supply costs from non-OPEC sources, lifting the world oil price to a new long-run level of between $25 and $30 per barrel. Others suggest there will be no upward pressure on the world oil price. In this Outlook, an upward ramp from $17/bbl to $25/bbl has been assumed from 2010 to 2015 as a response to the transition to non-conventional oil, with the oil price remaining at $25/bbl after 2015. All prices are quoted in 1990 US dollars.

A more optimistic view of oil reserves would assume an ultimate stock of recoverable conventional oil of 3 trillion barrels, compared with the lower assumption of 2.3 trillion barrels. This view postpones the production peak of conventional oil and the associated rise in world oil prices to 2020. The effect of the lower oil price on world oil demand is estimated to be small. A more conservative estimate of oil reserves at 2 trillion barrels would shift the production peak and possible oil price rise back to 2010.

The range of 2-3 trillion barrels represents our estimate of the uncertainty of the ultimate reserves of recoverable conventional oil. This includes allowances for expected new discoveries, upward revisions of the reserve estimates for identified fields and the impacts of new technologies. We are aware that experts differ - some more optimistic and some less so. It may be that new information in the future will cause us to revise our analysis, perhaps to reduce or to increase the range.

Gas Supply Prospects

Reserves of natural gas[4] are estimated to be equivalent to 1.9 trillion barrels of oil, similar in magnitude to the lower end of the range of reserve estimates for conventional oil. Although world demand for natural gas is growing faster than that for oil (2.6% per annum compared with 1.9%), it does so from a much lower base. World natural gas production is not expected to peak until well beyond 2020. A fuller discussion is provided in Chapter 8.

4. Masters, C. D. et al, World Petroleum Assessment and Analysis, Proc. 14th World Petroleum Congress, 1994.

Table 3.2: **Natural Gas Production and Net Imports (Mtoe)**

Indigenous Production			
	1995	**2010**	**2020**
OECD North America (including Mexico)	592	759	764
OECD Europe	199	276	238
OECD Pacific	31	77	68
Transition Economies	585	809	1116
China	17	57	81
Rest of World (excluding Mexico)	395	750	1208
World	**1818**	**2727**	**3474**
Net Imports			
	1995	**2010**	**2020**
OECD North America (including Mexico)	-2	-2	-2
OECD Europe	104	230	387
OECD Pacific	42	42	64
Transition Economies	-74	-162	-281
China	0	0	0
Rest of World (excluding Mexico)	-76	-114	-174

Table 3.2 shows BAU projections of indigenous gas production and net imports by region.

For regions other than OECD Europe and OECD North America plus Mexico, gas production is assumed to be determined by domestic demand until cumulative production reaches 60% of ultimate gas reserves in those regions. (This assumption allows for a possible increase in gas reserves in those regions as a result of new discoveries and of new technologies that would allow known reserves, now considered to be uneconomic, to be brought into production.) Beyond 60%, gas production is assumed to decline at 5% per annum.

In North America, both the Canadian and United States governments project rising gas production to 2020 at continuing low gas prices. They do not expect indigenous gas reserve constraints to limit supply or raise gas prices substantially over this period. This view is discussed in Chapter 8. The position taken in this study is that considerable uncertainty exists for North America over the impact of future technological developments on the extent of recoverable conventional gas reserves and on the costs of both conventional and unconventional gas production. It is possible that additional natural gas could be discovered and that the production costs of unconventional gas could remain low. It is also possible that some rise in gas prices would result from higher production costs, especially for large volumes of unconventional gas. A rise in gas price could stimulate further gas production from unconventional sources (coal-bed methane) or from coal gasification. We are extremely uncertain on these issues. We have assumed that gas prices in North America will increase linearly from $1.7 (in 1990 prices) per thousand cubic feet in 2005 to $3.5 in 2015 and then remain flat at that level. As a result, gas demand growth slows to 2020. Gas production in North America (including Mexico) is assumed to be sufficient to supply this demand. There is clearly a large potential for gas demand to grow in North America if gas prices do not rise.

In OECD Europe, gas production is assumed to grow at 2.2% a year[5], until cumulative production reaches approximately 60% of ultimate reserves, and gas production is assumed to decline at 5% p.a. after the production peak.

OECD Europe and OECD Pacific are projected to experience a downturn in gas production at some date during the second decade of the next century. The timing is uncertain, mainly because estimates of gas reserves (and gas demand growth) are uncertain. Gas imports into Europe are likely to continue to flow mainly by pipeline from Russia and North Africa. Gas imports into Japan and some Asian countries already arrive as LNG.

The assumption has been made that low-income Asian countries will not import large quantities of LNG before 2020 because of its high price. In the rest of non-OECD Asia, some countries are gas exporters and some importers. On balance, non-OECD Asia is not seen as a large net importer of gas.

World gas demand and supply are balanced in the projection by allocating world net imports to the principal gas exporting regions. A stable business and trading environment, together with adequate regulatory frameworks, will be needed to encourage the mobilisation of capital for developing gas production facilities and infrastructure. Only under these conditions will the future development of gas supplies be able to meet growing world demand for gas.

5. *IEA Natural Gas Security Study,* IEA/OECD Paris, 1995.

Coal Supply Prospects

World coal production is expected to match demand easily over the period to 2020. The main growth component in coal demand arises in power generation. The long lead time for power plant construction will allow the parallel development of coal-supply capacity. The international coal market has proven sufficiently flexible to overcome local supply deficiencies[6].

Electricity Supply Prospects

Power generation systems have been analysed for each region taking account of differing generating technologies. Requirements for new generating capacity have been calculated in light of the rapidly growing electricity demands in each region, the expected scrapping of ageing power plants and the reduction of currently large excesses of generating plant capacity over peak demand in some regions (OECD Europe and Transition Economies). Least-cost criteria are used for projecting the choice of new generating plants and the dispatching of power plants to meet demand from OECD regions. A detailed discussion of these topics is provided in Chapter 6.

Figure 3.10 : **World Power Generation Inputs by Fuel 1971-2020**

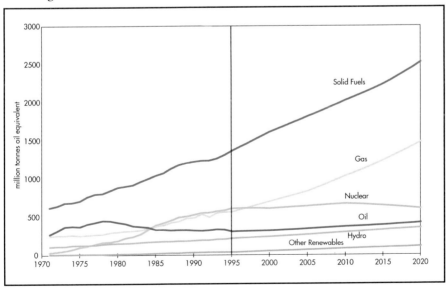

6. *International Coal Trade,* IEA/OECD Paris, 1997.

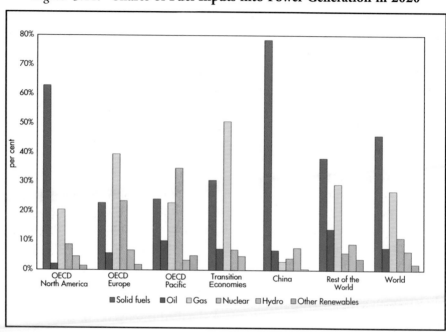

Figure 3.11: **Shares of Fuel Inputs into Power Generation in 2020**

Over the period 1995 to 2020, some 3500 GW of new electricity generating plant are required in the BAU projection. About half of the total is projected for China and the other developing countries and a third for OECD countries. This 3500 GW is estimated to have a capital cost of $3.28 trillion, i.e. an average capital cost of $937 per kW of capacity.

Fuels Used for Power Generation

Figures 3.10 and 3.11 plot the changing pattern of fuel use in power generation in each region. In our projection, future levels of nuclear power, hydro power and other renewable energy sources have been assessed on the basis of plans or targets announced by governments and current policies. Decisions on the use of these fuels are mainly political or are highly site-specific in nature. In OECD regions, the projected inputs of oil, gas and coal are calculated from a least-cost despatching model incorporating the higher thermal efficiencies of new generating plants. In other regions, the projections of fuel mix are based on country plans and on judgement.

Coal use in power generation continues to be important in North America, China and in many developing countries. Gas is expected also to be important, especially in the Transition Economies. Where supplies of natural gas are available or are imported, increasing volumes of gas are projected for use in combined-cycle generating plants. Oil will continue to be used in power generation at times of peak demand and, because it is easily stored, as a standby fuel for use when gas prices increase seasonally or where gas supplies are unreliable.

There are many uncertainties for future electricity developments, especially the pace of restructuring and changing the form of regulation of the industry in many countries. Expectations are that these developments will lead to greater efficiency and to electricity prices being more closely related to the full costs of supply. Decentralised sources such as combined heat and power production could also lead to increases in energy efficiency in this sector. As co-generation is already well established in industry, much will depend on the attraction of district heating or whether technological and regulatory developments will encourage the widespread use of micro-CHP units for use in individual buildings.

Projections of Biomass Use in Developing Countries

Unlike previous editions of the World Energy Outlook, this Outlook includes projections of biomass energy use in developing countries. According to IEA statistics, biomass's contribution to the world's total final energy consumption in 1995 was 930 Mtoe, comparable to those of electricity (932 Mtoe), coal (816 Mtoe) and gas (1019 Mtoe). In many developing countries, biomass (firewood, agricultural by-products, animal waste, charcoal and other derived fuels) provides a substantial share of energy needs, a third in developing countries on average, but as much as 80% in countries with very low per capita incomes. Some of this biomass is commercially exploited, but much is non-commercial. Hence, data on biomass use are difficult to collect and available statistics are of poor quality. However, it was felt that the omission of such an important energy source would distort the analysis of past trends in total energy use and lead to misleading indications for the future. Considerable work has been carried out by the IEA to assess the current status of biomass energy in developing countries and to include it in its modelling framework. An extensive discussion of these issues is provided in Chapter 10.

For the purposes of this chapter, biomass energy in non-OECD countries is excluded, so that projections are comparable with those presented in previous editions on the World Energy Outlook and with the projections done by other organisations. Tables summarising the projections of world energy demand and supply including biomass energy can be found in Chapter 10.

Similarly, in the Chapters 15 to 19 in Part III, the projections for regional energy demand and supply are shown with and without biomass energy. The analysis and projections for biomass can be found at the end of each chapter.

CHAPTER 4
CLIMATE CHANGE ANALYSES

At the time of writing, most governments that accepted greenhouse gas emission commitments at the Kyoto Conference have not yet determined the packages of policies they will adopt to meet their commitments. Some actions that reduce carbon dioxide emissions will take place without policy changes. Estimates of these reductions are already included in the BAU projection:

- the share of gas in primary energy supply rises relative to oil and coal, mainly in the provision of stationary energy services and power generation;
- some additional new nuclear plants are built;
- the use of renewables in power generation increases;
- energy use rises more slowly than economic activity.

But despite these actions, CO_2 emissions continue to rise in the BAU projection, as shown in Table 4.1.

Table 4.1: **Increases in Energy-Related CO_2 Emissions (million tonnes CO_2)**

	1990	BAU projection 2010	Projected increase 1990-2010	Reduction below BAU projection in 2010 required to meet Kyoto commitments	
OECD					
Europe	3659	4612	953	1246	27%
Pacific	1355	1774	419	461	26%
North America	5339	7041	1702	2076	29%
Transition Economies	4426	3852	-574		
Annex I	14779	17279	2500	3239	19%
China	2411	5322	2911		
ROW	3833	8034	4201		
World*	**21400**	**31189**	**9789**		

* Includes CO_2 emissions from marine bunkers.

The extent of the reduction in CO_2 emissions in the Transition Economies between 1990 and 2010 is especially uncertain. A fall of 1291 million tonnes CO_2 occurred between 1990 and 1995 and we project a rise of 717 million tonnes from 1995 to 2010. In order for the economies of these countries to grow, they must first modernise their industries and commerce. In doing so, they will become more energy efficient and switch to less carbon intensive fuels.

The increases in CO_2 emissions projected for China and the rest of the developing world between 1995 and 2010 are large - almost three quarters of the total increase for the world.

It is not possible to prepare a projection that describes the paths of energy demand and supply, and CO_2 emissions, for each world region where countries meet their Kyoto commitments in 2010 without first knowing what set of policies will be applied and analysing the effects of these policies and their interactions. The essential elements for that work do not yet exist. But it is possible to obtain some idea of where CO_2 emissions might be reduced and the types and magnitudes of actions that would be required of energy consumers.

Table 4.2: **OECD Energy-Related CO$_2$ Emissions in 2010 by Sector**

from:	million tonnes CO$_2$
Solid Fuels	722
Oil	5327
Gas	1625
Final Energy Consumption	7673
Solid Fuels	3698
Oil	331
Gas	1227
Electricity Generation	5257
Other Energy Transformation	496
Total Primary Energy Supply	13427
Reduction required to meet Kyoto commitments	3783

Table 4.2 shows the distribution of OECD energy-related CO_2 emissions in 2010 by sector compared with the reduction of 3783 Mt per annum required in 2010 from the BAU projection to meet the Kyoto commitment. The bulk of oil use in final energy consumption is used in transport and is unlikely to be replaced by gas before 2010.

CO_2 emissions from coal in final energy consumption are too small to allow the required savings to be achieved by fuel substitution in that category. This suggests that the main sources of the reduction (to the extent that it is realised within the OECD countries) must be energy saving in final energy consumption and the substitution of non-fossil for coal-fired electricity generation and we have arbitrarily allocated half of the needed reductions to these two sectors. As most new OECD generating plants in the BAU projection are gas-fired, coal use in power generation can be lowered only by reducing output from existing coal-fired power plants.

The analysis here, purely to illustrate the opportunities and constraints, is limited to the hypothesis that each OECD region seeks to meet its own Kyoto commitment in 2010. Within this constraint two analyses have been made. In the first, Kyoto Analysis 1, approximately half the reduction in CO_2 emissions is achieved by imposing a uniform additional reduction of 1.25% p.a. from 1998 to 2010 in energy intensity across all sectors of final demand in all three OECD regions. The other half of the CO_2 emission reductions is achieved by substituting non-fossil (nuclear or renewable) fuel for fossil fuel in power generation.

In the second analysis, Kyoto Analysis 2, the uniform reduction in energy intensity imposed in the first analysis is replaced by the addition to the prices of fossil fuels in each of the three OECD regions of a uniform carbon value, i.e. a uniform charge, reflecting the carbon content of each fuel, the imposition of which is sufficient to achieve approximately half the fall in CO_2 emissions necessary to meet the full Kyoto commitments.

The calculation of this value is fraught with difficulties. Partly because many other factors are at work and partly because end-user prices have not changed greatly in real terms over the data period, the estimation of price response coefficients for energy demand is an uncertain business. One uncertainty is the time lag between a price signal and the response, taking account of the rate of capital turnover. Further, the effects of large energy price increases on energy demand may be different from those of small price increases because of macroeconomic impacts and government policy changes to counteract them, as in the case of the oil price shock of 1973/74.

With these reservations in mind, the necessary carbon value has been calculated, using the price response coefficients estimated for the OECD regions. Built up linearly over the period 1998 to 2003, the required value reaches $250 per tonne of carbon in 2003.

This high value demands some explanation. The first reason is the short period (12 years) over which reductions in CO_2 emissions have to be achieved. This period requires the speeding up of the normal pace of turnover of capital stock; it does not provide time for new technologies to be developed and brought into significant use; and there is little opportunity for the normal learning process to reduce costs. The second reason is that the analysis makes no allowance for flexible measures that would allow the adoption of lower-cost CO_2 reductions in the developing countries and transition economies.

When such a carbon value is added to fossil fuel prices, the competitive position between different fuels changes, especially between fuels for electricity generation. In the original projection (BAU), substitution was allowed to take place between different types of fossil fuel-fired generating plants, but no substitution was allowed between fossil and non-fossil plants, i.e. the levels of power generation from nuclear and renewable fuels were determined in advance in each projection. This limitation was applied because generating cost was not thought likely to be the main determinant of new capacity construction for either nuclear or renewable generating plants over the period to 2020.

With these reservations in mind, there are striking differences between the impact of a common carbon value addition to fossil fuel prices in Kyoto Analysis 2 and the uniform reduction in energy intensity imposed in Kyoto Analysis 1. Because of different consumer reactions and dynamics, changes in fuel use in Kyoto Analysis 2 vary greatly between fuels and between different energy-related services. First, throughout the OECD, electricity use and fuel use for mobility are much less price-sensitive than fossil fuel use in stationary services. Second, energy demand and CO_2 emissions in North America are much more responsive to an increase in energy price than elsewhere in the OECD. This result has been reported in other studies.[1] The implication is that policies aimed at achieving a uniform reduction in energy intensities across sectors and across regions within the OECD are likely to result in a greater welfare loss to consumers than policies which are flexible and allow emissions trading or other mechanisms to equalise the actual (or implied) carbon values. As noted above, the possibility of Joint Implementation of obligations or emissions transfers between Annex 1 Parties, or of emissions trading, has not been allowed for. In part, this is because of the high level of regional aggregation employed in the study. In this regard, the large reduction in CO_2 emissions recorded for the

1. *The Costs of Cutting Carbon Emissions: Results from Global Models*, OECD Paris, 1993.

Transition Economies in the BAU projection (see Table 4.1) is very uncertain.

The substitution of non-fossil for fossil power generation required to meet the Kyoto commitments in addition to the changes made to final energy demand in the two Kyoto Analyses, is illustrated in Figure 4.1.

Figure 4.1: **Comparison of Power Generation by Fuel between BAU and Kyoto Analyses in 2010 for the Three OECD Regions**

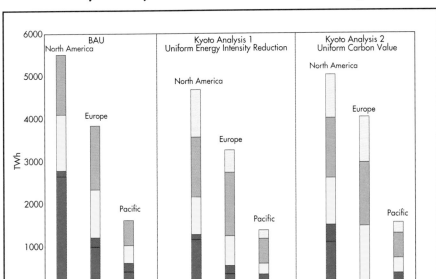

In OECD North America and OECD Pacific, total power generation is reduced because of the additional electricity saving imposed on final demand in Kyoto Analysis 1 or because of the carbon value added to fossil fuel prices in Kyoto Analysis 2. Electricity demand rises in OECD Europe with a carbon value added to fossil fuel prices because of a cross-price effect: electricity demand for space and water heating rises as gas prices rise, and this more than offsets the reduction in electricity demand as a result of the electricity price rise. Where electricity demand grows more slowly, less new generating plant is built. As this is mostly gas-fired, generation from gas is lower in the Kyoto Analysis than in the BAU projection. In order to meet Kyoto commitments in each region, additional non-fossil generation (nuclear or renewable) has progressively been substituted for coal-fired generating plant which has been scrapped early. In consequence, electricity generation from coal in the Kyoto Analyses is substantially less than that in the BAU projection in each region by 2010.

The Kyoto Analyses do not represent expected future outcomes. In practice, the policy response is likely to combine changes in price signals, either implicitly or explicitly, with the removal of barriers to the take-up of "no-regret" potential for energy-related CO_2 emission reductions. The latter could amount to 20-30% of business as usual consumption. There are many possible combinations of energy saving and fuel substitution that meet the Kyoto commitments. But all involve large deviations from past trends. It is clear that they will not happen unless adequate policies and measures are put in place by governments to make them happen. These policies will involve considerable practical difficulties, not least because of the relatively short time remaining to the period 2008-2012 in which the Kyoto commitments are to be met. The next step for governments is to identify that combination of policies and measures that best fits the circumstances of their respective countries, taking account of cost and political constraints. No account has been taken, in this assessment, of greenhouse gases other than CO_2.

The role of China and the other developing countries in determining growth in world CO_2 emissions (see Table 4.1) underlines the importance of these countries to the ultimate solution of the greenhouse gas problem and the opportunities which exist, in the context of such high rates of growth in energy demand, to invest cost-effectively in the minimisation of greenhouse gas emissions.

CHAPTER 5
CONCLUSIONS

The future development of energy demand, supply and prices in world regions is subject to many uncertainties. The business as usual projection, presented in this Outlook, provides a likely outcome if policies remain unchanged, but it is by no means the only outcome. Variations from the assumptions made for economic growth, reserves of fossil fuels, and hence world fossil fuel prices, and policies adopted to achieve environmental goals could all produce marked deviations from the projections presented in this volume.

The aim of this Outlook is to discuss the nature of these uncertainties. Not all types of uncertainty have been covered. The impacts of future changes in energy technologies are particularly difficult to capture. Specific electricity-generating technologies are identified, but further reductions in the unit costs of renewable energy technologies could occur before 2020, as experience is gained in their use. Further work on combined heat and power (CHP) plants is needed, particularly on the use of micro-CHP units in individual buildings.

For the OECD countries, persistent trends have been identified in the relations between economic activity (GDP) and energy use for mobility and electrical services. Changes in these trends are possible, for example, because of saturation in some areas of energy use or as a result of new policies to reduce the energy intensities of OECD economies. The past trends already reflect the many energy saving policies introduced by OECD countries since the first oil crisis in 1973/4. Stronger policies are likely to be needed in the future in order to meet environmental objectives, or, if circumstances demand, to assure stability in energy supplies. There is lively debate as to how much such policies will cost, but they are unlikely to be welcome to energy users, even if the reasons for them are well understood.

The choice of policies by countries to meet their Kyoto greenhouse gas emission commitments is perhaps the main policy uncertainty at present. It is hoped that the analysis presented here will provide useful input into the process of choice.

PART II

OUTLOOK FOR ENERGY SUPPLY

CHAPTER 6
POWER GENERATION

This chapter presents the BAU projection of electricity generation at world level and discusses the methods and assumptions used. Details of the projections for electricity demand and generation in each region are provided in the individual chapters in Part III. Tables giving BAU projections of electricity consumption, fuels used, electricity generation and generating capacities by region are provided in Part IV.

Electricity Generation

The BAU projections of electricity generation, fuel consumption and generating capacity are listed in Table 6.1 by energy source. Projected growth rates for fuel consumption are generally less than those for electricity generation, as new plants are more efficient than existing and retired plants. Except for "other renewables", projected growth rates for generating capacity are also less than those for generation. This reflects the assumption that current excess generating capacity in some regions (such as OECD Europe and the Transition Economies) will be absorbed over the projection period. The growth rates of generation and capacity also differ because plant load factors change over time, e.g. coal plants are used generally in base load and gas plants are used increasingly in medium load. "Other renewables" include wind, geothermal, solar and tidal power. The aggregate results depend on the mix of plant types, with different load factors and different conversion efficiencies (following IEA conventions). For example, wind power has a low load factor because of its intermittent nature, and 100 per cent conversion efficiency; geothermal power has high load factors but conversion efficiency is on the order of 10 per cent.

Table 6.1 shows that most new generating plants use gas, mainly in gas-fired combined-cycle turbines. These plants have low construction costs, are available in a range of small to medium sizes, have short construction times (2 to 3 years), are straightforward to build and operate. They also have high efficiency and low pollutant emissions. Provided gas is available at a competitive price, they are the generating plant of choice in the BAU projection[1].

Table 6.1: **World Electricity Generation, Fuel Consumption and Generating Capacity 1971-2020**

	1971	1995	2010	2020	Annual Growth Rate 1995-2020
Electricity Generation (TWh)	5248	13204	20852	27326	3.0%
Solid Fuels	2131	5077	7960	10490	2.9%
Oil	1100	1315	1663	1941	1.6%
Gas	691	1932	5063	8243	6.0%
Nuclear	111	2332	2568	2317	0.0%
Hydro	1209	2498	3445	4096	2.0%
Other Renewables	5	49	154	239	6.5%
Energy Inputs (Mtoe)	1269	3091	4470	5482	2.3%
Solid Fuels	618	1362	2023	2521	2.5%
Oil	268	308	367	418	1.2%
Gas	246	565	1034	1477	3.9%
Nuclear	29	608	670	604	0.0%
Hydro	104	215	296	352	2.0%
Other Renewables	4	34	80	110	4.9%
Capacity (GW)	-	3079	4556	5915	2.6%
Solid Fuels	-	1032	1362	1760	2.2%
Oil	-	404	527	604	1.6%
Gas	-	571	1309	2035	5.2%
Nuclear	-	347	375	334	-0.2%
Hydro	-	713	940	1109	1.8%
Other Renewables	-	13	43	73	7.2%

Solid fuel, mainly coal, retains a strong position in power generation. It is the favoured fuel where gas is unavailable or expensive (as in those developing countries that have coal available, like China and India), or in locations close to low-cost coal production

1 The circumstances in which electricity generation from gas has grown rapidly in the United Kingdom are discussed in *Energy Policies of IEA Countries: United Kingdom 1998 Review,* IEA/OECD Paris (forthcoming).

(parts of North America, Australia and South Africa). As indicated in Chapter 4, the main threat to coal use in power generation comes from future policies to reduce emissions of CO_2.

Oil use in power generation grows to 2020, but less quickly than total generation. Because of the relative ease and low cost of oil storage, it is an ideal generating fuel for remote locations where other fuels are difficult or costly to obtain, for standby or peaking plants and for use where seasonal variations in price make other fuels (especially gas) uncompetitive at certain times.

Nuclear generation remains stable in world terms to 2020 as the commissioning of new plants broadly matches plant retirements. New nuclear plants are built, in the BAU projection, in those countries that currently have nuclear power building programmes or have nuclear plants currently under construction.

Growth in the use of hydropower, for both base load and pumped storage for peaking purposes, is limited by the availability of suitable sites and environmental considerations, particularly in the OECD regions. Projections are based on announced building plans or the existence of substantial undeveloped hydro capacity.

Electricity generation from other renewable energy sources is the fastest growing category, but will still represent less than one per cent of world electricity generation by 2020.

World electricity generation by region and by type of fuel are shown in Figures 6.1 and 6.2. Generation grows strongly in all regions and is dominated by the OECD, whose world share, nevertheless, is projected to fall from 60% in 1995 to 47% in 2020. The generation share of China rises from 8% to 14%, for the Transition Economies it remains at 12% and for the rest of the world, rises from 19% to 27% over the period.

Solid fuels continue as the most important source of power generation in the BAU projection but with generation from gas rising more strongly. Hydropower and oil-fired generation continue to grow, but nuclear generation begins to decline from 2010.

The patterns of world fuel consumption for power generation by region and by fuel type in Figures 6.3 and 6.4 are similar to those shown for generation in Figures 6.1 and 6.2. They differ for the reasons discussed earlier in the chapter.

Figure 6.1: **World Electricity Generation by Region**

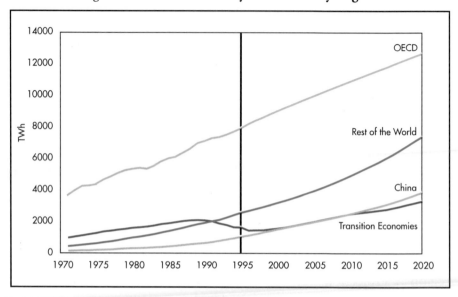

Figure 6.2: **World Electricity Generation by Fuel**

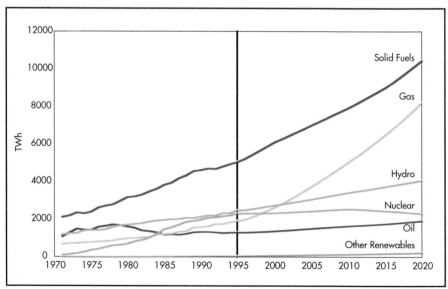

Figure 6.3: **World Fuel Consumption for Electricity Generation by Region**

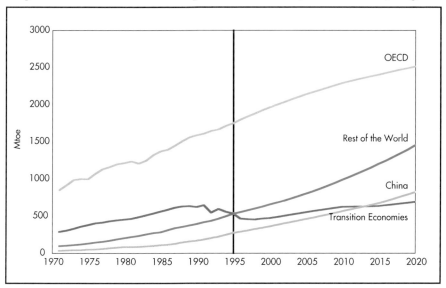

Figure 6.4: **World Fuel Consumption for Electricity Generation by Fuel**

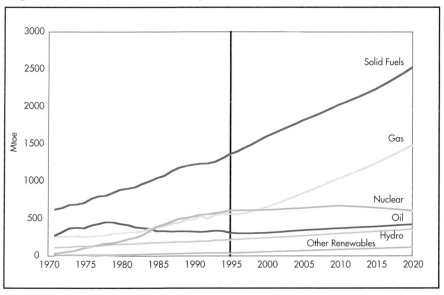

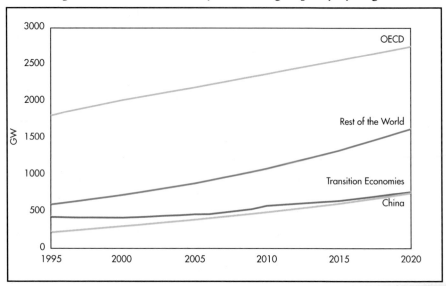

Figure 6.5: **World Electricity Generating Capacity by Region**

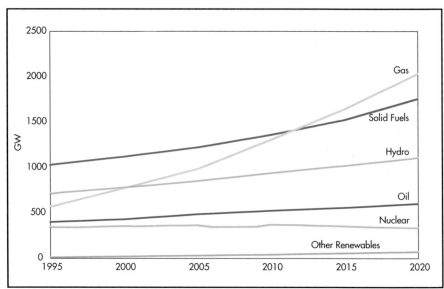

Figure 6.6: **World Electricity Generating Capacity by Fuel**

Generating Capacity

Between 1995 and 2020, world power generating capacity is projected to increase from 3079 to 5915 GW. New capacity requirement over the period is 3503 GW, including some 667 GW of existing plant expected to be retired over this period. The change in generating capacity from one year to the next is the net result of additions of new generating plants and the loss from plant retirements. Different types of generating plants are alloted fixed lives and plant retirements are determined by the history of plant commissioning and these fixed plant lives, on average 40-50 years.

The BAU projections for world generating capacity by region and by fuel type are shown in Figures 6.5 and 6.6. For the regions, the pattern is similar to those for generation shown in Figure 6.1. The projection of capacity by fuel type differs in some respects from that for generation in Figure 6.2. Figure 6.6 shows gas-fired capacity rising above coal by 2020, indicating the lower average load factor for gas-fired plants. The generating capacity for hydropower also appears relatively higher than for generation because it too has a low load factor.

The regional projections for generating capacity, new capacity and for plant retirements are listed in Table 6.2. Some of the oldest plants are located in the Transition Economies, in OECD Europe and in OECD North America.

Table 6.2: **New and Total Generating Plant Capacities and Plant Retirements 1995-2020**

	New generating plant capacity (GW)		
	1995-2010	**2010-2020**	**Total 1995-2020**
OECD Europe	263	267	530
OECD North America	309	260	569
OECD Pacific	98	97	195
Transition Economies	236	314	550
Latin America	158	167	325
Africa	56	61	118
Middle East	40	87	127
China	286	264	550
South Asia	113	105	218
East Asia	150	171	321
World	**1709**	**1794**	**3503**

Table 6.2 (continued)

	Generating plant capacity (GW)		
	1995	**2010**	**2020**
OECD Europe	628	853	1009
OECD North America	912	1159	1317
OECD Pacific	274	366	426
Transition Economies	434	586	776
Latin America	187	326	480
Africa	97	152	208
Middle East	89	126	206
China	227	501	757
South Asia	106	212	304
East Asia	126	275	432
World	**3079**	**4556**	**5915**

	Plant retirements (GW)		
	1995-2010	**2010-2020**	**Total 1995-2020**
OECD Europe	38	111	149
OECD North America	62	102	164
OECD Pacific	6	37	43
Transition Economies	84	125	209
Latin America	19	14	32
Africa	1	5	7
Middle East	2	8	10
China	12	8	19
South Asia	7	13	20
East Asia	1	13	14
World	**232**	**435**	**667**

About a third of the new capacity is projected to be built in the OECD region and about one half in China and the other developing regions. Projections of the capital expenditure needed for new capacity (excluding new transmission lines) are given in Table 6.3. Over the projection period, the capital expenditure remains a constant share of Gross Domestic Product, at around one third of one per cent.

Table 6.3: **Capital Expenditure on New Generating Plant**

| | $ Billion at 1990 prices | | |
	1995-2010	2010-2020	Total 1995-2020
OECD Europe	194	182	376
OECD North America	231	222	453
OECD Pacific	157	166	323
Transition Economies	207	222	429
Latin America	211	150	362
Africa	47	48	95
Middle East	40	68	108
China	323	306	629
South Asia	125	98	223
East Asia	137	144	282
World	**1673**	**1607**	**3280**

Projection Method for Power Generation

The projection method for power generation provides a simple, quantitative framework within which the many issues that arise in the sector may be analysed and quantified. Many of these issues involve current political or institutional trends in electric utilities, such as the future of nuclear power or large hydro schemes or the restructuring of electricity industries. In other cases, the absence of adequate, relevant data makes this quantification impossible (as for some developing countries). For those countries undergoing the transition from a centrally-planned to a market-oriented system, the pace of that transition and the ultimate form of the electricity industries that will emerge are very uncertain. In these cases, quantitative analysis provides little assistance, and judgements, supported by discussion of the issues, must be used. Even in these cases, however, a simple, quantitative framework is helpful in providing a basis for such a discussion.

The purpose of the power generation projection is to take electricity demand projections and assumptions for fossil fuel prices and availability and to calculate:
• the amount of any new generating capacity needed;
• the type of any new plant to be built;
• the amount of electricity generated by each type of plant;

- the fuels consumed to generate the estimated electricity demand;
- and the system short-run marginal cost of generation as the basis for the calculation of consumer electricity prices.

The calculation needs to simulate, albeit in a highly simplified manner, the way these outputs are determined in practice.

For market economies this means a lifetime, least-cost calculation for choice of new generating plants and a short-term, least-cost calculation for dispatching existing generating plants. Most state-owned monopolistic utilities have regulatory regimes that require cost minimisation, although examples are sometimes reported of choices of new plant decided on more political grounds. Where sufficient data are available on the existing stock of power plants and on the prices of generating fuels, a number of different ways exist for representing these two cost-minimising calculations.

Where plant or fuel price data do not exist, or where the choice of new plant or plant dispatching decisions are not made on a cost-minimising basis, more judgemental methods must be used, based on analysis of the data that do exist, on a review of the literature and on consultations with experts in the regions concerned. As more countries restructure their electricity industries and their associated regulatory systems on a market basis, it is likely that cost minimisation will become increasingly the norm over the period to 2020.

Structure of the Power Generation Model

In the power generation calculations, the demand for electricity (grossed up to take account of losses in transmission and own-use in the power sector) is combined with an assumed load curve to calculate peak load. The need for new generating capacity is calculated by adding a minimum reserve plant margin to peak load and comparing that with the capacity of existing plants less plant retirements using assumed plant lives. An allowance is needed for assumed plant availability. If new plant is needed, the choice is made on the basis of levelised cost. This is a technique widely used in the power sector by other modellers and by the IEA and NEA in their publications on comparative generating costs[2]. The levelised generating cost (expressed as money value per kWh) combines capital, operating and fuel costs over the whole operating life of a plant using a given discount rate and plant utilisation rate.

2 *Projected Costs of Generating Electricity,* IEA/NEA, OECD Paris, forthcoming.

Care has to be taken for each type of generating plant to ensure that sufficient supply of the resource or fuel is available to meet the demand for power generation (in addition to demand from other users) calculated for the region in the period in question. Most renewable resources are limited in capacity as is the availability of suitable sites. In some regions, the supply of natural gas may be limited by the resource available, the rate at which physical delivery systems and necessary regulatory structures may be put in place or the construction of LNG tankers, liquefying and gasifying facilities, etc. These problems are not assumed to apply to coal or oil. Because investments in nuclear and renewable plants have costs that are highly site- and country-specific and are frequently determined on a semi-political basis, they are determined by assumption. For reasons discussed earlier in the chapter, some allowance has to be made for oil use in peaking plant. The projection method ensures that annual oil use remains below 2500 hours in OECD Europe, 2250 hours in OECD North America and 3500 hours in the OECD Pacific region.

Once the existing set of plants has been determined, fossil fuel prices are used to load plants in ascending order of fuel and operating cost, allowing for assumed plant availability. Once the generation of each type of plant has been determined, the fuel requirements are calculated using plant efficiencies.

The marginal generating cost of each system is obtained by calculating the weighted average marginal cost over the load curve, using as weights the generation in each period.

Assumptions and Data Sources
New Generating Plants
Assumptions for the capital costs and efficiencies of new generating plants are listed in Table 6.4 by region. These figures are drawn from a wide variety of sources, including IEA studies[3], reports from the United States Energy Information Administration, national sources and the trade and business press. They should be treated with great caution. In a few cases they are based on observations made on actual new plants. In many cases, however, they are drawn from project proposals that may be subject to upward or downward bias. In any case, estimates vary widely in the literature, and some judgement has been exercised in choosing "typical" values. Capital costs are noticeably higher for new generating plants in Japan than elsewhere.

3. *Projected Costs of Generating Electricity,* IEA/NEA, OECD Paris, forthcoming.

Table 6.4: **Assumptions for Capital Costs and Efficiencies of New Generating Plants by Region 1995-2020**

	OECD Europe		OECD North America		OECD Pacific		China		Rest of World	
	1995	2020	1995	2020	1995	2020	1995	2020	1995	2020
Steam boiler - coal										
Capital cost ($/kW)	1025	1025	940	940	2130	2130	750	750	1000	1000
Efficiency %	38	40	38	40	40	42	35	38	35	38
CCGT - gas										
Capital cost ($/kW)	640	380	430	380	850	680	450	450	450	450
Efficiency %	52	60	52	60	47	56	50	55	50	55
GT - gas or oil										
Capital cost ($/kW)	340	310	270	260	640	510	275	275	275	275
Efficiency %	36	45	36	45	36	42	35	39	35	39
Nuclear										
Capital cost ($/kW)	2000	2000			3000	3000	2000	2000	2000	2000
Hydro										
Capital cost ($/kW)	2500	2500	2500	2500	3500*	3500*	2000	2000	2000	2000
Wind (availability 25%)										
Capital Cost ($/kW)	1000	1000	1000	1000			1000	1000	1000	1000
Geothermal										
Capital cost ($/kW)					2000	2000				

* pumped storage

Nuclear and Renewable Generation

Assumptions for future generating capacity and electricity generation by region for nuclear power are provided in Table 6.5 and for hydropower in Table 6.6. Detailed discussion of these assumptions may be found in Part III.

Table 6.7 provides similar information for four renewable categories. Again, some further details are given in Part III and in a forthcoming IEA report[4]. In many cases, the low or zero figures for developing countries represent a lack of adequate data, even for 1995.

4 *Renewable Energy Policy in IEA Countries,* Volume I (1997) and Volume II (forthcoming 1998), IEA/OECD Paris.

Table 6.5: **Assumptions for Nuclear Generating Capacity and Electricity Generation by Region 1995-2020**

	1995 Capacity (GW)	1995 Electricity (TWh)	2010 Capacity (GW)	2010 Electricity (TWh)	2020 Capacity (GW)	2020 Electricity (TWh)
OECD Europe	126	861	127	863	107	729
OECD North America	116	812	96	697	59	437
OECD Pacific	41	291	59	418	73	515
Transition Economies	41	216	44	257	29	181
Africa	2	11	2	12	2	12
China	2	13	11	72	20	127
East Asia	14	102	28	205	37	267
Latin America	3	18	4	30	4	30
Middle East	0	0	0	0	0	0
South Asia	2	8	3	15	4	19

Table 6.6: **Assumptions for Hydropower Generating Capacity and Electricity Generation by Region 1995-2020**

	1995 Capacity (GW)	1995 Electricity (TWh)	2010 Capacity (GW)	2010 Electricity (TWh)	2020 Capacity (GW)	2020 Electricity (TWh)
OECD Europe	167	486	188	585	201	629
of which Pumped Storage Hydro	30	-	32	-	34	-
OECD North America	165	648	172	680	177	703
of which Pumped Storage Hydro	22	-	22	-	22	-
OECD Pacific	56	126	69	145	73	152
of which Pumped Storage Hydro	23	-	30	-	33	-
Transition Economies	88	290	95	340	104	375
Africa	20	56	26	72	30	84
China	52	191	125	457	199	726
East Asia	25	78	40	131	55	185
Latin America	109	495	170	803	207	980
Middle East	5	16	10	32	10	32
South Asia	26	112	46	200	53	229

Note : Hydro output excludes output from pumped storage plants.

Table 6.7: **Assumptions for Generating Capacity and Electricity Generation from Renewable Energy Forms by Region 1995-2020**

	1995 Capacity (GW)	1995 Electricity (TWh)	2010 Capacity (GW)	2010 Electricity (TWh)	2020 Capacity (GW)	2020 Electricity (TWh)
OECD Europe						
Geothermal	0.7	4.1	1.6	10.2	1.9	12.7
Wind	2.3	4.0	15.0	32.9	30.0	65.7
Sol/Tide/Other	0.8	1.8	1.2	2.6	1.7	3.8
Waste	5.5	30.2	7.8	42.5	9.8	53.5
OECD North America						
Geothermal	3.0	14.9	3.0	19.6	3.0	19.9
Wind	1.9	3.3	3.5	7.7	5.5	13.0
Sol/Tide/Other	0.4	0.9	0.7	1.8	1.1	3.0
Waste	12.5	67.0	14.8	79.6	16.4	88.2
OECD Pacific						
Geothermal	0.8	5.3	2.1	14.5	3.3	22.9
Wind	0.0	0.0	1.0	3.1	2.9	8.6
Sol/Tide/Other	0.0	0.1	0.5	0.7	2.8	3.7
Waste	4.0	17.7	4.6	20.6	5.1	22.7
Transition Economies						
Geothermal	0.0	0.0	0.0	0.0	0.0	0.0
Wind	0.0	0.0	0.0	0.0	0.0	0.0
Sol/Tide/Other	0.0	0.0	0.0	0.0	0.0	0.0
Waste	0.6	2.8	0.6	2.8	0.6	2.8
Africa						
Geothermal	0.0	0.4	0.4	2.1	0.5	3.1
Wind	0.0	0.0	0.4	0.9	0.7	1.5
Sol/Tide/Other	0.0	0.0	0.0	0.0	0.1	0.1
Waste	0.1	0.3	0.1	0.6	0.1	0.6
China						
Geothermal	0.0	0.0	0.3	1.6	0.4	2.5
Wind	0.2	0.0	2.3	4.9	3.7	8.1
Sol/Tide/Other	0.0	0.0	0.1	0.1	0.1	0.2
Waste	0.0	0.0	0.1	0.4	0.2	0.7
East Asia						
Geothermal	1.4	8.0	6.1	33.8	8.8	48.7
Wind	0.0	0.0	0.0	0.0	0.0	0.1
Sol/Tide/Other	0.0	0.0	0.0	0.0	0.0	0.0
Waste	0.1	0.3	0.2	0.6	0.5	1.5
Latin America						
Geothermal	1.0	6.7	1.4	9.1	1.7	11.2
Wind	0.0	0.0	0.4	0.2	0.5	0.2
Sol/Tide/Other	0.0	0.0	0.0	0.0	0.0	0.0
Waste	2.0	9.6	3.0	13.1	3.9	17.1
Middle East						
Geothermal	0.0	0.0	0.0	0.0	0.0	0.0
Wind	0.0	0.0	0.0	0.0	0.1	0.0
Sol/Tide/Other	0.0	0.0	0.0	0.0	0.0	0.0
Waste	0.0	0.0	0.0	0.0	0.0	0.0
South Asia						
Geothermal	0.0	0.0	0.0	0.0	0.0	0.0
Wind	0.0	0.1	3.3	7.3	4.0	8.8
Sol/Tide/Other	0.0	0.0	0.3	0.5	0.5	1.1
Waste	0.1	0.0	1.0	4.6	1.7	7.3

Note: The sum of geothermal, wind, solar, tide and other is classified as "other renewables" in the regional chapters. Waste is included with solid fuel output.

Data on Existing Generating Plants

Data on capacities of generating plants by region and by fuel type as well as other characteristics of generating plants, such as operating efficiencies, plant lives, are drawn from a wide variety of sources, including estimations from IEA data, the Utility Data Institute[5], country statistical reports, consultants' reports and the business and trade press.

Limitations of the Power Generation Projection Method

Regional Variations in Fuel Prices

The power generation model considers each region as a single utility with a single price for each generation fuel. This is seldom the case for a single country, and is certainly not the case for any of the world regions considered in this Outlook. For example, in OECD Europe, coal prices are much higher in Germany and gas prices are generally lower in the Netherlands and in Italy than in other European countries. Adjustments for such regional differences in fuel prices are made in the projection both in the merit order calculation and in the choice of new plant, as well as in calculating the average prices for generating fuels for the region.

Uncertainties in Plant Parameters

The future values of capital and operating costs of different types of generating plants and their efficiencies are not known with precision and may vary from one country to another within a region. For this reason, formal cost-minimising calculations must be treated with caution. The actual outcome of dispatching and new-plant choice is likely to include some near-optimal options in addition to the optimal choices. In the projections, new plant technologies with levelised costs near the minimum value are included in the new-plant mix.

Uncertainties Faced by Utilities

When facing an uncertain future for prices of generating fuels and growth rate in electricity demand, utilities are likely to choose a portfolio of generating plant types rather than a single, optimal choice. This is another reason why some near-optimal choices for new generating plant types are included with the optimal choice calculated in the projection.

5 *World Power Plant Database,* Utility Data Institute, McGraw-Hill Co., Washington, DC, USA, 1996.

Local Constraints

For some countries within a region, capacity constraints on natural gas pipelines may limit the rate at which electricity generation from gas may grow. These are likely to be resolved over time in a developed region such as OECD Europe. More care needs to be taken on this issue for less developed regions such as Asia where there is greater reliance on seaborne LNG trade. In some cases, the existence of electricity transmission constraints may need to be taken into account. But no account has been taken of these constraints in this Outlook.

Environmental Constraints

Environmental regulations, including those for emissions of sulphur, NOx and particulates, are already in place in many countries and their impacts on plant dispatching and choice of new generating plants are likely to grow. These emission considerations are not explicitly included in the BAU projection. For new plants, these can, to some extent, be accommodated by limiting the range of new-plant technologies considered. The BAU projections do not include policies introduced to meet commitments made at the COP-3 Conference held in Kyoto.

Limits to Fuel Substitution

Changes in the prices for generating fuels can produce changes in the merit-order of plant and the dispatching programme. In practice, the opportunities for a coal plant in one country, for example, to substitute for a gas plant in another will depend on the capacity of international grid connectors and the arrangements for electricity trade. In general, these are limited, although electricity trade between world regions may grow in importance in the future. In the BAU projection, limits are included for the extent of fuel substitution arising from changes in relative prices to take account of international trading constraints.

Electricity Industry Restructuring

The restructuring of electricity industries from vertically-integrated utilities, each with its own service area, into more competitive structures with new types of regulation, has taken place in a number of countries: in the United Kingdom, the Nordic countries,

New Zealand, Australia, Chile, Argentina and elsewhere. The trading of electric power between regions has been widespread in the United States and many individual states are moving to more market-oriented systems. The 1996 electricity directive[6] in the European Union (EU) calls for increased competition in EU countries by 1999 (for Belgium and Ireland by 2000 and for Greece by 2001). Two alternative systems are allowed, the Third Party Access (TPA) system and the Single Buyer (SB) system. The degree of competition expected to result under this directive will depend on how the measures are implemented by individual countries. In some cases, for example in the United Kingdom, electricity-market restructuring has already been taken well beyond the requirements of the directive.

In many developing countries and countries in transition, restructuring is also taking place in electricity industries. The emphasis here is on privatisation and commercialisation, rather than on the creation of a competitive electricity industry. The more immediate aim is to improve the financial viability of the industry.

Some issues arising from increased competition in electricity industries are listed below.

Lower Generating Costs and Electricity Prices

Increased direct competition between generators is likely to lead to reductions in unit costs at power stations and headquarters of generating companies. Cuts in labour force of up to 50% were made in United Kingdom generating companies in the five-year period following restructuring in 1990, with increased power output. Where plant availability allows, greater competition is likely to see the increased use of low-cost generating plant as the competitive generating system seeks to minimise cost. Preliminary analysis by the US Department of Energy[7] suggests that increased use of existing low-cost coal-fired generating plants (by about 5%) may substitute for gas and oil-fired plant in the United States. The combined effect of these two factors will lower the costs of generation. Two other matters will affect electricity prices. The first is that commercial enterprises will seek a higher rate of profit on capital because of the more uncertain business environment in a competitive market, as well as the need to provide a sufficient dividend to shareholders and provide for growth in the

---

6. *Concerning Common Rules for the Internal Market in Electricity*, EU Directive, 1996.
7. *Modeling Electricity Restructuring using POEMS: Shaping Competitive Prices through Cost Sharing and Shifting*, John Conti et al., USDOE 1997.

business to maintain share price. In addition, reductions in overhead costs at headquarters, R&D expenditures, etc., can be expected to take place. The net effect of these trends is likely to be reductions in real electricity prices as electricity markets become more competitive. In the BAU projection, the mark-up from average generating system marginal cost to electricity price is reduced over the projection period.

Implications for Renewables

The emphasis on cost minimisation in a competitive market implies a stricter cost criteria for renewable technologies than in a monopoly structure. Under either structure, governments may, if they wish, provide financial support for some forms of renewable energy. This support can also be market-tested by inviting competitive tenders from renewable energy suppliers to provide specified elements of new capacity. In some cases, and in the longer term, greater market flexibility may provide scope for some renewable applications by electricity consumers. The contribution from renewables in the business as usual projection is based on assumptions.

Implications for Co-generation

Greater flexibility for autoproducers to sell their production in the electricity market may encourage cogeneration by industrial and large service-sector establishments. This would reduce electricity demand on other generators, reduce "heat" supplies from other sources and lead to increases in efficiency and lower emissions. In the BAU projection, a rising path of heat demand is assumed and corresponding reductions in fossil fuel consumption are made within a total projection of energy demand for stationary energy services (see Chapter 3). Electricity produced in association with this heat is included in the power generation projection.

Role of Merchant Generating Plants

A competitive electricity market provides increased opportunities for generators to invest in generating capacity, not just to meet capacity and reserve requirements, but to displace existing higher-cost plants. To be successful, these new plants must have a lower levelised cost (that takes account of all capital, operating and fuel costs) than the short-run marginal cost of the plant to be displaced. The result could be lower electricity prices.

Changes in the Shape of the Load Curve

The emergence of more differentiated electricity products - for example, wider and more flexible interruptible contracts - may lead to a flatter peak and higher shoulder sections in the load curve.

Conclusions

The projection method used for the power sector in this Outlook employs an explicit description of different electricity-generating technologies. It separates electricity demand, generation, generating capacity, new generating-plant construction, plant retirements, efficiencies and fuel consumption. It adopts cost minimisation in the choice of new generating plants and in the use of existing plants. Its structure, the numerical values of its parameters and assumptions, and its results are, however, subject to many uncertainties. A great many judgements, as well as considerable computation, have been made in the power projections presented here. In this sense, the projections follow the main thrust of this Outlook - to provide a quantitative framework for discussing the main factors and uncertainties affecting the future of energy supply and demand.

CHAPTER 7
OIL

Box 7.1: **Oil Supply**

Oil has the largest share of any fuel in world primary energy supply. Transport fuels are the fastest growing element and currently account for over half of oil demand. The remainder is used mainly for heating in buildings, industrial processes, power generation and for non-energy uses. Oil products can be easily transported and stored. Other fuels, such as coal, gas, nuclear power, hydro and other renewables are less flexible, but once the associated equipment, delivery infrastructure and contracts have been put in place, they tend to be used in preference to oil because they have a lower marginal cost in the short-term. In many countries, oil serves, in this sense, as a residual fuel.

This chapter presents projections of oil demand and supply. Definitions of the sources of oil supply, including production of conventional and unconventional oil, are provided in Box 7.2 together with definitions of oil reserves. Following a brief review of the business as usual projection of world oil demand, the chapter discusses the uncertainties surrounding future oil production and the extent of recoverable oil reserves, and analyses the relationship between them.

Box 7.2: **Definitions**

Oil is defined to include all liquid fuels and is accounted at the product level. Sources include natural gas liquids and condensates, refinery processing gains and the production of conventional and unconventional oil[1]. In the Outlook, stock changes are included in oil demand. Oil considered unconventional if it is not produced from underground hydrocarbon reservoirs by means of production wells and/or it needs additional processing to produce synthetic crude. More specifically, unconventional oil production is based on

1. The definition of unconventional oil is a shortened version of that given in *Oil Information,* IEA/OECD Paris, 1997.

the IEA's *Oil Market Report* (OMR) definitions and includes the following sources, listed in order from the heaviest to the lightest original resource:
- Oil Shales;
- Oil Sands-based Synthetic Crudes and Derivative Products;
- Coal-based Liquid Supplies;
- Biomass-based Liquid Supplies;
- Gas-based Liquid Supplies.

In 1996, production of unconventional oil, using this definition, amounted to 1.2 million barrels per day (Mbd). Production of natural gas liquids (including condensates) and refinery processing gains amounted to 6.7 Mbd and 1.5 Mbd respectively. Total oil supply in 1996 was 72 Mbd. Table 7.16 provides a breakdown of unconventional oil supplies and includes extra heavy oils such as Orinoco, as the latter has an API of less than 10°.

In this study, the term resources refers to oil in the ground, regardless of whether it can be recovered or not. The term reserves, or recoverable reserves, refers to that portion of resources that is believed to be recoverable with current or prospective technology and oil prices.

Ultimate reserves is the sum of production to date, identified and unidentified reserves. Identified reserves can be split into proved (high probability of being recovered), probable (medium probability) and possible (low probability) categories.

Oil Demand

The oil demand projections outlined in this chapter, and discussed in more detail in the regional chapters, have been prepared using a suite of regional energy models. The main assumptions used in preparing the BAU oil demand projections are shown in Table 7.1 below.

Table 7.1: **Oil Demand Assumptions for the BAU Projection**

	1997	1998-2010	2015	2020
Oil Price $ 1990/bbl	$16.1	$17	$25	$25
		1995 - 2020		
World GDP percent per annum		3.1%		

Table 7.2 shows that world demand is projected to increase from 3324 Mtoe in 1995 to 5264 Mtoe in 2020. During the period 1995 - 2010, the OECD's total demand is expected to grow at a little over 1% per annum on average and then to slow after 2010. Non-OECD demand is projected to grow strongly throughout the projection period at an average rate of 2.9% per annum. The general slowdown after 2010 results from an increase in world oil prices over the period 2010 to 2015, discussed later in this chapter. During the second decade of the 21st century, the non-OECD countries consumption of oil surpasses that of the OECD; by 2020 it is over 20% larger. The non-OECD's increase in demand for oil is likely to be dominated by demand growth in the Asian countries. Despite the recent economic difficulties experienced by some Asian countries, the demand for oil in Asia is projected to grow at an average rate of around 4% per annum during the projection period 1995-2020.

Table 7.2: **BAU Projection - Total Oil Demand (Mtoe)**

| | 1995 | 2010 | 2020 | 1995-2010 | 1995-2020 |
				Annual Growth Rates	
OECD	**1832**	**2158.7**	**2261.5**	**1.1%**	**0.8%**
North America	873.3	1025.3	1049.9	1.1%	0.7%
Europe	650.2	779.1	850.3	1.2%	1.1%
Pacific	308.7	354.3	361.3	0.9%	0.6%
Non-OECD	**1362.9**	**2135.2**	**2793.8**	**3.0%**	**2.9%**
Transition Economies	274.6	329.0	390.5	1.2%	1.4%
Africa	96.9	145.4	180.3	2.7%	2.5%
China	163.9	355.5	505.7	5.3%	4.6%
East Asia	263.9	471.5	639.1	3.9%	3.6%
South Asia	98.7	191.1	277.5	4.5%	4.2%
Latin America	281.5	423.8	519.7	2.8%	2.5%
Middle East	183.4	218.8	280.9	1.2%	1.7%
Total	**3195.1**	**4293.9**	**5055.3**	**2.0%**	**1.9%**
Maritime bunkers	129.2	174.7	208.7	2.0%	1.9%
World	**3324.3**	**4468.5**	**5263.9**	**2.0%**	**1.9%**

Transport Sector

The transport sector is projected to be the major source of oil demand growth. The non-OECD transport sector's demand is projected to grow on average by 3.6% per annum throughout the projection period. Growth in the OECD is somewhat lower, at an average of 1.5% per annum. In both cases, growth of aviation fuel demand is projected to be greater than that for surface transport. Despite its slower growth, the OECD is still projected to consume more oil in the transport sector than the non-OECD regions in 2020. This continued dominance of the OECD reflects higher average vehicle ownership and per capita income levels.

Table 7.3: **BAU Projection - Transport Sector Oil Demand[2] (Mtoe)**

	1995	2010	2020	1995-2010	1995-2020
				Annual Growth Rates	
OECD	**992.8**	**1317.5**	**1440.4**	**1.9%**	**1.5%**
North America	571.5	708.7	739.9	1.4%	1.0%
Europe	307.2	461.3	545.4	2.7%	2.3%
Pacific	114.1	147.5	155.2	1.7%	1.2%
Non-OECD	**483.2**	**843.2**	**1178.5**	**3.8%**	**3.6%**
Transition Economies	63.7	98.5	131.2	3.0%	2.9%
Africa	39.4	55.2	67.1	2.3%	2.1%
China	52.2	122.8	182.4	5.9%	5.1%
East Asia	94.8	205.1	312.6	5.3%	4.9%
South Asia	46.3	91.9	140.6	4.7%	4.5%
Latin America	130.4	202.3	260.8	3.0%	2.8%
Middle East	56.4	67.3	83.9	1.2%	1.6%
World	**1475.9**	**2160.7**	**2619.0**	**2.6%**	**2.3%**

Power Generation

Oil use in the OECD's power generation sector is projected to remain flat. A shift from fuel oil used in base and mid-load plants towards middle distillates used for peaking plants is expected. Some modest growth may occur in North America, but this is projected to be more than offset elsewhere in the OECD[3].

Power generators in Eastern Europe are expected to reduce their annual consumption of oil by around 1% per annum on average throughout the projection period due to fuel substitution and increased efficiency of use. Growth in other non-OECD countries is projected to offset the decline in Eastern Europe, with the result that

2. Excluding maritime bunkers.
3. Full details of the demand for energy in this sector can be found in Chapter 6.

oil demand in the non-OECD power generation sector is expected to grow on average by 1.7% per annum.

Table 7.4: **BAU Projection - Power Generation Sector Oil Demand (Mtoe)**

	1995	2010	2020	1995-2010	1995-2020
				Annual Growth Rates	
OECD	**107.2**	**104.3**	**110.7**	**-0.2%**	**0.1%**
North America	17.3	23.7	26.7	2.1%	1.8%
Europe	46.9	42.2	45.5	-0.7%	-0.1%
Pacific	43.0	38.4	38.5	-0.8%	-0.4%
Non-OECD	**200.4**	**263.2**	**307.1**	**1.8%**	**1.7%**
Transition Economies	62.6	50.4	49.6	-1.4%	-0.9%
Africa	12.8	21.2	22.2	3.4%	2.2%
China	13.4	36.1	55.1	6.8%	5.8%
East Asia	35.4	45.2	42.5	1.6%	0.7%
South Asia	6.9	13.8	21.8	4.7%	4.7%
Latin America	32.3	57.0	66.6	3.9%	2.9%
Middle East	37.0	39.4	49.4	0.4%	1.2%
World	**307.5**	**367.5**	**417.8**	**1.2%**	**1.2%**

Stationary Sectors

Demand for oil in the stationary sectors (industrial, commercial, residential, agricultural and non-energy use) is projected to decline slightly in the OECD, but to grow by 2.6% per annum in the non-OECD. Relatively modest growth in the Transition Economies is projected to be more than offset by rapid growth in Asia. In consequence, by 2020, the non-OECD region is projected to have an oil demand some 70% greater than that of the OECD. Increasing industrialisation in the non-OECD countries, switching away from non-commercial fuels and greater use of oil for heating purposes in the commercial and residential sectors explain much of this projected growth in demand.

Summary of Oil Demand

One clear message from the above analysis is that the transport sector will account for the bulk of the growth in oil demand during the period to 2020. Worldwide oil demand is projected to increase by 1940 Mtoe between 1995 and 2020; of this growth, 59% will come from the transport sector, 25% from the stationary sectors, 6% from the power generation sector and the remainder from other energy conversion industries.

Table 7.5: **BAU Projection - Stationary Sectors Oil Demand (Mtoe)**

	1995	2010	2020	1995-2010 Annual Growth Rates	1995-2020 Annual Growth Rates
OECD	**643.3**	**638.5**	**610.5**	**-0.1%**	**-0.2%**
North America	247.2	249.2	238.6	0.1%	-0.1%
Europe	259.8	239.2	223.1	-0.5%	-0.6%
Pacific	136.3	150.1	148.8	0.6%	0.4%
Non-OECD	**558.7**	**837.5**	**1055.8**	**2.7%**	**2.6%**
Transition Economies	117.2	141.9	165.2	1.3%	1.4%
Africa	38.6	60.0	79.5	3.0%	2.9%
China	79.8	157.4	212.9	4.6%	4.0%
East Asia	113.2	183.1	230.6	3.3%	2.9%
South Asia	40.6	76.0	101.6	4.3%	3.7%
Latin America	93.3	126.8	145.9	2.1%	1.8%
Middle East	75.9	92.3	120.1	1.3%	1.9%
World	**1202.0**	**1476.0**	**1666.3**	**1.4%**	**1.3%**

Figure 7.1: **BAU Projection - World Fuel Shares**

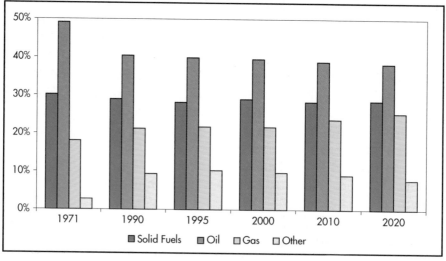

The increasing concentration of oil demand in transport reflects the loss of share in several non-transportation sectors to other fuels, particularly to gas. Oil demand is projected to increase on average by 1.9% per annum between 1995 and 2020, whereas gas is projected to grow by 2.6% per annum. Oil's share of world energy demand declines from 40% in 1995 to 38% by 2020. Despite this decline, oil is projected to remain the single largest energy source. The switch from oil to gas can be seen in Figure 7.1.

Units

So far, the discussion of oil demand has been in terms of millions of tonnes of oil equivalent. This is a unit of energy content appropriate for analysing the substitution between fuels in energy consumption. The data and analysis of oil production, on the other hand, is traditionally carried out in units of millions of barrels per day (Mbd), a production rate in volumetric units. In order to link the two analyses, conversion factors must be applied.

Table 7.6: **1995 World Oil Demand - Oil Market Report Basis**

	Inland Demand	Bunkers	Total	Total	Aggregate Conversion Factor
	Mtoe	Mtoe	Mtoe	Mbd	Barrels per toe
OECD	**1832.2**	**70.99**	**1903.2**	**40.6**	**7.79**
North America**	873.3	27.7	901.1	19.8	8.02
Europe**	650.2	36.0	686.2	14.1	7.50
Pacific**	308.7	7.3	316.0	6.7	7.74*
Non-OECD	**1362.9**	**58.2**	**1421.1**	**29.5**	**7.58**
Transition Economies**	274.6	1.5	276.1	6.0	7.93
Africa	96.9	8.3	105.2	2.2	7.63
China	163.9	2.6	166.5	3.3	7.23*
Other Asia**	362.6	22.4	385.0	7.9	7.49
Latin America**	281.5	8.6	290.1	6.0	7.55
Middle East	183.4	14.7	198.1	4.1	7.55
World	**3195.1**	**129.2**	**3324.3**	**70.1**	**7.70**

* The figure for China appears to be too low and that for OECD Pacific appears to be too high. These figures need further investigation.

** Pending submission of the detailed historical data needed to incorporate them into the OECD, the following OECD countries are shown in the IEA *Oil Market Report* (until August 1998) in the relevant non-OECD regions: the Czech Republic and Poland in Non-OECD Europe, Korea in Other Asia and Mexico in Latin America. Note also that, whereas the OMR mbd includes marine bunkers, the IEA Mtoe does not, except for the world.

Sources: Mtoe data are taken from the IEA statistical databases and the mbd (million barrels per day) are taken from the *Oil Market Report* (OMR) dated 11 May 1998.

Two problems arise. The first is that each oil product has its own barrel-to-tonne oil equivalent factor, so that a change in oil product mix alters the aggregate conversion factor for a region or country. The second problem is that oil consumption data and oil production data are collected from different sources. Inevitably, some differences exist between the data sources.

In order to deal with the above problems, the approach taken is to compare the databases expressed in tonnes and in barrels for 1995 and to apply the resulting regional conversion factors thereafter. The factors used are reproduced in Table 7.6.

Using the above conversion factors, the BAU oil demand projection is shown in Mbd terms in Table 7.7.

Table 7.7: **World Oil Demand (Business as Usual)**
Oil Market Report Basis (Mbd)

	1995	2010	2020	1995-2010 Annual Growth Rates	1995-2020
OECD	**40.6**	**48.1**	**50.7**	**1.1%**	**0.9%**
North America	19.8	23.4	24.1	1.1%	0.8%
Europe	14.1	17.0	18.7	1.3%	1.1%
Pacific	6.7	7.7	7.9	0.9%	0.7%
Non-OECD	**29.5**	**46.0**	**59.9**	**3.0%**	**2.9%**
Transition Economies	6.0	7.2	8.5	1.2%	1.4%
Africa	2.2	3.3	4.0	2.7%	2.5%
China	3.3	7.1	10.1	5.3%	4.6%
Other Asia	7.9	14.2	19.5	4.0%	3.7%
Latin America	6.0	9.0	11.0	2.7%	2.5%
Middle East	4.1	4.9	6.3	1.2%	1.7%
Total Demand (excl. stocks)	**70.1**	**94.2**	**111.0**	**2.0%**	**1.9%**

Note: The above table excludes stock changes but includes bunkers. In 1995 there was virtually no change in stocks (< 0.1 Mbd).

Oil Reserves and Production[4]

Previous versions of the World Energy Outlook did not place great emphasis on distinguishing between the different types of oil supplied to meet demand for petroleum products. The 1998 World

4. Some of the reserve estimates and charts shown in this chapter are based on work done by Jean Laherrère using the Petroconsultants database held in Geneva. The IEA would like formally to thank Petroconsultants for permission to reproduce the charts based on data taken from their database.

Energy Outlook differs from its predecessors in this respect, because the projection horizon has been extended from 2010 to 2020. For the first time, the WEO's oil supply projections have to consider the possibility that the production of conventional oil could peak before 2020. With this point in mind, supplies from conventional and non-conventional oil are considered separately and distinguished from other sources of supply (see Box 7.2 at the beginning of the chapter).

Conventional Oil Reserves

The level of future conventional oil production is ultimately determined by the quantity of remaining oil reserves and the recovery factor. It is therefore important that reliable estimates of remaining oil reserves are used when preparing long-term oil supply forecasts.

Perhaps the most widely used oil reserve estimates are those published annually by British Petroleum (BP)[5]. The chart in Figure 7.2, taken from the *BP Statistical Review of World Energy*, shows how estimates of these official world oil reserves and production have changed during the period 1961 - 1995.

Figure 7.2: **World Oil Official (proved) Reserves & Production**

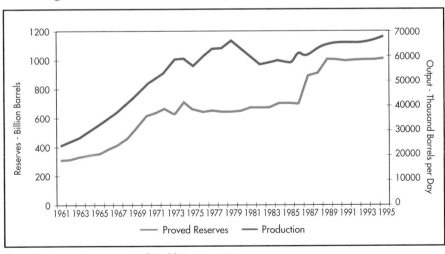

Source: *BP Statistical Review of World Energy,* 1997.

An interesting feature of Figure 7.2 is that these reserves increased dramatically in the mid- to late -1980s. Between 1985 and 1989, worldwide oil reserves increased by 43% or 304 billion barrels, up

5. BP's published oil reserves estimates are reproduced from the *Oil and Gas Journal.*

from 708 billion barrels in 1985. During the period, total oil discoveries amounted to approximately 65 billion barrels and cumulative production was around 91 billion barrels. Cumulative production exceeded new discoveries by 26 billion barrels. This 304 billion barrel increase in total reserves implies a worldwide oil reserve revision of 330 billion barrels. Such a huge increase raises the questions of why and where these revisions occurred.

In order to answer these questions, it is useful to divide worldwide conventional oil reserves between OPEC and non-OPEC areas. In Figure 7.3, it is clear that non-OPEC proved reserves remained broadly stable during the period 1970 and 1995 at around 200-250 billion barrels. Non-OPEC's oil production was rising during this period with new discoveries and reserve revisions increasing broadly in line with production. The bulk of the reserve revisions took place in the OPEC area as shown in Figure 7.4.

Figure 7.3: **Non-OPEC Official (proved) Oil Reserves & Production**

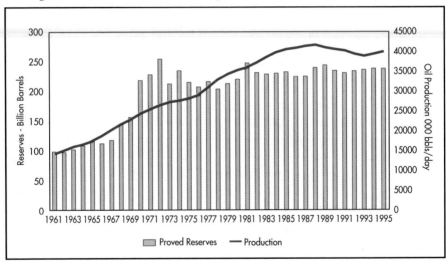

Source: *BP Statistical Review of World Energy,* 1997.

Total OPEC official oil reserves increased by almost 300 billion barrels between 1985 and 1989. Following the fall in the oil price in 1986, OPEC's oil production quotas became an important issue to its member governments. Since reserves were an important potential factor in determining quota allocations, every OPEC country had an incentive to increase its published reserve estimate. In the space of just four years, total OPEC oil reserves increased by 62%. Since then, OPEC's total oil reserves have remained virtually unchanged year after year.

Figure 7.4: **OPEC Official (proved) Oil Reserves**

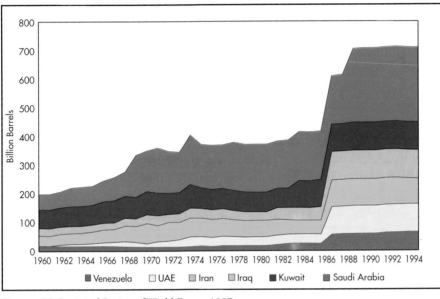

Source: *BP Statistical Review of World Energy,* 1997.

Because of this large, one-off increase in OPEC's oil reserves, many commentators have questioned the reliability of the reserves estimates data published in the BP Statistical Review of Energy and the Oil and Gas Journal. They have noted that, while the reserve estimates are described as proven (meaning a greater than 90% probability of being produced), a comparison with the Petroconsultants oil field database suggests that large quantities of probable and possible reserves may have been included in the OPEC estimates. Furthermore, large quantities of unconventional oil also appear to have been included in some OPEC member country estimates, possibly in order to obtain a larger oil production quota.

One commentator[6], Colin Campbell, has attempted to determine the size of the over-reporting of OPEC member country reserves by

6. *The Coming Oil Crisis,* CJ Campbell, Multi-Science Publishing Company and Petroconsultants S.A., Brentwood, UK, 1997.
The Status of World Oil Depletion at the end of 1995, C.J. Campbell, Energy Exploration and Exploitation, Volume 14, 1996, Number 1.
Better Understanding Urged for Rapidly Depleting Reserves, C.J. Campbell, Oil and Gas Journal, April 7, 1997, pp 51-54.

comparing their published estimates with those obtained from the Petroconsultants' oil field database. The results of his analysis for selected OPEC countries and three non-OPEC countries can be seen in Table 7.8.

Given the above, it is clear that official oil reserve estimates cannot be considered reliable indicators of remaining oil reserves. Because of these problems, many oil experts base their views on oil reserves on two principal sources of information. The first is the Petroconsultants oil field database, which is based in Geneva and concentrates on the world outside North America. The second is the United States Geological Service (USGS), which publishes estimates of worldwide oil reserves. These two sources are not entirely independent, as the USGS estimates are themselves partly based upon the Petroconsultants database, particularly for the world outside of North America. Despite this interdependence, it is not unusual for different reserve estimates to be obtained using the Petroconsultants database. For example, Jean Laherrère's 1997 estimate of worldwide discovered reserves (1530 billion barrels) differs from that of the USGS in 1997 (1608 billion barrels). This is despite the fact that both Laherrère and the USGS used exactly the same Petroconsultants database.

Table 7.8: **Reserve Estimates by Country[7] (billion barrels)**

	World Oil Estimate	Oil and Gas Journal (adjusted)* (1)	Campbell (median value) (2)	(2) - (1)
OPEC				
Saudi Arabia	260.00	252.98	189.73	-63.25
Iran	58.65	88.20	52.92	-35.25
Iraq	99.43	97.37	68.16	-29.21
Kuwait	95.20	91.74	59.63	-32.11
Venezuela	64.88	63.54	31.77	-31.77
Abu Dhabi	62.00	88.83	62.18	-26.65
Libya	36.57	29.50	22.13	-7.37
Non-OPEC				
Former Soviet Union	191.14	42.01	84.01	+42.00
Mexico	49.78	49.78	24.89	-24.89
China	30.20	17.70	28.32	+10.62

* Adjusted by Campbell to allow for years in which the published Oil and Gas Journal reserves did not alter to reflect the fact that oil production had taken place during the previous 12 months.

7. *The Status of World Oil Depletion at the end of 1995*, C.J. Campbell, Energy Exploration & Exploitation, Volume 14 1996, Number 1.

There are two main views on how to project future conventional oil supply: the pessimists' view, which makes a static assessment of reserves, and the optimists' view, which employs a continuous upward reappraisal of recoverable reserves. Summaries of these views are given below. Both make substantial use of the 1994 United States Geological Survey (USGS) estimates. In 1994, the USGS estimated that ultimate (total recoverable) oil reserves were around 2300 billion barrels (in a range of 2100 to 2800) and included the elements shown in Table 7.9.

The two competing views on oil supply deal only with conventional oil (see Box 7.2 at the beginning of the chapter).

Table 7.9: **1994 USGS Ultimate Oil Reserve Estimate as of 1/1/1993**

(modal estimates)	Billion Barrels
Cumulative Production to date	699
Remaining Identified Reserves	1103
Unidentified Reserves	471
Total Ultimate Recoverable Reserves	**2300 (rounded)**

Source: 14th World Petroleum Congress, *World Petroleum Assessment and Analysis* by Charles D. Masters, Emil D. Attanasi and David H. Root, US Geological Survey, National Centre, Reston, Virginia, USA, 1994.

The Pessimists' View

The pessimists treat the estimate of remaining reserves as a snapshot of the situation today with little or no anticipation of new information that may become available over time, from new technology or from variations in the oil price. Advances in new technology (3D seismic analysis and horizontal drilling) are seen as increasing the rate of production while having little impact on the estimate of recoverable reserves. Another example of how the pessimists' view differs from that of the USGS can be found in their estimates of undiscovered oil. The pessimists argue that the USGS's estimates are unduly high, given that most parts of the world have already been extensively explored. They argue that the USGS methodology, based in part on Delphi surveys, are not reliable. They prefer their statistical approach that yields more conservative results. Their estimate of ultimate recoverable reserves is around 1800 billion barrels, including cumulative production of around 800 billion barrels, as shown in Table 7.10.

Table 7.10: **Pessimists' View of Ultimate Oil Reserve Estimate as of 1/1/1997**

	Billion Barrels
Cumulative Production	784
Remaining Identified Reserves	836
Unidentified Reserves	180
Total Ultimate Recoverable Reserves	**1800**

Source: *The Coming Oil Crisis* by C.J. Campbell, Multi-Science Publishing Company & Petroconsultants S.A, page 175.

Since the purpose of this chapter is to assess oil supply, and not reserves, it is also important to note the pessimists' view of how the stock of oil (reserves) is transformed into supply. They assume that regional or global oil production follows a Hubbert curve in which oil production peaks when half of ultimate oil reserves has been produced. An ultimate reserve of 1800 billion barrels implies that the peak in conventional oil production will occur when 900 billion barrels have been produced. Campbell[8] has suggested that such a peak could come as early as 2001. However, this date implicitly assumes that a substantial increase in the oil price will occur once the share of world production from swing producers (Saudi Arabia, Iran, Iraq, Kuwait and the United Arab Emirates) reaches approximately 30%. In the absence of such an oil price increase, the IEA's long-term oil supply model suggests that even with ultimate of reserves of 1800 billion barrels, and assuming a Hubbert curve, worldwide oil production would not peak until around 2008 - 2009. An example of the Hubbert curve can be found in Figure 7.5.

Figure 7.5: **Generalised Hubbert Curve**

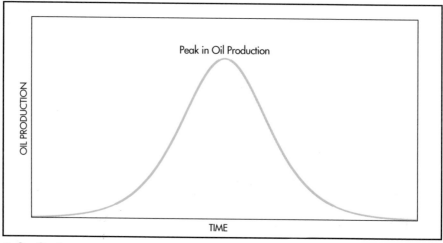

8. Op. Cit. 6.

Improving production technologies over time could result in the right hand tail of the Hubbert curve being somewhat fatter than the left hand tail. In addition, new technology could lead to an extension of peak production levels and a steeper eventual downturn in production. Thus, technical progress has the potential to change not only the area under the Hubbert curve, but also its shape. Part of the production increase in regions like the North Sea may be considered as a change in the shape of the Hubbert curve, i.e. allowing faster depletion. While it is recognised that the Hubbert curve may not be symmetrical, trying to adjust it to allow for this asymmetry is particularly difficult. The impact of technological progress in this Outlook is therefore confined to increasing the quantity of recoverable reserves under the Hubbert curve rather than trying to estimate how it might change its shape.

The issue of the size of conventional oil reserves and the level of production from them has been further complicated by a recent finding by Jean Laherrère[9]. Using the Petroconsultants database, he noted that only around 80% of oil reserves discovered are actually in production. As Figure 7.6 demonstrates, this finding holds true across all regions of the world. In the case of the Middle East, it is reasonable to argue that

Figure 7.6: **Percentage of Discovered Oil Reserves in Production**

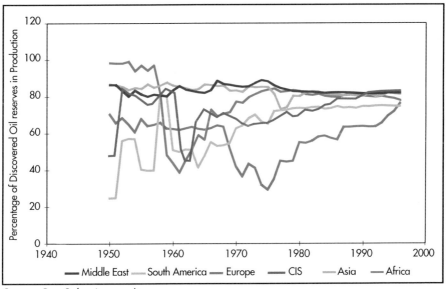

Source: Jean Laherrère, op.cit.

9. From a paper presented by Jean Laherrère to the 11 November 1997 Oil Reserves Conference held at the IEA in Paris, *Distribution and Evolution of Recovery Factor.* The original data for the chart were supplied by Petroconsultants.

production has been constrained by a staged approach to the development of output to follow demand growth. It is less easy to explain why other regions of the world are not producing at closer to 100% of oil discoveries.

On the other hand, the USGS found that between 1980 and 1993 there were some 925 reported discoveries[10] of oil and gas to which no reserves have been credited. Thus, whereas Laherrère's finding suggests that oil reserves may have been overstated, the USGS finding suggests some underestimating of oil reserves.

The Optimists' View

The optimists emphasise the roles of new information, technological advances and higher oil prices on ultimate oil reserves. For them, the current estimate of ultimate oil reserves is treated as nothing more than inventory that can grow as uncertainty is reduced, as technology advances or as the oil price rises. They believe that reserve growth from oil fields already discovered can occur from upward revisions of estimates of oil in place, or from increases in the recovery factor. Where the pessimists assume that the future recovery factor is unlikely to increase significantly, the optimists hold that oil fields already discovered, but previously considered uneconomic because of their size or location, can become economic through the application of new technology and a higher oil price. The pessimists do not rule out new technology and higher oil prices making marginal oil fields economic, but argue that these fields are typically small and would not augment reserves greatly.

Unlike the pessimists, the optimists do not assume that oil production follows a Hubbert curve. Indeed, the optimists say very little about how higher oil reserves are transformed into higher oil production or the date at which worldwide oil production will peak. When an explicit production assumption is made, it usually takes the form of a simple reserve to production (R/P) ratio. When the world's demand for oil is steadily rising, one cannot simply assume that world production will remain flat and then suddenly fall to zero when reserves are exhausted.

10. Op. cit. Table 7.9.

The 1998 WEO Approach

The conventional oil supply projections described in this chapter were prepared using the IEA's new long-term oil-supply model. This model comprises a suite of individual regional supply models, each of which incorporates specific regional factors such as estimates of cumulative production, remaining reserves and undiscovered oil. The approach taken here is to begin with a conservative estimate of ultimate recoverable reserves and then to increase this estimate over time to take account of new information and the application of new technology. For the purposes of this analysis, Campbell's 1996 conventional ultimate oil reserve estimate of 1800 billion barrels has been used as the starting point. The WEO approach to oil reserves and supply is a synthesis of static and dynamic views, as it makes use of the extensive geological data on which the pessimists' view is based, but permits the estimate of proven or probable recoverable oil reserves to increase over time. The next stage is to transform a stock estimate (ultimate recoverable reserves) into a flow (oil supply). The supply projections described in this chapter assume that oil production follows a Hubbert curve.

In order to take account of the uncertainty of ultimate recoverable reserves, a wide range of ultimate reserve estimates has been considered. The high estimates tend to be grouped around 3000 billion barrels and this figure is adopted as an upper bound. The lower bound is 2000 billion barrels. Since 1958, published ultimate oil reserve estimates have averaged 2032 billion barrels. Table 7.11 indicates how the WEO's range of 2000 - 3000 billion barrels of ultimate oil reserves is related to the pessimists' view of 1800 billion barrels. This range is somewhat wider than that suggested by the USGS of 2100-2800 billion barrels. The second column in Table 7.11 shows the increase from the base figure arising from additional new discoveries and upward revisions of identified reserves. These increases can arise as a result of a combination between the application of new technologies increasing the recovery factor, the acquisition of new information leading in upwards oil in place and reserves in revised estimates. The final column shows the implied recovery factor based on a fixed stock of conventional oil in place of 6000 billion barrels, a broadly accepted current estimate.

Table 7.11: **Assumed Ultimate Conventional Oil Reserves
(billions of barrels)**

Ultimate Oil Reserves	Increase from base of 1800 billion barrels from new information and technology	Implied Recovery Factor based on a fixed oil stock in place of 6 trillion barrels
1800	0	30%
2000	200	33%
2300	500	38%
3000	1200	50%

Note: The above table treats the oil stock as being fixed at 6 trillion barrels, and all increases in ultimate oil reserves as arising from improvements in the recovery factor. Identical ultimate oil reserve estimates could also be obtained if the oil stock in place were greater than 6 trillion barrels.

The range of ultimate conventional oil reserves of 2000 - 3000 billion barrels means that the supply projections examined in this chapter cover a wide spectrum of reserve estimates. This range only deals with conventional oil (see Box 7.2 at the beginning of the chapter).

Some experts[11] warn that all past attempts to forecast the timing of future reserve constraints on oil production and the associated rise in the world oil price have proved to be incorrect. We do not attempt to make such forecasts, but to discuss the current range of views held

Figure 7.7: **Oil Supply Profiles 1996-2030
Ultimate Conventional Oil Reserves of 2300 Billion Barrels**

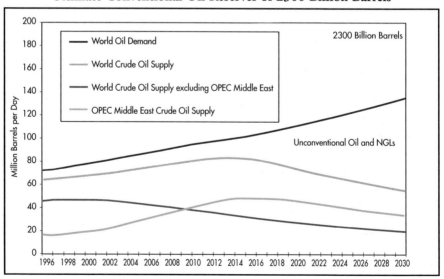

11. *The Failure of Long-Term Oil Market Forecasting,* M.C. Lynch in Advances in the Economics of Energy and Resources, Volume 8, pages 53-87, 1998.

by experts in the field. We do not foresee any shortage of liquid fuels before 2020, as reserves of unconventional oil are ample, should the production of conventional oil turn down. It may be that new oil discoveries, updated information on producing fields and future technology will increase the current estimates of ultimate conventional oil reserves. We cannot know that now. We take the view that current evidence and analysis supports a range of 2 to 3 trillion barrels of these reserves. As explained above, this range already takes account of estimates of undiscovered oil and growth in identified reserves.

Table 7.12: **Oil Supply 1996-2020 (million barrels per day)**

Ultimate recoverable reserves of 2300 Billion Barrels	1996	2010	2020	1996-2020 Annual Growth Rate
Total Oil Demand	**72.0**	**94.8**	**111.5**	**1.8%**
Oil Supplies by Source				
Natural Gas Liquids				
Middle East OPEC	1.3	2.8	3.7	4.5%
World excluding Middle East OPEC	5.3	8.5	11.5	3.3%
Total NGLs	**6.6**	**11.3**	**15.2**	**3.5%**
Identified Unconventional Oil				
Middle East OPEC	0.1	0.1	0.1	1.6%
World excluding Middle East OPEC	1.2	2.4	2.4	3.0%
Total Identified Unconventional Oil	**1.2**	**2.4**	**2.4**	**3.0%**
Processing Gains	**1.5**	**2.1**	**2.5**	**2.0%**
Conventional Crude Oil				
Middle East OPEC	17.2	40.9	45.2	4.1%
World excluding Middle East OPEC	45.5	38.0	27.0	-2.2%
Total Crude Oil	**62.7**	**79.0**	**72.2**	**0.6%**
World Oil Supply excluding Unidentified Unconventional Oil	**72.0**	**94.8**	**92.3**	**1.0%**
Balancing item: Unidentified Unconventional Oil	**0.0**	**0.0**	**19.1**	
Total Oil Supply (excl Processing Gains)				
Middle East OPEC	18.5	43.8	49.0	4.1%
World excluding Middle East OPEC	52.0	48.9	40.8	-1.0%
World	**70.5**	**92.7**	**89.9**	**1.0%**

Notes: Identified unconventional oil refers to relatively well defined projects.
Unidentified unconventional oil is from currently unknown or uncertain projects.
NGLs includes some condensates.

For the purposes of the WEO analysis, the USGS's estimate of 2300 billion barrels has been used for the BAU projection. Details of the oil production profile associated with ultimate reserves of 2300 billion barrels are shown in Figure 7.7. Details are provided in Table 7.12.

OPEC Middle East is treated as the residual supplier until its production begins to decline. Its conventional oil production is assumed to be capped by a maximum level of 47.9 Mbd. This ceiling has been taken from a study published by the US Department of Energy in 1983[12] and reproduced in a recent IEA publication[13]. The use of a lower ceiling on OPEC Middle East's production would bring forward the date at which global conventional oil production peaks, but would also lengthen the time during which OPEC Middle East could remain on plateau before production went into decline. Obviously, the ability of OPEC Middle East to expand its conventional oil production from the 1996 level of 17.2 Mbd to over 40 Mbd by 2010 depends on sufficient investment in additional capacity, availability of capital and the willingness of producers in the region to increase production.

Oil production outside of OPEC Middle East peaks early in the next century in the 2300 billion barrel case. Worldwide production of natural gas liquids (including some condensates) is assumed to grow at around 3% per annum. Were NGL production to grow less slowly than assumed, then conventional oil production and eventually unconventional oil production would have to increase in order to balance the oil market. Alternatively, the oil price would have to increase in order to restrain oil demand.

The oil price is assumed to increase from $17 to $25 (1990) per barrel (bbl) between 2010 and 2015. A ceiling of $25 bbl has been adopted, because above this level other liquids (non-conventional oils) could become increasingly competitive with conventional oil. This assumed increase in the oil price from $17 to $25 bbl between 2010 and 2015 is associated with the peak in conventional oil production that occurs around 2013 - 2014.

In this projection, Middle East OPEC conventional crude oil production increases its share of total oil supply from 24% in 1996 to 48% in 2014 and then declines. Production of conventional crude outside Middle East OPEC falls as a share of total oil supply from

12. Energy Information Administration, US Department of Energy, *The Petroleum Resources of the Middle East*, May 1983.
13. *Middle East Oil and Gas*, IEA/OECD Paris 1995.

63% in 1996 to 33% in 2014 and continues falling thereafter. Other oil production (natural gas liquids, processing gains and unconventional oil production) climbs steadily from 13% of total oil supply in 1996 to 19% in 2014 and then unconventional oil production expands rapidly in order to balance global demand and supply of oil. During the period up to 2014, in which Middle East OPEC increases its share of total oil supply, the potential for disruptions in world oil supply increases. The extent to which OPEC Middle East countries become more dependent on international trade and capital movements (e.g. if they become involved in downstream oil business in oil-consuming countries) will reduce the risks of such disruptions. The period following the transfer from OPEC Middle East to unconventional oil as the source of incremental supplies could also be one of instability of supply. The rapid expansion of unconventional oil production will require many multi-billion dollar greenfield production sites to come on stream. The potential clearly exists for mismatches between world oil supply and demand because of the long lead times involved. It will be important for major oil-importing countries to co-ordinate their arrangements for dealing with these supply disruptions. The IEA is already in discussions with major non-IEA Member countries on this subject.

Figure 7.8: **Oil Supply Profiles 1996-2030**
Ultimate Conventional Oil Reserves of 2000 Billion Barrels

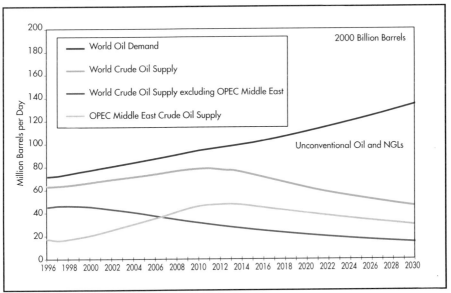

The above discussion is based on ultimate conventional oil reserves of 2300 billion barrels. Reducing the level of assumed ultimate oil reserves to 2000 billion barrels brings forward the date at which production peaks to around 2010. The oil supply production profile associated with ultimate conventional oil reserves of 2000 billion barrels is shown in Figure 7.8.

Figure 7.9: **Oil Supply Profiles 1996-2030**
Ultimate Conventional Oil Reserves of 3000 Billion Barrels

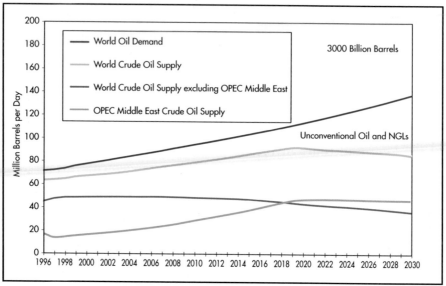

In the 3000 billion barrels case, oil prices are assumed to remain flat throughout the projection period at $17 bbl and total oil demand is somewhat higher than in the 2000 and 2300 billion barrels cases, which are based on the BAU oil demand projection. Despite the additional oil demand in the 3000 billion barrels case, the peak in oil supply is pushed back until 2020 as the higher reserves more than offsets the increase in demand. The general conclusion is that conventional oil production is likely to peak sometime between 2010 and 2020.

The range of 2000-3000 billion barrels of ultimate recoverable reserves of conventional oil provides a guide to the range of uncertainty currently expressed by experts. This Outlook, in common with those oil companies we have consulted, sees no shortage of oil supply. Yet it draws attention to the likely change from conventional to unconventional oil at the margin of oil supply between 2010 and 2020 and a possible increase in the oil price.

Increases in Estimates of Recoverable Reserves

Table 7.13: **North Sea Oil Fields' Recoverable Oil Reserves**[14]

	Million Tonnes of Oil			Block	Original Brown Book
	Original Brown Book Estimate	1996 Brown Book Estimate	Difference		
Auk (P+)	8	17	+9	30/16	1977
Beatrice	21	21	0	11/30a	1979
Beryl A (P+)	70	102	+32	9/13	1977
Brent (P+)	230	270	+40	211/29	1977
Buchan	7	16	+9	21/1	1979
Claymore	57	77	+20	14/19	1977
Cormorant South (P+)	20	29	+9	211/26	1977
Cormorant North (P+)	55	63	+8	211/21a	1980
Dunlin	80	55	-25	211/23	1977
Forties	240	334	+94	21/10	1977
Fulmar (P+)	70	74	+4	30/16	1979
Heather	20	14	-6	2/5	1977
Hutton North West	38	16	-22	211/27	1980
Magnus	60	106	+46	211/12a	1979
Maureen	21	29	+8	16/29	1979
Montrose	20	13	-7	22/17	1977
Murchison	51	46	-5	211/19	1979
Ninian	140	157	+17	3/3	1977
Piper	85	136	+51	15/17	1977
Statfjord	412	522	+110	211/24	1979
Tartan	2	14	+12	15/16	1979
Thistle	76	55	-21	211/18	1977
Totals	**1782**	**2167**	**+384**		

Source: UK Brown Book various annual editions, see for example Oil and Gas Resources of the United Kingdom, The Energy Report, Volume 2, 1998, Department of Trade and Industry, HMSO, London, 1998.

14. The UK Department of Trade and Industry has also examined the North sea's recovery factors, see *Estimation of ultimate recovery of UK oil fields; the results of the DTI questionnaire and a historical analysis,* J.M. Thomas, Petroleum Geoscience, Vol. 4, 1998, pp. 157-163. The paper compares reserve estimates for 1996 and 1998 and reaches less optimistic conclusions. It suggests that a large part of the reserve increase can be explained by exceptional circumstances not related to technological improvements, but to an initial underestimation of the efficiency of the water drive in North Sea's sandy reservoirs.
In *Geoscore: a method of quantifying uncertainty in field reserve estimates,* Dromgoole, P. and Speers R. Geoscience 3, 1997, the authors found that over a four-year period, low-complexity fields are underestimated by 20%, medium-complexity fields overestimated by 10% and higher-complexity fields overestimated by 15%. The paper also notes that most fields exhibited reserve growth in later life.

As noted above, the differences between ultimate oil reserves estimates arise from different assumptions about the impact of new information and technology developments. Unfortunately, obtaining reliable data on which to estimate this impact is not an easy task. Some data are available for the North Sea. Table 7.13 compares the 1996 estimates of recoverable oil reserves for 22 old North Sea oil fields with their estimated recoverable oil reserves in the late 1970s.

Table 7.13 shows that the total quantity of recoverable oil from the 22 oil fields examined increased by 22% in the space of less than 20 years. Total recoverable oil reserves from these fields therefore increased on average by around 1% per annum. Even this is an underestimate, as for six of the fields (indicated by a P+) the late 1970s recoverable oil estimate included more than just proven and probable recoverable oil reserves.

If the increase in recoverable reserves of 1% per annum held true elsewhere in the oil industry, then, assuming an initial recovery factor of 30%, the recovery factor could increase by 0.3 percentage points per annum[15]. Over the space of 25 years (1995-2020) this would increase the typical recovery factor from 30% to 38%. This would imply an increase in recoverable reserves of 500 billion barrels if the starting recovery factor of 30% were applied to a resource base of 6000 billion barrels (6000 x 0.3 = reserves of 1800 billion barrels).

The ultimate oil reserves range of 2000-3000 billion barrels used in this chapter is equivalent to a range in the recovery factors of 33% - 50%, assuming a certain resource base of 6000 billion barrels. Thus, if the oil resource base was 6000 Gb and ultimate reserves were to increase from 2000 to 3000 billion barrels, the recovery factor would have to increase by 17 percentage points, or 0.68 percentage points per annum, over a 25 year period. This increase is more than double that observed in the North Sea, according to the above table.

Another interesting approach is that of Jean Laherrère[16] using the Petroconsultants database. He compared recovery factor estimates prepared by Roadifer[17] for 300 giant fields in 1987 with his own estimates for 200 fields using Petroconsultants data for 1996. Figure 7.10 illustrates the distribution of recovery factors across oil fields in the two years. Between 1987 and 1996 virtually the whole giant oil field distribution moved to the right, indicating a general improvement in the recovery factor.

15. Work done by Jean Laherrère using the Petroconsultants database found some evidence of an improvement in recovery factors for large oil fields, but little or none for small fields.
16. Jean Laherrère, op. cit.
17. Roadifer R.E, 1987 *Size distributions of the World's largest known oil and tar accumulations*, AAPG studies in geology #25, pages 3 - 23.

Using data from Figure 7.10, it has been calculated that the average recovery factor for Roadifer's 1987 sample of 300 giant oilfields was 33.3%, compared to 38.6% for Laherrère's 1996 sample of 200 giant oilfields. This analysis suggests that the average giant oilfield's recovery factor increased by 5.3 percentage points in the space of nine years, or 0.6 percentage points per annum. In the unlikely event that giant oilfields' recovery factors were to continue to increase at 0.6 percentage points per annum, then by the year 2020 the average recovery factor would be some 14.2 percentage points higher than in 1996. The average giant oilfield in 2020 would therefore have an average recovery factor of 52.8%.

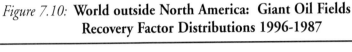

Figure 7.10: **World outside North America: Giant Oil Fields Recovery Factor Distributions 1996-1987**

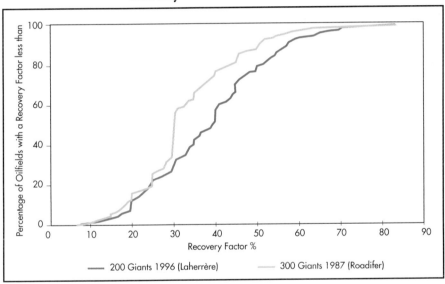

One criticism of this analysis is that it is based on two different sets of giant oil fields[18]. While this criticism undoubtedly has some validity, the sample sizes are sufficiently large for there to be

18 In discussions with the IEA about this comparison Jean Laherrère has made the point that the comparison is between two different distributions of fields. Each distribution therefore contains different fields and one is not directly therefore comparing like with like. Figure 7.10 was prepared by the IEA using data supplied by Jean Laherrère and the IEA therefore assumes full responsibility for Figure 7.10.

considerable overlap between them. Put simply, Figure 7.10 shows evidence of giant oil fields' recovery factors improving during the period 1987 - 1996. It may not be possible to extrapolate this result to all fields, see notes on Thomas and Dromgoole et al in reference to Table 7.13.

An alternative interpretation of the range 2000-3000 billion barrels for ultimate reserves of conventional oil is given in Box 7.3.

Box 7.3: Alternative Explanation of the Range in Estimated Ultimate Oil Reserves

An alternative explanation of the range in estimated ultimate oil reserves highlights growth factors applied to known oil fields. It argues that new discoveries will not contribute greatly to increases in ultimate reserves because the evolution of discovery statistics show that the pace of discovery is slow and the future potential for them is not large. The evolution of technology is recognized, but it is difficult to assess to what extent it simply accelerates depletion without extending reserves. The main determinant of the growth factor in oil reserve estimates is seen as arising from reassessment of the reserve sizes of individual known fields as new information becomes available and confidence builds. The wide range of high reserve estimates with low probability is usually ignored in preparing reserve estimates early in the life of an oil field. But it is taken into account as experience is gained later on. The size of the growth factor depends on two factors. The first is the rules governing declarations of reserve estimates which are for "proven" reserves in the United States, for "proven" and "probable" elsewhere. The second is the degree of riskiness and complexity of the field, since oil companies are likely to be more cautious in risky situations, leaving less room for upward revision later on. Indicative values of growth factors are:
- an initial US onshore proven barrel of oil grows to 6 ultimate reserve barrels;
- an initial US offshore proven barrel grows to 4 ultimate reserve barrels;
- an initial non-US probable barrel grows to 2 ultimate reserve barrels.

For a lower boundary, it is assumed that half the reserves (the largest fields) will grow by a factor of 2 and the other half will not grow at all, giving an average growth factor of 1.5. An average upper boundary growth factor is taken as 2, higher for the larger fields and lower for the others. These factors may be applied to the numbers in Table 7.10 to arrive at an alternative interpretation of the range of 2000-3000 billions barrels of ultimate conventional oil reserves. At the lower boundary, future discoveries of conventional oil just make up for overestimates of identified reserves and at the upper boundary unassessed identified reserves and future discoveries are taken as 300 billion barrels, larger than the 180 figure given in Table 7.10. The two bounds are calculated below:

	Billion Barrels
Lower Boundary	
Cumulative reserves	784
Remaining identified and unidentified reserves	836
Growth in remaining and unidentified reserves @ 50%	<u>418</u>
	<u>2038</u>
Upper Boundary	
Cumulative reserves	784
Remaining identified and unidentified reserves	1136
Growth in remaining and unidentified reserves @ 100%	<u>1136</u>
	<u>3056</u>

In this type of distribution, the expected (or mean) value of recoverable reserves is greater than the most likely (or modal) value. A range of uncertainty may be quoted for the size of the field, where 5 per cent of the probability lies below the "reasonable" minimum value and another 5 per cent lies above the "reasonable" maximum value. Early in the life of the field, insufficient weight is given to the higher reserve estimates. On average, as production flows and information is gathered on the characteristics of the field, the range of uncertainty narrows towards the expected value. This new information and increased confidence in the size of the reserves explains a major part of the growth in reserve estimates of existing fields.

Box 7.4: **Uncertainty of Reserve Estimates**

The probability distribution of the total recoverable oil in a field is typically a log-normal curve - it has a long tail, as shown below.

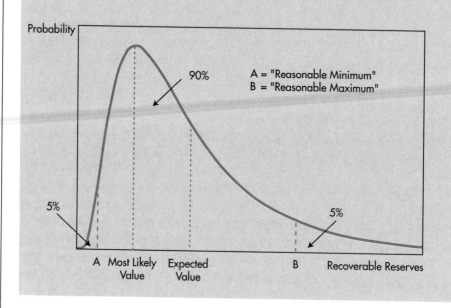

Unconventional Oil Reserves

The definition of unconventional oil used in this study is given in Box 7.2 at the beginning of this chapter. While some commentators argue that deep offshore oil should be classified as unconventional because of the difficulties of extraction, others note that substantial quantities of deep offshore oil are currently being produced and this oil should therefore be classified as conventional. Less contentious are the tar sands of Canada and Venezuela or the oil shales of the United States. A recent study of unconventional resources produced the estimates shown in Table 7.14.

Table 7.14: **Conventional and Unconventional[19] Oil Reserve Estimates**

Billion Barrels	Ultimate	Undiscovered	Yet-to-Produce
Conventional Oil	1700 - 1800 - 2300	200	1000
Conventional Gas Liquids	200 - 250 - 400	50	200
Unconventional Oil	300 - 700 - 2000	100	700
Total	**2300 - 2750 - 4000**	**350**	**1500 - 1900 - 3500**

Source: *The World's Non-Conventional Oil and Gas, Hydrocarbons of last recourse*, A. Perrondon, J.H. Laherrère and C.J. Campbell, published by the Petroleum Economist, March 1998, page 98. Note that the yet-to-produce estimates include undiscovered oil.

Based on the above estimates and their own definition of unconventional oil, Perrondon et al project production of unconventional oil to be 5.5 Mbd in 2000, 8 Mbd in 2010 and 11 Mbd in 2025. Unconventional oil production in each year is projected to be equally divided between extra-heavy oil/bitumen and ultra-deep-water and polar oil. This represents a conservative estimate of unconventional oil reserves based on a narrower definition of conventional oil and a wider definition of unconventional oil than those used in this study.

The United States Department of Energy's Energy Information Administration (USDOE/EIA) is more optimistic than Perrodon in its prospects for unconventional oil. The USDOE notes that the resource base could be at least 5 trillion barrels, only part of which could actually be produced, and that as much as 15 Mbd could become available by 2020. This assumes that the world oil price rises to $25 per barrel early in the 21st century[20]. In an earlier publication[21] the USDOE noted that, with current technology,

19. The Perrondon et al study defines conventional oil as having an API of greater than 10° and residing in water depths of less than 1000 metres. All oil not satisfying at least one of these two criteria is classified as unconventional.
20. *International Energy Outlook 1998, With Projections Through 2020*, USDOE/EIA, April 1998, DOE/EIA - 0484(98), page 38.
21. *International Energy Outlook 1997, With Projections to 2015*, April 1997 DOE/EIA - 0484(97), page 37.

around 550 billion barrels of unconventional oil could be produced at a cost of $30 per barrel or less. With significant technological advances, approximately 2 trillion barrels of unconventional oil could become economic to produce by 2020 at a cost of $30 per barrel. The USDOE thus envisages unconventional oil resources lying in the range of 550-2000 billion barrels between now and 2020. It should be noted that 2000 billion barrels is similar in magnitude to the USGS' estimate of ultimate conventional oil (2300 billion barrels). Unlike conventional oil, very little unconventional oil has been produced to date.

One interesting unconventional oil source is gas-to-liquids (GTL) technology. GTL was first developed in 1923, but has only recently come of age. Recent cost reductions mean that GTL could be on the verge of being economic. GTL is important as there are an estimated 1488 trillion cubic feet (tcf) of gas finds, each at least 5 tcf, that cannot be marketed because of their geographical location. This "stranded gas" is too far from existing pipeline grids or LNG liquefaction plants for it to be economic to use, but if the gas could be converted into liquid via GTL it could be transported to market in tankers. Converting the 1488 tcf of stranded gas into liquids via GTL would produce the equivalent of 150 billion barrels of oil. This is a large quantity and is broadly similar in size to some reserve estimates for the Caspian Sea.

A crucial factor in determining the future production of unconventional oil is its production cost. Table 7.15 presents cost information (IEA Secretariat estimates) for existing or likely projects before 2005. Note that this cost information is unlikely to apply to all of the unconventional oil recoverable reserves in a region, since the cheaper reserves are invariably produced first and the more expensive reserves later in a province's lifetime.

All of these estimates are at or below average world crude oil prices and refer to projects likely to enter into production before 2005. The IEA projections of oil supply described earlier envisage a very rapid expansion of non-conventional supplies following a peak in production of conventional oil in the period 2010 to 2020. The impact of rapid expansion of large scale non-conventional oil production facilities on unit costs is unknown, but might be higher than for the current, relatively small scale activities. To allow for the possibility of higher production costs, the world oil price has been increased from $17 to $25 (1990 prices) over the period 2010-2015 in the BAU projection. In practice, advances in technology may well limit the extent of such a price rise. On the other hand, more stringent environmental controls in the future could increase it. There is inevitably uncertainty on this issue.

Table 7.15: **Production Cost Estimates**

	Generally Accepted Unconventional Oil Projects			
	Operating cost $/bbl	Capital cost contribution $/bbl	Total Costs $/bbl	Recoverable Reserves (billion barrels)
Canada Alberta Oil Sands	9 - 10	3 - 5	12 - 15	300
Venezuela Orinoco	8 - 10	5 - 7	15 - 17	300
Gas to Liquids			>18	150
	Other Unconventional / Conventional Oil Projects		
	Operating cost $/bbl	Capital cost $/bbl	Total Costs contribution $/bbl
California Heavy Crude Oil (EOR)	5 - 9	2.5 - 3	7.5 - 12
Western Canada Heavy Crude Oil (EOR)	3 - 5	2.5 - 3	5.5 - 8
Mexico Heavy Crude Oil	1	5 - 6	6 - 7
US Gulf of Mexico Deepwater (>200 metres)	3	3.5 - 5.5	6.5 - 8.5
Brazil Offshore Deepwater (>200 metres)	3.5	1.5 - 4	5 - 7.5
Alaskan Oil	3.5 - 4.5	2 - 3	5.5 - 7.5
US Stripper Wells	6 - 16	n.a.	6 - 16

Note: Cost data are only for those projects likely to enter into production before 2005.

All of these estimates are at or below average world crude oil prices and refer to projects likely to enter into production before 2005. The IEA projections of oil supply described earlier envisage a very rapid expansion of non-conventional supplies following a peak in production of conventional oil in the period 2010 to 2020. The impact of rapid expansion of large scale non-conventional oil production facilities on unit costs is unknown, but might be higher than for the current, relatively small scale activities. To allow for the possibility of higher production costs, the world oil price has been increased from $17 to $25 (1990 prices) over the period 2010-2015 in the BAU projection. In practice, advances in technology may well limit the extent of such a price rise. On the other hand, more stringent environmental controls in the future could increase it.

Table 7.16: Identified Unconventional Oil Supply - Thousand Barrels per Day

	1995	1996	1997	1998	1999	2000	2001	2002	2003	2004	2005
Venezuela Total	36	72	103	123	235	330	415	620	705	790	900
Orinoco Upgrading Joint Ventures				13	100	170	230	410	470	530	615
Orimulsion	36	72	103	110	135	160	185	210	235	260	285
Canada: Synthetic Crude Total	281	279	287	311	335	365	435	520	545	570	595
Syncrude	205	201	209	219	235	260	285	310	335	360	385
Suncor	76	78	78	92	100	105	150	210	210	210	210
US: Other Hydrocarbons Total	306	301	341	345	349	353	357	361	365	369	373
Brazil: Alcohols Total	219	247	262	276	280	280	280	280	280	280	280
South Africa: Total	195	190	185	180	175	170	165	160	155	150	150
Sasol	150	150	150	150	150	150	150	150	150	150	150
Mossgas	45	40	35	30	25	20	15	10	5	0	0
Rest of World	104	121	113	102	102	102	112	124	137	147	147
World	**1141**	**1210**	**1291**	**1337**	**1476**	**1600**	**1764**	**2065**	**2187**	**2306**	**2445**

There is inevitably uncertainty on this issue.

The role of unconventional oil in the WEO projections is to act as the residual producer once OPEC Middle East is no longer able to fulfil this role. Thus, once global conventional oil production peaks, all additional oil demand is sourced from unconventional oil reserves. Estimated identified unconventional oil production for the period 1995 - 2005 is shown in Table 7.16.

Net Oil Imports and Stocks[22]

Oil companies hold oil stocks equivalent to around 55-65 days of consumption for operational purposes. IEA member countries are required to hold emergency oil stocks equivalent to at least 90 days of net imports. A number of European IEA Member countries hold stocks in excess of this minimum to meet European Union (EU) obligations to hold stocks equivalent to 90 days of oil consumption. Some IEA Member governments hold strategic stocks in addition to the stocks held by oil companies. Although Canada and Norway are net oil exporters, they also hold oil stocks. Details of IEA oil emergency measures, including stockholding obligations, may be found in relevant IEA publications[23]. The oil supply projections in this chapter point to increasing reliance by oil-importing countries on Middle East producers in the first decade of the next century. For this reason, consuming countries may wish to increase their stockholdings. There are many uncertain factors at work, and trying to project future OECD stocks is a difficult task. For the purposes of these projections, it has been assumed that the OECD's regional oil stocks (as of the end of 1997) rise at the same rate as net oil imports.

Outside of the IEA, most countries do not yet have any formal policy for maintaining strategic oil stocks. Historical data on non-OECD oil stocks are poor and so projecting non-OECD oil stocks is even more difficult than for the OECD countries. The assumption made in these projections is that the non-OECD regions hold oil stocks equivalent to 55 days of oil consumption. This assumption is also applied to the base year 1997 in order to provide a starting point for the oil stock projections.

To summarise:

---

22. For projection purposes, oil is assumed to include both conventional and unconventional oil.
23. *Oil Supply Security: The Emergency Response Potential of IEA Countries,* IEA/OECD Paris, 1995.

- OECD stocks are assumed to rise at the same rate as net imports;
- non-OECD stocks are assumed to be equal to 55 days of oil consumption.

Changes in estimates of oil stocks from one year to the next are included in Table 7.18 as an element of oil demand.

Table 7.17: **Oil Stocks (million barrels)**

	End 1997	**2010**	**2020**
Total OECD	**3708.0**	**5710.5**	**6421.2**
OECD North America*	1724.2	2666.3	2763.8
OECD Europe	1248.1	2165.5	2749.0
OECD Pacific	735.8	878.8	908.4
Total Non-OECD	**1749.0**	**2516.1**	**3277.2**
Transition Economies	313.5	395.7	469.7
Africa	126.5	180.0	222.7
China	220.0	391.4	555.8
Other Asia	495.0	782.0	1075.2
Latin America**	363.0	495.3	607.1
Middle East	231.0	271.7	346.7
World	**5457.0**	**8226.6**	**9698.4**

Note: OECD data are for total stocks on land. IEA *Oil Market Report,* 11th May 1998, Table 7. They include oil in pipelines and other operational stocks that are excluded from data in IEA statistical publications. Non-OECD stock data were obtained by multiplying the oil demand data for 1997 shown in Table 1 of the IEA's *Oil Market Report* (11th May 1998) by 55 days.
* Excluding Mexico.
** Including Mexico.

Table 7.18 presents the net import position for each of the WEO's regions. Since, by definition, the source of the unidentified unconventional oil is unknown, it is not possible to include this oil in the net import calculations. Since most of the world's unconventional oil reserves are situated in the Americas, particularly Canada and Venezuela, the net import positions of OECD North America and Latin America are likely to be lower by 2020 than the above table suggests.

Table 7.18: **Oil Demand, Supply and Net Imports**
Conventional Oil Reserves of 2300 Billion Barrels - BAU Projection (million barrels per day)

	Demand 1996	Supply 1996	Net Imports 1996	Demand 2010	Supply 2010	Net Imports 2010	Demand 2020	Supply 2020	Net Imports 2020
OECD North America	20.3	11.1	9.3	23.4	8.6	14.8	24.1	8.9	15.1
OECD Europe	14.4	6.7	7.7	17.0	4.5	12.5	18.7	2.8	15.9
OECD Pacific	6.7	0.7	6.0	7.7	0.3	7.4	7.9	0.3	7.6
Total OECD	**41.4**	**18.4**	**23.0**	**48.1**	**13.4**	**34.7**	**50.7**	**12.0**	**38.7**
Transition Economies	5.5	7.3	-1.8	7.2	10.2	-3.0	8.5	9.4	-0.9
Africa	2.2	7.7	-5.5	3.3	7.8	-4.6	4.0	6.3	-2.2
China	3.6	3.1	0.5	7.1	3.2	3.9	10.1	2.0	8.1
Other Asia	8.5	3.7	4.8	14.2	2.9	11.3	19.5	2.4	17.2
Latin America	6.3	9.8	-3.5	9.0	10.4	-1.4	11.0	8.6	2.5
Middle East	4.1	20.4	-16.3	4.9	44.7	-39.7	6.3	49.2	-42.9
Total Non-OECD	**30.4**	**52.1**	**-21.9**	**46.0**	**79.3**	**-33.4**	**59.9**	**77.9**	**-18.0**
World Conventional, Identified Unconventional and NGLs excluding stock changes.	71.7	70.5	1.1	94.2	92.7	1.5	111.1	89.9	21.1
Unidentified Unconventional Oil			0.0			0.0			19.1
Processing Gains		1.5			2.1			2.5	
Stock Change	0.3			0.6			0.4		
World	**72.0**	**72.0**	**0.0**	**94.8**	**94.8**	**0.0**	**111.5**	**92.4**	**19.1**

Note: The World Energy Model's projections are based on the Mtoe statistics shown in the IEA statistical publications. Inevitably, there are some differences between that database and the separate *Oil Market Report* database which uses million of barrels per day (Mbd) as its unit of measurement. In order to deal with this problem the Mtoe data has been converted to mbd using regional conversion factors; these were discussed earlier in the chapter. Because of these conversion difficulties, there are sometimes small differences between the sum of the regions and the world totals.
Source: 1996 supply and demand data taken from the May 1998 *Oil Market Report*, tables 1 and 4.

The following table shows how the OECD's oil dependence (i.e. net imports as a percentage of oil demand) is projected to rise during the period to 2020. After peaking early in the next century, OECD Europe's conventional oil production is projected to decline. This results in the region's net import position worsening considerably. The OECD will become increasingly dependent on OPEC Middle East until conventional oil production in that region peaks around 2013/2014. Beyond that date, the OECD will need increasingly to derive its supplies of oil from unconventional sources.

Table 7.19: **Oil Import Dependence (per cent)**

	1996	2010	2020
OECD North America	45	63	63
OECD Europe	53	74	85
OECD Pacific	90	96	96
Total OECD	**56**	**72**	**76**

Note: These figures exclude stock changes, processing gains and unidentified unconventional oil.

Table 7.19 includes NGLs. Since worldwide demand for gas is projected to grow on average by 2.6% per annum in the BAU case, it is expected that considerable quantities of associated liquids (NGLs and condensates, etc.) will be produced with this gas. Since worldwide gas production is not expected to peak until well after 2020, production of associated liquids from gas production is also unlikely to peak until then. In some regions of the world, declining gas production will reduce the production of NGLs, and so in practice there is likely to be considerable regional variation in NGL production. On the other hand, use of gas-to-liquids technology could result in liquids production from gas reservoirs increasing at a faster rate than gas demand. In view of these difficulties, trying to be precise about the likely net import position of the OECD during the projection period is particularly difficult, especially after 2010. One strong conclusion is that the OECD's net import requirement will rise during the projection period. Whether market forces result in the OECD's meeting additional oil demand via imports from OPEC Middle East or by increasing unconventional oil production will have important consequences for the future energy security of the OECD.

Oil Supply Projection Comparisons

The only other major organisation that regularly publishes a long-term world oil supply projection is the United States Department of Energy[24]. It adopts a somewhat different approach and does not distinguish explicitly between conventional and unconventional sources of oil.

Table 7.20: **Oil Supply USDOE / EIA - Reference Case
(million barrels per day)**

	1996	2010	2020
Middle East OPEC	18.5	27.2	47.3
World excl. Middle East OPEC	53.5	59.0	68.6
World	**71.8**	**95.5**	**115.9**

Note: The above table includes all sources of oil, e.g. NGLs, processing gains, unconventional and conventional oils.

Although the total oil supply projections in the two cases are very similar, the disaggregation is very different. In the IEA's projection, production of conventional oil from the world excluding Middle East OPEC peaks early in the 21st century; in the USDOE's projection it continues to grow throughout the projection period. One region where there are considerable differences between the two projections is Europe. In 2010, the USDOE's supply projection for Western Europe is some 3 mbd higher than this Outlook's projection for OECD Europe (7.5 versus 4.5 Mbd). By 2020, the difference expands to 3.5 Mbd (6.3 versus 2.8 Mbd). A 1996 IEA study[25] indicated that the UK's offshore oil production from currently known fields would peak during 1999 and then go into decline. Given this projection, and the likely peaking of Norwegian offshore production early in the following decade, the USDOE's projection appears very optimistic. A similar question arises with respect to North American production (excluding Mexico). The USDOE projects oil supply to be virtually flat throughout the period, while the IEA projects supply to fall. In 2020, the IEA projects that North American oil production will be 8.9 mbd compared to the USDOE's projection of 11.9 Mbd.

24. USDOE/EIA, *International Energy Outlook 1998 - With Projections Through 2020,* page 179.
25. *Global Offshore Oil Prospects to 2000,* IEA/OECD 1996.

Table 7.21: **Oil Supply IEA WEO 1998 - BAU**
(million barrels per day)

2300 Gb Conventional Oil Reserves	1996	2010	2020
Conventional & NGLs			
Middle East OPEC	18.5	43.7	48.9
World excluding Middle East OPEC	50.8	46.5	38.5
Sub-Total	69.3	90.2	87.4
Unconventional Oil	1.3	2.4	21.5
Processing Gains	1.5	2.1	2.5
Sub-Total	2.8	4.5	24.0
Total	**72.0**	**94.8**	**111.5**

When examining the two oil supply projections, it is important to remember that in the IEA's Outlook projection there is an explicit link between oil production and reserves in the form of the Hubbert curve. This is an important difference, as the USDOE projection appears to assume that continuing improvements in technology will allow oil reserves and oil production to increase without an explicit link between them. In the USDOE's projections, only two producers (US and Western Europe) are projected to have lower oil production in 2020 than in 1996. Even these declines are very modest, just 0.9 and 0.7 Mbd respectively over a period of 24 years.

Great uncertainties exist for the Transition Economies. The IEA projection shows supply from this region increasing from 7.3 Mbd in 1996 to 10.2 Mbd and then declining to 9.4 Mbd by 2020. The USDOE projection, by contrast, shows a continual increase in production to 13.2 Mbd in 2020. This region includes the Caspian Sea and Russia. Russia is a mature production province and the Caspian Sea an emerging one. In recent years, FSU oil production has been depressed by a lack of investment, particularly in existing Russian oilfields, and there have been considerable difficulties in bringing the Caspian Sea's oil reserves to market. Trying to project how production from either of these two provinces will develop during the next 20 years is a task fraught with difficulties. Combining production from both provinces into a single Transition Economies projection further compounds these difficulties. It is therefore too early to say whether the IEA or USDOE's projection is likely to prove more accurate in 2020.

World Energy Outlook

In summary, the USDOE oil supply projections are considerably more optimistic than the BAU projection (based on 2300 billion barrels conventional oil reserves). One major reason for the difference is the absence of an explicit quantitative link in the USDOE's projection between production and reserves. At some point in the future, worldwide conventional oil production must peak, just as it did in the United States, for example. Worldwide conventional oil production cannot rise year after year and then rapidly fall to zero when reserves are exhausted. It seems more likely that conventional oil production will decline gradually during the post-peak period. Considerable uncertainties remain, on current estimates of recoverable reserves of conventional oil, on the likely impacts of new technologies, and on the costs of unconventional oil supplies when they are required. One purpose of this chapter has been to highlight these uncertainties.

CHAPTER 8
GAS

Box 8.1: **Gas Supply**

The demand for gas is growing rapidly worldwide. Where gas is available and the delivery system to the market is in place, or can be built, gas is the preferred fuel for power generation, heating in buildings and in industrial applications. Once the substantial capital investments in gas delivery systems have been made, the marginal cost of delivering gas in the short term is low, provided spare capacity to deliver exists. Hence demand will be encouraged until full capacity is reached. On a long-term basis, demand will only grow if gas prices are sufficient to cover the full costs of delivering additional gas and the necessary supply infrastructure. Price signals[1] will identify bottlenecks in the gas chain and must be strong enough to attract the investment needed to overcome them. In practice, the limiting factors on the growth in gas consumption will vary from region to region. They include the size and cost of indigenous gas reserves, the distance from exporting countries, competition from competing fuels (especially coal in North America and China) and the size of the local energy market.

This chapter presents the business as usual (BAU) gas demand and supply projections.

Gas Demand

Table 8.1 shows that over the period 1995 - 2020, worldwide gas demand is projected to grow at an average annual rate of 2.6%. Non-OECD demand is projected to grow more quickly, at 3.5% per annum, and OECD gas demand more slowly, at 1.7% per annum. Rapidly expanding non-OECD gas demand is 40% larger than OECD gas demand by 2020.

Total Final Consumption

One reason why the OECD's gas demand is expected to grow more slowly than in the rest of the world is saturation of gas demand in several sectors. The share of gas in most OECD final consumption sectors is already high. For example, in 1995 the share of gas in total

---

1. *Natural Gas Pricing in a Competitive Environment,* IEA/OECD Paris (forthcoming).

Chapter 8 - Gas **123**

Table 8.1: **Total Primary Energy Supply of Gas (Mtoe)**

	1995	2010	2020	1995 - 2020 Annual Growth Rate
OECD	**949.8**	**1329.5**	**1433.4**	**1.7%**
North America	575.9	704.6	676.2	0.6%
Europe	301.3	506.1	625.2	3.0%
Pacific	72.7	118.8	132.0	2.4%
Non-OECD	**860.6**	**1391.6**	**2034.9**	**3.5%**
Transition Economies	498.3	646.7	835.2	2.1%
Africa	39.2	70.5	102.2	3.9%
China	16.7	56.6	80.7	6.5%
East Asia	75.8	178.8	289.5	5.5%
South Asia	33.7	89.9	160.4	6.4%
Latin America	92.7	185.1	306.0	4.9%
Middle East	104.3	164.2	261.0	3.7%
World	**1810.4**	**2721.1**	**3468.3**	**2.6%**

Note : OECD North America in the above table excludes Mexico, which is included in Latin America. 1 tcf = 23.31 Mtoe

fossil fuel consumption in the stationary sectors was 43%. Historically, much of the growth in gas demand has come from fossil fuel switching in the residential, commercial, public administration and industrial sectors. In these sectors taken together, the share of gas in total fossil fuel consumption had reached 57% by 1995. Considerable scope for switching away from other fossil fuels to gas still exists: oil demand in the industrial sector still exceeds that of gas, for example. But the contribution of fuel switching to the future growth in gas demand is likely to be more modest than in the past. Saturation in some end-uses, particularly the residential sector's space and water heating, is also likely to limit the future rate of growth in OECD gas demand. In North America, a higher gas price will tend to switch gas use from industrial boilers to combined-cycle gas turbines for power generation.

It is not surprising, then, that the OECD's total final consumption of gas is projected, as shown in Table 8.2, to be virtually flat during the projection period, growing at an annual average rate of just 0.2%. Elsewhere, the share of gas in total final consumption of fossil fuels was just 18% in 1995, compared to 26% in the OECD, and so the potential for fuel switching to gas is greater. Furthermore, per capita energy consumption is typically lower in the non-OECD regions and so the saturation of some end-uses is less of a restraining factor. When these factors are taken into account, it is estimated that non-OECD gas demand will grow during the projection period at an annual average rate of 3.5%, well above the 0.2% projected for the OECD.

Table 8.2: **Total Final Gas Consumption (Mtoe)**

	1995	2010	2020	1995 - 2020 Annual Growth Rate
OECD	**634.9**	**704.7**	**661.2**	**0.2%**
North America	379.2	384.8	345.7	-0.4%
Europe	225.5	280.5	274.2	0.8%
Pacific	30.3	39.4	41.3	1.2%
Non-OECD	**383.7**	**644.3**	**899.1**	**3.5%**
Transition Economies	232.0	331.6	428.3	2.5%
Africa	11.3	17.5	23.5	2.9%
China	13.1	36.2	46.7	5.2%
East Asia	19.2	45.1	71.4	5.4%
South Asia	18.9	54.8	91.8	6.5%
Latin America	49.8	94.3	133.8	4.0%
Middle East	39.4	64.8	103.6	3.9%
World	**1018.6**	**1348.9**	**1560.3**	**1.7%**

Table 8.3: **Stationary[2] Sector Gas Demand (Mtoe)**

	1995	2010	2020	1995 - 2020 Annual Growth Rate
OECD	**612.8**	**673.6**	**623.3**	**0.1%**
North America	357.6	354.1	308.1	-0.6%
Europe	225.1	280.1	273.9	0.8%
Pacific	30.1	39.4	41.2	1.3%
Non-OECD	**369.2**	**621.1**	**866.2**	**3.5%**
Transition Economies	219.1	311.0	398.7	2.4%
Africa	10.8	17.0	23.0	3.1%
China	13.0	36.1	46.6	5.2%
East Asia	19.2	45.0	71.4	5.4%
South Asia	18.9	54.8	91.8	6.5%
Latin America	48.8	92.4	131.2	4.0%
Middle East	39.4	64.8	103.6	3.9%
World	**982.0**	**1294.7**	**1489.5**	**1.7%**

2. The Stationary Sectors are defined in Part IV.

Details of the stationary sectors projected gas demands are shown in Table 8.3.

Power Generation

Gas demand is projected to grow especially quickly in power generation[3]. The high efficiency of combined cycle gas turbines (CCGTs), and their low emissions of CO_2 and SO_2, make them particularly attractive for generating electricity. Within the OECD, growth in the use of gas for power generation is projected to be rapid, at an annual average rate of 4.5%. OECD Europe's growth in gas demand for power generation is the most rapid of all OECD regions, at 7.3% per annum. In the other two OECD regions, growth is projected to be more modest, at around 3%, because coal or nuclear power will often remain the preferred option for base load electricity generation.

Table 8.4: **Power Generation Gas Demand (Mtoe)**

	1995	2010	2020	1995 - 2020 Annual Growth Rate
OECD	**227.4**	**525.2**	**678.1**	**4.5%**
North America	131.6	253.5	270.7	2.9%
Europe	55.0	194.4	318.9	7.3%
Pacific	40.8	77.3	88.5	3.1%
Non-OECD	**337.2**	**508.6**	**798.9**	**3.5%**
Transition Economies	228.0	267.1	350.8	1.7%
Africa	15.3	33.6	52.9	5.1%
China	0.7	12.4	23.6	14.9%
East Asia	27.1	64.8	108.9	5.7%
South Asia	11.8	26.4	54.1	6.3%
Latin America	20.7	48.7	112.4	7.0%
Middle East	33.5	55.6	96.2	4.3%
World	**564.6**	**1033.8**	**1477.0**	**3.9%**

Although gas demand growth in the non-OECD's power generation sector is projected to be somewhat lower than in the OECD, 3.5% compared to 4.5% per annum, non-OECD demand in this sector already exceeds that from the OECD. Gas demand in the non-OECD is dominated by the Transition Economies, where gas has often been used in the past to free up other fossil fuels, particularly oil,

---

3. See Chapter 6 and Part III for more information on the increasing use of gas for power generation.

for export. If the Transition Economies are excluded from the non-OECD figures, then gas demand in the power generation sector is projected to grow at an annual average rate of 5.8%

Table 8.5 summarises the demand and supply gas projections in terms of million tonnes of oil equivalent (Mtoe).

Table 8.5: **Summary Table for the BAU Gas Projection (Mtoe)**

Indigenous Production	1995	2010	2020
OECD North America (including Mexico)	592	759	764
OECD Europe	199	276	238
OECD Pacific	31	77	68
Transition Economies	585	809	1116
China	17	57	81
Rest of World (excluding Mexico)	396	750	1208
World	1818	2727	3474
Net Imports	**1995**	**2010**	**2020**
OECD North America (including Mexico)	-2	-2	-2
OECD Europe	104	230	387
OECD Pacific	42	42	64
Transition Economies	-74	-162	-281
China	0	0	0
Rest of World (excluding Mexico)	-76	-114	-174
World	-8	-6	-6
Total Primary Gas Supply	**1995**	**2010**	**2020**
OECD North America (including Mexico)	602	756	762
OECD Europe	301	506	625
OECD Pacific	73	119	132
Transition Economies	498	647	835
China	17	57	81
Rest of World (excluding Mexico)	319	636	1033
World	**1810**	**2721**	**3468**

Units and Regions

The following section presents the Outlook's gas supply projections. Whereas the Outlook's demand projections are prepared in terms of million tonnes of oil equivalent (Mtoe), gas supply is traditionally measured in trillion cubic feet (tcf)[4] and the BAU supply projections are presented in these units in Table 8.6.

4. Throughout this Outlook the following conversion factor has been applied 1 Mtoe = 0.0429 tcf.

While Mexico is included under Latin America elsewhere in the Outlook, in the gas supply analysis Mexico is included in OECD North America. This alternative definition arises from Mexico's extensive gas reserves, which could in the long run be exported to the US. These exports would require large capital investments in pipeline infrastructure, but could come into service before 2020 if the US were unable to satisfy gas demand from Canadian and domestic reserves. Currently, the US is a net exporter of gas to Mexico, but this position could be reversed towards the end of the projection period if US gas reserves proved to be less abundant than assumed by some commentators.

Table 8.6: **Total Primary Energy Supply (tcf)**

	1995	2010	2020	1995-2020 Annual Growth Rate
OECD	**41**	**57**	**61**	**1.7%**
North America (excl. Mexico)	25	30	29	0.6%
Europe	13	22	27	3.0%
Pacific	3	5	6	2.4%
Non-OECD	**37**	**60**	**87**	**3.5%**
Transition Economies	21	28	36	2.1%
Africa	2	3	4	3.9%
China	1	2	3	6.5%
East Asia	3	8	12	5.5%
South Asia	1	4	7	6.4%
Latin America (incl. Mexico)	4	8	13	4.9%
Middle East	4	7	11	3.7%
World	**78**	**117**	**149**	**2.6%**

1 Mtoe = 0.0429 tcf

Gas Supply

This section presents the BAU projections for gas supply, including conventional and unconventional gas. For the world as a whole, our calculations indicate that cumulative consumption of gas to 2020 will be less than one half of the United States Geological Survey (USGS) ultimate conventional gas reserves. In world terms, therefore, reserves are not expected to constrain gas production in the Outlook period. At present, the world gas market can be considered as five separate markets:

- Europe, North Africa and the Transition Economies
- North America and Mexico
- Asia Pacific
- Middle East
- Latin America

The markets are linked by LNG trade, a large part of which serves Japan. In the future, major new pipelines and increased LNG trade are expected to increase the linkages between markets. Attention therefore needs to be given to gas trade prospects.

For regions outside North America, the projections in this Outlook have been prepared using the 1994 USGS[5] estimates of ultimate[6] conventional gas reserves. The 1994 USGS estimated that global conventional ultimate gas reserves were around 11500 tcf, or approximately 2000 billion barrels of oil. Details of this estimate can be found in Table 8.7. The 1994 USGS' ultimate gas reserves estimate is at the lower end of the range of ultimate oil reserves assumed in this Outlook[7]. Perrondon et al provide similar estimates of ultimate gas reserves to that of the USGS and estimate a range of 9000-13000 tcf with a mean of 10000 tcf[8].

The USGS' estimated ultimate conventional gas reserves are shown in Table 8.7. Cumulative world production to 1993 had reached only 15.3% of the USGS estimate of ultimate reserves of conventional gas. The figures for OECD North America are misleading in this table, as gas production in this region includes substantial amounts of unconventional gas (mainly coal bed methane and tight reservoir gas). For this reason, gas supply projections for North America are considered separately below. Gas supply in OECD Europe has been the subject of an IEA study[9] and is also treated separately.

Estimates of gas reserves are expected to grow over time because uncertainty is reduced and technology develops, new gas is discovered and upward revisions are made to identified reserves. In many parts of the world, gas reserves are known to exist, but the lack of a suitable

5. *World Petroleum Assessment and Analysis,* Masters, C.D et al, Proceedings of the 14th World Petroleum Congress, 1994, Published by John Wiley and Sons.
6. Ultimate reserves = Cumulative Production + Remaining Recoverable Reserves + Undiscovered.
7. See Chapter 7 for details of the 2000 - 3000 billion barrels range of ultimate oil reserves.
8. *The World's Non-Conventional Oil and Gas, Hydrocarbons of last recourse,* A. Perrondon, J.H. Laherrère and C.J. Campbell, published by The Petroleum Economist Ltd in March 1998 (ISBN 1 86186 062 5), see page 98 for further details.
9. *The IEA Natural Gas Security Study,* IEA/OECD Paris, 1995.

infrastructure to get them to consumers means that they are not currently considered economic. These finds are referred to as "stranded" gas. It is likely that this gas will increasingly be exploited as existing pipeline systems are extended, as markets are developed closer to stranded gas reserves or via Gas-to-Liquids technology (see Chapter 7). In addition, unconventional gas reserves may be exploited as technology develops and gas prices rise to make it economic to do so.

Table 8.7: **USGS Ultimate Conventional Gas Reserves (tcf)**

Region	Ultimate Reserves	Production (1992)	Cumulative Production (end 1992)	Cumulative Production / Ultimate Reserves
OECD North America	2151.9	23.3*	899.1*	41.8%*
OECD Pacific	113.2	1.1	10.2	9.0%
OECD Europe	655.7	7.6	159.8	24.4%
Africa	746.6	3.0	31.1	4.2%
Latin America	485.4	2.3	39.7	8.2%
S and E Asia	596.0	5.1	51.8	8.7%
Transition Economies	3886.6	27.5	493.5	12.7%
Middle East	2585.6	3.7	49.8	1.9%
China	227.0	0.6	15.2	6.7%
World	**11448.0**	**74.2**	**1750.2**	**15.3%**

Note : Ultimate Reserves = Cumulative Production + Remaining Recoverable Reserves + Undiscovered.
1 Mtoe = 0.0429 tcf or 1 tcf = 23.31 Mtoe.
* Production in OECD North America includes unconventional gas.

Simple models have been adopted for gas supply. For regions other than North America and OECD Europe, gas production is assumed to follow a modified Hubbert Curve[10] to ensure that a link exists between cumulative gas production and estimated recoverable reserves of gas. In order to allow for further increases in gas reserve estimates, gas production is allowed to increase until 60% (instead of the normal 50%) of the USGS' estimated ultimate conventional gas reserves for the region have been produced. Once that threshold has been reached, gas production is assumed to decline by 5% per annum. The difference between a region's consumption and post-peak production is met by imports of gas from other regions. Gas imports are allocated to gas exporting countries on the basis of judgement. They are especially uncertain.

10. Chapter 7 discusses the Hubbert Curve.

North America

As noted in relation to Table 8.7, the cumulative production of gas is already approaching 50% of the 1994 USGS estimate of ultimate reserves of conventional gas. Account needs to be taken therefore of both the production of unconventional gas and the substantial increase in estimates of North American gas reserves since the 1994 USGS estimates.

The United States

According to Perrondon et al[11], unconventional gas currently contributes up to 20% of total gas production in the US and accounts for three out of every four gas wells drilled. Since 1990, Perrondon et al state that unconventional gas has accounted for almost all the growth in US gas production[12].

Table 8.8 compares the 1994 USGS[13] estimate of remaining conventional gas reserves for the United States at 1/1/93 of 632 tcf with the resource assumptions underlying the USDOE/EIA Annual Energy Outlook 1998[14]. The higher USDOE/EIA conventional resources reflect the substantial increase in conventional inferred reserves as of 1/1/94 in a later 1995 USGS assessment.

Calculation of the ratio of cumulative gas production to ultimate reserve estimate indicates that some 65% of the latest reserve estimate will be produced by 2020 in the Reference Case of the USDOE/EIA 1998 Annual Energy Outlook, and gas production will still be rising at that point. If gas supply tightened, gas prices would rise. A modest rise in gas prices is included towards 2020 in the USDOE/EIA Outlook. The IEA Outlook takes the view that some increase in the gas price is likely to be necessary to match gas supply and demand, but the price rise is assumed not to be sufficient to attract significant LNG imports into the United States.

The uncertainties on gas reserves and gas production in the United States over the period to 2020 are clearly substantial. The USDOE's assumption, in Table 8.8, that new technology will add

11. op.cit.
12. *The World's Non-Conventional Oil and Gas, Hydrocarbons of last recourse,* A. Perrondon, J.H. Laherrère and C.J. Campbell, published by The Petroleum Economist Ltd in March 1998 (ISBN 1 86186 062 5), see page 24 for further details.
13. *World Petroleum Assessment and Analysis,* C.D. Masters, E.D. Attanasi and D.H. Root, Proceedings of the 14th World Petroleum Congress, 1994.
14. *Annual Energy Outlook 1998,* Energy Information Administration, US Department of Energy, USDOE/EIA- 0383(98), December 1997.

some 30% to gas reserves by 2020 is uncertain, as gas reservoirs have much higher recovery factors than oil reservoirs, leaving less room for new technology to increase recoverable reserve estimates. Less than 30% of the USDOE's (1998) existing conventional gas reserves are proven. Finally, the costs of much of the remaining unconventional gas reserves are unknown.

Table 8.8: **Estimates of Gas Reserves in the United States**

	tcf
USGS (Masters 1994)	
Remaining conventional reserves at 1/1/93	632
US EIA/DOE (1998) remaining reserves to 1/1/97	
Conventional proved, inferred and undiscovered	731
Unconventional	247
Upgrade from 1997 to 2020 technology	316
Current remaining reserves	1294
Cumulative production to 1/1/97	871
Cumulative production 1997-2020	567
Cumulative production to 2020	1438
Cumulative production to 2020	1438
Ultimate reserves	(871 + 1294)
	= 66%

Canada

A similar position exists in Canada with respect to the uncertainty surrounding the quantity of gas reserves, as Table 8.9 demonstrates. Table 8.9 can be compared with the USGS' (1994) estimates of Canadian conventional ultimate gas reserves of 485 tcf, of which 82 tcf had been produced as of 1/1/1993.

According to this table, recoverable reserves of Canadian conventional gas could be in the range from 93 - 292 tcf. In the case of unconventional gas, recoverable reserves are clearly substantial but are even more difficult to estimate.

The above estimates suggest that although considerable reserves of unconventional gas exist in North America, there is much uncertainty about their size, cost and future production levels.

It is possible to develop a wide variety of gas supply projections for the region. One scenario was examined by the IEA in early 1998, for the G8 Ministerial Meeting. It used the USGS' estimates of

OECD North America's conventional gas reserves in conjunction with an assumption that regional gas production would peak when 65% of the region's reserves had been produced[15]. That scenario led to a large import requirement of LNG. We have rejected this scenario on the grounds that the rise in gas price necessary to attract LNG imports would probably reduce demand and stimulate additional indigenous gas supply sufficiently to render the imports unnecessary. In this Outlook, an alternative scenario has been developed in which it is assumed that a combination of a gas price increase, improvements in technology and greater use of unconventional gas allows OECD North America to meet the projected increase in gas demand during the period 1995 - 2020 from domestic sources. For the purposes of the BAU projection, it has been assumed that between 2005 and 2015 the price of gas increases linearly from $1.7 to $3.5 (US dollars) per thousand cubic feet. Increasing the gas price in this manner means that although limited imports of LNG may occur, they will most likely reflect local mismatches in supply and demand.

Table 8.9: **Estimates of Canadian Gas Reserves (tcf)**

	Canada's Energy Outlook 1996 - 2020		Canadian Gas Potential Committee 1997	
Conventional Gas	Proven	Potential	Recoverable	Initially In Place
Conventional Areas	68	255	185	448
Frontier Areas	25	270	107	121
Total	93	525	292	569
Unconventional Gas				
Coal Sources	20	250 - 2600	135 - 261	n.a.
Tight Gas / Shale Gas	n.a.	n.a.	n.a.	175 - 3500

Sources: *Canada's Energy Outlook 1996 - 2020,* Natural Resources Canada.
Natural Gas Potential in Canada, A Report by the Canadian Gas Potential Committee, 1997.

OECD Europe

OECD Europe's gas production is assumed to grow by 2.2% per annum[16] until cumulative production reaches 60% of the USGS'

15. *World Energy Prospects to 2020,* paper prepared by the IEA for the G8 Energy Ministers' Meeting held in Moscow on the 31st March 1998.
16. This assumption has been taken from Table 3.18, page 75 of *The IEA Natural Gas Security Study,* IEA/OECD Paris 1995.

Table 8.10: **BAU Gas Supply and Demand Projections (tcf)**

	1995	2010	2020	Annual Growth Rate
Indigenous Production				
OECD	**35.2**	**47.7**	**45.9**	**0.7%**
OECD North America (including Mexico)	25.4	32.5	32.8	0.7%
OECD Pacific	1.3	3.3	2.9	2.1%
OECD Europe	8.5	11.8	10.2	0.5%
Non-OECD	**42.8**	**69.3**	**103.2**	**3.6%**
Africa	3.2	5.6	8.3	3.4%
Latin America (excluding Mexico)	2.9	5.7	9.4	4.4%
South and East Asia	6.2	11.7	17.9	3.8%
Transition Economies	25.1	34.7	47.9	3.0%
Middle East	4.7	9.2	16.1	4.5%
China	0.7	2.4	3.5	5.0%
World	**78.0**	**117.0**	**149.0**	**2.5%**
Net Imports				
OECD	**6.2**	**11.6**	**19.3**	**3.9%**
OECD North America (including Mexico)	-0.1	-0.1	-0.1	0.0%
OECD Pacific	1.8	1.8	2.8	1.7%
OECD Europe	4.5	9.9	16.6	4.3%
Non-OECD	**-6.4**	**-11.8**	**-19.5**	**3.8%**
Africa	-1.5	-2.6	-4.0	3.2%
Latin America (excluding Mexico)	0.0	0.0	0.0	0.0%
South and East Asia	-1.5	-0.1	1.4	n.a.
Transition Economies	-3.2	-6.9	-12.0	4.5%
Middle East	-0.2	-2.1	-4.9	9.1%
China	0.0	0.0	0.0	n.a.
World	**-0.2**	**-0.2**	**-0.2**	**0.0%**
Total Primary Energy Supply				
OECD	**41.9**	**59.3**	**65.2**	**1.4%**
OECD North America (including Mexico)	25.8	32.5	32.7	0.7%
OECD Pacific	3.1	5.1	5.7	1.9%
OECD Europe	12.9	21.7	26.8	2.4%
Non-OECD	**35.8**	**57.5**	**83.6**	**3.5%**
Africa	1.7	3.0	4.4	3.6%
Latin America (excluding Mexico)	2.9	5.7	9.5	4.4%
South and East Asia	4.7	11.5	19.3	5.0%
Transition Economies	21.4	27.7	35.8	2.6%
Middle East	4.5	7.0	11.2	3.4%
China	0.7	2.4	3.5	5.0%
World	**77.6**	**116.7**	**148.8**	**2.5%**

1 Mtoe = 0.0429 tcf or 1 tcf = 23.31 Mtoe.

estimated ultimate reserves, at which point production is assumed to decline by 5% per annum thereafter.

Table 8.10 presents the gas supply projections for the BAU projection.

Gas Trade

The dependence of OECD Europe and OECD Pacific on non-OECD supplies of gas steadily increases throughout the projection period. Gas imports into OECD Europe triple during the projection period, mainly by pipeline from the Transition Economies and North Africa. Imports of gas from new sources, such as the Middle East and countries surrounding the Caspian Sea, are also possible by the end of the projection period. It is likely that these new gas imports would have to come by pipeline via Turkey (large imports of LNG would almost certainly be too expensive). The main problem is one of transporting the gas to OECD Europe rather than gas reserve limitations.

As these additional sources of imports would have to compete on price with gas from Russia and Algeria in order to win market share, there may be some downward pressure on the import price of gas. Current cost estimates suggest, however, that gas from the Caspian is not competitive with either Algerian or Russian pipeline gas[17]. For example, the cost of supplying Turkmen gas to Western Europe ranges from $127 - $152 per thousand cubic metres compared to Algerian pipeline gas at $64 per thousand cubic metres and Russian pipeline gas at $113 - $131 per thousand cubic metres. Imports of Caspian gas into OECD Europe may therefore have to wait until cheaper additional supplies of gas from Algeria and Russia have been exhausted, or until the higher costs of new sources of gas can be justified on the grounds of diversification of supply. It should also not be forgotten that Norway is a major supplier of gas to other OECD Europe countries and that increases in the gas price would almost certainly result in additional volumes of Norwegian gas being delivered.

Another possible source of imports into OECD Europe is liquid natural gas. As LNG trade grows, an LNG spot market could develop over time as a result of a number of factors in much the same way as for oil during the last 30 years.

17. *Caspian Oil and Gas, The Supply Potential of Central Asia and Transcaucasia,* IEA/OECD Paris 1998, page 107.

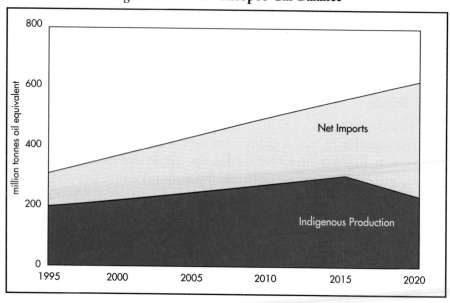

Figure 8.1: **OECD Europe's Gas Balance**

OECD Pacific's net imports of gas are projected to rise by 56% during the projection period. The import position of this region is complicated by the fact that whereas Japan is a net importer of gas, Australia exports LNG and plans to increase its exports. This difference in Australia and Japan's net import positions explains why the region's indigenous gas production is projected to rise at an annual average rate of 2.1%, while, at the same time, net imports grow at 1.7%.

Total gas demand outside the OECD is projected to grow at an annual average rate of 3.5% (2.1% for the Transition Economies and 4.9% in the developing countries) during the projection period; however, gas production will grow slightly more rapidly, at 3.6% per annum, in order to satisfy the OECD's need for gas imports. Within the non-OECD, South and East Asia will switch from being a net exporter of gas to become a net importer. Net exports of gas from the Transition Economies, Africa and the Middle East are all projected to rise during the projection period and this will result in the non-OECD's exports of gas more than tripling between 1995 and 2020.

Despite projected rapid growth in non-OECD gas production, none of the individual non-OECD regions is expected to have reached the 60% point of ultimate gas reserves by 2020, the point at which gas production is assumed to go into decline in these projections. Thus, gas production in all non-OECD regions is projected still to be increasing in 2020. The position of the non-OECD in 2020 contrasts sharply with that of the OECD, in which 70% to 80% of the USGS' estimated ultimate conventional gas reserves will have been produced.

Table 8.11: **Cumulative Gas Production as a Percentage of the USGS' Estimated Conventional Gas Reserves**

	1995	2010	2020
OECD North America	n.a.	n.a.	n.a.
OECD Pacific	12.3%	43.4%	72.9%
OECD Europe	28.1%	51.5%	69.8%
Africa	5.4%	14.3%	23.5%
Latin America excluding Mexico	9.8%	22.8%	38.6%
South and East Asia	7.7%	29.6%	54.7%
Transition Economies	14.7%	25.3%	35.7%
Middle East	2.4%	6.4%	11.2%
China	7.6%	17.9%	30.9%
World	**17.1%**	**29.7%**	**41.3%**

Note : Only conventional gas reserves are considered in the above table.

Figure 8.2: **World Gas Production**

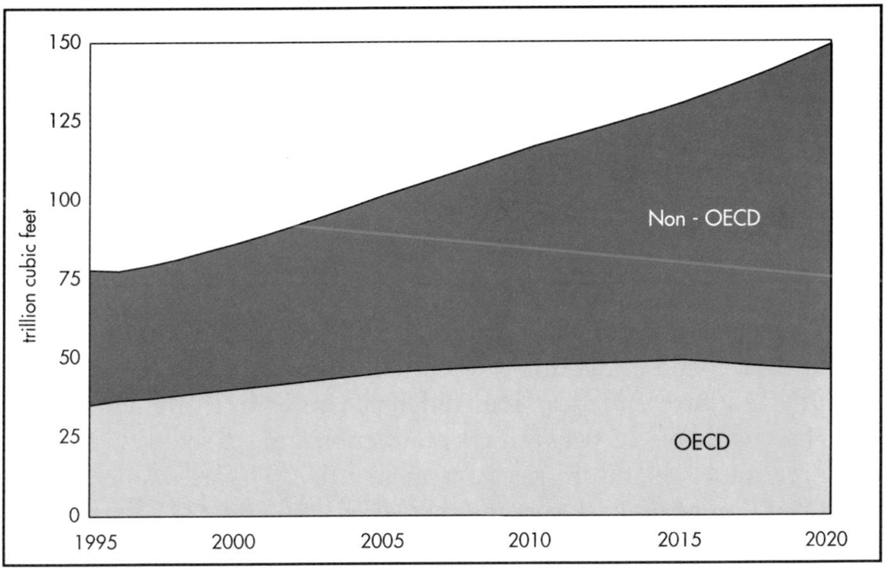

Worldwide gas production is not expected to peak until well after 2020. Over the whole of the projection period, gas supply is projected to grow by 91%. The assumption is made that OECD North America's gas supply and demand will be in balance throughout the projection period. Production in OECD Europe and in OECD Pacific will be declining as 2020 approaches.

Comparisons with Other Organisations' Gas Projections

The International Energy Outlook 1998[18] published by the USDOE/EIA provides regional gas consumption projections against which the BAU's TPES projections described earlier can be compared. The USDOE publication does not provide sufficient information for a comparison to be made of gas production. Table 8.12 compares the two demand projections.

Table 8.12: **USDOE versus IEA Gas Demand Projections**
Annual Growth Rates 1995 - 2020

	USDOE Reference Case	IEA BAU Projection
OECD	**2.5%**	**1.7%**
OECD North America	1.6%	0.6%
OECD Europe	3.8%	3.0%
OECD Pacific	1.6%	2.4%
Non-OECD	**3.9%**	**3.5%**
Transition Economies	2.4%	2.1%
South and East Asia	7.3%	5.8%
China	7.5%	6.5%
Middle East	2.6%	3.7%
Africa	2.8%	3.9%
Latin America	6.1%	4.9%
World	**3.3%**	**2.6%**

One of the most notable features of Table 8.12 is the lower growth rate in gas demand in the IEA projection than in the USDOE projection for OECD North America. This difference arises from the link in the IEA's gas supply model between gas production and gas reserves. Because of uncertainties on future gas reserves in OECD North America, the IEA's BAU projection assumes that between 2005 and 2015 the price of gas increases linearly from $1.7 to $3.5 per thousand cubic feet. Whereas in the IEA projection, gas demand in OECD North America

18. *International Energy Outlook 1998,* USDOE/EIA-0484(98), Energy Information Administration, US Department of Energy, April 1998.

actually declines slightly between 2010 and 2020 because of the gas price increase, in the USDOE projection, gas demand continues to grow.

A second projection against which the Outlook's gas projections can be compared is that of the European Union. The EU's publication *European Energy to 2020: A Scenario Approach*[19] provides projections on both gas production and consumption. For the purposes of this comparison, the EU's Conventional Wisdom (CW)scenario has been used as it represents the closest match, in terms of assumptions, to the IEA's BAU projection. Table 8.13 compares the IEA, USDOE and EU gas consumption projections.

Table 8.13: **EU versus IEA Gas Demand Projections Annual Growth Rates 1995 - 2020**

	EU (1990 - 2020) Conventional Wisdom	IEA BAU Projection
OECD	**2.3%**	**1.7%**
OECD North America	n.a.	0.6%
OECD Europe	n.a.	3.0%
OECD Pacific	n.a.	2.4%
Non-OECD	**2.9%**	**3.5%**
Transition Economies	1.5%	2.1%
South and East Asia *	6.4%	5.8%
China *	6.4%	6.5%
Middle East	3.7%	3.7%
Africa	5.0%	3.9%
Latin America	5.6%	4.9%
World	**2.7%**	**2.6%**

Note : The EU projections are two years older than either the IEA or USDOE projections and, so, at the time they were being prepared, 1995 energy data were unavailable. The EU's publication reference year is therefore 1990 and not 1995. However, the omission of 1995 alone should not greatly alter its projections.
* The EU projections do not separate China from the rest of Asia.

Probably the most significant difference between the EU and IEA projections concerns the Transition Economies. The EU growth projection is 0.6 percentage points below that of the BAU projection (2.1% versus 1.5%). Since the Transition Economies accounted for

19. *European Energy to 2020: A Scenario Approach, Energy in Europe,* DG XVII, European Commission, Special Issue - Spring 1996.

38% of global gas consumption in 1990, small variations in the region's growth rate can have large impacts on the projected non-OECD gas consumption. Thus, the EU's lower projected growth rate for the Transition Economies results in their projection for the non-OECD's being lower than that projected by the BAU. At the world level, however, there is little to choose between the two projections, with the EU projecting faster growth in the OECD's gas consumption than the IEA. This difference almost exactly offsets the difference in projections for the Transition Economies, with the result that at a global level there is little difference between the two organisations' gas projections.

Interestingly, the EU's rapid growth rate in OECD gas consumption suggests that either it does not have an explicit link between gas reserves and production in its gas supply model (as with the USDOE), or it is projecting large gas imports into OECD North America. Table 8.14 compares the BAU and EU gas balances for the OECD in 2020.

Table 8.14: **OECD Gas Balances in 2020 IEA BAU versus EU CW (Mtoe)**

	IEA BAU	EU CW	Difference
Production	1070	811	259
Net Imports	449	802	-353
TPES	1519	1612	-93

It is evident from the above table that when allowance is made for the difference in TPES projections (93 Mtoe in 2020), gas production in the BAU projection is approximately 260 Mtoe higher than in the EU projection. Similarly in the EU projection, adjusted net imports are around 260 Mtoe higher than in the BAU projection. The EU projections do not separate out total OECD into its three regions, but they provide separate gas production projections for the USA and EU. An examination of these projections shows the USA's gas production falling from 419 Mtoe in 1990 to 364 Mtoe in 2020. Similarly, the EU's gas production starts at 133 Mtoe in 1990, and then rises to 174 Mtoe in 2000 before declining to 131 Mtoe in 2020. Since the EU is projecting total OECD gas production to increase from 714 Mtoe in 1990 to 811 Mtoe in 2020, it expects gas production in countries such as Canada, Mexico, Norway[20] and Australia to offset the decline in gas production from the EU and USA.

The principal difference between the Outlook's BAU projection and the EU's Conventional Wisdom projection lies in the growth of gas production and net imports. In the BAU projection, it has been noted that imports of LNG into OECD North America would require a substantial gas price increase and that, as the price increased, additional unconventional and possibly also conventional gas production would be forthcoming. Also, since the BAU projection assumes that OECD North America's gas price more than doubles between 2005 and 2015, the projected increase in gas demand is moderated by this price increase. In the EU's projection, there seems to be a large increase in OECD imports of gas without any mention of the gas price increasing in order to encourage these imports. Even if the increase in net imports were restricted to OECD Europe, there would still be some upward movement in the price of gas imports and, therefore, in the delivered gas price.

The important point to note from the comparisons between the IEA, USDOE and EU's gas projections for the OECD is that eventually rising gas demand will necessitate some increase in gas prices. This price increase will occur in North America in order to ensure that either indigenous gas production or net imports rise sufficiently to meet gas demand. The link that exists between gas reserves, production and net imports in the IEA's gas supply model is therefore important, as it ensures that gas demand is not allowed to increase without questions being answered about the sources and about the prices at which this additional demand can be supplied.

The uncertainties in these projections are very substantial and the data available today for resolving the uncertainties are limited. This is why a comparison of projections can better identify the uncertainties and throw more light upon them.

---

20. Recall that Norway is a Member of OECD but voted not to become a Member of the EU.

CHAPTER 9
COAL

Box 9.1: **Coal Supply**

Coal is used mainly in power generation, in industry and in the residential sector. Demand in the non-power generation sectors has been static in the OECD region for a number of years but is growing elsewhere. Consumption for power generation is growing worldwide. Two major factors will affect projections of coal demand. The first will be the outcome of competition between coal and gas in power generation. The second will be the choice of policies by governments to meet the greenhouse gas commitments entered into at Kyoto in 1997.

Introduction

This chapter considers the prospects for coal during the projection period 1995 to 2020. Unlike conventional oil, sufficient reserves of coal exist to meet world demand for the foreseeable future. Coal reserves are generally much more evenly distributed throughout the world than oil or gas reserves and strong competitive pressures exist to minimise production costs. Security of supply is not an issue as lower coal production from one supplier can relatively easily be substituted by additional production from another.

Because of the wide diversity of existing and potential coal suppliers, a separate coal supply model has not been developed for this Outlook. Instead, the approach taken is to assume that all the projected increase in coal demand can be met from known reserves and that competition between suppliers will determine regional shares in meeting global coal demand. Information on the prospects for each region's coal supply are presented in the relevant regional chapter.

Previous versions of the World Energy Outlook aggregated coal and biomass[1] into a category called solid fuels. This Outlook makes use of recent IEA analysis to separate biomass and coal demand projections for the first time, in non-OECD regions.

1. Also known as Combustible Renewables and Waste (CRW).

Coal Demand

Total Primary Coal Demand

Global demand for coal is projected to grow at an annual average rate of 2.2%. Overall, OECD demand is projected to grow at less than half the rate of non-OECD demand. Within the OECD there are marked differences. North America's[2] coal demand is projected to grow at close to the global rate. In OECD Europe, demand is projected to decline by 0.6% per annum. Similarly, OECD Pacific's demand for coal is projected to grow much more slowly than that of OECD North America, at an annual average rate of just 0.5%. This substantial increase in OECD North America's coal demand arises from an assumed rise in the gas price, producing lower gas demand and higher coal demand than would otherwise be the case. The reason for the high gas price in North America is discussed in Chapter 8.

Table 9.1: **Total Primary Coal Demand (Mtoe)**

	1995	2010	2020	1995 - 2020 Annual Growth Rate
OECD	904.4	1096.5	1219.0	1.2%
North America	500.8	649.3	835.2	2.1%
Europe	282.4	314.0	245.4	-0.6%
Pacific	121.3	133.2	138.3	0.5%
Non-OECD	1300.5	2013.4	2556.1	2.7%
Transition Economies	300.2	357.0	359.6	0.7%
Africa	81.6	111.7	136.9	2.1%
China	663.7	1086.7	1415.9	3.1%
East Asia	84.5	145.5	218.8	3.9%
South Asia	139.8	255.6	347.7	3.7%
Latin America	25.2	44.2	59.0	3.5%
Middle East	5.4	12.7	18.2	5.0%
World	2204.9	3109.9	3775.1	2.2%

Despite recent economic difficulties in Asia, the long-term outlook for the region's coal demand remains strong. Asian demand

---

2. Unless otherwise stated, OECD North America excludes Mexico, which is instead included under Latin America.

outside China is projected to grow at an annual rate of around 3.8% and in China at 3.1%. The Middles East's demand for coal is projected to grow at 5% per annum. Around two-thirds of the additional Middle East's coal demand is for power generation, principally in those countries without large oil and gas reserves, such as Israel. Most of the remaining increase is likely to occur in those sectors, such as iron and steel making, where coal has few substitutes. Coal demand in the Transition Economies is projected to grow only slowly, reflecting the large potential for energy savings that still exists in these countries and the increasing use of oil and gas. Given the uncertainties surrounding the rate of economic growth and improvements in energy efficiency, it is difficult to say how rapidly the Transition Economies' coal demand will grow.

Total Final Consumption

Table 9.2: **Total Final Consumption (Mtoe)**

	1995	2010	2020	1995 - 2020 Annual Growth Rate
OECD	**155.7**	**145.6**	**150.2**	**-0.1%**
North America	38.8	38.8	43.5	0.5%
Europe	72.7	66.4	67.6	-0.3%
Pacific	44.1	40.4	39.1	-0.5%
Non-OECD	**660.2**	**906.0**	**1067.8**	**1.9%**
Transition Economies	109.5	119.5	121.2	0.4%
Africa	20.7	25.5	29.3	1.4%
China	415.9	617.3	755.4	2.4%
East Asia	46.7	53.5	56.7	0.8%
South Asia	50.4	69.9	81.5	1.9%
Latin America	15.8	18.6	21.4	1.2%
Middle East	1.2	1.6	2.3	2.7%
World	**815.9**	**1051.6**	**1218.0**	**1.6%**

Within the OECD, virtually all of the region's total final consumption of coal is consumed in the stationary sector and is projected to decline slightly throughout the projection period. In OECD Europe, a return to average winter temperatures, from the warm winters experienced for most of the 1990s, is expected to result in a small short-term increase in coal demand. In the longer term, however, the switch to other fuels, principally gas, will more than offset this short-term effect.

Non-OECD final consumption of coal is projected to increase by over 400 Mtoe between 1995 and 2020. Growth is expected to be dominated by China, which already accounts for 63% of total non-OECD coal demand. By 2020, China's share of non-OECD coal demand is projected to increase to 71%. China's share of global final coal consumption leaps from 51% to 62% between 1995 and 2020. By 2020, China's final consumption of coal is expected to be over five times greater than that of the entire OECD.

Power Generation[3]

With the exception of OECD Europe, coal demand for power generation is projected to increase in every region. But, tighter emission controls and the switch to gas will reduce the extent to which coal consumption can grow in many regions. In the case of OECD Europe, these factors combine with the cost competitiveness of CCGT plants relative to coal plants to lower coal demand by 16% in 2020 compared with 1995. In North America, coal demand is projected to grow at an annual average rate of 2.2%. Growth in OECD Pacific is projected to be more modest, at 1.2% per annum.

Total non-OECD demand for coal in this sector grows at an annual average rate of 3.6%, more than twice the OECD's growth rate. Growth in non-OECD demand will, however, be dampened by low demand growth in the Transition Economies. This low rate of growth results in China increasing its share of non-OECD coal demand from 41% to 46% during the projection period. Elsewhere in Asia, coal demand for power generation is also expected to grow rapidly, at an annual average rate of 4.9%. In Latin America and the Middle East, demand will grow even more rapidly than in Asia, but the current low level of coal demand in these regions means that the additional volumes demanded by 2020 will be relatively modest.

In sum, the power sector's demand for coal will increasingly be dominated by Asia. Asia's share of world demand is projected to increase from 28% in 1995 to 43% by 2020. OECD North America will remain the largest consuming region, but China's rapid growth during the projection period will reduce the size of North America's lead considerably by 2020.

---

3. The prospects for coal in power generation are discussed in each of the regional chapters in Part III and in Chapter 6. This section therefore highlights the main global trends.

Table 9.3: **Power Generation (Mtoe)**

	1995	2010	2020	1995 - 2020 Annual Growth Rate
OECD	**719.6**	**921.7**	**1039.5**	**1.5%**
North America	456.1	604.3	784.8	2.2%
Europe	197.9	235.9	166.9	-0.7%
Pacific	65.6	81.5	87.8	1.2%
Non-OECD	**586.9**	**1038.4**	**1413.7**	**3.6%**
Transition Economies	163.9	210.5	212.3	1.0%
Africa	43.8	65.1	83.3	2.6%
China	240.7	458.7	647.5	4.0%
East Asia	33.5	87.1	157.0	6.4%
South Asia	92.6	181.8	261.7	4.2%
Latin America	8.3	24.3	36.1	6.1%
Middle East	4.2	11.0	15.8	5.5%
World	**1306.5**	**1960.1**	**2453.3**	**2.6%**

Coal Supply

Reserves

Whereas oil reserves are concentrated in the Middle East and gas reserves in the Middle East and Former Soviet Union (FSU), coal can be found in large quantities throughout the world. Coal reserves at the end of 1996 are shown in the following table, along with production.

The global ratio of coal reserves to production was 224 years at the end of 1996. For the OECD, the ratio was even larger at 237 years. Coal reserves are not expected to act as a constraint on coal supply until well into the next century. In order to obtain a view on which countries are likely to be major coal suppliers during the projection period, Table 9.5 lists the top-10 countries in terms of coal reserves and their shares of world coal reserves.

Table 9.4: **Coal Reserves and Production**

	Reserves - End 1996 (Billion Tonnes)	Percentage of Total	Production - 1996 (Mtoe)	Percentage of Total
OECD	**430**	**41.6%**	**920.8**	**40.7%**
OECD North America*	250	24.3%	611.7	27.0%
OECD Europe**	87	8.5%	173.2	7.6%
OECD Pacific***	92	8.9%	135.9	6.0%
Non-OECD	**602**	**58.4%**	**1343.3**	**59.3%**
Transition Economies	310	30.1%	310.8	13.7%
Africa	617	6.0%	114.5	5.1%
China	115	11.1%	680.6	30.1%
Other Asia	105	10.2%	209.0	9.2%
Latin America	10	1.0%	27.1	1.2%
Middle East	0.2	0.0%	1.3	0.1%
World	**1032**	**100%**	**2264.1**	**100%**

Source: *British Petroleum Statistical Review of World Energy,* 1997.
*   Including Mexico.
**   Excluding Poland and Hungary.
***   Excluding the Republic of Korea.

Table 9.5: **Percentage of World Coal Reserves by Country (1996)**

FSU	23.4
USA	23.3
China	11.1
Australia	8.8
India	6.8
Germany	6.5
South Africa	5.4
Poland	4.1
Indonesia	3.1
Canada	0.8
Total	**92.5**

Source: *British Petroleum Statistical Review of World Energy,* 1997.

A strong relationship exists between this ranking and the top 10 countries in terms of production shown in Table 9.6.

Table 9.6: **Percentage of World Coal Production by Country (1996)**

China	30.1
USA	25.0
FSU	8.5
India	6.2
Australia	5.7
South Africa	4.8
Poland	3.8
Germany	3.1
Canada	1.8
UK	1.4
Total	**90.4**

Source: *British Petroleum Statistical Review of World Energy,* 1997.

The level and pattern of regional coal production during the projection period will be determined by competition within each country between indigenous production and coal imports. Currently the proportion of coal traded internationally is small in proportion to world coal production. In the case of hard coal, the proportion of coal traded internationally is about 13%. The proportion is higher for coking coal than for steam coal. Despite the low percentage of internationally-traded coal, a number of countries are likely to increase their level of coal exports. The prospects for each region's coal production are briefly outlined below, with special emphasis on the expanding international coal market[4].

Asia

China and South Asia are both projected to increase their demand for coal by more than 3% per annum during the projection period. Coal demand in South Asia will continue to be dominated by India. China and India will therefore exert a large influence on the level of Asian coal production and international coal trade. China could retain its position as a significant exporter of coal throughout the projection period. In 1996, China was responsible for 8.3% of total world steam coal exports. China could also import coal into its Southern regions.

4. Further information on the evolution of the international coal market can be found in *International Coal Trade: The Evolution of a Global Market,* IEA/OECD 1997.

In India, the future level of coal production will primarily depend on the availability of finance to expand production capacity, washing plants and infrastructure. India could, in future, import coal from Indonesia, South Africa and New Zealand, in addition to current imports from Australia. Currently, however the protection enjoyed by domestic coal, port capacity and facilities restrain the level of imports. The distribution of these imports is also limited to a small coastal area because of rail capacity and costs. India has ample coal reserves from which to supply its growing domestic market. The problem is not one of reserves, but the rate at which production capacity can be expanded and its location relative to potential consumers. Currently, India's coal production and transportation capacity is not expanding rapidly enough to satisfy domestic coal demand.

North America

The United States is a major player in the international steam coal market. Considerable excess production and export capacity exists in the US, and this effectively places a limit on the extent to which internationally traded coal prices can rise. The relatively high price level at which US producers enter the export market provides some shelter for the development of new capacity in other less expensive regions, such as Latin America, Indonesia and China.

Canada's exports are primarily coking coal, although some steam coal is also exported. Canadian exports face the challenge that the mines are situated more than 1000 kilometres from the nearest international deep-water port on the west coast and so transportation costs are a major element in the total delivered cost of Canadian coal exports.

Latin America

There is a large amount of pre-production capacity at an advanced stage of planning in this region. Much of Latin America's new capacity during the projection period is likely to be relatively low cost. The main export markets for Latin American coal are the US and Europe. Since European coal demand is projected to decline during the projection period, any additional Latin American coal production exported to Europe will have to first displace existing coal suppliers.

Colombia and Venezuela currently dominate Latin America's coal production. Colombia is already an established steam-coal exporter, with plans for significant expansion. With vast reserves of low-cost, low-sulphur, low-ash coal, Colombia has the potential to increase its coal exports significantly during the projection period. Colombia is within good shipping distances of the US and European markets, although currently most coal exports go to Europe. In the past, lack of infrastructure has limited Colombia's coal production, but if the deepwater port at Puerto Bolivar were expanded, and improvements made to railway and handling facilities, Colombia's export capacity could double. In 1996, Colombia exported 24.9 million metric tons (Mt) of its total coal production of 30.1 Mt.

Venezuela is currently a small exporter but has considerable scope for expansion. It is similarly placed to Colombia with good quality coal and access to European and US markets. Currently, Venezuelan exports of coal are around 4 Mt per annum and will remain limited to this level without construction of a dedicated rail link and improved port facilities. One proposal for a new rail link and coal terminal would allow exports to be increased to 10 Mt per annum. The limiting factor on Venezuela's future coal exports is not therefore lack of reserves but infrastructure.

Transition Economies

The future of coal production in Eastern Europe depends heavily on the successful implementation of current restructuring plans, particularly in Poland, Ukraine and Russia. The Outlook for these restructuring plans is not favourable, and production destined for export is likely, at best, to stabilise at current levels for the foreseeable future.

Pacific

Australia and Indonesia are the major producing countries in this region. In Australia, there is a large quantity of pre-production capacity at an advanced stage of planning, while in Indonesia considerable flexibility exists. In the immediate future, Australia represents a likely source of additional supplies of coal to the world market. Australia is well situated to be the natural supplier of coal to the growing Asian markets. How successful the country will be in increasing its exports to Asia will depend on its ability to compete with Indonesia and China. Australia will also face competition from South African exports of coal into the Asian markets. A key factor determining Australia's future level of coal production will be its ability to contain production and transportation costs. Improving industrial relations will be important. The Australian Bureau of

Agricultural and Resource Economics has estimated that an additional 47 Mt of capacity could be developed quickly, if returns are judged sufficient.

Between 1980 and 1996, Indonesian coal production increased from 0.3 to 45 Mt. This exceptional growth has been driven by large reserves of good quality coal, proximity to markets, high labour productivity and low labour costs. Government policies have encouraged foreign investment in the coal industry. Historically, Indonesian coal production has been dominated by exports (over 75% of production was exported in 1995), but during the projection period the domestic market is expected to become increasingly important. In the past, some doubts have been expressed about physical limits on export-quality Indonesian coal resources, but recent IEA research suggests that they may be less serious than previously thought. Exports are thought likely to continue to expand.

Southern Africa

South Africa is well situated to meet the growing demand for coal imports into both Europe and Asia. Since the Europe-Atlantic market for coal has a large number of competing suppliers and the Asia-Pacific market a much narrower range of suppliers, South Africa can choose to supply the market offering the highest price. South African arbitrage means that the world coal market tends to act as a single market rather than several regional ones.

Despite South Africa's ability to meet the growing global demand for coal, the outlook for coal production in the country is highly uncertain. South Africa faces two main problems: location of additional export coal production capacity and port capacity. The coal export fields that are currently operating are approaching the ends of their economic lives and new production will have to come from coal reserves that are less well located for either domestic or export use. Traditionally, production of export-quality coal has resulted in large quantities of discards, which have been used domestically for power generation. The competitiveness of South African exports depends, in part, on the use of discards and high-ash coal in the domestic market. Potential production areas in the northern part of the country do not have a domestic market, and this lack is likely to act as a constraint on coal production, even if the infrastructure problems can be solved.

Most exports of South African coal use the Richards Bay Coal Terminal. This port was already operating at close to full capacity in

1995, and although an expansion in capacity is planned for 1999, further port capacity will be necessary if exports are to continue to increase. High rail-freight costs mean that the port of Maputo in Mozambique is not currently a serious competitor to Richards Bay, but this may change during the projection period. For the foreseeable future, Richard Bay offers the only realistic outlet for any significant expansion in South African coal exports[5]. South Africa's coal export industry is currently a mid- to high-cost supplier when compared to other countries. Productivity rates are lower than in Australia and Indonesia. This suggests that even if the infrastructure problems are solved, South African production costs may need to fall, or the Rand to depreciate, for coal exports to be sufficiently competitive to win new markets in Asia and Europe.

Western Europe[6]

The general outlook for coal production in Western Europe is not bright. Increasing pressure to reduce subsidies to the domestic coal industry means that the region's production looks certain to continue its decline. In Germany and Spain, political pressures appear likely to delay the full removal of subsidies, and to maintain some supported production on social and regional grounds. Falling indigenous production will inevitably provide scope for a slight growth in imports of cheap coal into Western Europe, but competition from low-cost gas, particularly in power generation, is expected to limit the increase in coal imports into Western Europe.

Supply Overview

One common feature running through the above analysis is uncertainty, principally the potential impact of climate change policies on coal demand. As argued in Chapter 4, it would be necessary to reduce coal demand from the levels projected in the BAU projection if the commitments entered into at Kyoto in December 1997 are to be met.

Given these uncertainties, we have not made long-term projections of regional coal production. The approach taken in this Outlook has been to project regional demand for coal, and to assume that the resulting global demand can be adequately sourced from the large number of potential suppliers. Figure 9.1 shows the BAU's projected increase in global coal supply.

5. *Energy Policies of South Africa,* IEA/OECD, 1996.
6. The coal supply outlook for Western Europe is considered in more detail in the OECD Europe chapter.

Figure 9.1: **World Coal Supply and Demand (Mtoe)**

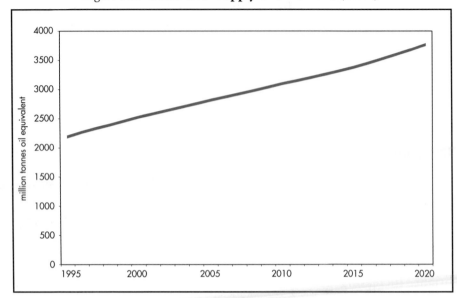

In practice, coal demand for the period to 2000 could be lower than shown in Figure 9.1 because of the lack of orders for coal-fired plants in North America since the early 1980s.

Comparison with Other Projections

Table 9.7 compares our projected regional coal demand and global supply with projections prepared by the United States Department of Energy[7] (USDOE) and European Union[8] (EU). It should be noted that the EU projections cover all solids and therefore include combustible renewables and waste in addition to coal. A strict comparison with the IEA projection is therefore not possible.

Two features stand out in comparing the USDOE and IEA projections. First, both projections show global coal demand and supply growing at an annual average rate of around 2%. Second, in the majority of regions, the USDOE is more pessimistic about future demand growth than the IEA. The factor resulting in similar demand

---

7. See Table A5, page 138, of the USDOE/EIA *International Energy Outlook 1998: With Projections Through 2020,* April 1998.
8. *Energy in Europe: European Energy to 2020 A Scenario Approach,* European Commission, DGXVII, Special Issue - Spring 1996.

growth rates is the USDOE's high growth rate for Chinese coal demand. Since China is already the world's largest consumer of coal, small changes in its projected demand growth rate have a large impact on global coal demand. If China is assumed to source its additional coal demand from indigenous sources, projecting higher demand growth for China means that a higher percentage of global coal supply will come from China in the USDOE projection than in the IEA projection.

Note that the EU projection does not separate out the three different parts of Asia, namely China, East Asia and South Asia. The EU's aggregate Asian growth rate has therefore been shown in the above table for all three Asian regions.

Another interesting feature of the above table is the much slower growth rate in OECD North America's coal demand in the USDOE projection than in the IEA projection. This difference arises mainly from the fact that the IEA has matched North American gas demand with supply. The result of that analysis (see Chapter 8 for details) implies an increase in the North American gas price. A consequence of this approach is that the IEA projection contains higher coal demand but lower gas demand than does the USDOE projection.

Table 9.7: **Total Primary Energy Supply (1995 - 2020)**
Annual Growth Rates

	USDOE Reference Case	EU (1990 - 2020) CW Scenario	IEA BAU Projection
OECD	**0.8%**	**0.2%**	**1.2%**
North America	1.2%	n.a.	2.1%
Europe	0.1%	n.a.	-0.6%
Pacific	0.6%	n.a.	0.5%
Non-OECD	**2.8%**	**1.6%**	**2.7%**
Transition Economies	-0.6%	-1.4%	0.7%
Africa	0.9%	3.1%	2.1%
China	4.3%	2.4%	3.1%
East Asia	1.8%	2.4%	3.9%
South Asia	2.5%	2.4%	3.7%
Latin America	2.4%	3.7%	3.5%
Middle East	2.6%	4.4%	5.0%
World	**2.1%**	**1.1%**	**2.2%**

CHAPTER 10
BIOMASS[1]

Introduction

Biomass energy currently represents approximately 14% of world final energy consumption, a higher share than that of coal (12%) and comparable to those of gas (15%) and electricity (14%). In developing countries[2], in which three-quarters of the world's population live, biomass energy (firewood, charcoal, crop residues and animal wastes) accounts, on average, for one-third of total final energy consumption and for nearly 75% of the energy used in households. For large portions of the rural populations of these countries, and for

Figure 10.1: **Per Capita Biomass versus per Capita GDP in Developing Countries**

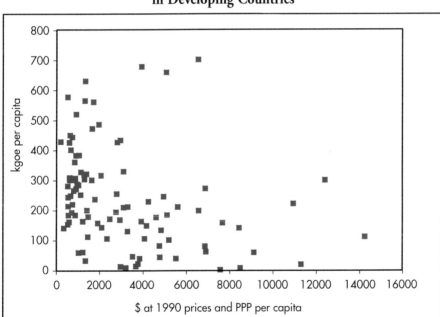

1. The IEA has organised two workshops on biomass energy. See *Biomass Energy: Key Issues and Priority Needs. Conference Proceedings,* IEA/OECD, Paris, 1997, and *Biomass Energy: Data, Analysis and Trends.* Conference Proceedings, IEA/OECD, Paris, forthcoming. The IEA has received finance and support for this work from NUTEK (the Swedish National Board for Industrial and Technical Development) and the European Commission (Directorate General XII).
2. In this chapter, we define (developing countries) as the non-OECD countries of Africa, Latin America and Asia. Geographic coverage of each regional grouping is provided in the Definitions in Part IV.

the poorest sections of urban populations, biomass is often the only available and affordable source of energy for basic needs such as cooking and heating. Although biomass energy is predominantly used in households, it also provides an important fuel source for traditional village-based industries, as well as for many small- to medium-scale services and industries in and around cities[3].

The importance of biomass in the economy and in the household sector varies widely across countries and regions, broadly reflecting their level of economic development (see Figure 10.1).

The share of biomass in final energy consumption is generally lower in countries with higher levels of income and industrialisation. On the other hand, in countries with low per capita incomes, which are predominantly rural and rely heavily on subsistence agriculture, this share can reach 80% and more (for example Ethiopia, Mozambique, Tanzania, Democratic Republic of Congo, Nepal and Myanmar).

In spite of its significance at world level and its vital importance for developing countries, biomass is often treated as a footnote item by most sources of global energy statistics. This exclusion is usually justified on the grounds that data on traditional biomass are too scarce and unreliable to be presented alongside commercial energy data[4]. For the same reason, biomass has been largely excluded from analyses of global energy demand trends. The omission of such a critical and dominant fuel has several important implications leading to potentially serious shortcomings in global analysis[5]. First, it substantially understates the actual level of energy consumption of developing countries. Second, the omission of biomass not only affects the level but also the rate of change of indicators such as energy intensity and per capita energy consumption, giving misleading indications in cross-national or inter-temporal comparisons. Third, in projecting future energy trends, the dynamics of the inter-fuel substitution from biomass to commercial energy cannot be captured and quantified. This sets an important limitation on the reliability of long-term energy demand projections for developing countries,and for the world in general.

3. See Hall, D.O. (1991), *Biomass Energy*, Energy Policy, Vol.19, No.10.
4. For example, the *BP Statistical Review of World Energy* does not include biomass, with the argument that "fuels such as wood, peat and animal waste, though important in many countries, are unreliably documented in terms of consumption statistics" (British Petroleum, *BP Statistical Review of World Energy*, British Petroleum Company plc, London, June 1998).
5. See *World Energy Outlook, 1996 Edition*, IEA/OECD, Paris; and Guerer, N. (1997), Implications of Including Biomass in Global Energy Analysis, in IEA, *Biomass Energy: Key Issues and Priority Needs*. Conference Proceedings, IEA/OECD Paris, 1996.

Definitions

Discussions of biomass are often clouded by problems of definition. Several "labels" are used to refer to the same concept, or tightly overlapping ones: biomass fuels (or biofuels), non-commercial energy, traditional fuels, etc.

The IEA uses the term combustible renewables and waste (CRW) to include all vegetable and animal matter (biomass) used directly or converted to solid fuels, as well as biomass-derived gaseous and liquid fuels, and industrial and municipal waste converted to energy. In practice, there is limited use of municipal or industrial waste for energy in developing countries. The main biomass fuels are fuelwood (or firewood), charcoal, agricultural residues and dung.

It is incorrect to equate biomass with non-commercial fuels, because an increasing share of fuelwood and practically all charcoal is traded. In many developing countries these markets rival electricity sales in monetary value. Similarly, the terms traditional as opposed to modern or efficient fuels are misleading because the same fuel (e.g. fuelwood) can be used in a traditional three-stone cooking stove or in a modern industrial boiler to generate electricity or heat. Although the majority of biomass energy use in developing countries is still in the form of direct combustion of unprocessed solid fuels, the proportion of biomass being used in larger-scale industries (such as pulp and paper and agro-industries) and in other "modern" processes, such as electricity generation and the production of transport fuels, is steadily growing.

In this study, the term "biomass" is used to designate the aggregate combustible renewables and waste. All other non-biomass fuels are referred to as conventional fuels; these include fossil fuels as well as electricity and non-combustible renewables (hydro, geothermal, wind and solar).

Data Availability

National biomass statistics are inadequate both in quantity and quality. Official sources frequently restrict themselves to the marketed (and therefore more easily measurable) component of the energy picture. In developing countries, there is often a lack of expertise as well as financial and human resources for adequate data collection and estimation, a task rendered more difficult by the decentralised (mostly rural) and largely non-marketed nature of biomass energy use. As a consequence, in many countries, the data available are at best estimates or extrapolations based on partial consumption studies, as regular country-wide surveys are extremely costly.

The statistics of the Food and Agriculture Organisation (FAO), although extensively used as the best available data at a macro level for a large number of countries, provide data only for fuelwood and charcoal. These are based mainly on the availability of forestry resources[6] and thus ignore a substantial amount of informal wood-gathering in rural areas. Furthermore, time-series by the FAO are estimates often based on simple relationships with population. United Nations energy statistics draw largely on FAO data for firewood, adding estimates of other biomass fuels, such as agricultural residues, animal waste, and other waste (e.g. municipal, pulp and paper)[7].

Information on biomass use can also be found in an increasing number of detailed, ad-hoc surveys carried out by various regional or international organisations and independent researchers. While these studies may give interesting indications as to the local situation, they are generally limited in time and scope, and do not generally cover non-household biomass energy.

The lack of uniform definitions and the use of different units and conversion factors, make aggregation and comparison of data from different sources a hazardous task. Problems of data quality may also arise from insufficient coverage, both geographical and temporal. Biomass energy consumption levels can vary significantly, even in a relatively small geographical area. Thus, the extrapolation to national level of data collected in a small number of villages may lead to erroneous conclusions. Similarly, the extrapolation to a whole year of data collected at a certain time of the year can be very misleading. The types and quantities of biomass fuels used can vary significantly according to the time of the year, because of changing supply availability (abundance of certain crop residues at the time of harvesting) or changing demand due to seasonal temperature variations or social and religious behaviours. As a result, there may be considerable discrepancies among country figures compiled from different sources.

Finally, most surveys tend to give a "point-in-time" picture of biomass use, with little or no indication of historical trends. Coherent historical series, necessary for the dynamic assessment of biomass use, are available only for a few countries.

6. *FAO Yearbook of Forest Products*, FAO, Rome, annual.
7. *The United Nations Statistics Database*, United Nations Statistical Office (UNSO), New York, annual.

If consumption figures are uncertain, data on biomass supply and resources, which are necessary to determine whether biomass energy use is sustainable or not, are even more sparse and inadequate. As a result, the analysis of biomass fuel scarcity is largely based on anecdotal information and secondary indicators, such as the time spent in fuel collection, distance travelled and purchases of alternative fuels.

The IEA Biomass Database

For the first time, the IEA has prepared a database for biomass energy use in non-OECD countries. Data are included for more than 100 non-OECD countries. Wherever possible, data are disaggregated into five main product categories and more than 30 individual products. Sectoral disaggregation follows IEA statistical conventions for conventional fuels. Historical data generally do not amount to coherent time series, as they usually come from different sources or have been obtained with different methodologies. Where historical series are incomplete or unavailable, data have been estimated.[8] The biomass database is updated on a regular basis, and its contents are published annually in the IEA series Energy Statistics and Balances of Non-OECD Countries.

From the IEA Biomass Database it is possible to extract two types of data-set for use in the analysis:
- Figures of biomass consumption for the latest available year for more than 100 non-OECD countries, allowing cross-country comparisons and tests.
- Time series of consistently collected primary data for a number of countries (mostly Latin American countries and a few Asian and African countries), which may be used in regression analysis to estimate relationships between biomass energy use and selected driving variables.

Basic Framework and Key Assumptions

General Observations

The literature at hand and the data available suggest that:
- Biomass in general accounts for a smaller share of energy consumption in countries with a higher per capita income. The amount and type of biomass energy used is very site-specific and

---

8. See the 1998 edition of the IEA's *Energy Statistics and Balances of Non-OECD Countries,* for details on methodology and coverage.

influenced by many non-income-related factors, such as climate, geography, land use, preferred foods and cooking techniques, availability and price of different conversion equipment (stoves), availability and reliability of supply of alternative fuels and their relative costs, socio-economic organisation, culture and tradition.

- A common theory in household energy analysis is that of the "energy transition" along a "fuel ladder". It suggests that, with socio-economic development, households move up their "ladder of fuel preferences" from low-quality fuels, such as biomass, to more convenient, efficient fuels, such as kerosene, bottled gas and electricity[9].

- Although evidence exists for the presence of an energy transition in the household sector, the decline of the share of biomass in the energy mix accompanying economic development is mainly due to the rapid growth of the industrial, transport and other sectors which rely on conventional fuels. Indeed, in many countries total biomass consumption is still increasing and in some countries, even per capita biomass use is still growing.

- Availability and accessibility of biomass fuels is an important factor determining levels of consumption in rural areas. Availability also influences prices of biomass fuels in urban areas.

- It is important to distinguish between rural and urban areas, as patterns and determinants of energy use are fundamentally different in these two environments. This is because:
  - In rural areas, biomass fuels are mainly collected by users, whereas in urban areas they are mostly marketed. The importance of income and relative fuel prices arises mainly in urban areas.
  - The availability of alternative conventional fuels is often limited or unreliable in rural areas.
  - Substitution processes may differ substantially in urban and rural areas. When a given biomass fuel becomes scarce, people may go up the "fuel ladder" in urban areas, but down the "fuel ladder" in rural areas.
  - Finally, when increases in GDP are accompanied by a worsening of income distribution, the benefits of economic growth do not reach rural areas, where the large majority of

9. See Leach, G., *The Energy Transition*, Energy Policy, February 1992, and Davis, M., *Rural Household energy consumption: The effects of access to electricity, evidence from South Africa*, Energy Policy, February 1998.

biomass use is concentrated.
- It is important to distinguish between different types of biomass fuels (wood, charcoal and others). In fact:
  - Substitution between biomass fuels may be a more general phenomenon than substitution with conventional fuels, especially in rural areas. For example, a reduced availability of woody biomass may not necessarily lead to an increasing use of alternative conventional fuels, because there may be a switch to a lower-quality but freely available biomass fuel, such as crop residues or dung.
  - "Intra-biomass" substitutions are not 1-to-1 switches, because different biomass fuels are used in stoves with different efficiencies.
  - In the case of substitution of charcoal for wood and other residues (which is often a consequence of urbanisation, especially in Africa), total final consumption of biomass may decrease because of the higher end-use efficiency and calorific value of charcoal. But the low energy efficiency of the techniques used in many countries to produce charcoal will inevitably result in an increase in the amount of primary wood used.

Methodological Approach

Primary supply of biomass is calculated by adding the following three components:
- final end-use consumption of biomass;
- biomass used for electricity and CHP generation;
- losses in charcoal production, i.e. the difference between the energy content of the wood input and that of the charcoal output.

Following the approach used for conventional fuels, biomass inputs in power generation (including CHP) are analysed separately (see Chapter 6) from end-use consumption. The calculation of losses in charcoal production involves ad-hoc assumptions on the evolution of the share of charcoal in biomass consumption, as well as on the current and future efficiency of the charcoal transformation process, which is high in Brazil and lower in Africa and Asia. The approach used for projecting final consumption of biomass is described below.

As in the case of conventional fuels, the analysis and projections for biomass demand are prepared on a regional basis. This involves aggregating countries which are very different in many aspects. The following discussion concerns the five regions that have a high share of biomass use: Africa, Latin America, China, East Asia and South Asia[10].

Biomass is not a homogeneous fuel. It differs widely in its original forms and production techniques. Solid, liquid and gaseous fuels can be produced from dry and wet feedstocks. Furthermore, it is used in a variety of processes with a large range of efficiencies. The level of geographical aggregation and the problems of data quality and availability limit the degree of detail in the analysis and "biomass" is considered here as a single fuel with a single end-use[11].

With these limitations in mind, several methods and approaches have been explored, but no single approach was found suitable for all regions. The methodology used is therefore mainly an assumption-driven accounting framework.

In order to isolate the effect of growing population, per capita biomass consumption was chosen as the dependent variable. The variables most likely to influence it are:
- available income (GDP per capita)
- level of conventional energy use
- price of alternative fuels (where available, the domestic price of LPG, kerosene, diesel and fuel oil, or a weighted average of all these - otherwise, world oil price as a proxy)
- share of urban population
- availability of supply of biomass fuels
- price of final biomass fuels

The choice of quantitative measures for the above variables was determined by the possibility of obtaining readily available projections over the period 1995-2020. For this reason, for example, we use GDP per capita rather than household income.

It proved very difficult to find a simple quantitative measure for "availability of supply of biomass fuels" for a large number of countries. While shortages may constrain biomass consumption locally (or, more often, induce shifts in the type of biomass used), it is not clear what effect local shortages would have on aggregated biomass consumption at national level (this is especially true for very large countries, such as India, China, or Indonesia). To account for the large differences in geography that could have an impact on the supply of biomass, we have tried to include the "share of forested land" as a proxy.

---

10. See Definition in Part IV.
11. Except for Latin America, where we distinguish biomass energy used in the industrial sector and in other sectors (mainly households, but also agriculture and small services).

Assumptions on the levels of parameters, such as elasticities, fuel shares and growth rates, were derived from:

- econometric tests on countries with sufficient biomass data time series
- an analysis of socio-economic structure
- conventional energy developments
- other studies
- cross-country analysis (classification methods, principal components analysis)
- expert judgement.

Using available historical series for a number of Latin American and Asian countries, and one or two countries in Africa, several equations were estimated to test the relationships between the level of biomass per capita, or the share of biomass in total energy consumption, and different sets of determining variables.

It was found that the most important variable is per capita income, while the price effect (the price of alternative fuels) was generally small or insignificant. This is largely due to the fact that most biomass is used in rural areas, where prices are generally not relevant. Urbanisation was found to be too highly correlated with income to be included in the equations.

The levels and arithmetic signs of the coefficients were as expected. Income elasticities were found to be negative (but smaller than 1), implying that per capita use of biomass decreases as per capita income increases. Price elasticities (for the price of competing fuel), when significantly different from zero, were found to be positive though small, implying that per capita biomass use will grow if the price of the competing fuel increases (for example if subsidies were removed).

Econometric tests on the cross-country data-set confirmed these results, while classification methods and principal components analysis showed that the regional groupings are homogeneous, although with a few overlapping areas and some outliers.

The values chosen for the elasticities in future years are based on the econometric results above, as well as on a critical review of the available literature. They are not constant but vary throughout the projection period to reflect the changing economic and energy structure.

The methodology for Latin America is slightly different from that used for the other regions, because disaggregated historical series are available. Since in Latin America the share of biomass use in the industrial sector is significant, industrial biomass and non-industrial biomass were projected separately. The elasticities for both the industrial and household models are based on a combination of econometric analysis and expert judgement.

The key underlying assumptions on economic and demographic trends, as well as on the evolution of fossil fuel prices are the same as those used in the conventional energy model[12]. The resulting trends in terms of regional per capita income levels are illustrated in Table 10.1.

Table 10.1. **Per Capita GDP, Levels and Growth Rates**[13]

$ at 1990 prices and PPP per capita	1995	2000	2010	2020
China	2822	4029	6143	8933
East Asia	4259	4987	6929	9600
South Asia	1271	1432	1863	2433
Latin America	5510	6105	7489	9022
Africa	1521	1503	1496	1542
Average Annual Growth Rate (%)	1971-1995	1995-2000	2000-2010	2010-2020
China	6.9	7.4	4.3	3.8
East Asia	4.8	3.2	3.3	3.3
South Asia	2.3	2.4	2.7	2.7
Latin America	1.2	2.1	2.1	1.9
Africa	-0.1	-0.2	-0.1	0.3

Summary of Results

Final Consumption

Projections of biomass energy consumption are shown in Table 10.2. Final consumption of biomass in developing countries is projected to continue to increase, rising from 825 Mtoe in 1995 to 1071 Mtoe in 2020, although at a lower rate than population and a much lower rate than conventional energy use.

This rising trend is, broadly speaking, the result of two contrasting trends. On one hand, the expected growth in average per

12. See Chapter 2 for a detailed discussion of GDP, population and fossil fuel prices assumptions.
13. Attention is drawn in Chapters 2 and 15 to the difficulties encountered in measuring and projecting gross domestic product in China.

capita GDP is assumed progressively to lead to lower per capita biomass use, as people, especially in urban areas, gradually switch to conventional fuels, and biomass end-use efficiency slowly increases. On the other hand, the still significant rate of population growth means that an increasing number of people will use biomass, driving up total consumption.

The rate of growth of total biomass consumption is relatively low and slowing down: it is projected to be 1.2% between 1995 and 2000, 1.1% between 2000 and 2010 and 1% between 2010 and 2020.

During the same periods, final consumption of conventional fuels is projected to grow at much faster rates (4.3%, 3.5% and 3.1% per annum respectively), so that the share of biomass in total final consumption will decline from 34% in 1995 to 22% in 2020. There are significant regional differences in the rates of growth and resulting shares, as illustrated in Table 10.2. Consumption of biomass is expected to grow much faster in Africa (2.4% per annum) than in other regions, as a result of sluggish economic growth, rapidly increasing population and relatively low growth in conventional fuel consumption.

Adding to these figures and projections those for combustible renewables and waste (CRW) consumption in OECD regions, as well as rough estimates of CRW consumption in the Transition Economies and in the Middle East, world biomass consumption is projected to grow from 930 Mtoe to 1193 Mtoe between 1995 and 2020. Its share in total final energy consumption will decrease from 14% to 11%.

Power Generation

Biomass-fuelled power generation is still marginal in developing regions, but it is projected to rise rapidly, nearly tripling during the forecast period from 10 TWh in 1995 to 27 TWh in 2020. Accordingly, biomass inputs in power (and CHP) generation will also triple from 4 Mtoe in 1995 to 12 Mtoe in 2020. The share of biomass in total electricity generation does not rise, however, because of the even more rapid increase of other types of power generation. Most biomass-fuelled power generation is concentrated in Latin America. Projections of power generation are discussed in Chapter 6.

Charcoal Production

Charcoal is a secondary product, included in the final consumption of biomass. For the calculation of the primary supply of

Table 10.2. **Total Final Energy Supply including Biomass Energy (Mtoe)**

	1995				2020				Annual Growth Rate (%) 1995-2020		
	Biomass	Conventional Energy	Total	Share of Biomass	Biomass	Conventional Energy	Total	Share of Biomass	Biomass	Conventional Energy	Total
China	206	649	855	24%	224	1524	1748	13%	0.3	3.5	2.9
East Asia	106	316	422	25%	118	813	931	13%	0.4	3.8	3.2
South Asia	235	188	423	56%	276	523	799	35%	0.6	4.2	2.6
Latin America	73	342	416	18%	81	706	787	10%	0.4	2.9	2.6
Africa	205	136	341	60%	371	260	631	59%	2.4	2.6	2.5
Total developing countries	**825**	**1632**	**2456**	**34%**	**1071**	**3825**	**4896**	**22%**	**1.0**	**3.5**	**2.8**
Other non-OECD	24	1037	1061	1%	26	1669	1695	1%	0.3	1.9	2.8
Total non-OECD	**849**	**2669**	**3518**	**24%**	**1097**	**5494**	**6591**	**17%**	**1.0**	**2.9**	**2.5**
OECD countries	81	3044	3125	3%	96	3872	3968	2%	0.7	1.0	1.0
World	**930**	**5713**	**6643**	**14%**	**1193**	**9365**	**10558**	**11%**	**1.0**	**2.0**	**1.9**

biomass it is necessary to know the amount of wood used in charcoal production. For many countries, this amount is not known, so that assumptions have to be made on the efficiency of the charcoal transformation process.

Available data and estimates for 1995 show that charcoal consumption in developing countries amounted to approximately 22 Mtoe, roughly equally divided between Africa, Asia and Latin America. Most of charcoal use in Latin America is concentrated in Brazil (5 Mtoe), where it is produced in large, highly efficient modern kilns and used mainly in the production of steel. In Africa and Asia, charcoal is largely produced with traditional techniques, in small village kilns with low transformation efficiencies, and used in the domestic sector, especially in urban areas. Thailand accounts for 65% of charcoal use in Asia and is one of the countries with the highest share of charcoal in biomass consumption in the world (39%). In China, charcoal use is virtually non-existent because of the extensive use of coal briquettes.

Table 10.3. **Charcoal Production (Mtoe)**

	1995	2010	2020	1995	2010	2020
	East Asia			South Asia		
Share in final biomass	5%	7%	8%	2%	3%	4%
Charcoal production/use	5.6	7.8	9.2	3.5	7.9	11.1
Wood input	16.5	21.7	25.1	12.6	28.2	39.5
Losses in charcoal transformation	**10.8**	**14.0**	**15.9**	**9.1**	**20.3**	**28.4**
	Latin America			Africa		
Share in final biomass	9%	9%	9%	3%	6%	8%
Charcoal production/use	6.4	7.0	7.2	6.8	19.1	30.8
Wood input	13.2	14.5	14.9	27.0	72.1	112.1
Losses in charcoal transformation	**6.8**	**7.5**	**7.7**	**20.3**	**53.0**	**81.3**

Future charcoal use and wood inputs into charcoal production were calculated using ad-hoc assumptions on the evolution of the share of charcoal in biomass consumption and the efficiency of the transformation process. The share of charcoal in biomass consumption is expected to rise in all regions as a result of the switch in cities from wood and agricultural residues to charcoal, which is a more convenient fuel and more economical to transport over long distances than wood. The resulting projections are summarised in Table 10.3 below.

Primary Energy Supply

Primary consumption of biomass has been calculated by adding final end-use consumption of biomass (including charcoal), biomass used for electricity and CHP generation and the energy losses in charcoal production.

Primary consumption of biomass in developing countries is projected to increase from 876 Mtoe in 1995 to 1216 Mtoe in 2020, at an average of 1.4% per annum. This is a slightly higher growth rate than that for final consumption due to the rapidly increasing, though still small, use of biomass in electricity generation and the increasing use of charcoal. Table 10.4 shows the projections by region.

Adding the OECD, Transition Economies and Middle East regions, world primary consumption of biomass is expected to grow from 1046 Mtoe to 1418 Mtoe between 1995 and 2020. Its share in total final consumption will decrease from 11% to 9%.

More details on biomass consumption in each region are given in the chapters in Part III.

Uncertainties and Limitations

The uncertainties and limitations linked to these projections are substantial, mainly due to problems of data availability and quality. As a result, the figures presented in this chapter should be read as indications of the orders of magnitude involved and the changing patterns that can be expected.

The main objective of the exercice was to demonstrate the importance of including biomass in global energy analysis, and illustrate the shortcomings deriving from its exclusion. The integration of the analyses and projections of conventional and biomass fuels provides a more complete picture of future energy trends in developing countries and allows a better understanding of the dynamics of the transition from non-commercial biomass to commercial fuels. It is hoped that better data and further investigation will become available so that this work may be deepened and extended.

Table 10.4. Total Primary Energy Supply including Biomass Energy (Mtoe)

	1995				2020				Annual Growth Rate (%) 1995-2020		
	Biomass	Conventional Energy	Total	Share of Biomass	Biomass	Conventional Energy	Total	Share of Biomass	Biomass	Conventional Energy	Total
China	206	864	1070	19%	224	2101	2325	10%	0.3	3.6	3.2
East Asia	117	464	581	20%	136	1275	1411	10%	0.6	4.1	3.6
South Asia	244	284	528	46%	308	811	1119	28%	0.9	4.3	3.0
Latin America	83	452	535	16%	95	986	1081	9%	0.5	3.2	2.8
Africa	225	226	451	50%	453	432	886	51%	2.8	2.6	2.7
Total developing countries	**876**	**2291**	**3166**	**28%**	**1216**	**5696**	**6221**	**16%**	**1.3**	**3.6**	**3.1**
Other non-OECD	28	1449	1477	1%	30	2228	2258	0%	0.3	1.7	3.1
Total non-OECD	**904**	**3739**	**4643**	**19%**	**1246**	**7833**	**9080**	**14%**	**1.3**	**3.0**	**2.7**
OECD countries	142	4330	4473	3%	172	5535	5707	3%	0.8	1.0	1.0
World *	**1046**	**8199**	**9245**	**11%**	**1418**	**13577**	**14995**	**9%**	**1.2**	**2.0**	**2.0**

* Includes marine bunkers.

PART III

OUTLOOK FOR WORLD REGIONS

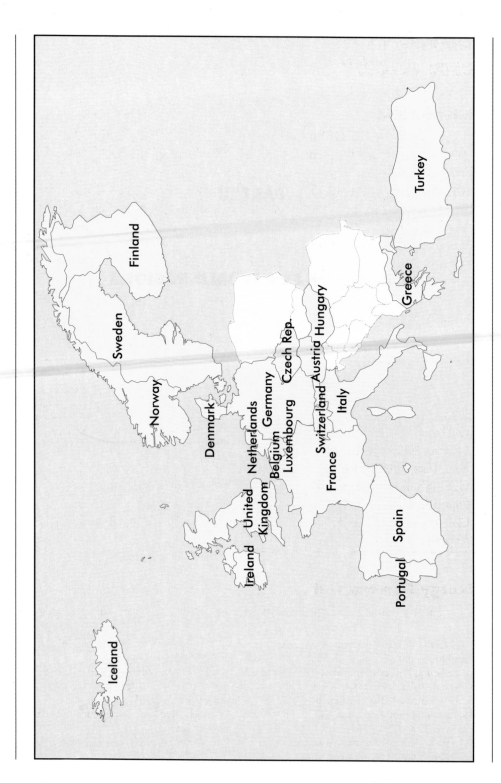

CHAPTER 11
OECD EUROPE[1]

Introduction

In 1995, OECD Europe accounted for 35% of OECD's and 19% of the world's primary commercial energy demand. OECD Europe's share of world energy demand, in the business as usual projection, declines to 15% by 2020 as energy demand in the non-OECD regions grows more rapidly. The main assumptions used in deriving OECD Europe's energy projections are shown in Table 11.1. A static population results in GDP and per capita income growing together by almost two-thirds between 1995 and 2020 providing upward pressure on energy demand. In most other regions of the world the population is assumed to grow, consequently per capita incomes rise less quickly than GDP.

Table 11.1: **Assumptions for OECD Europe**

	1971	1995	2010	2020	1995-2020 Annual Growth Rate
Coal Price ($1990 per metric ton)	44	40	42	46	0.5%
Oil Price ($1990 per barrel)	6	15	17	25	2.1%
Natural Gas ($1990 per toe)	n.a.	90	103	150	2.1%
GDP ($Billion 1990 and PPP)	3929	6965	9803	11524	2.0%
Population (millions)	410	466		468	0.0%
GDP per Capita ($1990 and PPP per person)	9587	14944			2.0%

Energy Demand Outlook

Total primary energy demand is

1. OECD Europe in this Outlook comprises the fo
Republic, Denmark, Finland, France, Germar
Luxembourg, Netherlands, Norway, Portugal, Sp
Kingdom. Poland acceded to the OECD on
Poland's historical data had not been incorp
details can be found on page XXXI of the (
Countries 1994-1995, 1997.
2. Some revisions to historical data may be
data from Eastern European countries.

projection, at an annual average rate of 1.1% between 1995 and 2020. Other (non-hydro) renewables are the most rapidly growing component of TPES, at an annual average rate of 5.1%, from a low base in 1995. Gas is projected to be the most rapidly growing fossil fuel with an annual average demand growth rate of 3%, compared to 1.1% for oil and -0.3% for solid fuels. Hydro power grows at an annual average rate of 1% during the projection period.

Table 11.2: **Total Primary Energy Supply (Mtoe)**

	1971	1995	2010	2020	1995-2020 Annual Growth Rate
TPES	1151	1554	1944	2046	1.1%
Solid Fuels	370	331	371	310	-0.3%
Oil	652	650	779	850	1.1%
Gas	86	301	506	625	3.0%
Nuclear	13	225	225	190	-0.7%
Hydro	28	42	50	54	1.0%
Other Renewables	2	4	11	16	5.1%
Other Primary	0	1	1	1	0.0%

Total Final Energy Consumption

Total final energy consumption (TFC) is projected to grow at an annual average rate of 1.3% between 1995 and 2020. Coal demand remains virtually unchanged, although there will be some variations in intra-regional composition. Electricity is the most rapidly growing energy type within TFC and grows at slightly more than the average rate of GDP growth. Among the fossil fuels, oil grows most quickly, at annual average rate of 1.2%. This growth is mainly driven by ... for mobility-related energy, growing at an annual average rate ... he demand for gas rises at a modest rate of 0.8%, reflecting ... demand for energy in the stationary sector (excluding ... wly during the projection period. With relatively flat ... ssil fuels in the stationary sector, a large portion ... d arises from substitution for coal and oil.

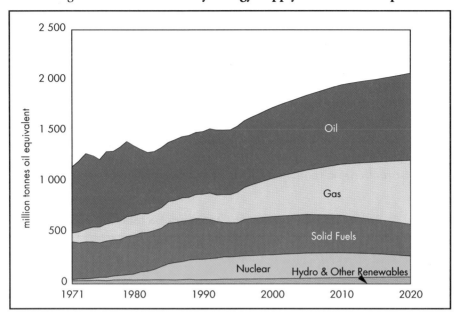

Figure 11.1: **Total Primary Energy Supply in OECD Europe**

Table 11.3: **Total Final Energy Consumption (Mtoe)**

	1971	1995	2010	2020	1995-2020 Annual Growth Rate
TFC	**887**	**1120**	**1403**	**1529**	**1.3%**
Solid Fuels	196	109	106	109	0.0%
Oil	523	567	701	768	1.2%
Gas	71	225	280	274	0.8%
Electricity	95	195	280	329	2.1%
Heat*	3	23	36	48	2.9%

* Includes renewables.

Stationary Sectors[3]

Stationary uses of fossil fuels are projected to remain essentially flat over the projection period, as they have been since the early 1980s.

3. Stationary uses are all non-electricity consumption in the following final consumption sectors - industry, agriculture, commercial, public services, residential, non-specified and non-energy uses. It can be calculated as Total Final Consumption less Total Final Electricity Consumption less Total (non-electricity) Transport Consumption.

This projection reflects the saturation of residential space and water heating in some OECD Europe countries and the continuing trend towards less energy-intensive industries. The consumption of oil in stationary uses is projected to continue to decline. Gas increasingly substitutes for oil with the result that 75% of the projected increase in gas demand during the period 1995 to 2020 arises from oil-to-gas substitution. Around a third of the total increase in demand is met by gas with the remainder met by heat in district heating systems and sales of steam in industry. The consumption of heat is projected to grow at 2.9% per annum, with the increased use of combined heat and power units being a major factor in increasing projected heat demand.

Table 11.4: **Energy Use in Stationary Sectors (Mtoe)**

	1971	1995	2010	2020	1995-2020 Annual Growth Rate
Total	636	617	661	655	0.2%
Solid Fuels	192	109	106	109	0.0%
Oil	370	260	239	223	-0.6%
Gas	71	225	280	274	0.8%
Heat*	3	23	36	48	2.9%

* Includes renewables.

Figure 11.2: **Fossil Fuel & Heat in Stationary Sectors**

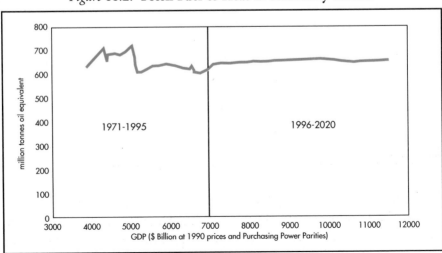

Figure 11.3: **Stationary Energy Uses by Fuel**

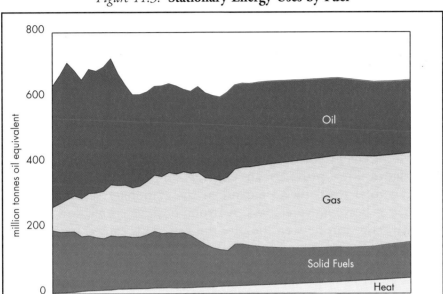

Figure 11.4: **Heating Degree Days**

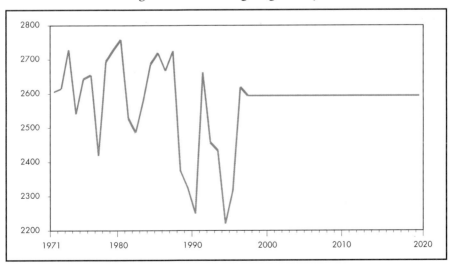

One of the difficulties in projecting energy demand in the stationary sectors is that much of the demand is sensitive to the weather. Energy demand for space heating in the residential and service sectors are clear examples. Less obvious examples include energy used in blast furnaces and kilns. During the period 1971 to 1996, the average number of heating degree days in OECD Europe was 2556[4], however, as Figure 11.4 indicates, the number of heating degree days has fallen sharply since 1987. Since that year, only 1991 has had anything like a typical number of heating degree days. 1991 was clearly exceptional as the eruption of Mount Pinatubo in the Philippines in that year cooled the earth for about two years. Had Mount Pinatubo not erupted, the number of heating degree days may have been lower and with it energy consumption.

Figure 11.5 provides an example of the broad relationship between total fossil fuels demand in the stationary sectors and the number of heating degree days. A strong positive correlation between the two series can be seen, despite the variations caused by changing levels of GDP and energy prices.

Figure 11.5: **Stationary Sectors Energy Demand 1971 - 1995**

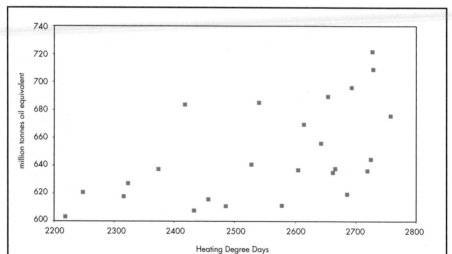

It should be clear from the discussion above that the heating-degree assumptions used in preparing the stationary sectors energy projections can alter the results by as much as 10% over the range of 2300-2700 heating degree days. The approach adopted here has been to examine the average number of heating degree days experienced up

4. Heating degree days are a measure of the extent to which the mean daily temperature falls below an assumed base temperature. The exact base temperature used in the calculation varies across countries.

until 1991 (inclusive) and to set the assumed future number with reference to this average for the period 1971 to 1991. This approach therefore excludes the early years of the 1990s, during which the number of heating degree days was unusually low. If emissions of greenhouse gases are having a warming impact on the climate, as suggested by a number of climate change experts, then continued growth in the demand for fossil fuels could result in a lower number of heating degree days than assumed in this analysis. Were this to happen then a downward adjustment to the stationary sectors' fossil fuel demands would be required.

Mobility[5]

The increasing demand for mobility is a major reason for the growth in total oil demand in recent years. Since the demand for transport-related services increases with income, and this relationship shows no sign of ending, oil demand in OECD Europe and in many other regions is becoming increasingly concentrated in the transport sector. The demand for road and aviation fuels has dominated the demand for energy in the transport sector and is likely to continue to do so. The demand for road fuels will ultimately be limited by factors such as congestion and the saturation of vehicle ownership, but within OECD Europe there exists a wide diversity of vehicle ownership levels. Merely raising car ownership levels in each country to the highest country level in OECD Europe would increase the demand for energy in this sector. Similarly, for aviation, although the number of aircraft movements at an airport and traffic volume have an upper limit, the income-related trend toward taking long-distance holidays by air would increase energy demand unless there were offsetting improvements in aircraft efficiency.

Table 11.5: **Energy Use for Mobility (Mtoe)**

	1971	1995	2010	2020	1995-2020 Annual Growth Rate
Total	157	308	462	546	2.3%

5. Mobility includes all energy consumption in the transport sector except electricity and bunkers.

The total demand for mobility-related fuels (excluding electricity) continues the linear link with GDP established over the last 24 years. From Table 11.5, the annual growth rate of 2.3% for energy use in mobility is somewhat greater than the 2.0% annual average growth rate in incomes assumed for the projection period.

Figure 11.6: **Energy Use in Mobility**

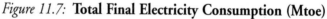

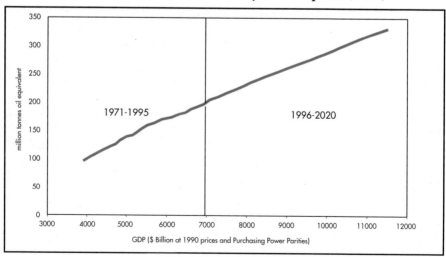

Figure 11.7: **Total Final Electricity Consumption (Mtoe)**

Total Final Electricity Consumption

The projected demand for electricity continues the link with GDP established since 1971. During the period 1971 to 1995, electricity demand grew faster than GDP in OECD Europe (3.1% versus 2.4% per annum). During the period 1995 to 2020 the relationship is expected to be closer than in the past, with electricity demand projected to grow at an annual average rate of 2.1% compared to the assumed GDP growth rate of 2.0%.

Table 11.6: **Total Final Electricity Consumption (Mtoe)**

	1971	1995	2010	2020	1995-2020 Annual Growth Rate
Electricity	95	195	280	329	2.1%

Power Generation

Electricity generation in OECD Europe is projected to grow at an average annual rate of 2.1%, increasing from 2678 TWh in 1995 to 4492 TWh by 2020.

By 2020, the electricity generation mix in OECD Europe is projected to be quite different from that of today. Most of the incremental demand for electricity is expected to be met by natural gas, and its share in generation increases rapidly, from 10% at present, to 45% in 2020. Coal and nuclear power, which today are Europe's most important sources of electricity, together supplying more than 60% will decline to 34% in 2020.

Table 11.7: **Electricity Generation in OECD Europe (TWh)**

	1971	1995	2010	2020
Solid Fuels	557	828	997	801
of which CRW	*6*	*30*	*43*	*53*
Oil	316	237	214	230
Gas	74	255	1131	2021
Nuclear	51	861	863	729
Hydro	320	486	585	629
Wind	0	4	33	66
Other	3	6	13	16
Total	**1322**	**2678**	**3836**	**4492**

Until recently, coal was the most important source of electricity supply in OECD Europe. It was overtaken by nuclear power in 1993. Coal accounted for 42% of electricity generation in 1971. By 1995, it had fallen to 31% and is projected to fall to 18% in 2020. After an initial increase in the period to 2010, coal-fired generation decreases, as older plants are retired. Although its significance in electricity generation decreases, coal is likely to maintain its position in base-load generation, particularly as oil and gas prices begin to rise, making coal more competitive. This position could only be threatened by further tightening of environmental controls, responding to concerns about future emission levels of CO_2 and sulphur dioxide.

Since 1971, the share of oil in the electricity-output mix has fallen from nearly one quarter to less than 10%. The first oil price shock in 1973 effectively ended oil's position as the least expensive power generation fuel[6]. Concerns in some countries about security of supply also contributed to oil's decline. At current oil prices, heavy fuel oil is too expensive for normal base-load generation, and its main use is in delivering power at peak periods in existing oil-fired boilers. In the future, oil distillates may play that role in new simple turbines. Oil is an ideal fuel for use in peaking plant or as a standby fuel in case of emergency, as it has a low storage cost and the capital costs of turbine plant are also low. Over the Outlook period, electricity output from oil is projected to continue to decrease slightly, with its share falling to around 5%.

Nuclear power grew strongly in the 1970s and 1980s. The average annual growth in the period 1971 to 1995 was 12.5%. In this period, nuclear power was perceived as economically viable and as enhancing the security of supply of electricity. Nuclear power increases slightly in the late 1990s, as new stations in France and the Czech Republic are brought on line, while existing plants are upgraded and operate at higher capacity factors. After 2010, nuclear power plant retirements are frequent, as nuclear plants reach their assumed 40-year lifetime.

Hydroelectricity increases by 1% per annum. Most hydro sites in OECD Europe have already been exploited. Currently, there is little activity in new hydro building, but small capacity additions in several countries of the region could lead to a 29% increase in hydroelectric generation. The largest additions are expected in Turkey, which has significant untapped hydro resources and a rapidly growing electricity sector.

6. *Oil in Power Generation*, IEA/OECD Paris, 1997.

Other renewable energies are growing fast, although from a very low basis. The most significant increase is expected in wind power, which could grow from 4 TWh in 1995 to 66 TWh in 2020. The share of non-hydro renewable energy for electricity generation will still remain low, at about 1.8% of total electricity generation in 2020.

Electricity generation from combined heat and power (CHP) plants is projected to grow at around 3% per annum. In 1995, CHP plants generated 243 TWh of electricity, which was about 9% of total electricity generation. By 2020, this figure could rise to 508 TWh and could account for 11% of total generation. Heat output from CHP plant increases from 17.4 Mtoe in 1995 to 42.2 Mtoe by 2020.

Electricity Generating Capacity

Installed capacity in OECD Europe is projected to increase by 1.9% per annum in the period 1995 to 2020. The growth in capacity is less than the growth in electricity demand. This is due partly to current excess capacity in OECD Europe, because of overbuilding in the 1980s. In the projected capacity mix there is less hydro power and most new capacity is in CCGT plant, with high availability compared to that of a coal fired plant.

Table 11.8: **Electricity Generating Capacity by Fuel (GW)**

	1995	2010	2020
Solid Fuels	173	160	129
of which CRW	*6*	*8*	*10*
Oil	84	82	80
Gas	75	279	459
Nuclear	126	127	107
Hydro	167	188	201
Of which Pumped Storage	*30*	*32*	*34*
Wind	2	15	30
Other	2	3	4
Total	**628**	**853**	**1009**

Most new capacity is expected to be natural gas-fired, particularly in combined cycle gas turbine (CCGT) plants, because of their economic and environmental advantages.

As shown in Table 11.9, installed CCGT capacity in OECD Europe has increased rapidly over the past few years.

Table 11.9: **Combined Cycle Gas Turbine Capacity (MW)**

	1995	2010	2020
Belgium	186	1202	1196
Italy	115	1508	2470
Netherlands	1710	2255	4827
Spain	936	967	1311
UK	0	9185	12303
Other	1203	2302	2565
Total OECD Europe	**4150**	**17419**	**24672**

Source: IEA data.

There are a number of reasons for the new popularity of gas. The lifting of the European Commission's ban upon the use of natural gas for power generation was a significant factor. It coincided with an economic and political climate favourable to the expansion of gas fired generation. The economics of power generation have moved in the direction of natural gas as has the requirement to fit pollution-control equipment to coal-fired generation plants. This and the environmental advantages of natural gas have resulted in it becoming the preferred fuel for new power generation capacity across most of OECD Europe.

In addition, the increasing deregulation of electricity markets favours the use of gas in power generation, as smaller companies entering the market will be attracted by the lower overall cost of gas-fired power generation and by the shorter lead times and lower capital costs. Many countries have announced plans to build more gas-fired capacity, in both the public and private sectors.

Nuclear capacity in OECD Europe peaks around the year 2000, with the completion of new units, as shown in Table 11.10, and some capacity upgrades in Finland, Belgium and Switzerland. After that, capacity decreases and falls to 107 GW in 2020, as the nuclear units that were built in the 1970s are retired. It is assumed in this Outlook that nuclear units are decommissioned after 40 years of operation. One should not, however, exclude the possibility that, in order to achieve emission reduction targets, some countries could extend the lives of their nuclear plants. On the other hand, some of Europe's nuclear plants may be retired earlier. Recently, the Dodeward BWR 55 MW unit in the Netherlands was permanently shut down after 30 years of operation. In France, the 1200 MW Superphenix fast breeder reactor was shut down after 12 years of operation. The Swedish

World Energy Outlook

government has stated its intentions to phase out nuclear power entirely by 2010, although this could create tension between satisfying electricity requirements and achieving other environmental objectives. The first two Swedish units to be retired were Barsebaeck 1 in 1998 and Barsebaeck 2 in 2001. However, in the beginning of May 1998, the country's Supreme Administrative Court ruled that the decommissioning of the country's oldest reactor could be unlawful.

Power station fuel requirements are projected to increase by 39% above their current levels. This is an average annual increase of 1.3% over the projected period and is substantially lower than growth in output. The power sector becomes more efficient as highly efficient CCGT plants are introduced. It is assumed that the efficiency of new combined cycle plant increases over time, from 52% at present to 60% in 2020. The average efficiency of coal burning increases from 34% to 37%, as other less efficient units are retired, especially toward the end of the projection period. Natural gas requirements for electricity generation grow sixfold, from 55 Mtoe in 1995, to 319 Mtoe by 2020. More than half the region's total gas demand in 2020 is projected to come from power stations. Solid fuel consumption increases from 208 Mtoe in 1995 to 250 Mtoe by 2010 and falls to 184 Mtoe in 2020.

Figure 11.8: **Fuels used in Power Generation in OECD Europe 1971-2020**

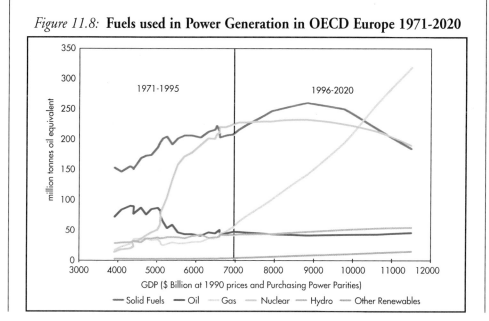

Table 11.10: **Nuclear Plants Under Construction and Completed: 1995 - 2000**

Plant Name	Capacity (MW)	Country	Year on Line
Sizewell B	1188	UK	1996
Chooz B1	1455	France	1996
Chooz B2	1455	France	1997
Civeaux 1	1450	France	1997
Civeaux 2	1450	France	1999
Temelin 1	910	Czech Republic	1999

Source: Various industry sources.

Demand for oil products remains almost flat throughout the period and represents a small share of the fuel mix, 8% in 1995, falling to 6% by 2020. The mix of oil used is expected to change towards lighter distillates.

Oil[7]

In 1997 OECD Europe produced 6.7 million barrels per day (Mbd) of oil[8]. Of this total the UK and Norway together produced over 6 Mbd. The overwhelming majority of the region's oil production is from the North Sea. A recent IEA study of offshore prospects projected that UK offshore oil production would peak around 1999[9]. The same publication shows Norwegian offshore oil production peaking a year later in 2000[10]. During early 1997, Norway announced an increase in its combined oil and gas reserves. Most of this increase arose from the assumption that new technologies would improve the recovery factors of new and existing fields. It is too early yet to say how these new technologies might alter future Norwegian oil production profile, but, as the oil production profiles considered in this WEO are based on a range of ultimate oil reserve estimates, it is reasonable to assume that the upper portion of the range incorporates Norway's technology-induced reserve upgrades.

The oil balance for OECD Europe is shown in the table below, see Chapter 7 for further details.

7. The methodology used to derive the oil production projections can be found in Chapter 7.
8. Table 1, *April 1998 Oil Market Report,* IEA/OECD.
9. Table 11, page 44. *Global Offshore Oil Prospects to 2000,* IEA/OECD Paris, 1996.
10. Ibid., Table 23, page 66.

Table 11.11: **OECD Europe Oil Balance (mbd)**

	1996	2010	2020
Demand	14.4	17.0	18.7
Supply	6.7	4.5	2.8
Net Imports	7.7	12.5	15.9

Note: The above table includes all liquids.

Gas[11]

Indigenous gas production in OECD Europe was 199 Mtoe in 1995. In addition, the region had net imports of 104 Mtoe. Some 93% of OECD Europe's gas production in 1996 was concentrated in just five countries; Norway (33%), UK (31%), Netherlands (14%), Germany (8%) and Italy (7%). OECD Europe's share of world proven gas reserves is relatively modest, at around 4%[12]. This region's share of ultimate gas reserves[13] was estimated by the USGS at 5.7% in 1993. The following table provides details of this estimate.

Table 11.12: **OECD Europe's Gas Reserves at 1/1/1993 - Trillion Cubic Feet (tcf)**

Cumulative Production	160
Identified Reserves	290
Undiscovered	206
Ultimate Reserves	**656**

Source: Masters C., Attanasi E. and Root D., US Geological Survey (USGS), *World Petroleum Assessment and Analysis*, in Proceedings of the Fourteenth World Petroleum Congress (New York, NY: John Wiley and Sons, 1994). World total ultimate gas reserves are estimated by the USGS to be 11448 tcf. Note 1 Mtoe = (42.9 / 1000) tcf.

With the exception of OECD North America, OECD Europe has produced the highest percentage of its ultimate gas reserves of any of the 10 regions examined here, some 28% by the end of 1995. Given the region's modest remaining gas reserves and projected growth in gas demand of around 3% per annum, the scope for large gas

11. The methodology used to derive the gas production projections can be found in Chapter 8.
12. See page I.44 of *Natural Gas Information, July 1997*, IEA/OECD Paris 1997.
13. Ultimate reserves is the sum of cumulative production, remaining reserves (usually proven + probable) and estimated undiscovered reserves.

imports into OECD Europe is considerable during the projection period. It is assumed that gas production will grow at 2.2% per annum until 60% of OECD's Europe ultimate gas reserves have been produced[14]. Production is then assumed to decline by 5% per annum. The resulting gas production projections are shown below.

Figure 11.9: **Gas Balance for OECD Europe**

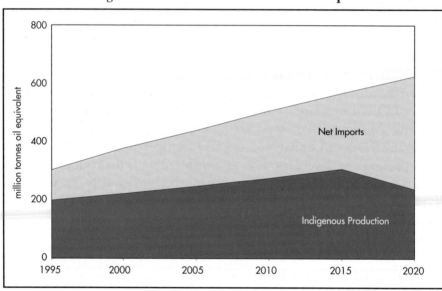

Table 11.13: **Gas Balance for OECD Europe (Mtoe)**

	1995	2010	2020
Production	199	276	238
Imports	164	290	447
Exports	-59	-59	-59
Stock Changes	-2	0	0
TPES	301	506	625

Note: 1 Mtoe = (42.9 / 1000) tcf.

Based on Figure 11.9 and Table 11.13, it is clear that OECD Europe's gas security of supply situation will alter radically during the

14. This estimated growth in OECD Europe's gas production has been obtained from the analysis shown on page 75 of *The IEA Natural Gas Security Study,* IEA/OECD 1995. The analysis in that publication only examined the period 1992 to 2010, but since OECD Europe's gas production is projected to reach the 60% inflection point by 2015, using the same growth rate in production for the five years beyond 2015 is not an unreasonable assumption to make.

projection period. Whereas in 1995 OECD Europe produced around two-thirds of the gas it consumed, and imported the remaining 35%, by 2020 the region will be importing over 70% of its gas requirements.

Coal[15]

In 1996, 140 million tonnes (Mt) of hard coal were produced in OECD Europe. Of this total Germany, Spain and France produced 77 Mt[16]. Of the remaining 63 Mt, the majority was produced by the United Kingdom (49.8 Mt). In Germany and Spain, hard coal production remains heavily subsidised. In the UK, however, subsidies fell by 95% between 1983 and 1995 as the government has sought to put the coal industry onto a commercial footing. During the same period, German coal subsidies increased by 86%. In Spain, coal subsidies increased by 142% during the period 1986 - 1995[17].

The amount of financial support that Governments are prepared to give to their indigenous hard coal industry will be a major determinant for the future of a substantial proportion of hard coal production in OECD Europe. In Belgium and Portugal, hard coal production has ceased, while in France production is planned to close by the year 2005. In both Germany and Spain, pressures to maintain regional employment will inevitably mean that restructuring and the reduction of subsidies will remain politically contentious. However, in Germany the 1997 agreement between the Government, the affected Länders, the coal companies and the trade unions to reduce subsidies is expected to cut production from some 51 million tonnes in 1997 to about 30 million tonnes by the year 2005. In Spain the Government has announced the continuation of subsidised coal production over the next ten years under the terms of a framework agreement for the electricity sectors, signed with national generators. This agreement, designed to phase-in deregulation, will continue to guarantee that the share of domestic coal used in power generation will be a minimum 15 percent (down from about 40 percent currently). Production is currently planned to decrease from 18 million tonnes in 1997 to 14.7 million tonnes by the end of 2001.

15. Information in this section is taken from the recent IEA publication *International Coal Trade - The Evolution of a Global Market*, IEA/OECD 1997.
16. See page 95 op. cit.
17. These figures refer to IEA estimates of Total Producers Subsidy Equivalent for coal production. See Table 15, page 106 op. cit.

As the amount of subsidies provided by Member governments have such a crucial impact on a major part of coal production in OECD Europe, it is not possible to provide firm projections of the level of future production. Subsidies are likely to continue into the foreseeable future, for essentially social and regional reasons, but coal production will decrease significantly. An indication of the scope of possible reductions can be seen from the fact that, whereas 77 million tonnes of coal was produced in Germany, Spain and France in 1995, only between 10 and 30 million tonnes of this could be considered economic[18].

OECD Europe's hard coal imports trebled between 1968 and 1995. This trend towards growing import dependence looks set to continue as domestic production declines. The introduction of deregulation and Third Party Access rights in the European gas market from 1999 will restrain coal demand and hence coal imports. Security-of-supply issues are less of a concern for coal than for either oil or gas, as coal reserves are much more widely dispersed than is the case for the other two fossil fuels. The following table indicates the geographical diversity of OECD Europe's steam coal imports (101 Mt in 1996)[19].

Table 11.14: **OECD Europe 1996 Steam Coal Imports by Source (percentage)**

South Africa	32
Latin America (Colombia and Venezuela)	18
United States	15
Poland	13
Former Soviet Union	5
Australia	5
Indonesia	3
China	1
Other	8
Total	**100**

The table above shows that no single region or country supplies more than a third of OECD Europe's imports and so security of supply is not a significant concern. Furthermore, since excess capacity exists in the US and, to a lesser extent, in some other coal exporting countries, an increase in coal prices is unlikely. Therefore, domestic

18. See page 96 of *International Coal Trade - The Evolution of a Global Market*, IEA/OECD 1997.
19. See page II. 41 of *Coal Information 1996*, IEA Statistics, IEA/OECD 1997.

coal producers in OECD Europe cannot rely on higher world prices to improve their competitiveness vis-à-vis coal imports. In summary, the outlook for OECD Europe's coal production remains weak and any additional volumes will be met by low-cost imports rather than high-cost domestic production. The share of the three largest suppliers is likely to increase, because restructuring in the Transition Economies will reduce the amount of coal they have available for export. In addition, the transport costs from suppliers remote from Europe are high and are unlikely to be competitive in the European market.

Projections from Other Organisations

Two other major organisations produce European energy demand projections: the European Union (EU) and the United States Department of Energy (USDOE). The last set of energy projections produced by the EU was in 1996[20] and the Conventional Wisdom (scenario) is used here for comparison purposes. The USDOE's reference case projection, published in 1998[21], is the other projection considered in this chapter. Neither the EU[22] nor the USDOE's[23] projections are exactly comparable with those of the World Energy Outlook as their geographic coverage differs from that used in this Outlook.

European Union Conventional Wisdom Projection

Apart from the differences in geographical composition between the EU and OECD Europe, there are also differences in GDP assumptions. In order to normalise both projections (as far as possible)

---

20. *Energy in Europe, European Energy to 2020 - A Scenario Approach,* Directorate General for Energy DGXVIII of the European Commission.

21. *International Energy Outlook 1998 - With Projections to 2020*, April 1998 DOE/EIA.

22. The European Union includes the following 15 Member countries - Austria, Belgium, Denmark, Finland, France, Germany, Greece, Ireland, Italy, Luxembourg, Netherlands, Portugal, Spain, Sweden and the United Kingdom. Thus the EU definition excludes the Czech Republic, Hungary, Iceland, Norway, Switzerland and Turkey which are included in the OECD Europe definition adopted in this chapter.

23. The USDOE projections cover Western Europe defined as the following 18 countries - Austria, Belgium, Denmark, Finland, France, Germany, Greece, Iceland, Ireland, Italy, Luxembourg, Netherlands, Norway, Portugal, Spain, Sweden, Turkey and the UK. This is basically the same definition as that used for OECD Europe in this chapter but with the Czech Republic and Hungary omitted. In common with the definition used in this chapter, Poland is not included in the USDOE's Western Europe aggregation.

onto a comparable basis, the ratio of energy consumption to GDP is used in the following analysis. The energy ratio has then been put into index form (1995 = 100) to adjust for differences in geographical coverage.

Using the above approach, Figure 11.10 compares the EU Conventional Wisdom (CW) scenario with the 1998 WEO's business as usual projection.

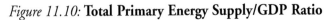

Figure 11.10: **Total Primary Energy Supply/GDP Ratio**

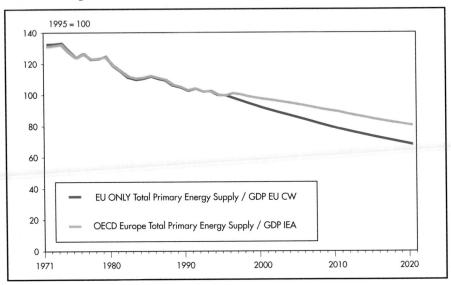

The important point to note is that the EU appears to be assuming a much greater decline in the ratio between energy and GDP. In the EU projections, the energy ratio declines at an annual average rate of 1.5% compared to 0.9% in the WEO projection. The EU projections assume a somewhat higher oil price than in the WEO case. The EU's projection assumes that the oil price increases smoothly from $17.60 in 1995 to $21/bbl in 2000, $29/bbl in 2010 and $31/bbl in 2020. In our projection, the oil price does not start to increase until 2010 and then only reaches $25/bbl in 2015. Nevertheless, this price difference is too small to explain the difference in the decline in the energy ratio.

The difference between the EU and WEO projections is more marked for transport. The two projections foresee very different paths for the mobility energy ratio. In our case, the mobility energy ratio continues to grow in line with past experience (see Figure 11.11). In the EU's projections, the mobility energy ratio declines at an annual average rate of 1%. The higher oil price assumed in the EU projection may explain some of the difference, but it is clear that the EU's projections assume that other factors such as saturation, new technologies and changes in consumer behaviour result in a declining energy ratio in the transport sector. This assumption represents a clear break with past experience.

Figure 11.11: **Transport Energy Demand/GDP Ratio**

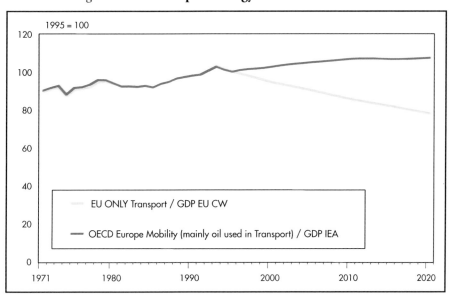

The comparison between the WEO and EU projections is equally marked when the ratios of final electricity demand to GDP are compared, as Figure 11.12 indicates.

The BAU case projects that this ratio will flatten out in line with past experience. In the EU projection, however, the ratio of final electricity demand to GDP declines at an annual average rate of 0.9%, which is considerably different from that observed historically. As in the transport sector, energy prices, assumptions about new technologies and changes in consumer behaviour appear to play a significant role in the EU's projections.

Outside the transport sector and total final demand for electricity, there is very little difference between the two projections, as Figure

11.13 indicates for the stationary sectors. Both projections show a similar decline in the ratio of energy demand to GDP as in the past.

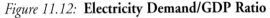

Figure 11.12: **Electricity Demand/GDP Ratio**

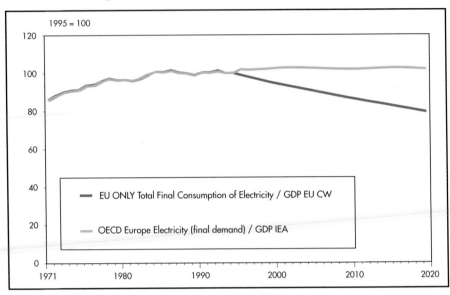

Figure 11.13: **Stationary Sectors Energy Demand/GDP Ratio**

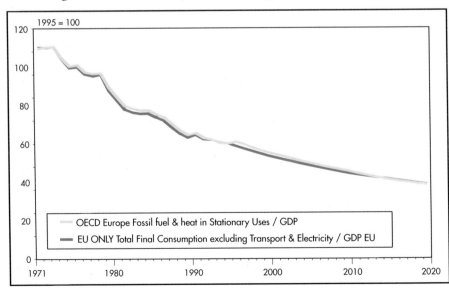

Comparison of EU and IEA Electricity Generation Projections

These projections are not directly comparable as previously stated, because the EU projection only covers its 15 member countries, whereas the Outlook's projections are for OECD Europe, which has 21 member countries. Table 11.15 shows the composition of the electricity generation mix in the two regions in 1995.

Table 11.15: **Electricity Generation in OECD Europe and European Union - 1995 (TWh)**

	OECD Europe	Per cent	E U	Per cent
Total generation	**2678**	**100%**	**2308**	**100%**
Solid Fuels	828	31%	742	32%
Oil	237	9%	225	10%
Gas	255	10%	233	10%
Nuclear	861	32%	810	35%
Hydro	486	18%	287	12%
Other Renewables	10	0%	10	0%

As Table 11.15 indicates, electricity generation in 1995 in OECD Europe as a whole, was about 16% higher than in EU member countries. Hydroelectricity makes up more than half the difference (non-EU countries with high reliance on hydro are Norway, Switzerland and Turkey). Over the projection period, total electricity generation in OECD Europe increases by 2.1% per annum, whereas in the EU scenario the growth is 1.3%. Fuel consumption in the period to 2020 increases at an annual rate of 1.3% in the IEA's projections. The corresponding growth rate in the EU projections is 0.6%.

The following observations can be made on Table 11.16:
- Coal use declines at rates lower than 1% in both projections.
- Oil consumption is slightly higher in the IEA scenario.
- Gas consumption increases faster in the IEA's projection. This is due to the fact that most of new generation comes from gas-fired stations. Since the IEA projects higher electricity demand, gas requirements are also higher.
- Nuclear power declines faster in the EU's projections. In our projections, there is additional new nuclear capacity in OECD Europe, outside EU countries.

- Hydro power increases faster in the IEA projections; most of this increase is expected to take place in OECD countries outside the EU.
- The IEA estimates on combustible renewables and waste are more conservative than those of the EU.
- Other renewable energies (solar, wind, geothermal) grow faster in the IEA's projections.

Table 11.16: **Comparison of Power Generation Projections 1995 - 2020**

	IEA % per annum 1995-2020	EU % per annum 1995-2020
Total Generation	**1.3**	**0.6**
Coal only	-0.7	-0.3
Oil	-0.1	-2.4
Gas	7.3	4.8
Nuclear	-0.7	-1.5
Hydro	1.0	0.7
Waste	2.3	7.0
Other Renewables	9.2	6.4

Figure 11.14: **Electricity Generation (1995 = 100)**   *Figure 11.15:* **Fuel Use in Power Stations (1995 = 100)**

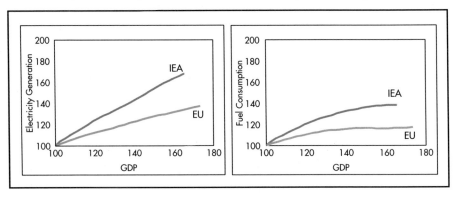

Figure 11.14 plots electricity generation against GDP for the two different projections. Figure 11.15 shows fuel consumption against GDP. In both charts, GDP and energy have been indexed to 1995. The gap between the two sets of projections is somewhat narrower in

Figure 11.15. This implies that the IEA fuel mix is slightly more efficient. Indeed, average fossil fuel efficiency in the IEA's projections increases from 36% in 1995 to 47% in 2020. In the EU projections, efficiency increases from 38% to 45%. The difference can be attributed to higher demand for gas in the IEA projections; this gas is burned mostly in combined cycle gas turbine plants that are more efficient than the conventional steam technologies, currently in use.

Finally, the IEA's total electricity generation is more efficient because of the higher percentage of hydro in OECD Europe's fuel mix (the conversion efficiency for hydroelectricity is assumed to be 100%).

United States Department of Energy's Reference Case Projection

The USDOE's 1998 International Energy Outlook contains somewhat less detail than the EU's 1996 publication, but it still provides a useful benchmark against which to compare our projections for OECD Europe. Table 11.17 compares the projected growth in TPES during the period 1995 - 2020.

Table 11.17: **WEO 1998 BAU versus IEO 1998 Reference Case**

Annual Growth Rates 1995-2020	USDOE 1998 IEO	IEA WEO 1998
Total Primary Energy Supply	**1.2%**	**1.1%**
Solid Fuels	-0.1%	-0.3%
Oil	0.3%	1.1%
Gas	3.8%	3.0%
Nuclear	-1.2%	-0.7%
Hydro / Other	2.1%	1.6%

Note: USDOE projection refers to Western Europe whereas IEA projection refers to OECD Europe.

Both organisations project TPES to grow at a similar rate of 1.1% - 1.2%, considerably higher than the EU's 0.7%. Both the USDOE and the EU have lower projections than the IEA for oil and nuclear power. An interesting feature of the USDOE projection is the high projected growth rate in gas demand of 3.8%. This is, in part, because gas replaces oil in heat production. The USDOE also projects that total final electricity demand will grow at an annual average rate of 2.4%, slightly faster than projected by the IEA for OECD Europe but more than a percentage point greater than projected by the EU.

USDOE 1998 IEO	IEA WEO 1998 BAU	EU 1996 CW
2.4%	2.1%	1.3%

With the USDOE projecting that TPES will grow at 1.2% and assuming that GDP growth will average 2.4% during the period 1995 to 2020, the TPES energy ratio (TPES / GDP) is projected to decline at an annual average rate of 1.2%. This decline is somewhat faster than 0.9% projected here for OECD Europe. The higher GDP growth rate assumed in the USDOE projections may explain why the USDOE's gas and electricity demands grow faster than in the 1998 WEO. Higher economic growth would lead to a more rapid turnover of the capital stock and thereby increase the potential for gas and electricity to substitute for coal and oil. The decline in the USDOE projected energy ratio is very similar to that observed during the last quarter of a century and consistent with our own projection.

The oil price assumptions made by the IEA (BAU), USDOE (reference case) and EU (CW) are shown below.

Table 11.19: **Oil Price Assumptions Real $ per Barrel**

	1995	2000	2010	2020
WEO 1998 BAU	$15	$17	$17	$25
USDOE 1998 IEO	-	$19	$20	$22
EU 1996 CW	$17.6	$21	$29	$31

Note: The oil prices in the above table are in the following units: WEO real 1990$, USDOE real 1996$ and EU real 1993$.

The USDOE and WEO oil price assumptions are broadly similar, although the EU's oil price assumption for 2020 is somewhat higher than in either of the other studies. Some additional incentive to reduce energy demand may therefore exist in the EU's projections when compared to the USDOE and IEA's projections.

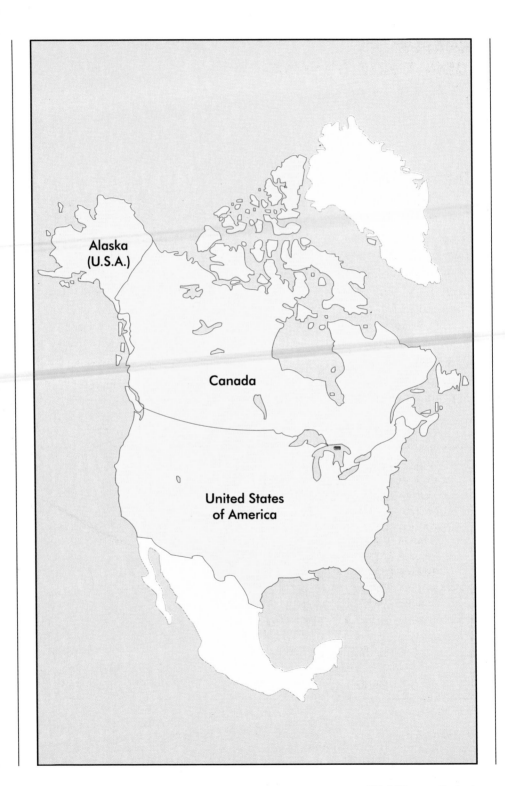

Alaska
(U.S.A.)

Canada

United States
of America

CHAPTER 12
OECD NORTH AMERICA

Introduction

OECD North America[1] (the United States and Canada) is a homogenous region in terms of energy and economic structure. In 1996, it accounted for more than a quarter of world primary energy demand and around half of OECD demand. At the same time, the region has large hydrocarbon and hydropower resources. The US is the largest oil-consuming and oil-importing country in the world and is the second largest producer of oil after Saudi Arabia[2].

Compared to other OECD countries, the US and Canada have high ratios of energy use to GDP. Many factors combine to produce this effect. Among the most important are low energy prices, high incomes per head, large distances between centres of population and extreme climate conditions in both winter and summer.

Figure 12.1: **Energy Intensities of Selected OECD Countries**

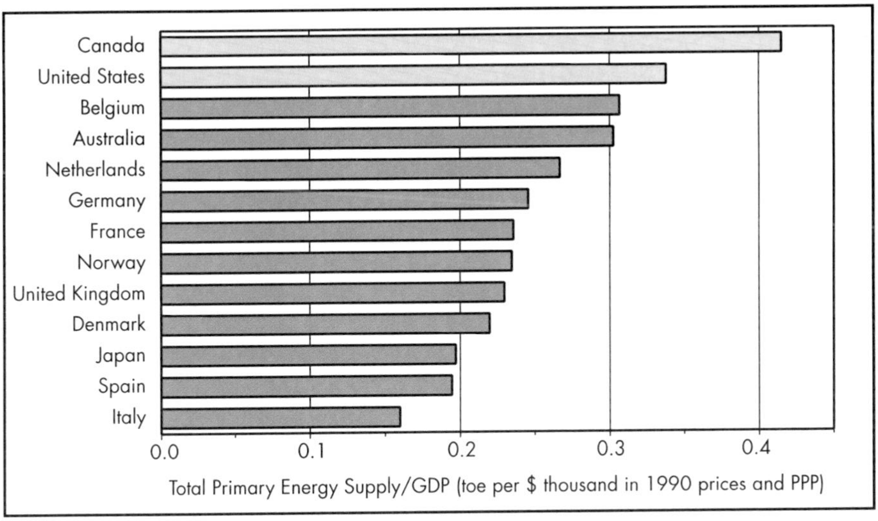

Total Primary Energy Supply/GDP (toe per $ thousand in 1990 prices and PPP)

---

1. Although Mexico joined the OECD in 1994, it has been considered together with the Latin American region for projection purposes.
2. When natural gas liquids and alcohols are included.

Table 12.1 provides a comparison of gasoline prices in different OECD countries. In absolute terms, European gasoline taxes in 1996 were some 8 times higher than those in the US. The low level of taxes on transportation fuels in the US, make that country's oil demand particularly sensitive to changes in world crude oil prices.

Table 12.1: **Retail Gasoline Prices and Taxes 1997 (US cents per litre)**

	Retail Price	Tax	Tax (%)
US	37.4	10.1	27
Canada	43.5	20.8	48
Japan	96.0	53.6	56
France	120.7	94.6	78
Germany	111.0	79.6	72
Italy	118.5	85.4	72

Source: *Energy Prices and Taxes 1998*, IEA

The United States is the largest economy in the world, with a GDP of about $6.3 trillion (at 1990 prices and PPP) in 1996, accounting for about 37% of total OECD and more than one-fifth of world GDP. Canada had a GDP of $600 billion in 1996 and accounts for about 3.3% of the OECD's total GDP. Following a recession in the early 1990s, the economies of the US and Canada have recovered with economic growth rates for both countries in 1997 close to 4%. For the US, this growth was a nine-year high, the unemployment rate was at its lowest level for a generation and inflation down to rates last seen in the mid-1960s. This is the third longest expansion period since the Second World War. The Canadian economy, which is closely linked to that of the US, has also continued to grow at a healthy pace.

Our business as usual assumptions suggest a soft landing for the US economy with growth easing back and inflation staying under control. GDP in OECD North America is expected to grow at an average annual rate of 2.1% between 1995 and 2020, a slowdown compared to the annual average growth rate of 2.7% in the period 1971 to 1995. Continued immigration and an increasing birth rate contribute to a growth in population of slightly below 1% per annum. In consequence, per capita incomes are expected to increase by 1.3% a year to 2020, a lower rate than has been experienced over the last two decades.

Table 12.2 lists the principal economic and demographic assumptions made for OECD North America in the BAU projection. These assumptions are discussed in Chapter 2. The most significant feature is a rise in gas prices from $1.7 per thousand cubic feet in 2005 to $3.5 in 2015, reflecting some tightness in the North American gas market and increasing use of unconventional gas supplies. These issues are discussed later in this chapter and in Chapter 8.

Table 12.2: **OECD North America Assumptions**

	1971	1995	2010	2020	1995-2020 Annual Growth Rate
Coal Price ($1990 per metric ton)	44	40	42	46	0.5%
Oil Price ($1990 per barrel)	6	15	17	25	2.1%
Natural Gas ($1990 per 1000 cubic feet)	0.6	1.3	2.6	3.5	3.9%
GDP ($ Billion 1990 and PPP)	3580	6710	9432	11175	2.1%
Population (millions)	230	293	331	357	0.8%
GDP per Capita ($ 1000 1990 and PPP per person)	16	23	29	31	1.3%

Throughout the United States, restructuring is taking place toward more competitive electricity and gas markets. The outcome of these market reforms poses additional uncertainties for the projections presented in this Outlook.

Box 12.1: **Energy Market Reforms in US**

Restructuring of the electricity sector in the US is expected to have a major impact on electricity consumption trends. The bulk market was opened to further competition by the Federal Energy Regulatory Commission (FERC) in April 1996. FERC has not opted for the most radical approach to liberalisation: full vertical separation of transmission from generation and supply. Rather, it has chosen a set of grid access rules with control of day-to-day operations of the transmission grid to be transferred to newly-created institutions called Independent System Operators. It is generally believed that within the next three to five years, at least half of the US citizens will obtain the right to choose their electricity supplier. Estimates of the results of competition in the market for electric power vary widely. The US government projects price decreases of some 10% in the short term, and an additional 11% by the year 2015[3].

Further liberalisation of the US natural gas market is unlikely to have a major impact on overall energy consumption, as the market is already largely deregulated[4]. FERC liberalised bulk transactions at the federal level in 1992. At present, about half of all final gas sales are made by suppliers other than the local distribution company. More importantly, it is estimated that large industrial customers and power plants can already switch suppliers in some 75% of all cases. The remainder of the gas market is not seen as attractive to gas suppliers, as it mainly consists of small customers with low load factors; they mainly consume gas during the heating season, and are thus expensive to serve. Further market opening in the gas sector may not lead to large increases in gas demand[5].

Energy Demand Outlook

Overview

In OECD North America, primary energy demand is expected to grow by 0.8 per cent per annum over the projection period. This increase is low by historical standards and lower than the projected OECD average of 1% per annum. In addition to GDP and the evolution of oil and gas prices, other important factors contributing to the slowing of energy demand growth include the saturation of

3. *Electricity Prices in a Competitive Environment: Marginal Cost Pricing of Generation Services and Financial Status of Electric Utilities: A Preliminary Analysis through 2015,* Department of Energy (DOE)/Energy Information Administration (EIA), Washington, DC, August 1997.
4. *Natural Gas Pricing in a Competitive Market,* IEA/OECD, (forthcoming).
5. *Energy Policies of IEA Countries - United States 1998 Review,* IEA/OECD, 1998 and *Energy Policies of IEA Countries - Canada 1996 Review,* IEA/OECD, 1996.

markets for domestic appliances, already high vehicle ownership levels and expected improvements in energy efficiency, especially in the power generation sector.

Table 12.3: **Total Primary Energy Supply (Mtoe)**

	1971	1995	2010	2020	1995-2020 Annual Growth Rate
TPES	1724	2312	2724	2846	0.8%
Solid Fuels	338	582	737	927	1.9%
Oil	789	873	1025	1050	0.7%
Gas	548	576	705	676	0.6%
Nuclear	12	212	182	114	-2.4%
Hydro	37	56	58	60	0.3%
Other Renewables	1	13	18	18	1.4%

In terms of total primary energy demand, consumption of solid fuels is expected to grow rapidly. This is mainly due to changes in the fuel mix of the power generation sector as a result of rising gas and oil prices. The fall in the use of nuclear power in electricity generation will be largely taken up by coal. Consumption of oil and gas are expected to grow rather slowly at 0.7% and 0.6% per annum on average. As a result, the market shares of oil and gas in total primary energy demand are expected to decline slightly, and solids are expected to increase their market share by over 7 percentage points over the outlook period. As shown in Figure 12.2, the share of nuclear is projected to fall by about 5 percentage points in 2020, compared to the current level.

As Table 12.4 shows, total final energy consumption (TFC) is expected to grow at an annual rate of 0.7%. Electricity is the main driver of final energy demand. It is projected to grow at a rate slightly higher than that of GDP. The current 19% share of electricity in total final energy consumption is expected to reach 25% by 2020. Final oil and solids demands are expected to increase at a similar pace to that of aggregate final demand and gas demand is projected to decline after 2010 due to an increase in gas prices. Heat demand grows the fastest, from a low base in 1995.

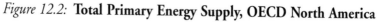

Figure 12.2: **Total Primary Energy Supply, OECD North America**

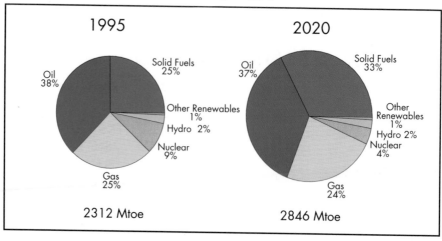

Table 12.4: **Total Final Energy Consumption (Mtoe)**

	1971	1995	2010	2020	1995-2020 Annual Growth Rate
TFC	**1289**	**1581**	**1836**	**1891**	**0.7%**
Solid Fuels	100	76	80	87	0.6%
Oil	709	819	958	978	0.7%
Gas	339	379	385	346	-0.4%
Electricity	140	300	402	464	1.8%
Heat	0	8	12	16	3.0%

Stationary Sectors

As shown in Table 12.5, consumption in stationary uses of fossil fuels is projected to increase slightly till 2010 and to decline thereafter. Key influences on the energy outlook of the residential and commercial sectors will be increases in personal incomes, movements in energy prices, demographic trends, appliance penetration and efficiency trends in the energy-using equipment in these sectors. Annual population growth of 0.8% for the projection period, against the last two decades' average of 1.1%, is a contributing factor to slowing energy demand in the residential sector. Markets for many major appliances (space heaters, water heaters) in the US and Canada are already tending to saturate. It is also expected that the average efficiency of the stock of appliances will increase, mainly as a result of technological innovation and stock turnover. In the commercial sector, saturation trends will contribute to the declining pace of energy demand growth. Lower growth in industrial output, in line with the assumptions made for GDP growth, is the underlying factor for the decreasing trend of industrial energy demand. The increasing predominance of less energy-intensive industries is a further contributing factor.

Figure 12.3: **Stationary Uses by Fuel**

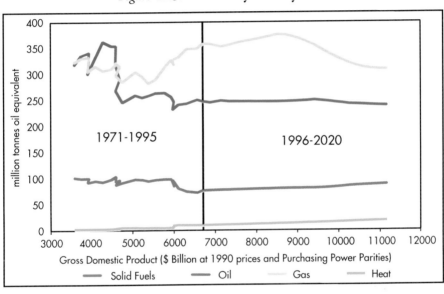

Table 12.5: **Energy Consumption in Stationary Sectors (Mtoe)**

	1971	1995	2010	2020	1995-2020 Annual Growth Rate
Total	739	688	695	650	-0.2%
Solid Fuels	100	76	80	87	0.6%
Oil	317	247	249	239	-0.1%
Gas	322	358	354	308	-0.6%
Heat	0	8	12	16	3.0%

Mobility

Energy demand for mobility in OECD North America is projected to increase broadly in line with GDP to the year 2010. It begins to slow thereafter due to an assumed rise in the world oil price. Total energy demand for mobility is expected to grow by 1.5% per annum between 1995 and 2010 and 1.1% for the whole projection period. This compares with the 1.6% growth rate of the last two decades. The OECD North American region has the highest level of car ownership of all OECD regions. This is expected to approach saturation.

Figure 12.4: **Mobility**

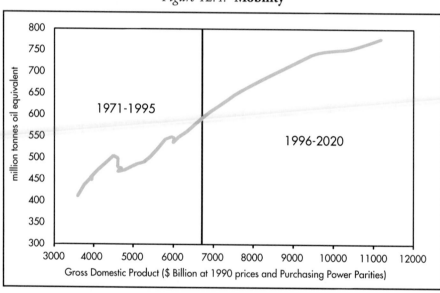

Table 12.6: **Fossil Fuel Use for Mobility (Mtoe)**

	1971	1995	2010	2020	1995-2020 Annual Growth Rate
Total	409	593	739	777	1.1%

Figure 12.4 shows sharp declines in energy use for mobility after the oil price shocks and the resulting government action to improve

energy efficiency, especially the Corporate Automobile Fuel Efficiency (CAFE) standards. The evolution of transportation fuel efficiency over the projection period is an important source of uncertainty for the projections presented here. Similarly, the future of alternative-fuel vehicles, following legislative mandates at the Federal and State level in the US, may well alter future trends of mobility energy use.

Oil is the predominant transport fuel, accounting for approximately two-thirds of total primary oil consumption in OECD North America and 17% of total world oil consumption. As shown in Figure 12.5, oil for mobility accounted for all the growth in oil demand between 1971 and 1995 and is expected to do so again over the outlook period.

Figure 12.5: **Incremental Changes in Oil Consumption**

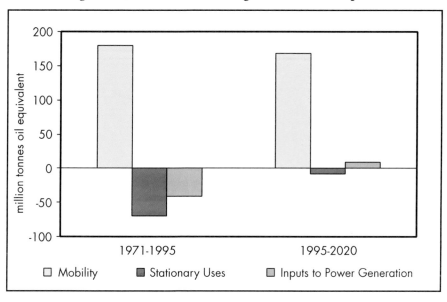

Electricity

Figure 12.6 shows OECD North America electricity demand rising regularly along with increasing income. This continues the established past trend. The income elasticity shows a corresponding slowly declining trend. It was close to 2 in the 1960s and declined to about 1.2 in the last two decades. It is projected to decrease to 1 over the outlook period. The underlying factors expected to contribute to this trend include market saturation of electrical appliances and improvements in appliance efficiency.

A major uncertainty affecting the electricity demand projections is the expected impact of market reforms. As discussed in Box 12.1, price reductions due to increasing competition in the energy sector could lead to additional electricity demand. On the other hand, new air-quality standards prepared by the US Environmental Protection Agency may cause significant increases in the generating costs of power that could lead to upward pressure on retail electricity prices and reduce electricity demand. However, the sharp increases in prices at the time of the oil shocks did not lead to a major change in electricity demand on a short-term basis, so a rapid deviation from the BAU trend should not be expected.

Figure 12.6: **Electricity Demand**

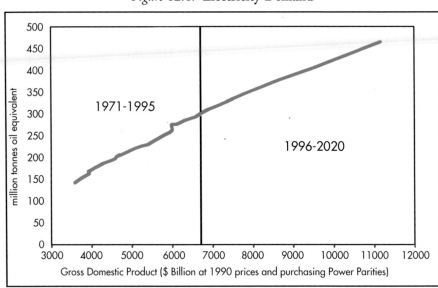

Table 12.7: **Total Final Electricity Demand (Mtoe)**

	1971	1995	2010	2020	1995-2020 Annual Growth Rate
Electricity	140	300	402	464	1.8%

Supply

Power Generation

In the BAU projection, electricity generation in North America increases at an average rate of 1.8% per annum. This may be compared with a growth rate of 3.2% per annum experienced since 1971. By 2020, annual generation could represent 6363 TWh, a 55% increase above current levels. Coal and gas are expected to be the key fuels in the projected electricity mix. Gas-fired generation appears to be the most economic option for new plant, particularly in the first half of the outlook. In the second half, higher gas prices, associated with higher gas production costs, could switch the economics of power generation in favour of coal. Consequently, although the share of natural gas generation increases from 13% in 1995 to 24% of total in 2020, coal will continue to supply the bulk of electricity in the region. The role of oil is expected to remain marginal, as oil-fired plants will continue to be called at times of peak load. Nuclear electricity decreases, as no new nuclear plants are built and nuclear plant retirements accelerate in the second half of the outlook period. Hydropower shows a small increase. Other renewables increase slightly, as their costs remain high.

Figure 12.7: **North American Electricity Output**

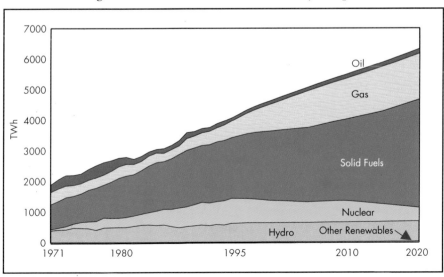

Table 12.8: **Electricity Generating Capacity by Fuel (GW)**

	1995	2010	2020
Solid Fuels	372	418	564
of which CRW	*12*	*15*	*16*
Oil	45	51	58
Gas	209	415	450
Nuclear	116	96	59
Hydro	165	172	177
of which Pumped Storage	*22*	*22*	*22*
Other Renewables	5	7	10
Total	**912**	**1159**	**1317**

Most of the region's net increase in capacity is expected to come from natural gas fired plants in the form of combined cycle gas turbines (CCGTs), where medium- to base-load capacity is required, and simple cycle combustion turbines (which can use either gas or oil distillates depending on their cost competitiveness) where new or replacement peaking capacity is needed. Natural gas fired capacity has increased significantly over the past few years and is expected to go on doing so while gas prices remain low. The following table shows planned capacity additions for US utilities for the period 1996 to 2005; around two thirds of this capacity is gas-fired.

Table 12.9: **Planned Capacity Additions in US Electric Utilities, 1996 to 2005**

	Capacity (MW)	% of Total
Coal	4845	12
Oil	5951	15
Gas	27371	68
Hydro	431	1
Nuclear	1170	3
Other	383	1
Total	**40151**	**100**

Source: *Inventory of Power Plants in the United States,* 1997, US EIA/DOE, Washington DC, 1998.

A number of factors have changed the relative advantages of power generation technologies to favour gas-fired turbines in simple or combined cycle configuration. Lower gas prices since the mid-1980s have made gas attractive for medium and, in some cases, baseload applications. The removal of most of the restrictions of the Power Plant and Industrial Fuel Use Act (PIFUA) in the US in 1990 eliminated an important barrier to increased use of gas by utilities. Combustion turbines are now more efficient and more reliable than they were a few years ago and their capital costs have fallen. The new generation of CCGT plants is approaching 60% efficiency. Environmental restrictions favour gas, as it is free of sulphur and emits less carbon dioxide and other pollutants when combusted than other fossil fuels. For example, the New Source Performance Standards (NSPS) impose capital-intensive technological control on new coal plants. Natural gas consumption in power stations is projected to double by 2020 and to account for more than 40% of North American gas demand.

Figure 12.8: **Comparison of the Generating Costs of New Steam Coal and CCGT Plants, 2000**

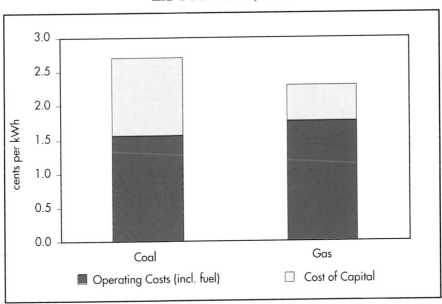

Coal-fired generation is projected to increase by 2.3% per annum. By 2020, coal-fired plants could supply more than half of the region's electricity. Coal-fired capacity increases at a lower rate of 1.7% per annum. This means that coal capacity is used more intensively in baseload, particularly when nuclear units serving baseload duty are retired. Figure 12.8 compares the costs of new coal and CCGT plants in the year 2000. Overall, CCGT plants are more economic to build, but coal plants have lower running costs and therefore, once they are built, are more economic for baseload use. Higher use of the existing stock could also result from the restructuring of the electricity industry that is currently taking place in the US.

Oil use in power generation in North America is the lowest in the OECD. It currently accounts for 2% of total generation and is projected to maintain this share throughout the projection period. In absolute terms, it shows a modest increase, from 98 TWh in 1995 to 151 TWh by the end of the outlook period.

There are no plans to build new nuclear power plants in the US or Canada in the foreseeable future; unfavourable economics combined with siting and permit problems lead to a significant decline of nuclear power. The last unit to be commissioned in the region was Watts Bar 1 in Spring City, Tennesee, in 1996. It is a 1170 MW pressurised water reactor that will supply enough electricity for 200 000 Tennesse Valley households. Nuclear capacity in the region in 1995 was 116 GW. By 2020, some 58 GW of nuclear plants could be retired, bringing nuclear capacity down to 59 GW.

Table 12.10: **Canadian Nuclear Plants Temporarily Shut Down**

Unit Name	Unit Size (MW)	Commercial Operation
Pickering 1	542	1971
Pickering 2	542	1971
Pickering 3	542	1972
Pickering 4	542	1973
Bruce 1	904	1977
Bruce 2	904	1978
Bruce 3	904	1979

Canadian nuclear capacity stood at 16.4 GW at the beginning of 1995, representing 14% of the country's installed capacity. At the end of this year, unit 1 at Bruce Power Station was shut down after twenty years of operation. No nuclear units have been commisioned in the country since 1993. In August 1997, Ontario hydro decided temporarily to shut down 7 of its 19 nuclear units in order to refurbish them and extend their lives to 40 years. The 7 units are scheduled to be brought back into operation before 2010 and this has been taken into account in the BAU projection. There is, however, some uncertainty as to whether this will happen.

Recently, two nuclear power plants in the United States applied for extension of their licences. Similar applications for other plants may follow. For several years, nuclear plants had very low running costs, but they have risen since the mid-1980s. Fossil fuel prices have fallen since 1986, so that by 1996 the average production cost of fossil-fuelled steam plants was only 3% higher than that of nuclear plants, as shown in Table 12.11. There would have to be significant increases in fossil fuel prices for new nuclear plants to become competitive again, based on a comparison of full generating costs.

Table 12.11: **Average Power Production Expenses for US Nuclear and Fossil-fuelled Steam Plants (cents per kWh), 1996**

	Fuel	Operation	Maintenance	Total
Fossil Fuel	1.65	0.23	0.25	2.13
Nuclear	0.55	0.95	0.57	2.10

Source: *Financial Statistics* of *Major US Investor-Owned Electric Utilities 1996,* Washington, DC, 1997.

Hydroelectric capacity in Canada is assumed to increase by about 12 GW in the period 1995 to 2020. Most of the increase will come from new plants in Quebec. The 828 MW Sainte Marguerite plant is expected to come on line in 2001. Five more power stations, Eastmain 1, Mercier, Kipawa, Haut Saint Maurice and Ashuapmushan, totalling 2015 MW, are expected to be developed during the outlook period. The largest new hydro project is Grande Baleine, in the same province, but only part of it is expected to be completed before 2020. Other new Canadian hydro projects include the Wukswatim and Notigi stations (405 MW) in Manitoba[6]. In the United States, only small capacity increases are expected, primarily because of lack of new sites, high construction costs, environmental considerations and competing uses for water resources.

The BAU projection of renewable energy for electricity

6. *Canada's Energy Outlook 1996-2020,* Natural Resources Canada, 1997.

generation is based partly on national forecasts (USDOE and Natural Resources Canada) and partly on internal IEA sources and estimates. In both countries, most incremental generation from renewables is expected to come from biomass and waste. Other sources, such as wind and solar power, show only small increases. Electricity generation from renewable energies is costly compared with conventional fossil fuel technologies. Increased use of these sources could be expected only if encouraged by specific supportive strategies. For example, in the United States, a very popular approach is the renewable portfolio standard (RPS), which specifies a certain percentage of electricity that must be supplied by renewable energies. Canada's strategy to stimulate renewable electricity generation is outlined in its Renewable Energy Strategy.

Oil

The following table summarises OECD North America's oil balance until 2020. Details on how the oil balance was obtained can be found in Chapter 7.

Table 12.12: **OECD North America's Oil Balance (Mbd)**

	1996	2010	2020
Demand	20.3	23.4	24.1
Supply	11.1	8.6	8.9
Net Imports	9.3	14.8	15.1

North America's position as the world's most mature oil producing region means that oil reserve constraints are likely to continue to be a major determinant of the region's oil production. During the projection period, some increase in production will come from offshore[7] oilfields, particularly in the Gulf of Mexico. Prospects for growth in onshore oil production are less optimistic, although the development of new technologies may lower the rate of decline in some fields.

Given these reserve constraints, the long-term outlook is one of steadily rising net oil imports. Towards the end of the projection period, rising unconventional oil production in Canada could reduce

7. The prospects for offshore oil production have been examined in a recent IEA publication, *Global Offshore Oil Prospects to 2000*, IEA/OECD Paris, 1996.

the region's reliance on oil imports. Since it is uncertain how future unconventional oil production will be split between Canada and Venezuela, where the two largest deposits of unconventional oil are situated, the above oil balance table includes only those unconventional oil projects for which production plans are at an advanced stage of preparation, or are already in production.

Gas

Prospects for gas supply in North America are discussed in detail in Chapter 8. The estimates for gas reserves quoted there are substantial for both the United States and Canada, especially if unconventional gas sources (coal bed methane and tight reservoir gas) are included. Indeed, unconventional gas has played a significant role since 1990, accounting for almost all the growth in US gas production[8]. The main uncertainties are the level of ultimate recoverable gas reserves in the region in relation to the size of cumulative gas production by 2020, the cost of incremental gas supplies and the balance among gas demand, supply and price in the North American market.

Official forecasts for the United States and Canada take the view that gas reserve estimates are likely to increase further and that indigenous gas supply will be sufficient to meet growing gas demand to 2020 at a price less than $3 per thousand cubic feet (tcf). This view is shared by major gas suppliers in the region, at least up till 2015.

As Chapter 8 indicates, current estimates of North American gas reserves differ, and projections of the US gas supply-demand balance to 2020 indicate some tightness in supply towards the end of the period. Considerable uncertainty exists on gas production costs, once the lowest-cost sources are used up. For these reasons, we adopt a less optimistic view. In the BAU projection, the gas price is assumed to double (at 1990 prices) from $1.7 per tcf in 2005 to $3.5 in 2015 and then to remain at that level to 2020. Most other projections expect the gas price to remain below $3 per tcf.

We assume that a price level of $3.5 is not likely to attract bulk imports of LNG into North America, and indigenous supply and demand are expected to balance to 2020. The gas price rise will restrict gas demand growth, however. We do not doubt the importance of

8. *The World's Non-Conventional Oil and Gas, Hydro-carbons of last recourse,* A. Perrondon, J.H. Laherrère and C.J. Campbell, Petroleum Economist, March 1998.

technological developments in gas exploration, development and production, nor the enterprise and innovation of gas companies. However, we feel that the assumption that gas production in North America can continue to grow at low production costs till 2020 requires further analysis. Until that analysis is completed, we prefer a more cautious approach.

The following table shows how OECD North America's gas balance is projected to develop over the projection period. Chapter 8 provides a discussion on how this supply projection was obtained.

Table 12.13: **OECD North America's Gas Balance (Mtoe)**

	1995	2010	2020
Demand	602	756	762
Supply	592	759	764
Net Imports	-2	-2	-2

Coal

The US is the world's second largest producer of coal, after China. In 1996, its coal production reached 878 million tonnes (Mt), about 24% of world coal supply. The US has vast coal resources, estimated at around 650 000 Mt. More than half of US electricity generation is supplied from coal, and about 85% of coal production is sold to domestic utilities. It is expected that power generation will account for an increasing share of US coal production as other fuels are substituted for coal in other energy-consuming sectors.

The share of the US in the internationally-traded coal market fell significantly, from about 50% in 1970 to about 17% in 1995. US producers effectively set the upper limit to world prices by their capacity to enter the market whenever the price is high and exploit their excess capacity. US coal producers make decisions on investment in new capacity according to their expectations of future coal demand from the domestic market. US fields are closing faster than they are being replaced, because of low returns on investment. Although domestic prices have fallen, they are currently above export prices. In this situation, where exports are marginal, production costs are covered by domestic sales. Otherwise, it is unlikely that the situation could be sustained; either prices will rise or less export coal will be available, particularly for low and medium volatility metallurgical coal and low-sulphur steam coal. Supply can be expected to continue to tighten for better quality coal, leaving higher-sulphur coal for export.

Figure 12.9: **Hard Coal Production and Exports**

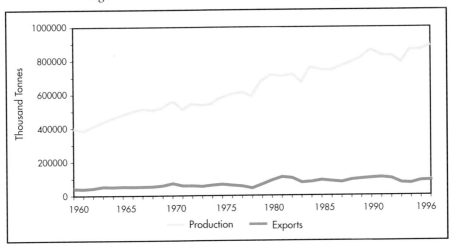

Because of their high level of dependence on the electricity sector, restrictions on emissions under the Clean Air Act, and deregulation and restructuring in the electricity sector, could have a significant impact on US coal producers. In general, the changes in the US domestic market are pushing coal producers to investment in low-sulphur coal for the domestic market, leaving surpluses of higher sulphur coal for export in the medium term, but creating uncertainty as to the level and grades of coal available for export in the longer term.

Canada supplies about 1% of the world's hard coal production and 4% of the world's brown coal production. In 1996, Canada produced about 40 Mt of coal and exported more than three quarters of this amount, primarily to Japan, Republic of Korea, Chinese Taipei and Brazil.

Comparison of Projections with Other Organisations

This section compares the projections of the US Department of Energy with the BAU projections presented here. As shown in Table 12.14, assumptions for GDP growth rates, the main driver of energy demand, are the same. For future world oil price developments, both of the organisations assume increases, albeit at different paces and different times. The main difference between USDOE and WEO 98 assumptions lies in the evolution of gas prices. Because of assumed rising North American gas production costs, the BAU projection assumes significantly higher natural gas prices than is assumed in the USDOE's projection.

Table 12.14: **Comparison of Key Assumptions for the USDOE and the BAU Projections**

	USDOE		WEO 98	
	1995-2010	1995-2020	1995-2010	1995-2020
GDP Growth Rates	2.3%	1.9%	2.3%	2.1%
Population Grawth Rates	0.8%	0.8%	0.8%	0.8%

Over the period 1995-2020, the USDOE reference case projections[9] for the US foresee a higher pace of energy demand growth than does the BAU projection. As shown in Table 12.15, USDOE projects an average growth of primary energy demand of 1.2% per annum against 0.8% for this Outlook. This difference can be largely attributed to the assumed increase in oil price over the period 2010 to 2015, and of the gas price from 2005 to 2015, in the IEA projections. Figure 12.10 compares the OECD North America oil and natural gas price assumptions of the two models over the projection period.

Table 12.15: **Comparisons of Growth Rates of Total Primary Energy Supply for the USDOE and the BAU Projections**

Average Annual Growth Rates	USDOE 1995-2020	WEO 98 1995-2020
TPES	1.1%	0.8%
Solid Fuels	1.0%	1.9%
Oil	1.3%	0.7%
Gas	1.6%	0.7%
Nuclear	-2.2%	-2.4%
Hydro	0.1%	0.3%
Other Renewables	1.7%	1.4%

9. *Annual Energy Outlook 1998 - With Projections through 2020,* December 1997, USDOE/EIA.

Figure 12.10: **Comparison of the Price Assumptions for the USDOE and the IEA Projections**

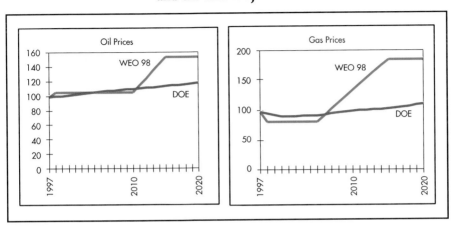

In the IEA projection, the higher energy price environment leads to a slowdown in energy demand, in particular that of oil and gas. This region is very responsive to energy prices, and the greater sensitivity of energy demand to higher prices in OECD North America compared with other OECD regions has been reported in several studies[10]. For the period 1995 to 2010, our projection confirms this finding: total primary energy demand is expected to grow 1.1% per annum in the BAU projection which is similar to that of USDOE.

As a result of the above differences in projected energy demand patterns over the period 1995-2020, the projected energy intensity improvement rates of the two models diverge significantly. Whereas the USDOE expects a decline in energy intensity of 0.8% per annum on average, the WEO 98 BAU case projects a decline of 1.2% annually.

The two projections also differ in respect to growth in final electricity demand. The IEA projection has higher demand for electricity; 1.8% per annum compared with 1.4% per annum for USDOE. The slower pace of electricity demand growth in the USDOE projections is explained by the factors "saturation, utility investments in demand-side management programmes and legislation establishing more stringent equipment efficiency standards"[11].

10. See, for example, *The Costs of Cutting Emissions: Results from Global Models,* OECD, 1993, amongst others.
11. See page 50 of *Annual Energy Outlook 1998-With Projections Through 2020,* December 1997, DOE/EIA, for a detailed discussion.

The differences with OECD North America oil demand projections are mainly due to expected developments in the transportation sector. While USDOE projects a growth rate of 1.6% per annum, the BAU projection has an annual increase of 1.1% in the period of 1995-2020. This can be mainly attributed to the oil price increase in the period 2010-2015.

For power generation, the assumed increases in the gas price leads to less use of gas and consequently more coal in the BAU projection. This is reflected in the higher growth rate of solids in total primary energy demand in Table 12.15. The BAU projection has similar nuclear capacity figures but a somewhat higher estimate of wind power in 2020.

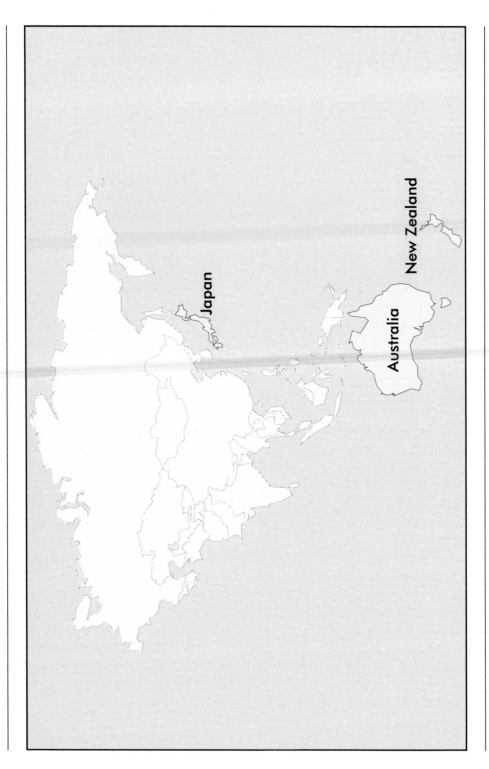

CHAPTER 13
OECD PACIFIC

Introduction

The OECD Pacific region[1] is diverse in terms of both its energy and economic structures. Japan, the OECD's second largest energy consumer, is the dominant energy user in the region with total primary energy demand of 510 Mtoe in 1996. This is more than 80% of the region's total consumption. Australia is a major producer of coal and New Zealand has a large supply of hydropower.

In 1996, the region accounted for 14% of total OECD commercial primary energy demand, compared with 10% in 1971. This increasing share results partly from relatively high economic growth in the region over the last 25 years (3.5% per annum compared with 2.7% for the total OECD).

Compared to most OECD economies, Japan has a low energy intensity level, 0.2 toe per $1000 in 1990 prices and purchasing power parity (PPP) terms. This is some 30% less than that of the OECD, and is partly due to the country's limited energy resources and traditionally high energy prices. Australia and New Zealand have higher energy intensities than Japan, around 0.3 toe per $1000 (at 1990 prices and PPP). End use prices in Japan are significantly higher than in the United States and are comparable to those in some European countries. High energy costs and high tax rates are the main reasons for this. Taxes account for more than half of the total price of automotive fuels both in Japan and Australia. Gasoline prices in Japan are almost twice as high as in Australia and about three times as high as in the United States. Industrial energy prices in Japan have historically been subject to very low taxes in comparison with other OECD countries.

Box 13.1 discusses the possible impact on end-user prices of planned deregulation and institutional reform in the Japanese energy sector. The uncertain outcome of these reforms contributes to the overall uncertainty of the projections in this study.

---

1. The region consists of Japan, Australia and New Zealand. Although the Republic of Korea joined the OECD in 1996, it has been included with other East Asian countries for modelling purposes.

The OECD Pacific region is diverse in terms of economic structure. The manufacturing sector accounts for 24% of GDP in Japan, compared with 15% and 18% in Australia and New Zealand. The high share of manufacturing in Japan is reflected in the 40% industrial share in total final energy consumption, significantly higher than the OECD average of about 30%.

In the business as usual case, GDP in the OECD Pacific region is assumed to increase at an average annual rate of 1.8% over the outlook period, a slowdown compared to the 3.2% achieved between 1971 and 1995. The recent Asian financial crisis is assumed to contribute to the future slowdown in economic growth. The OECD Pacific region's trade and other economic linkages with the industrialising Asian countries and China have strong impacts on the economy and energy sectors of the region. The OECD[2] projects a rather weak recovery for Japan, which is expected to register a zero or negative growth in 1998 for the first time in more than two decades. This is expected to be followed by only modest growth.

Population in the OECD Pacific region is assumed to increase by only 0.1% per annum over the Outlook period, compared with 0.7% from 1971 to 1995. It is even expected to start decreasing at some point before 2020. The age structure of the population is expected to shift towards more older people. It is estimated that Japan's working-age population, which peaked at about 90 million in the mid-1990s, will shrink to about 70 million by 2030[3].

The Japanese CIF import price for LNG has broadly followed crude oil prices over the past two decades (see Figure 2.2, in Chapter 2). It is assumed that LNG prices will increase from $126 per toe in 1995 to $210 in 2020, following a path similar to that of crude oil prices. The price of internationally-traded hard coal is not expected to increase substantially, due to abundant world supply.

Box 13.1: **Regulatory Reforms in Japan and their Impacts**

In recent years, an increasing number of countries have launched ambitious regulatory reform programmes to increase competition and cost effectiveness. Energy is one of the sectors affected.

In May 1997, the Japanese Cabinet approved An Action Plan

2. *OECD Economic Outlook,* OECD Paris, June 1998.
3. *Japan Review of International Affairs,* Fall 1997, pp. 219-233.

for Economic Structure Reform, in which deregulation measures are proposed as a means of promoting market mechanisms to fulfil electric-power-load needs and improve the operation of the petroleum market. The action plan builds on the Programme for Economic Structure Reform (approved in December 1996) that aimed to ensure, through competition, that the electricity, gas and petroleum industries provide services at an international standard of performance, including costs, by 2001.

The main objective of deregulation in the Japanese electricity sector is to bring electricity costs in line with international levels. Measures to achieve this goal include:

- improvements to the electricity system load factor through actions by the government, utilities, manufacturers and users, such as the promotion of heat-storage air conditioners, gas-fired air conditioners and load-reflective tariffs;
- more active use of independent power producers (IPPs) including a study of their possible supply capacity and targets for their introduction;
- acceleration of utilities' efforts to improve administrative efficiency.

According to the report of the Study Group on the Economic Effects of Deregulation, an advisory committee of the Ministry of International Trade and Industry (1997), the increase in the efficiency of the electricity sector as a result of deregulation would significantly lower electricity prices. It would ameliorate the price disparities that currently exist between Japan and, for example, Germany, which has a comparable energy situation. Similarly, a general review of petroleum policies has been initiated with a goal of deregulation and institutional reform by 2001.

It is expected that regulatory reforms in general will stimulate economic growth by increasing productivity, which lowers prices and creates additional demand for goods and services. MITI estimates that, as a result of regulatory reforms, Japanese real GDP could be increased by 6 percentage points over time.

Table 13.1: **Assumptions for the OECD Pacific Region**

	1971	1995	2010	2020	1995-2020 Annual Growth Rate
Coal Price ($1990 per metric ton)	44	40	42	46	0.5%
Oil Price ($1990 per barrel)	6	15	17	25	2.1%
LNG price ($1990 per toe)	n.a.	126	141	210	1.6%
GDP ($Billion 1990 and PPP)	1249	2848	3856	4445	1.8%
Population (millions)	121	147	153	153	0.1%
GDP per Capita ($1000 1990 and PPP per person)	10	19	25	29	1.6%

Energy Demand Outlook

Overview

Total primary energy demand in the OECD Pacific region increased by 2.6% per annum in the period 1971 to 1995. This compares with 1.2% in OECD North America and 1.3% in OECD Europe. Despite this relatively high growth, the OECD Pacific region improved its energy intensity level at an annual average rate of 0.9%.

In the business as usual case, primary energy demand is projected to grow at an annual rate of 1.2% over the outlook period. Consumption of oil is expected to grow rather slowly, at 0.6% per annum. The present 51% share of oil in total primary energy demand declines to 47% in 2010 and to 44% in 2020.

Table 13.2: **Total Primary Energy Supply (Mtoe)**

	1971	1995	2010	2020	1995-2020 Annual Growth Rate
TPES	**329**	**607**	**755**	**815**	**1.2%**
Solid Fuels	82	134	148	154	0.6%
Oil	229	309	354	361	0.6%
Gas	5	73	119	132	2.4%
Nuclear	2	76	109	134	2.3%
Hydro	9	11	12	13	0.8%
Other Renewables	1	5	13	20	5.6%

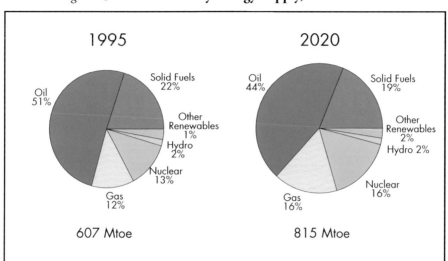

Figure 13.1: **Total Primary Energy Supply, OECD Pacific**

As shown in Table 13.2 and Figure 13.1, future consumption of gas, nuclear power and other renewables is expected to grow strongly. Gas increases its market share by 4 percentage points over the outlook period. Nuclear power in Japan, the only country in the region with a nuclear programme, is expected to increase by 2.3% per annum. Other renewables, mainly wind and geothermal, grow rapidly, albeit from a low base in 1995.

As summarised in Table 13.3, total final energy consumption is projected to grow at an annual rate of 1% over the outlook period. Electricity is expected to grow most rapidly, at an annual rate of 1.8%, which is identical to that assumed for GDP growth. Final gas demand increases at a significantly slower rate than the growth in primary gas demand, indicating a growing input to power generation. Oil is expected to grow at a slower rate than total final consumption, mainly driven by the demand for mobility. Solid fuels demand is projected to stagnate over the Outlook period.

Table 13.3: **Total Final Energy Consumption (Mtoe)**

	1971	1995	2010	2020	1995-2020 Annual Growth Rate
TFC	**257**	**424**	**516**	**547**	**1.0%**
Solid Fuels	45	52	49	49	-0.2%
Oil	171	250	298	304	0.8%
Gas	8	30	39	41	1.2%
Electricity	34	90	122	141	1.8%
Heat*	0	1	8	12	8.9%

* Includes renewables.

Energy Related Services

Stationary Sectors

As seen in Table 13.4, stationary uses of fossil fuels are expected to increase rather modestly over the Outlook period. There are many factors underlying this projection. A major reason is the relocation of industries. As demand for steel fell in the recession following the oil crises of 1973 and 1979, older plants in OECD countries closed and new plants elsewhere were more competitive. In the case of Japan, the trend in relocation to other countries of energy-intensive heavy industries, such as iron and steel, automobile and heavy engineering industries is an important determinant of the slowdown in domestic fuel demand. Another reason for low growth rate for stationary fuel demand is the declining trend of energy intensities in many heavy industrial branches. As illustrated in Figure 13.3, almost all major energy-intensive industries in Japan have experienced substantial energy-intensity improvements, particularly in the 1970s and 1980s, due partly to technological innovation. For example, the energy-intensity improvement in the iron & steel and chemical industries, which together account for about 50% of total industrial fuel demand, reached about 30% and 50% respectively over the past two decades. In this Outlook, further improvements in energy intensity in the industrial sector are projected.

Table 13.4: **Energy Use in Stationary Services (Mtoe)**

	1971	1995	2010	2020	1995-2020 Annual Growth Rate
Total	**173**	**220**	**246**	**251**	**0.5%**
Solid Fuels	44	52	49	49	-0.2%
Oil	121	136	150	149	0.4%
Gas	8	30	39	41	1.3%
Heat*	0	1	8	12	8.9%

* Includes renewables.

Figure 13.2: **Energy Intensity Developments by Industry 1974=100**

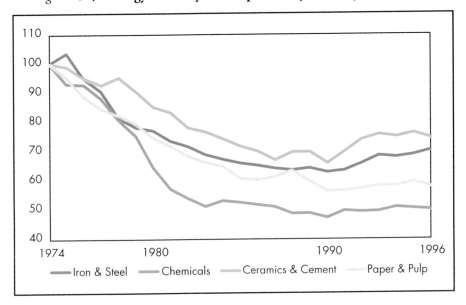

The projection of stationary fuel demand in stationary services reflects expected saturation for residential space and water heating in the region. While oil is projected to retain the largest share of stationary fuel demand, it is expected that gas will increasingly substitute for coal. Around 42% of incremental demand over the Outlook period is expected to be met by gas and the rest by oil. The strong increase in gas underlines the importance of Japanese long-term LNG supply and related trade linkages.

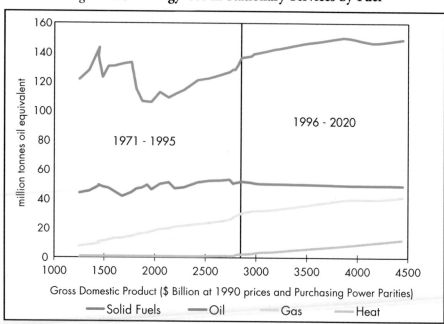

Figure 13.3: **Energy Use in Stationary Services by Fuel**

y-axis: million tonnes oil equivalent

x-axis: Gross Domestic Product ($ Billion at 1990 prices and Purchasing Power Parities)

1971 - 1995

1996 - 2020

Solid Fuels   Oil   Gas   Heat

Mobility

The demand for mobility in the OECD Pacific region is expected to rise along with GDP. The recent sharp increase can be explained partly by the shift to larger cars in Japan. The share of passenger cars with an engine capacity more than 2000 cc increased from 4.1% in 1989 to 21.1% in 1996. The slowing down effect of the increase in transport fuel prices on demand for mobility due to increasing world oil prices after 2010 (see Chapter 2 for details) can be seen in Figure 13.4. It can also be seen that, during the 1990s and despite the economic slowdown in Japan, the energy demand for mobility has increased at a quicker pace than in the 1980s. As in other OECD regions, demand in the OECD Pacific for transport-related services could show some saturation, especially beyond 2010. This could arise from constraints on road traffic, including congestion, limitations on infrastructure development and saturation in vehicle ownership levels. However, OECD Pacific car ownership levels are still significantly lower than in other OECD regions. In 1996, per capita passenger car ownership in Japan was about 0.37, compared to 0.52 in USA and 0.50 in Germany. It is also expected that changes in the GDP structure, away from heavy industry towards services and towards lighter materials, could reduce the additional tonne-kilometres required for transport.

Figure 13.4: **Energy Demand for Mobility**

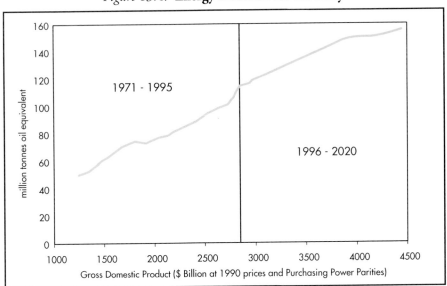

1971 - 1995

1996 - 2020

million tonnes oil equivalent

Gross Domestic Product ($ Billion at 1990 prices and Purchasing Power Parities)

Figure 13.5: **Ownership of Passenger Cars in Japan (More than 660 cc)**

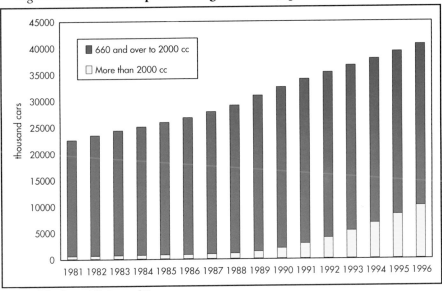

■ 660 and over to 2000 cc

☐ More than 2000 cc

thousand cars

Source: The Japan Ministry of Transport.

Total energy demand for mobility is expected to grow by 1.2% per annum. Demand for aviation fuel is expected to increase faster than for road fuels, due to the effects of rising per capita income levels and to the expected further decline in the cost of international travel.

About 70% of the increase in total oil demand is projected to arise from increased mobility. By the year 2020, it is expected that the current 37% share of mobility in total oil demand will have risen to 43%.

Table 13.5: **Energy Use for Mobility (Mtoe)**

	1971	1995	2010	2020	1995-2020 Annual Growth Rate
Total		50	114	148	155	1.2%

Electricity

Total electricity demand in the OECD Pacific region is projected to rise with increasing GDP. As seen in Figure 13.6, this is broadly in line with the almost linear trend since 1971. Such a linear trend is associated with a decreasing GDP elasticity of electricity demand with a gradual decline from a level of 2 in the 1960s to just over 1 at present. Over the outlook period, this elasticity is expected to be about 1, a 1.8% electricity growth compared to assumed GDP growth of 1.8%.

Table 13.6: **Total Final Electricity Demand (Mtoe)**

	1971	1995	2010	2020	1995-2020 Annual Growth Rate
Electricity		34	90	122	141	1.8%

Strong demand growth leads to significant penetration of electricity in final energy consumption of the region. In 1971, electricity accounted for 13% of OECD Pacific final consumption; by 1995, this had increased to 21% and it is projected to rise to 26% by 2020.

The regulatory reforms in the electricity industry (see Box 13.1) or saturation of electricity uses in the household and services sectors could affect these projected electricity demand trends.

Figure 13.6: **Total Final Electricity Demand**

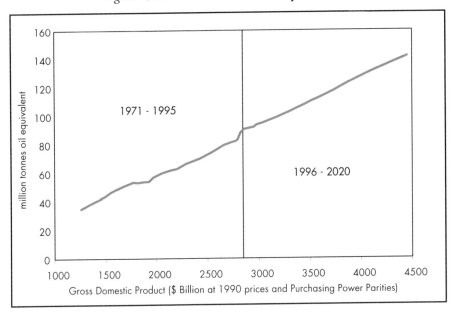

Gross Domestic Product ($ Billion at 1990 prices and Purchasing Power Parities)

Supply

This section provides an overview of the supply side of OECD Pacific energy markets. While energy demand in this region is dominated by Japan, Australia is the major supplier of coal and gas.

Power Generation

Electricity generation in the OECD Pacific region is dominated by Japan, which accounts for 82% of the region's total generation. About half of Japan's electricity supply comes from nuclear and oil-fired power plants, more than 80% of Australia's electricity is generated by domestic coal and three quarters of New Zealand's electricity comes from hydropower. The region's electricity mix, for 1995, is summarised in Table 13.7.

By the end of the projection period, annual power plant output in the region could be 57% above its 1995 level, in line with the 1.8% per annum growth projected for electricity demand.

Electricity generated by solid fuels is projected to grow at an average annual rate of 1.2%, and its share in total generation could decline from 27% to 24%. Japan imports most of the coal it uses in power stations. However, the utilities do buy a certain amount of domestic coal. Domestic coal is highly priced; in 1996, a tonne of domestic coal cost about 20000 Yen, whereas imported coal cost 5500 Yen per tonne. The share of domestic coal in power station use has been in decline; in 1982, it was two thirds of power station coal use, but only 15% in 1995. This share declined further after the closure of Japan's largest mine in March 1997.

Table 13.7: **Electricity Generation Mix, 1995 (TWh)**

	Australia	**Japan**	**New Zealand**	**Pacific**
Solid Fuels	137	189	3	327
Oil	3	224	0	227
Gas	18	191	5	214
Nuclear	0	291	0	291
Hydro	16	82	27	126
Other Renewables	0	3	2	5
Total	**173**	**981**	**36**	**1190**

As elsewhere in the OECD, natural gas is the fastest growing fuel; its use is expected to grow by 3.6% per annum over the projection period and to increase its share in electricity output from 18% in 1995 to 28% in 2020. All three countries have plans to increase gas use in their power generation sectors. In Japan, where almost all fossil fuels are imported, this will be in the form of imported liquefied natural gas (LNG). LNG is used, along with coal, to cover daily mid-load demand whereas oil covers seasonal, mid- and peak-load demand. Small increases in gas-fired capacity are expected in Australia and New Zealand using indigenous resources.

Oil-fired generation is marginal in Australia and New Zealand, but accounts for more than 20% of electricity generation in Japan. Official plans call for oil-fired generation to fall to 8% of total by 2010. However, as oil-fired plants have aged, pressure has been increasing to allow the replacement of oil-fired capacity. A study group of the Electric Utility Industry Council argued that retiring oil-fired power plants should be replaced by new oil-fired plants so as to maintain an appropriate fraction of oil-fired generation in Japan's power generation mix[4]. The share of oil is projected to decline from

4. *Oil in Power Generation*, OECD/IEA, 1997.

19% of total generation in the OECD Pacific in 1995 to 11% by 2020. In absolute terms, oil-fired generation declines slightly from 227 TWh to 204 TWh over the same period.

Nuclear power, concentrated in Japan, increases significantly; its share of total generation increases from 24% in 1995 to 28% in 2020. The first commercial nuclear plant in Japan was commissioned in 1966 in Ibaraki prefecture. At the end of 1996, there were 54 reactors in the country, with a total capacity of 44 GW.

Figure 13.7: **Fuel Consumption in Power Generation**

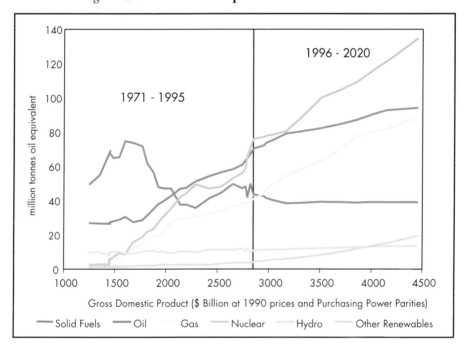

Nuclear power is considered by the Japanese authorities as an important energy source in a country that lacks natural resources. In addition to reducing demand on imported oil and gas, it is seen as a means of reducing environmental problems such as acid rain and global warming. The government's target is to have 66 to 70 GW of nuclear capacity by the year 2010. This means that more than 20 GW of new capacity will be needed over the next 12 years. At the time of writing, there is only one nuclear unit under construction: Onagawa-3, a boiling water reactor (BWR), of 796 MW is expected to become operative in 2002 or 2003. There are four other units firmly committed. These are also BWRs with overall gross capacity of 4.7 GW. We assume in this Outlook that by 2010, installed nuclear capacity will be lower than the official target, at around 60 GW, reaching 73 GW by the end of the Outlook period. If Japanese nuclear power plants operate for 40 years, then in the second half of the projection period, a few plants could be decommissioned, requiring further nuclear plants to be built.

Over the past few years, public opposition to Japan's nuclear power programme has increased, following a number of nuclear incidents in Japan. In 1996, a referendum in the town of Maki in Niigata prefecture rejected the planned construction of the Maki-1 nuclear plant. In March 1997, Kyushu Electric announced the cancellation of plans to build a nuclear power plant[5] in Miyazaki due to strong local protests.

Electricity generation from hydro power plants in the region is expected to increase by 0.8% per annum. Most of the additional hydro power production is expected to be in Japan as pumped storage to ease the daily peak. There is little activity in Australia and New Zealand. The latter already depends heavily on hydro power for its electricity supplies, but there are no plans to build large new hydro stations because of their relatively high cost. There are plans to upgrade the large Manapouri station, which would add an extra 175 MW by 2000, and some small-scale hydro plants are under construction[6].

Hydro power in Japan gained momentum after the oil crises in the 1970s. Most of the sites available for large-scale facilities have now been used and recent development has been on a smaller scale. On the other hand, development of pumped storage facilities that provide electricity for peak demand continues. Over the 25-year horizon of the Outlook, it is expected that about 7 GW of new conventional hydro plant and 10 GW of new pumped storage stations will be constructed in the region, largely in Japan.

Non-hydro renewable generation is set to increase seven-fold. Both Japan and New Zealand have geothermal energy; in 1995, production was 3.2 and 2 TWh respectively. Total geothermal capacity is expected to reach 3.3 GW in 2020. In New Zealand, geothermal energy supplies about 6% of electricity and, depending on cost and discount rate assumptions, there is potential for an additional annual

5. *Atoms in Japan*, September 1996, Vol. 40, No. 8, pp 5-7.
6. *Energy Policies of IEA Countries, New Zealand, 1997 Review*, IEA/OECD, 1997.

supply of 4.1 TWh. Wind and solar power generation are also expected to increase, reaching 8.6 and 3.7 TWh respectively by 2020.

Table 13.8: **Non Hydro-Renewable Electricity Generation (TWh) and Capacity (MW)**

	1995		2010		2020	
	TWh	MW	TWh	MW	TWh	MW
Wind	0.01	3	3.2	1050	8.6	2855
Geothermal	5.3	756	14.5	2071	22.9	3272
Solar	0.05	27	0.7	500	3.7	2800

Over the Outlook period, installed generating capacity in the region is expected to increase about one and a half times, from 274 GW in 1995 to 426 GW in 2020. This is almost in line with electricity demand, at an average rate of 1.8% per annum. However, more new plants will be needed, as some 55 GW of existing plant are expected to be retired by the end of the Outlook period.

Table 13.9: **Electricity Generating Capacity (GW)**

	1995	2010	2020
Solid Fuels	57	65	71
of which CRW	4	5	5
Oil	60	69	73
Gas	58	101	128
Nuclear	41	59	73
Hydro	56	69	73
Other Renewables	1	4	9
Total	**274**	**366**	**426**

Fossil fuel inputs to power stations increase 43% above their 1995 levels by 2020. This increase is lower than the increase in the corresponding output, due to efficiency improvements in generating plants. Japan is already one of the most efficient countries in the world in terms of power generation, but average fossil-fuel conversion efficiency could increase further with the increased use of CCGT plants rather than boilers for gas burning.

Table 13.10: **Fuel Consumption in Power Generation (Mtoe)**

	1995	2010	2020
Solid Fuels	70	87	94
of which CRW	5	5	6
Oil	43	38	39
Gas	41	77	89
Nuclear	76	109	134
Hydro	11	12	13
Other Renewables	4	12	19
Total	**245**	**336**	**387**

Oil

In 1996 OECD Pacific produced just 1% of global oil production but accounted for 9% of global oil demand. The region is therefore a large net importer of oil, around 90% of demand in 1996 and projected to rise to 96% by 2020.

Table 13.11: **OECD Pacific Oil Balance (Mbd)**

	1996	2010	2020
Demand	6.7	7.7	7.9
Supply	0.7	0.3	0.3
Net Imports	6.0	7.4	7.6

In the short term Australian offshore oil production is expected to increase, but the current low level of regional oil production means that the impact on the region's net oil imports will be minimal. In the longer term, OECD Pacific's relatively modest remaining oil reserves of around 2.5 billion barrels (discovered and undiscovered) will prevent oil production from increasing. Cumulative regional oil production at the end of 1996 was around 4.5 billion barrels and so it can be seen that this region has already produced the majority of its original oil reserves. Further information on the oil supply projections can be found in Chapter 7.

Gas

Table 13.12 presents the region's gas balance until 2020. It is important to note that the countries in this region are somewhat different, for example whereas Japan is a large net gas importer, Australia is a large net gas exporter. Both countries are expected during the projection period to increase their respective roles as net importers and exporters.

Table 13.12: **OECD Pacific Gas Balance (Mtoe)**

	1996	2010	2020
Demand	73	119	132
Supply	31	77	68
Net Imports	42	42	64

Australia has substantial gas reserves and is a significant gas producer and exporter. In 1996, Australia produced about 98% of the total OECD Pacific gas production equal to a total of 30 billion cubic meters (bcm). About two thirds of this amount was consumed in the domestic market and around 10 bcm was exported. In 1996, 95% of this gas was exported to Japan, and the rest to Turkey and Spain.

The Carnarvon basin provides about half of Australian gas production. It is assumed by the Australian Government that the current gas export level will more than double by the year 2010. In addition, Australia has the world's fourth largest coal-seam gas resources, after Russia, Canada and China. It is expected that this industry will develop during the coming decades[7].

A specific feature of the OECD Pacific region is its dominant role in the world LNG market. Almost all of Japan's gas requirements are imported, and all in the form of LNG. About three-quarters is used in power generation. In 1996, Japan accounted for 60% of the world's LNG imports. Most of this gas comes from Southeast Asia, 40% from Indonesia alone. The Asia-Pacific region is the world's largest market for LNG, with Japan, the Republic of Korea and Chinese Taipei accounting for about three-quarters of total world LNG trade.

Japan's contracted imports of LNG as of 1998 are up to 53.3 million tonnes per annum. There is considerable uncertainty regarding the new sources which will meet the expected 80% increase in gas demand in the OECD Pacific by 2020. With natural gas demand in

7. *Energy Policies of IEA Countries: Australia 1997 Review* (IEA, 1997) provides a detailed assessment of gas production trends of Australia.

Asia expected to grow substantially in the next two decades, additional extensive investments in the region's gas infrastructure, in particular pipelines such as those from East Siberia, are likely to be necessary. Such plans, however, are still in the very early stages.

Japanese LNG import prices are 30-40% higher than the border price of gas transported to European countries via pipeline, mainly due to substantial costs of processing and transporting LNG. Despite the 40% increase in the real LNG price assumed in the projections presented here, there is still considerable uncertainty about whether the expected demand can be met by available supply. However, it is assumed here that adequate investment for LNG capacity expansion will be made and that Japan will not face a lack of physical supply over the projection period.

Coal

Australia is the world's largest exporter of coal. In 1996, its coal production was 195 Mt, an increase of 2% over 1995. Since 1970, coal production has increased more than fourfold, making Australia the world's fifth largest coal producer with about 6% of the world total. Most of the increase in production has been exported. Coal exports have risen from about 40% of total hard coal production in 1970 to about 70% now.

Australian coal mines are close to the sea and within reasonable shipping distance of Asian markets where coal consumption is increasing rapidly. Despite coal industry restructuring in Europe and, until recently, the embargo on South African coal, Australian exports to Europe have not shown any consistent growth trend, partly because of high ocean freight costs.

Hard coal exports have increased by 8% per year since 1973, reaching 140.4 Mt in 1996. Steam coal exports rose more quickly than those of coking coal. In 1980, steam coal represented 21% (8.9 Mt) of total coal exports, but this rose to 45% in 1996 (62.8 Mt). In contrast, coking coal exports rose from 33.8 Mt in 1980 to 77.6 Mt in 1996. Japan takes the largest share of Australian coal exports, 47% in 1996, followed by the Republic of Korea (14% in 1996) and Europe (11%). Exports to the Republic of Korea have risen over the past few years, while exports to Europe have fallen. In the next two decades, exports are likely to continue to account for the majority of Australia's coal production.

So far, Japan has played a major role in establishing the reference coal price in Asian markets. Real coal prices have been falling for over a decade. Australia-Japan benchmark prices for thermal and hard coking coals have fallen by 2.5% and 3.4% a year in real terms from 1985 to 1997[8]. This trend reflects increased competition among suppliers with lower production costs because of higher labour and capital productivity. An important feature of coal pricing in recent years is the increased use of the spot market in Asian coal trade with a reduction in the price premium for reference coal[9]. This is expected to introduce a greater degree of transparency into the market and to keep prices low.

In this Outlook, coal prices are assumed to remain constant up to 2010 in real terms and show a slight increase thereafter, mainly due to increased freight costs. Although consumption growth is projected to be significant, supply growth is expected to be sufficient to meet higher demand.

Comparison of Projections with Other Organisations

This section provides a general comparison of some other energy projections with those presented in this Outlook. There are (at least) three other international organisations that produce long-term energy projections for the OECD Pacific region; the Asia Pacific Energy Research Centre (APERC), the European Union (EU) and the United States Department of Energy (USDOE). For the sake of comparability, the comparison is based only on the business as usual cases of each model. Table 13.13 gives the key assumptions for the models discussed.

Table 13.13: **Comparison of Assumptions for the OECD Pacific Region**

	APERC		USDOE		EU		WEO 98		
Levels	1995	2010	1995	2020	1992	2020	1995	2010	2020
Oil Price	17.0	17.0	17.0	22.3	17.6	31.0	15.0	17.0	25.0
Growth Rates	1995-2010		1995-2020		1992-2020		1995-2010	1995-2020	
GDP	2.6%		2.3%		2.1%		2.0%	1.8%	
Population	0.3%		n.a.		0.3%		0.3%	0.1%	

Note: Oil prices are quoted in real terms for the following years: APERC: $1995, USDOE: EU: $1993, WEO 98: $1990. LNG prices are quoted in $1990/toe.

8. *Coal Information,* IEA/OECD, 1998.
9. *International Coal* Trade, IEA/OECD, 1997.

APERC assumes the strongest increase in GDP while the WEO 98 assumes the lowest. As for world oil prices, APERC assumes a flat price, while EU, USDOE and WEO 98 all foresee future increases. All three organisations assume broadly similar price levels except for the rather higher 2020 price assumption of the EU study.

APERC projections

In a recently published report[10], APERC provides its first long-term energy outlook for APEC member countries[11]. The projections are made on a country-by-country basis for the period 1995 to 2010. APERC uses a "hybrid methodology" that combines econometric modelling and end-use approaches.

In order to compare the OECD Pacific projections of WEO 98 with those of APERC, the projections of the latter for Japan and Australia are added together. A comparison of projections is provided in Table 13.15.

APERC projects total primary energy supply to grow rapidly, at an annual rate of 2.2% against 1.2% for WEO 98. This can be mainly attributed to the higher GDP growth rate assumption made by APERC. APERC projects an average energy intensity decline of 0.4% per annum, as compared with 0.5% per annum for WEO 98.

Table 13.14 **Comparisons of Projections of Total Primary Energy Supply by Fuel for the OECD Pacific Region**

	APERC 1995-2010	USDOE 1995-2020	EU 1992-2020	WEO 98 1995-2020
TPES	2.2%	1.3%	1.3%	1.2%
Solid Fuels	2.3%	0.7%	1.0%	0.6%
Oil	1.3%	1.4%	1.4%	0.6%
Gas	4.5%	1.6%	0.3%	2.4%
Nuclear	2.3%	1.2%	2.6%	2.3%
Hydro/Other Renewables	3.1%	1.7%	0.3%	3.0%

There is a difference in the change in the market share of coal in TPES. While WEO 98 projects a market loss of 2 - 3 percentage points for coal for the period 1995-2010, APERC expects no increase.

10. *APEC Energy Demand and Supply Outlook*, APERC, 1998.
11. These 18 countries are: Australia, Brunei Darussalam, Canada, Chile, China, Hong Kong (China), Indonesia, Japan, the Republic of Korea, Malaysia, Mexico, New Zealand, Papua New Guinea, Philippines, Singapore, Chinese Taipei, Thailand, and the US.

This is mainly due to the differences in power generation projections, as illustrated on Table 13.15.

The oil share in the power input mix declines more rapidly in WEO 98 than in the APERC projections while WEO 98 projects higher market penetration rates for gas. APERC projects nuclear's share as declining, also contrary to our expectations.

EU and USDOE Projections

Both the EU[12] and the USDOE[13] provide long-term energy projections for the OECD Pacific region on a regular basis. The EU modelling approach includes the same countries as WEO 98 for the definition of OECD Pacific, while USDOE has the identical grouping of Industrialised Pacific countries. In terms of TPES, all three models project a similar annual growth rate up to 2020 as shown in Table 13.14.

A striking feature of the EU's projection is that gas demand is expected to show almost no growth at TPES level. Both USDOE and WEO 98 project gas to be the most rapidly increasing fuel type. For oil, EU and US DOE projections are higher than that of WEO 98. EU and WEO 98 project similar growth trends for transportation, 1.3% and 1.2% per annum respectively. The main difference between the EU and WEO 98 oil figures is in the assessment of the power generation sector. While WEO 98 expects a declining trend of 0.4% per annum, the EU projects a doubling of oil in power generation, implying a growth rate of 2.6% up to 2020. For hydro and renewable energy sources, both organisations project significantly more conservative trends than does WEO 98.

Table 13.15: **Comparison of Power Generation Projections**

Electricity and CHP Plants	1995		APERC	WEO 98
	Mtoe	Share	2010-Share	2010-Share
Solid Fuels	70	29%	33%	26%
Oil	43	18%	16%	11%
Gas	41	17%	20%	23%
Nuclear	76	31%	28%	32%
Hydro	11	4%	3%	4%
Other	4	2%	0%	3%
Total	245	100%	100%	100%

12. *International Energy Outlook 1998 - With Projections to 2020,* April 1998, DOE/EIA.
13. *Energy in Europe, European Energy to 2020 - A Scenario Approach,* Directorate General for Energy DGXVIII of the European Commission, 1996.

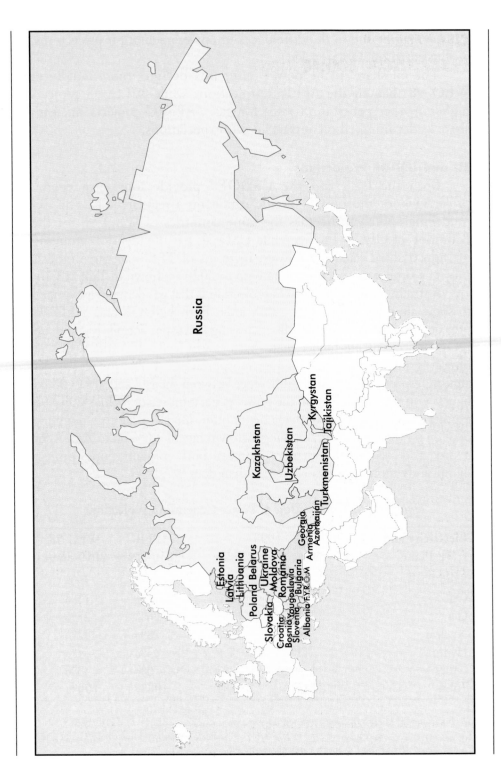

Russia

Kazakhstan

Uzbekistan

Kyrgystan

Turkmenistan

Tajikistan

Estonia

Latvia

Lithuania

Poland

Belarus

Ukraine

Moldova

Romania

Slovakia

Croatia

Yugoslavia

Bosnia

Slovenia

Bulgaria

Albania

F.Y.R.O.M

Georgia

Armenia

Azerbaijan

CHAPTER 14
TRANSITION ECONOMIES[1]

This chapter describes the business as usual (BAU) energy projection for the former centrally-planned economies of the Soviet Union and Eastern Europe. A common feature of these countries is that they are at various stages in the transition to market economies. Following the dissolution of the Soviet Union in the late 1980s, disruptions occurred in the collection of energy statistics. Energy data reflecting the new economic order started to become available in 1990, however, anomalies remain. Given the inadequacies of the GDP and the energy data for these countries, and the fundamental changes taking place in their economies, the margin for error associated with the projection described in this chapter is much greater than for most other regional energy projections in this Outlook. Because of these problems, the projections presented in this chapter have been prepared using a simulation approach rather than one based on econometric methods. The principal parameters used in constructing the energy projections are shown below.

The values of the above parameters are highly uncertain and depend on a number of factors such as future restructuring of the economy, energy prices in relation to costs of supply, energy consumption metering and investment in new energy-using and energy-producing capacity. Different values of these parameters would produce different projections and the above tables are therefore designed to inform the reader of the values assumed rather than provide a definitive statement about their values.

---

1. This chapter covers the combined energy projections of non-OECD Europe (Albania, Bulgaria, Poland, Romania, Slovak Republic and Former Yugoslavia) and the Former Soviet Union (Armenia, Azerbaijan, Belarus, Estonia, Georgia, Kazakhstan, Kyrgyzstan, Latvia, Lithuania, Moldova, Russia, Tajikistan, Turkmenistan, Ukraine and Uzbekistan). Poland joined the OECD on 22 November 1996, but at the time that the energy projections were being developed for this Outlook, Polish energy data had not been incorporated into OECD Europe. For statistical reasons, this region also includes Cyprus, Gibraltar and Malta.

Table 14.1: **Eastern European Parameters (excluding Russia)**

Energy Efficiency Improvement per annum	
Industry	0.6%
Commercial, Public Service, Residential and Non-Specified	0.5%
Agriculture	1.0%
Transport	0.5%
Output/Income Elasticities	
Industry	0.8
Commercial, Public Service, Residential and Non-Specified	0.6
Agriculture	0.9
Transport	1.1
Energy Price Elasticities	
Industry	-0.2
Commercial, Public Service, Residential and Non-Specified	-0.1
Agriculture	-0.2
Transport	-0.2

Table 14.2: **Russian Energy Parameters**

Output/Income Driver Elasticities	
Industry	0.9
Commercial, Public Service, Residential and Non-Specified	0.8
Agriculture	0.8
Transport	1.1
Energy Price Elasticities	
Industry	-0.10
Commercial, Public Service, Residential and Non-Specified	-0.05
Agriculture	-0.10
Transport	-0.10

Table 14.3: **GDP Assumptions**

$ Billion 1990 and PPP	1995	2010	2020	1995 - 2020 Annual Growth Rate
Transition Economies excl. Russia	679	1061	1464	3.1%
Russia	690	1086	1603	3.4%
Total	**1369**	**2146**	**3066**	**3.3%**

The GDP assumptions used in the BAU projection for this region are shown in Table 14.3.

Total Primary Energy Supply

During the period 1990 to 1994, energy demand and GDP in the Transition Economies fell continuously. GDP, for example, declined at an annual average rate of 10.4%. By 1995, there was some evidence that the Transition Economies had stabilised. This stability, however, masks considerable inter-regional differences, as economic recovery and higher energy demand in non-OECD Europe was partly offset by continued decline in the former Soviet Union.

Figure 14.1: **Transition Economies Energy and GDP 1990-1995**

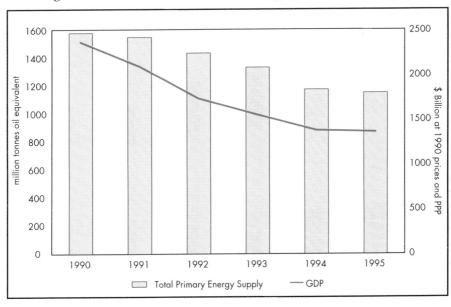

As Table 14.4 and Figure 14.2 indicate, the decline in Total Primary Energy Supply was spread across all fuels, with the exception of hydropower. Oil experienced the largest fall in demand, declining at an annual average rate in excess of 10% per annum. This rapid decline partly reflects the desire of the region's oil producing countries to maintain oil exports at the expense of domestic oil demand.

Table 14.4: **Total Primary Energy Supply by Fuel (Mtoe)**

	1990	1991	1992	1993	1994	1995	1990 - 1995 Annual Growth Rate
Solid Fuels	412	374	357	341	309	300	- 6.1%
Oil	473	461	416	347	278	275	-10.3%
Gas	614	632	582	563	511	498	- 4.1%
Nuclear	63	63	61	62	54	57	- 2.2%
Hydro	24	25	24	25	25	25	1.2%
Other	-2	-1	0	-1	-1	-1	-11.0%
TPES	**1584**	**1554**	**1440**	**1336**	**1177**	**1154**	**- 6.1%**

Figure 14.2: **Total Primary Energy Supply by Fuel (Mtoe)**

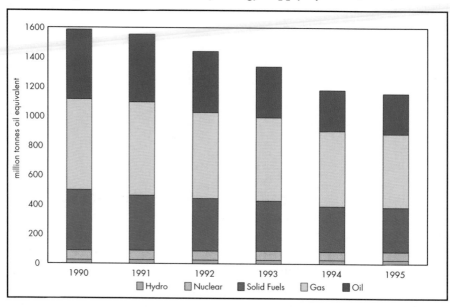

TPES declined at a slower rate than did GDP. Energy intensity therefore increased from 1990 to 1995, rising from 0.7 in 1990 to 0.8 in 1995. To produce one unit of GDP in 1995 required 25% more energy than in 1990. One obvious problem with this comparison is the development of a large black economy during this period, which has resulted in some under-recording of GDP. If electricity consumption were taken as a proxy for GDP evolution, then the under-recording could be as large as 30%. The Transition Economies true energy intensity is unlikely to have worsened by 25%. There is some evidence that rather than rationalising production by closing factories, and concentrating it in the most efficient plants, production has been maintained at low levels across many plants resulting in large energy overheads per unit of output.

Table 14.5: **Total Primary Energy Supply (Mtoe)**

	1995	**2010**	**2020**	**1995 - 2020 Annual Growth Rate**
Solid Fuels	300	357	360	0.7%
Oil	275	329	390	1.4%
Gas	498	647	835	2.1%
Nuclear	57	67	48	-0.7%
Hydro	25	29	32	1.0%
Other	-1	-1	-1	0.0%
TPES	**1154**	**1429**	**1664**	**1.5%**

Table 14.5 shows that in the BAU projection, the demand for gas grows more rapidly than for any other fuel. Gas already has the highest share of any fuel in the TPES fuel mix (43%). By 2020, gas is projected to account for just over half of the Transition Economies total energy demand. Oil is projected to grow considerably more slowly, but is still projected to grow twice as fast as coal demand. This will result in oil overtaking coal to become the second most important fuel in the fuel mix by 2020.

The relationship between TPES and official GDP has in the past been erratic, as Figure 14.3 indicates. TPES is projected to grow at half the rate of GDP until 2010. Between 2010 and 2015, the oil price is assumed to increase from $17/bbl to $25. During this period, energy demand growth slackens, but begins rising again once the oil price stabilises.

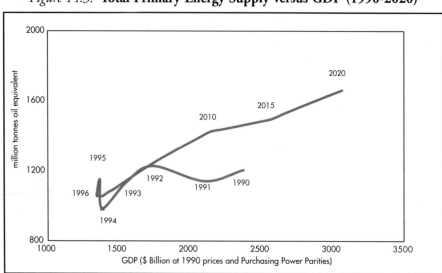

Figure 14.3: **Total Primary Energy Supply versus GDP (1990-2020)**

Total Final Consumption

Total final energy consumption (TFC) of energy fell continuously between 1990 and 1995. Those fuels delivered by a fixed infrastructure (gas, electricity and heat) declined less rapidly than fuels that require physical deliveries (solid fuels and oil). In several parts of the region, household consumption of gas and electricity is either unmetered or sold at a very low price. Therefore, little price-related incentive exists to reduce consumption.

Table 14.6: **Total Final Energy Consumption 1990-1995 (Mtoe)**

	1990	1991	1992	1993	1994	1995	1990 - 1995 Annual Growth Rate
Solid Fuels	175	143	149	144	117	109	- 9.0%
Oil	356	346	272	227	172	181	-12.7%
Gas	318	296	277	245	227	232	- 6.1%
Electricity and Heat	272	272	398	378	340	318	3.2%
Total	**1121**	**1057**	**1097**	**993**	**856**	**840**	**- 5.6%**

During the Outlook period, total final consumption is projected to grow at an annual average rate of 1.7%, compared to 3.3% for

GDP. Again, gas is projected to be the most rapidly growing fossil fuel. Among all energy types, electricity is projected to grow the most quickly, at an annual rate of 3.4%. Despite electricity's rapid growth, gas will remain the most important fuel, accounting for 33% of total final energy consumption in 2020. The increased demand for gas is likely to arise primarily from industrial and heating end-uses.

Table 14.7: **Total Final Energy Consumption (Mtoe)**

	1995	2010	2020	1995 - 2020 Annual Growth Rate
Solid Fuels	109	119	121	0.4%
Oil	181	240	296	2.0%
Gas	232	332	428	2.5%
Electricity	102	169	233	3.4%
Heat	216	216	216	0.0%
Total	**840**	**1077**	**1295**	**1.7%**

Projections of total final energy consumption were prepared using GDP as the main economic variable with a fixed elasticity, which implicitly assumes that the structure of GDP remains unchanged, or continues to change in the future in much the same way as in the past. The difficulties associated with underestimating GDP in this region are well known, and the share of the service sector also tends to be underestimated. Since the service sector is generally less energy intensive than industry, a failure to record its growing share in GDP may have resulted in aggregate energy intensity being seriously over-estimated. Clearly, if the service sector's share of GDP increases faster than it has in the past, as the OECD expects it is likely to do, then some over-estimation of future energy consumption might also have occurred. The extent of this over-estimation will vary by country. In the case of Russia, its rich resource base means that it is likely to keep a high degree of heavy industry.

A factor restraining total final energy consumption in these countries is the low level of official per capita incomes which do not by definition take account of unrecorded income. Part of the unrecorded GDP will be increasingly included in official data between now and 2020 and this party explains the low GDP elasticity.

Table 14.8: **Per Capita Income Comparison (Based on Official Data)**

Transition Economies	1995	2010	2020
Population (millions)	395	395	396
GDP per Capita ($1990 and PPP per person)	3470	5430	7749
OECD Europe	**1995**	**2010**	**2020**
Population (millions)	466	472	468
GDP per Capita ($1990 and PPP per person)	14944	20774	24640

Figure 14.4: **Total Final Energy Consumption versus GDP (1990-2020)**

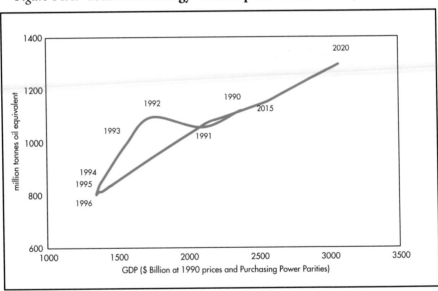

Stationary Sectors[2]

The general approach used in this Outlook to model the stationary sectors fossil fuel demands has been to model total energy demand and then to separately model individual fossil fuel shares. In the case of the OECD regions fossil fuel share equations have been used that include fossil fuel cross-prices. In the non-OECD regions a less formal approach has been adopted, mainly because of data difficulties. In these regions, such as the Transition Economies, a more judgmental approach has been adopted that takes into account information on domestic production of fossil fuels (availability) and transmission networks etc.

Table 14.9 indicates how total fossil fuel demand in the stationary sectors varied from 1990 to 1995. Coal, oil and gas all declined reasonably smoothly, but the heat series exhibited a marked increase in 1992 and so cannot be used for comparison purposes as some problems of data classification appear to exist.

Table 14.9: **Energy Consumption in Stationary Sectors (Mtoe)**

	1990	1991	1992	1993	1994	1995	1990 - 1995 Annual Growth Rate
Solid Fuels	171	140	149	143	117	109	- 8.6%
Oil	213	179	141	144	111	117	-11.2%
Gas	312	290	232	231	214	219	- 6.8%
Heat	140	142	274	263	236	216	9.0%
Total	**836**	**750**	**795**	**780**	**677**	**661**	**- 4.6%**

Figure 14.5: **Energy Consumption in Stationary Sectors versus GDP (1990-2020)**

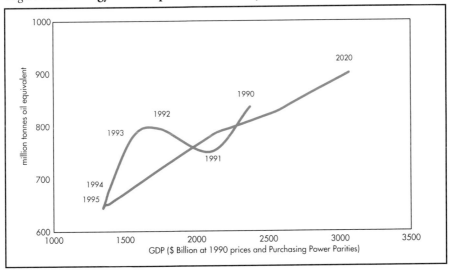

2. Note that in the case of this region, final consuming sector energy demand data are highly uncertain. For example, industry's use of oil for transportation has often been recorded as part of industry's energy demand rather than under transport. Undue weight should not therefore be applied to past movements in sectoral energy demand as they are sometimes the result of changing classifications rather than actual variations in energy demand.

Although energy demand in the stationary sectors is projected to increase from its 1995 trough, it is not expected to surpass its 1990 level until after 2010. Gas is projected to grow more quickly than the other fossil fuels reinforcing its dominant position in this sector. Consumption of heat, mainly in the form of district heating, is of major importance in this region.

The relationship between energy demand and GDP during the projection period is shown in Figure 14.5.

Table 14.10: **Energy Consumption in Stationary Sectors (Mtoe)**

	1995	2010	2020	1995 -2020 Annual Growth Rate
Solid Fuels	109	119	120	0.4%
Oil	117	142	165	1.4%
Gas	219	311	399	2.4%
Heat	216	216	216	0.0%
Total	**661**	**787**	**900**	**1.2%**

Mobility

As has already been noted, there are considerable problems with the region's transport sector energy consumption data, as it was common practice in the past to record industry's consumption of transport fuels under industry and not the transport sector. In any event, there is a clear downward trend in the Transition Economies' energy consumption. Some stabilisation of transport sector energy demand occurred in 1994-1995. Overall consumption in 1995 was still around half of its reported 1990 level.

Table 14.11: **Energy Demand for Mobility (Mtoe)**

	1990	1991	1992	1993	1994	1995	1990-1995 Annual Growth Rate
Transition Economies excl. Russia	77	49	53	45	39	38	-13%
Russia	77	128	124	53	37	39	-13%
Total	**154**	**177**	**177**	**97**	**75**	**77**	**-13%**

Given the difficulty in distinguishing between energy consumption in the transport sector and other final consumption sectors, projecting energy consumption in this sector is a particularly difficult task. While acknowledging these difficulties, the following chart presents the Outlook's energy projection for the Transition Economies' transport sector. Note that, as in the stationary sector, the transport sector's energy demand is not projected to exceed the 1990 level until well after 2010.

Figure 14.6: **Mobility versus GDP 1990 - 2020 (Mtoe)**

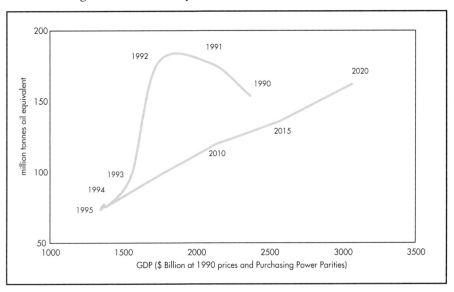

Energy demand in this sector is projected to grow at an annual average rate of 3%, slightly less than that of GDP (3.3%). Currently, car ownership levels in the region are low by OECD standards and so energy demand in this sector is likely to continue to expand for the foreseeable future.

Table 14.12: **Energy Demand for Mobility (Mtoe)**

	1995	2010	2020	1995 -2020 Annual Growth Rate
Total	77	120	162	3%

Electricity

Total final consumption of electricity has been shown in many countries to be correlated with economic activity.

Table 14.13: **Total Final Electricity Consumption (Mtoe)**

	1990	1991	1992	1993	1994	1995	1990-1995 Annual Growth Rate
Transition Economies excl. Russia	57	60	59	54	49	49	-3%
Russia	74	70	66	61	55	53	-6.5%
Total	**131**	**130**	**124**	**115**	**104**	**102**	**-4.9%**

Electricity consumption fell considerably less rapidly than GDP during the period 1990 to 1995 (4.9% versus 10.4% per annum), which suggests that some under-recording of GDP took place during this period. As with the transport sector's energy consumption data, there is some evidence of economic stability's having returned in 1994 and 1995.

During the projection period, total final consumption of electricity[3] is projected to grow at a rate slightly faster than that of GDP, 3.4% and 3.3% espectively. In the short term, electricity demand growth may be constrained by inadequate distribution networks and the small sizes of some apartments. In the longer term, electricity demand is likely to grow somewhat faster, as real incomes grow and the demand for electrical appliances increases. The total final electricity consumption projection is shown in Figure 14.7.

---

3. Table 14.7 gives details of the electricity demand projection.

Figure 14.7: **Total Final Electricity Consumption versus GDP (1990 - 2020)**

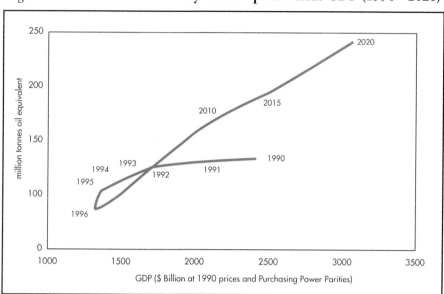

Power Generation

The Transition Economies have significant variations in their electricity output mix. Electricity generation in Poland and Kazakhstan is almost entirely based on coal; natural gas is the most significant source of power for Russia, Moldova, Uzbekistan and Belarus; Lithuania, Slovakia and Bulgaria generate large shares of their electricity from nuclear power; Tajikistan, Kyrgyzstan and Albania rely almost exclusively on hydropower. In aggregate, the region relies most heavily on coal and gas: in 1995 each accounted for about 30% of electricity production. The Russian Federation dominates the region, accounting for more than half electricity output.

Electricity generation in the region has been declining since 1990. In 1995, output had fallen to 1631 TWh, about the same level as in 1981, and some 28% lower than in 1990. Over the Outlook period, economic growth is assumed to resume and demand for electricity to grow at an average annual rate of 2.9%.

Installed capacity in the Transition Economies stood at 434 GW in 1995. Solid fuels accounted for 32% of total capacity, oil for 11%, gas for 28%, nuclear for 9% and hydro for 20%. The average utilisation factor was 43%, implying that there was substantial surplus capacity in the region, although the availability of most plants is low compared to that in OECD countries. Fossil-fired thermal plants, in particular, operate at low load factors (mid or peak load), since generation from nuclear and hydro has lower running costs and so there is an incentive to operate these plants as much as possible (base load). The surplus capacity is sufficient to meet some of the projected growth in electricity demand and this has been taken into account in the projection.

Over the Outlook period, a substantial increase in gas fired generation is projected, as gas supplies from Russia and the Caspian region (mainly Turkmenistan[4]) become increasingly available. The share of gas in the output mix is projected to increase from 30% in 1995 to 54% in 2020.

Table 14.14: **Electricity Generation in the Transition Economies (TWh)**

	1995	2020	1995-2020 Annual Growth Rate
Solid Fuels	498	770	1.8%
Oil	140	179	1.0%
Gas	487	1793	5.4%
Nuclear	216	181	-0.7%
Hydro	290	375	1.0%
Total	**1631**	**3298**	**2.9%**

Coal will remain an important fuel for electricity generation. Although it is projected to lose share to gas, coal increases in absolute terms from 498 TWh in 1995 to 770 TWh by 2020. Its share declines over the same period from 31% to 23%. Oil-fired generation, currently accounting for 9% of the total, is projected to increase at 1% per annum. Its share could fall to 5% of the electricity generation mix by 2020.

Nuclear power is assumed to increase to 2010 and to start declining afterwards, as several nuclear power stations are decommissioned in that period and capacity additions are not expected to keep pace with retirements. Current capacity is about 41 GW, most of it in Russia and Ukraine. By the end of the Outlook period, nuclear capacity in the region could be 29 GW.

4. *Caspian Oil and Gas,* IEA/OECD Paris, 1998.

Table 14.15: **Nuclear Power Statistics, 1995**

	Installed Capacity (GW)	Output (TWh)
Russia	19.9	99.5
Ukraine	12.1	70.5
Bulgaria	3.5	17.3
Lithuania	2.8	11.8
Slovakia	1.6	11.4
Slovenia	0.6	4.8
Armenia	0.4	0.3
Kazakhstan	0.1	0

Romania's first nuclear plant, the Canadian built Cernavoda-1 (660 MW), came on line in 1996. A number of reactors are under construction in the region. The following plants could be operational around the year 2000:

- the 2x388 MW Mochovce plant in Slovakia
- Khmelnitski-2 (950 MW) and Rovno-4 (950 MW) in Ukraine
- Rostov-1(950 MW), Kalinin- 3(950 MW) and Kursk-5 (925 MW) in Russia.

All of these are of Russian VVER design with the exception of Kursk-5 which is an RBMK type of reactor. More nuclear plants could be built in the longer term, although the ability to finance these projects remains uncertain. Russia has plans to build several reactors in Siberia and the Far East. Lack of funding for new plant may lead to an extension of the lifespan of some of the older reactors.

Hydropower in the region is assumed to increase at 1% per annum, bringing installed capacity from 88 GW currently to 104 GW by 2020. Part of the incremental capacity could come from upgrading existing plants.

Combined heat and power is widely used in the region, but the quality of the available data is poor and it is very difficult to make future projections. It is, however, widely reported that conversion efficiencies are low and losses high. Large scale CHP facilities could progressively be replaced by small-scale and more efficient gas-fired CHP plants.

Most of the coal used in the region is of low quality and has much higher ash and sulphur content than those considered to be economic in OECD countries[5]. In 1995, brown coal accounted for 37% of coal inputs to power stations compared with 18% in the OECD. In Poland, higher grades of coal are exported and only the lower grades are used for domestic consumption. Use of low-quality coal combined with an absence of environmental pollution control equipment has led to acute environmental pollution problems in Central & Eastern European countries, particularly acid rain. Some efforts have been undertaken by countries in the region to improve the environmental performance of coal-fired plants. Low NOx burners are being installed in Poland and there are plans to use them in Bulgaria and Romania; circulating fluidised bed combustion is being installed or planned in Poland and Romania; electrostatic precipitators are widely used, although they are often inefficient; several flue gas desulphurisation systems have been installed or are planned in Poland, Russia and Ukraine[6].

Electricity tariffs in the region are low compared with OECD countries, and, unlike the OECD, residential sector tariffs are lower than industrial tariffs[7]. An important problem is non-payment of electricity bills by customers (especially industrial and government bodies). Even the countries themselves are often unwilling or unable to pay for their electricity imports or imported fuel supplies to generate electricity. Such practices have left the power sector without sufficient working capital and investment funds.

Reform of the electricity sector will be necessary to finance adequate maintenance and growth and to ensure that electric utilities are financially viable. Such reforms will also be necessary in order to create a level playing field encouraging investment in existing and new assets and allowing greater competition. Most of the countries in the region have already started this process.

Fossil Fuel Supply

The individual chapters on oil, gas and coal describe the regional supply prospects for each of these three fuels. The following table presents the 1995 energy balance for the Transition Economies as a group.

5. *Air pollution control for coal-fired power stations in Eastern Europe,* IEA Coal Research, 1996.
6. op. cit.
7. *European Bank for Reconstruction and Development, Transition Report,* 1996.

Table 14.16: **Transition Economies Energy Balance 1995 (Mtoe)**

	Non-OECD Europe	FSU	Transition Economies
Indigenous Production	168	1204	1372
Imports	87	4	91
Exports	-36	-248	-284
Net Imports	*52*	*-244*	*-193*
Marine Bunkers	-1	0	-2
Stock Changes	1	9	9
TPES	**219**	**968**	**1188**

Source: *Energy Statistics and Balances of non-OECD countries 1994-1995,* IEA/OECD Paris, 1997.

Oil

Oil production is projected to recover from the sharp decline since the dissolution of the Soviet Union. In the short to medium term, the region's oil supply has the potential to recover more quickly than demand. In the longer term, rising domestic oil demand is likely to reduce net exports of oil.

Table 14.17: **Transition Economies Oil Balance - Million Barrels per Day**

	1996	2010	2020	1996 - 2020 Annual Growth Rate
Demand	5.5	7.2	8.5	1.8%
Supply	7.3	10.2	9.4	1.1%
Net Imports	**-1.8**	**-3.0**	**-0.9**	**-2.8%**

Chapter 7 discusses the many uncertainties surrounding the estimation of oil reserves and future oil production. These problems are particularly acute for the FSU, as Soviet oil reserve estimates included oil that is considered neither economically or technically recoverable and substantial quantities of unconventional oil.

Many Russian oil fields suffer from a lack of maintenance and investment. Future production from these fields is therefore heavily dependent on new expenditure on production facilities. Production from the largely untapped Caspian Sea area is currently hindered by limited export routes[8]. Only when the major problems in the Caspian Sea area have been settled, such as pipeline routes and sovereignty issues, is oil production likely to expand rapidly. The date by which these outstanding issues are likely to be settled is highly uncertain and so is therefore the future oil production profile from this province.

For the purposes of the BAU oil supply projection, Table 14.18 sets out the assumptions made for the region's oil reserves.

Table 14.18: **Transition Economies Conventional Oil Reserves (Billion Barrels)**

Cumulative Oil Production (end 1996)	134.1
Remaining Discovered Reserves (end 1996)	99.8
Undiscovered Oil Reserves (end 1996)	48.9
Additional Reservers from new technology and information	79.1
Ultimate Oil Reserves	361.9

Table 14.18 presents the Transition Economies ultimate oil reserves including the contribution made by new technologies and better information after 1996. The important point to note is that allowing new information and technologies to increase the level of oil reserves results in the region's ultimate oil reserves varying with time. It is the enhanced estimate of ultimate oil reserves of 361.9 billion barrels that determines the date at which the peak in the Transition Economies oil production will occur.

Total remaining recoverable oil reserves are of the order of 150 billion barrels. This is a large quantity, and further emphasises the point that infrastructure improvements (pipelines, maintenance and oil field investment) are a key factor in raising the region's oil production. With the exception of the Caspian area, the rest of the region is a mature province with average output per well less than 100 barrels per day. In such a context, close to the average of the US lower states, investment and technology deployment are likely to be the major determinants of the region's future oil production.

Gas

Gas production is also projected to increase during the period 1995 to 2020. Full details of the gas production projection for this

8. A recent IEA publication examines the Caspian Sea's future prospects in some depth, see *Caspian Oil and Gas,* IEA/OECD Paris, 1998.

region can be found in Chapter 8. Table 14.19 summarises the main features of the gas balance during the projection period.

Table 14.19: **Transition Economies Gas Balance 1995 - 2020 (Mtoe)**

	1995	**2010**	**2020**	**1995 - 2020 Annual Growth Rate**
Indigenous Production	585	809	1116	2.6%
Net Imports	-74	-162	-281	5.5%
TPES	**498**	**647**	**835**	**2.1%**

Gas exports rise by 5.5% per annum, mainly to meet OECD Europe's rising demand. The widespread introduction of CCGTs into OECD Europe's power generation sector and falling indigenous gas production in the region after 2010, provides the Transition Economies with a ready market for their substantial gas reserves. Exports of gas double as a percentage of total gas production, from under 13% in 1995 to over 25% by 2020. These large exports of gas together with huge oil exports, will provide the Transition Economies with the much needed hard currency revenue. These revenues are likely to provide a useful shelter under which the long-term restructuring of the region's economy can proceed.

Only a minority of countries in this region are likely to be net gas exporters, but several countries, such as Ukraine and Belarus, are expected to earn substantial revenues for allowing gas to pass through their territory to OECD Europe. In the longer term, the structure of gas exports from the region is likely to change, as Siberian exports will have to increasingly compete with large quantities of gas produced in the Caspian area. Currently Caspian gas exports are expected to enter OECD Europe via Turkey, rather than taking the northern Black Sea route, as the latter route would require Russian agreement to transport the gas. Such an agreement is unlikely to be easily forthcoming since Turkmen gas (for example) would be in direct competition with Russia's own gas exports. Furthermore, European gas consumers are likely to push for diversification in both their origin of gas and in its transport route. Currently, Turkmen gas is expensive when compared to imports into OECD Europe from Algeria and Russia, but this position could change toward the end of the projection period when both of these countries will be much higher up their gas supply curve than is currently the case.

Coal

The Outlook for coal production is highly uncertain. The FSU's coal reserves are the largest in the world, accounting for 23% of the world reserves. Coal production from the FSU, however, makes up a much smaller share of global output then its coal reserves would suggest, at just 8.5%. The region's future coal production will depend heavily on its ability to compete successfully in the international coal market. For this to happen, current restructuring plans in Poland, Ukraine and Russia must be successfully implemented. The current outlook for these restructuring plans is not good, and the region's coal exports are assumed, at best, to stabilise at current levels.

Comparisons with Other Organisations' Projections

Energy Demand

This section compares the Outlook's BAU energy projection with equivalent projections prepared by the United State Department of Energy and Energy Information Administration (USDOE)[9]. The European Union (EU) also produced a set of energy projections for this region in 1996, but the base year used in those projections was 1990 and not 1995. Given that for several fuels and end-uses the changes in demand that occurred from 1990 to 1995 are of a similar magnitude to that projected for 1995 to 2020 in the Outlook's projection, a direct comparison with the EU's projection is not possible. The USDOE projections are shown below.

Table 14.20: **Annual Growth Rates of Total Primary Energy Supply (1995 - 2020)**

	USDOE	IEA BAU
Solid Fuels	-0.6	0.7
Oil	2.2	1.4
Gas	2.4	2.1
Nuclear	0.5	-0.7
Hydro	2.1 *	1.0
Other Renewables	2.1 *	-1.5
Other Primary	2.1 *	0.0
Total	**1.7**	**1.5**

* The USDOE projection does not distinguish between these three different energies instead an "Other" category is shown.

9. *International Energy Outlook 1998 - With Projections Through 2020*, USDOE/EIA-0484(98), April 1998, Table A2, page 134.

At first sight, there would appear to be a number of differences between the two sets of energy projections. However, given the data problems and other uncertainties, these differences are not very significant. Both projections suggest total energy demand will grow by around 1.5% per annum. Both projections also show gas as the most rapidly growing fuel, followed by oil. Although the two projections predict different paths for coal and nuclear, the annual average growth rates are less than plus or minus 1%. In both projections nuclear and coal are largely stagnant during the projection period. "Other" fuels are dominated by hydro, according to IEA statistics. In the BAU projection, hydro increases from 25 Mtoe in 1995 to 32.3 in 2020, an annual average growth rate of 1%. If the USDOE's "other" fuels projection starts at 25 Mtoe in 1995 then it grows to 42 Mtoe by 2020. Given that both sets of projections suggest that TPES will exceed 1500 Mtoe in 2020 a difference of 10 Mtoe in the "other" fuels category is marginal.

The USDOE and IEA appear to be telling broadly similar stories about how the Transition Economies energy demand will develop during the period 1995-2020. Some differences do exist, such as the USDOE's higher growth rate for oil consumption, but these differences are small when measured against the huge uncertainties that surround the region's future.

Energy Supply

On the supply side, the USDOE publishes only oil production capacity projections. It is, however, highly unlikely that the Transition Economies will do anything but produce at full capacity, whether it be pipeline capacity or oil field capacity, and so a direct comparison with the BAU oil production projections is possible. The following table summarises the main features of the comparison.

The USDOE reference case projection is much more optimistic than the BAU projection on both demand and supply. In 2020, oil demand is 1.6 Mbd higher and oil supply 4.2 Mbd higher than in the BAU projection. Thus, even with higher oil demand, the USDOE expects oil exports to double between 1996 and 2020, although, as in the BAU projection, there is some decline in net exports after 2010, as increases in domestic oil demand start to outstrip oil production. An important consequence of the USDOE's oil production forecast is that oil exports remain at relatively high levels and this reduces the quantity of non-conventional oil that may be required to balance world oil demand and supply.

Table 14.21: **Transition Economies Oil Balance (Mbd)**

IEA -BAU	1996	2010	2020	1996 - 2020 Annual Growth Rate
Demand	5.5	7.2	8.5	1.8%
Supply	7.3	10.2	9.4	1.1%
Net Imports	**-1.8**	**-3.0**	**-0.9**	**-2.8%**
USDOE - Reference Case	**1996**	**2010**	**2020**	**1996 - 2020 Annual Growth Rate**
Demand	5.7	7.8	10.1	2.4%
Supply	7.4	12.5	13.6	2.6%
Net Imports	**-1.7**	**-4.7**	**-3.5**	**-3.1%**

While the Caspian Sea is effectively a new oil province, oil production in many other parts of the FSU is mature. On the basis of the oil reserves estimates used in the IEA's oil supply model, the FSU had already produced 37% of its ultimate oil reserves by 1997. The Hubbert Curve peak in the FSU's oil production occurs around 2012 in the BAU projection, when cumulative oil production surpasses 50% of ultimate oil reserves. Since the USDOE's oil production continues to expand beyond 2012 the USDOE must be assuming a higher level of remaining oil reserves, or else there is no link between oil production and oil reserves in the USDOE oil model. For example, the USDOE presents analysis for the Caspian Basin which shows that, while minimum expected oil reserves are only 32.5 billion barrels, there are another 186 billion barrels of potential resources[10]. It is important to note that potential resources have a much lower probability of actually being produced than proven reserves, because the former are based on seismic and other tests rather than actual drilling. When the USDOE's proven reserves and potential resources are added together, the result is in an estimate of total resources of

10. See page 34 of *International Energy Outlook 1998: With Projections Through 2020*, USDOE/EIA - 048(98).

218 billion barrels for the Caspian Basin. If such a large oil reserve estimate for the Caspian Basin is added to the estimated oil reserves for parts of the region, the USDOE's oil production forecast becomes feasible. Since, however, over 85% of the USDOE's Caspian Basin oil resources are potential, not proven, reserves, the USDOE's oil production forecast is likely to be towards the top of the range of possible oil production forecasts.

Summary

The central theme of this chapter has been uncertainty, both on the demand and supply sides of the energy balance. All the countries in this region have been undergoing fundamental changes in recent years. Trying to project energy demand and supply for these countries in 25 years time is not an easy task. The energy projections presented in this chapter should therefore be considered as work in progress and likely to change as the region develops and our knowledge base expands.

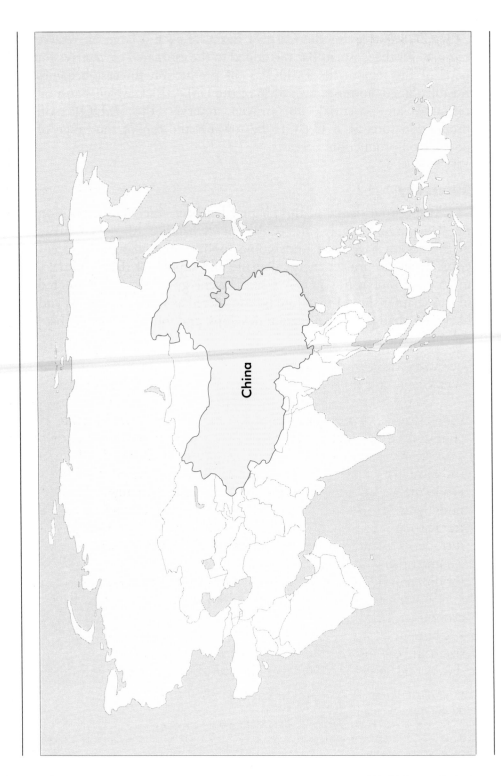

China

CHAPTER 15
CHINA[1]

Introduction

This chapter provides a summary of China's energy situation and examines likely energy developments over the period to 2020. The objective is to increase the understanding of China's energy system and its driving forces as well as to present the underlying uncertainties, rather than to forecast energy developments over the next 25 years. It is important to emphasise that the projections included in this chapter are based on a wide range of assumptions, some of which are made on relatively scarce information. Data on much of the Chinese energy system, and on important energy demand drivers, are rather poor or are available for a very limited period of time, making standard econometric analysis difficult. Problems also exist for the main macroeconomic indicators, especially GDP and its components.

Even without data problems, the dramatic changes in the Chinese economy and energy system over the past 15 years would make any standard econometric techniques inappropriate for deriving projections. In the past, energy consumption was allocated rather than individually chosen. Policy mechanisms and the behaviour of economic agents are in the process of substantial change. The model underlying the projections presented here is primarily an accounting framework. The main drivers are assumed activity levels. Deregulation introduces elements of market economies, like price signals. It is assumed that market reforms in China will continue. Price elasticities for different fuels/sectors are imposed throughout the Outlook period.

There are many reasons for China's growing importance in economic, energy and environmental terms. With a population of over 1.2 billion, China is the most populous country in the world. If the size of its economy is measured using purchasing power parities, it is the second largest economy in the world[2], after the United States.

1. In this Outlook, Hong Kong is included in China. Hong Kong became a Special Administrative Region of China in 1997.
2. The use of market exchange rates to make the comparison provides a significantly different picture. GDP calculated on a purchasing power parity approach is six times as large as that based on market exchange rates.

China is one of the largest trading economies, ranking fifth after the EU, the US, Japan and Canada. China is likely to become progressively more important if its economy continues to expand at or near recent rates. This will lead to increasing influence both in the Pacific region and in the world economy. Since China already accounts for more than a tenth of world carbon emissions, the way in which its growing energy needs will be met will be critical for its own and the world's environment over the next two decades and beyond. Table 15.1 highlights China's increasing significance in the world.

Table 15.1: **Importance of China in the World (Percentage of World Total)**

	1971	1995	2010	2020
GDP in PPP terms	3	12	17	20
Population	23	21	20	19
Primary energy demand (excl. CRW*)	5	11	14	16
Primary energy demand (incl. CRW*)	n.a.	12	14	16
Coal Demand	13	28	33	36
Oil Demand	2	5	8	10
Power Generation	3	9	13	15
CO_2 Emissions	6	14	17	19

* CRW - Combustible renewables and waste.

Given the specific nature of China's economy, the Asian financial crisis does not appear to have affected China as severely as elsewhere in the region. However, China has not been completely immune to its impacts. It is expected that the Asian crisis could cause a decline in foreign investment.

China's present level of primary energy consumption is equivalent to one-fifth of the OECD total and one-tenth of the world total. Its expected contribution to the increase in world energy consumption over the Outlook period will be very important. For example, the projected increase in China's energy consumption is expected to be equal to that of the OECD, and to account for almost a quarter of the increase in world demand, as shown in Figure 15.1.

Based on official Chinese statistics, its economic performance over the past 15 years has been impressive, not only because of the fast economic growth achieved, but also because of the relatively modest growth in its energy needs. Between 1981 and 1995, China's primary energy demand grew at more than 5% per annum, significantly less than the economic growth rate of over 9%. Such a decline in energy intensity is an achievement rarely accomplished in countries at this level of development. However, the reliability of country's official GDP statistics has been questioned. In the projections presented here, official GDP statistics have been used. The next section provides a discussion of the statistical measurement of China's GDP.

Figure15.1: **Shares in Incremental World Primary Energy Demand (1995-2020)**

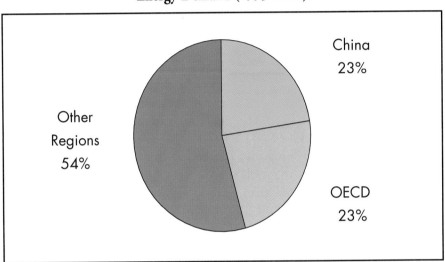

One of the key features of the Chinese economy is its large share of industry. This could be due to the political emphasis given to heavy industry up until the early 1980s. The share of industry in GNP in the last two decades did not change: it accounted for 48% in 1978, the same as now[3]. However, the share of agriculture in GNP dropped significantly, from 28% in 1978 to around 20% in 1995, and the share of the service sector grew from 24% in 1978 to 31% in 1995[4].

China is the second largest energy consuming country in the world behind the US. The most striking feature of the Chinese energy market is its extreme dependence on coal. In 1996, coal accounted for more than three quarters of primary energy supply and around two

3. For comparison, the share of industry in the GDP of OECD countries was around 40%, on average, in 1960 and has declined gradually to around 30% in 1995.
4. *China Statistical Yearbook,* State Statistical Bureau, China, 1996.

thirds of final commercial energy consumption. Oil accounted for about 20% with gas and hydro sharing the remainder. Final gas consumption in China is insignificant. This is used mostly for the production of chemicals and fertilisers. The share of electricity in final consumption, slightly higher than 10%, is low compared to other countries, reflecting the low stage of economic development in China. Nearly three quarters of electricity generation is from coal-fired plants with the bulk of the remainder coming from hydroelectricity.

These figures refer to commercial energy use. However, China is estimated to use about 206 Mtoe of non-commercial biomass energy. This currently represents about 19% of China's total primary energy demand. Biomass energy consumption is analysed at the end of this chapter and in Chapter 10.

A specific feature of the Chinese energy system is the uneven distribution of energy resources between regions. While major coal and oil resources are in the North, the main energy consuming regions are in the South. This underlines the crucial importance of the transportation network.

Energy prices in China are, in varying degrees, controlled by the government. Almost all fuel prices are significantly below full economic costs. Since the early 1980s, successive Chinese governments have introduced different measures to reform the energy pricing mechanism, but these efforts have been limited in scale. In June 1998, following the Asian financial crisis and the oil price fall, the State Council decided to link crude oil prices closely to the international price on a monthly basis.

China's GDP

A major uncertainty for energy analysis of China is the quality of China's GDP statistics. It is widely agreed that the figures published by China's statistical authorities underestimate China's GDP level and overestimate the GDP growth rate, at least in the last two decades.

Two recent studies, both launched by the OECD Development Centre, have produced new estimates of China's GDP using internationally accepted methodological approaches[5]. Both these reports aim at providing more accurate and internationally

5. *Measuring Chinese Economic Growth and Levels of Performance,* Angus Maddison, OECD Paris, 1997 and China's Economic Performance in an International Perspective, Ren Ruoen, OECD Paris, 1997.

comparable measures. Although the two authors do not use the same approaches, their findings are similar.

Maddison[6], along with a number of other authors, claims that official statistics tend to underestimate the level of national income in Chinese currency, mainly for the following reasons:

- The current Chinese national accounts remain a mixture of the old Material Production System (MPS) and the United Nations System of National Accounts (SNA). Official statistics for some service sectors are still weak.
- The national accounting system provides incomplete coverage of the national economy. Up to 1978, the Chinese national accounting system did not include non-productive services, such as banking and insurance and passenger transport, which are included in standardised national accounts of OECD countries.
- Agricultural value-added is understated.

Although some "non-material product" services have been included since 1987, the notion of comparable prices, which understates inflation, is still used to deflate national income in money terms in order to calculate growth rates in real terms. This means that inflation rates have been underestimated and real economic growth rates overestimated in official Chinese statistics.

Maddison (1997) re-estimates Chinese GDP using a different measurement technique, closer to western national accounting practice, and making use of 1987 weights. He comes to the conclusion that for the period of 1952 to 1978, his overall GDP measure records an average growth rate of 4.4% per year, compared with the official growth rate of 6%. For 1978 to 1994, these figures are 7.4% and 9.8% respectively. Similarly, Ren Ruoen (1997) made several calculations for China's GDP and found that applying a producer price index to official GDP for the period of 1986 to 1994, produces 6% growth rate instead of the official 9.8%. Applying ICP-based dollar series (United Nations International Comparison Project), he estimated GDP growth at 8.4%. A similar exercise with the ICOP (International Comparison of Output and Productivity) provided 7.3%, all significantly below the official figure. Strong growth rates in some industrial sectors suggest that costs, prices and

6. See, e.g., World Bank (1992), *China: Statistical System in Transition,* Washington, DC, and X.H. Wu (1993) The "Real" Chinese Gross Domestic Product (GDP) for the Pre-reform Period, 1955-1977, Review of Income and Wealth, Series 39, No. 1.

value-added have been declining as a result of economies of scale. If true, this could lead to even lower measures of economic growth.

Table 15.2: **Estimates of China's GDP ($Billion 1990 and PPP) and GDP per Capita ($ per person)**

	GDP	GDP per capita
Kravis	4 834	4 264
Summer and Heston (1993)	3 061	2 700
Ren and Kai (1993)	1 983	1 749
Ren and Kai (1994)	2 661	2 347
Taylor (1991)	1 286	1 135
Maddison (1997)	2 105	1 856
Official Statistics	1 830	1 614

Source: Maddison[7] (1995) and IEA calculations.

Impacts on Energy Analysis

The exceptionally rapid decrease of energy intensity of China has been questioned by several authors. Based on official figures, Chinese commercial energy intensity in the last 15 years has decreased by 5.6% per year on average. This trend contrasts with increases of 1.4% per year for India and 1.2% for the East Asia region. Empirical evidence shows that the "typical" energy intensity curve of a country increases during the development phase, then peaks and, after reaching a certain level of economic development, begins to fall. The opposite behaviour of energy intensity evolution in China has been explained as "unique" or "a result of statistical problems". Using the GDP estimates of Maddison (1997) for energy intensity calculations provides a "more typical" picture. As can be seen in Figure 15.2, the decline of energy intensity is less sharp. By using Maddison's figures, the average commercial energy intensity decline in the last 15 years falls to 3.4% per year. This dampens significantly the improvement in energy intensity officially claimed for China.

Alternatively, if one were to assume that the relationship between energy consumption and GDP in China were similar to that observed in other developing countries, then the implied GDP growth rates, based on actual consumption of electricity and primary energy, would be less than the official figures.

7. *Monitoring the World Economy 1820-1992*, Angus Maddison, OECD Paris, 1995.

World Energy Outlook

The same issue arises in the calculation of the income elasticity of energy demand, the main parameter determining long-term energy demand projections. Official statistics show an income elasticity of roughly 0.5, while for a developing country one would expect a value of around 1.

Figure 15.2: **Comparison of Energy Intensities Based on Official and Maddison GDP Figures (1978 = 100)**

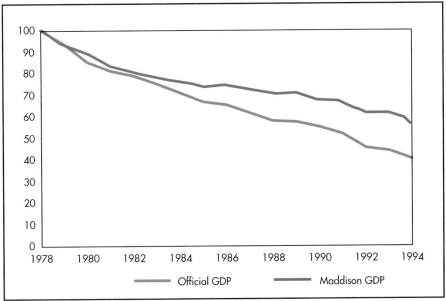

Although official GDP statistics are used for the projections presented here, the issue of the reliability of these figures represents a key uncertainty for this analysis.

In the business as usual case assumptions, the economy is projected to grow at 5.5% per annum from 1995 to 2020. The assumed GDP growth rates for China are consistent with official data and are higher than those assumed for any other region in this Outlook. If realised over the next 15 to 20 years, China would become the largest economy of the world in purchasing power parity terms. It is assumed here that policy reform will continue in China. As state-owned enterprises still dominate the Chinese economy, problems involved in transforming these enterprises and transferring them successfully to the private sector, as well as bottlenecks in many critical sectors of the economy, may dampen this assumed growth. It is assumed that China will be successful in limiting growth in population to an average of 0.8% per annum over the Outlook period.

Table 15.3: **Assumptions for China Region**

	1971	1995	2010	2020	1995-2020 Annual Growth Rate
Coal price ($1990 per metric ton)	44	40	42	46	0.5%
Oil price ($1990 per barrel)	6	15	17	25	2.1%
LNG price ($1990 per toe)	n.a.	126	141	210	2.1%
GDP ($Billion 1990 and PPP)	484	3404	8426	13123	5.5%
Population (millions)	845	1206	1372	1469	0.8%
GDP per capita ($1000 1990 and PPP per person)	0.57	2.82	6.14	8.93	4.7%

Energy Demand

Overview

Using the same methodology (i.e. extrapolating past GDP and related energy growth), primary energy demand in China is expected to grow at 3.6% per annum over the Outlook period. This increase is lower than historical growth rates (5.5% in the period 1971 to 1995). The difference can be attributed largely to slower economic growth. It is assumed that, as a result of increased liberalisation in many sectors, fuel prices will begin gradually to play a role in energy consumption decisions and slow energy demand growth. These assumptions lead to a further decline of energy intensity by 1.8% per annum on average.

In terms of total primary energy demand, solid fuels are expected to grow the slowest, at 3.1% per annum. As a result, the current 77% market share of solid fuels declines by about 10 percentage points by 2020, but solid fuels remain dominant. The main driver of solid fuel demand is power generation. Oil demand is projected to grow by 4.6% per annum, resulting in a significant market share increase by 2020. Gas is expected to grow very strongly, at 6.5% per annum, but its share of total primary energy demand remains limited. As discussed in the power generation section, in order to meet the high electricity demand growth, both nuclear and hydro power plants are expected to increase their shares in the primary energy mix. Over the

Outlook period, nuclear is expected to grow by 9.6% and hydro by 5.5% per annum.

Table 15.4: **Total Primary Energy Supply (Mtoe)**

	1971	1995	2010	2020	1995-2020 Annual Growth Rate
TPES	**239**	**864**	**1559**	**2101**	**3.6%**
Solid fuels	190	664	1087	1416	3.1%
Oil	43	164	355	506	4.6%
Gas	3	17	57	81	6.5%
Nuclear	0	3	19	33	9.6%
Hydro	3	16	39	62	5.5%
Other Renewables	0	0	2	3	-

Figure 15.3: **Total Primary Energy Supply**

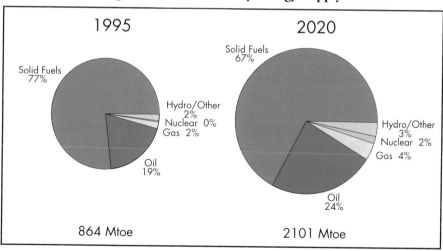

As shown in Table 15.5, total final consumption is projected to increase by 3.5% per annum to 2020. Electricity is expected to grow the most rapidly, followed by heat and gas. Final solids demand is projected to grow by only 2.4% on average, reflecting significant loss of market share in the industrial and residential/commercial sectors.

Table 15.5: **Total Final Energy Consumption (Mtoe)**

	1971	1995	2010	2020	1995-2020 Annual Growth Rate
TFC	**195**	**649**	**1145**	**1524**	**3.5%**
Solid Fuels	147	416	617	755	2.4%
Oil	37	132	280	395	4.5%
Gas	1	13	36	47	5.2%
Electricity	10	68	165	255	5.4%
Heat	0	19	46	71	5.3%

Stationary Sectors

As shown in Table 15.6, energy demand in stationary uses of fossil fuels is projected to increase at 3% per annum, more than doubling over the Outlook period. The main expected change in the residential/commercial sector fuel mix is the rapid penetration of oil and gas at the cost of coal. Partly for environmental reasons, official policy encourages the use of gas in residential areas. Gas networks already exist in many large cities, although much of the gas used is derived from coal. In rural areas, coal will continue to be the major fuel, increasingly substituting for non-commercial biomass. Future trends in residential/commercial energy demand will largely depend on: the speed of substitution of non-commercial fuels by commercial energy (mainly in rural areas); the increase in building space for both residential and commercial purposes; efficiency trends of new buildings and appliances; and the rate of appliance penetration, which depends in turn on growth in household disposable income.

The industrial sector in China accounted for about 66% of total final energy consumption in 1995, an unusually large proportion when compared with other countries. In the OECD, for example, the industry sector accounted on average for only 31%, while in the Republic of Korea the share of industry was around 47% in 1995. As for fuel mix, it is expected that, as in the residential/commercial sector, the coal share will decline and the oil and gas shares will grow.

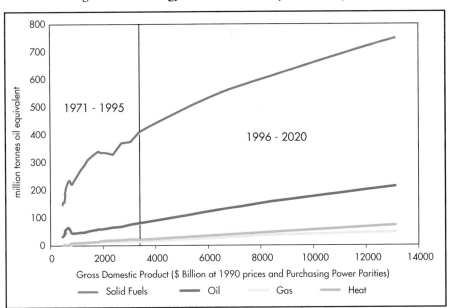

Table 15.6: **Energy Use in Stationary Sectors by Fuel (Mtoe)**

	1971	1995	2010	2020	1995-2020 Annual Growth Rate
Total	**179**	**521**	**850**	**1079**	**3.0%**
Solid Fuels	147	409	610	748	2.4%
Oil	31	80	157	213	4.0%
Gas	1	13	36	47	5.2%
Heat	0	19	46	71	5.3%

In preparing the projection of energy demand in the industrial sector, special attention was paid to the iron & steel and chemical industries, due to their combined share of total industrial fuel demand of about 50%. About 85% of energy consumption in the iron and steel industry is coal and oven coke. China appears to be one of the most steel-intensive countries in the world[8]. The Chinese steel industry uses, on average, one-

8. As with energy intensities, international comparisons of steel intensities are subject to severe interpretation and measurement problems. See the 1996 edition of the IEA's *World Energy Outlook* for a detailed discussion of energy demand in the iron & steel sector.

third more energy per tonne of steel than the US industry. Similarly, in the chemical industry, the use of coal as a feed stock in small-scale plants involves large inefficiencies. Future heat demand trends will be largely affected by the patterns of technological development in industry.

Mobility

China's energy demand for mobility is low, both in absolute terms and in comparison with the total energy used in the country. In 1995, energy used in transportation was 33% of total final energy demand in OECD countries and 23% in developing countries as a whole, but only around 9% in China[9]. The Chinese demand for mobility is projected to grow broadly in line with GDP over the Outlook period. As shown in Table 15.7, total demand for mobility is expected to grow at 4.8% per annum to the year 2020, more than tripling in this period. This expected growth is almost the same as the assumed increase average GDP per capita for the period.

Figure 15.5: **Energy Use for Mobility**

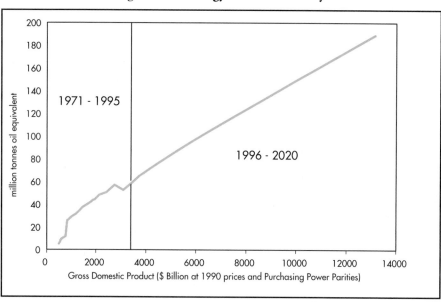

A key uncertainty for projections of mobility is the future increase in vehicle ownership in China. Currently, passenger vehicle ownership

9. Due to the methodology of data collection in China, the official numbers on oil consumption by the transportation sector, as reported by IEA Statistics, are very likely to be underestimated.

per 1000 people is about 3 compared with 27 for Thailand and 498 for Germany[10]. Official policies may play a role in affecting future private car ownership trends.

Table 15.7: **Energy Use for Mobility (Mtoe)**

	1971	1995	2010	2020	1995-2020 Annual Growth Rate
Total	6	59	130	190	4.8%

Electricity

China's electricity demand more than doubled in the last decade and is projected almost to quadruple by 2020. As shown in Figure 15.6, electricity demand rises linearly with income. It is expected that electricity demand will increase at 5.4% per annum over the Outlook period, almost equal to the assumed GDP growth rate. In 1995, about 68% of electricity was consumed in the industrial sector and 23% in the residential/commercial sector.

Figure 15.6: **Total Final Electricity Demand**

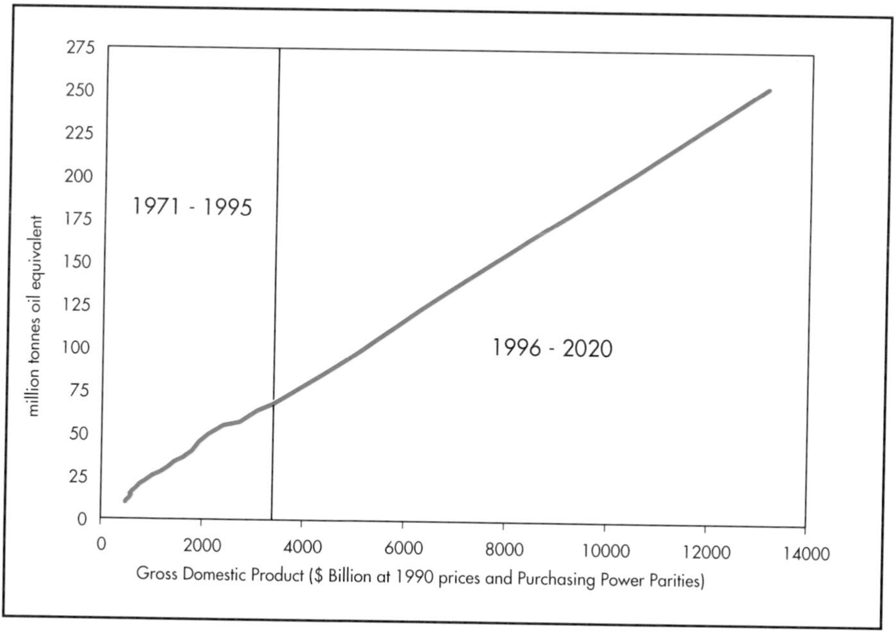

10. *World Road Statistics '98*, International Road Federation, 1998.

Table 15.8: **Total Final Electricity Demand (Mtoe)**

	1971	1995	2010	2020	1995-2020 Annual Growth Rate
Total	10	68	165	255	5.4%

As a result of technological innovation and an assumed shift in the industrial structure towards less energy intensive industries, it is expected that electricity will substitute for coal in many industries over the Outlook period. In the residential/commercial sector, energy demand growth will be increased by the further penetration of electrical appliances. As shown in Table 15.9, the level of electrical appliances has grown at high rates in the last decade, mainly as a result of increasing income levels. The penetration of refrigerators has increased by 10 times in urban households and about 50 times in rural households over the last ten years. The penetration of washing machines in urban households has grown to almost 90% in 1995 from less than 50% in 1985, and to 17% from 2% for rural households. Penetration ratios for television sets and electric fans are already beyond 100% in urban households, and more than 80% in rural households. Based on these past trends and expected strong growth in income per capita, it is very likely that penetration of many appliances will continue to grow and strongly affect the future trends of electricity demand. Only about 80% of the population is now connected to China's electrical grid so that continued electrification in rural areas over the Outlook period will be another factor for increasing electricity demand.

Table 15.9: **Ownership of Major Durable Consumer Goods per 100 Households**

	Urban			Rural		
	1985	1990	1995	1985	1990	1995
Washing Machines	48.3	78.4	89.0	1.9	9.1	16.9
Refrigerators	6.6	42.3	66.2	0.1	1.2	5.2
Television Sets	84.6	111.4	117.8	11.3	44.4	80.7
Electric Fans	73.9	135.5	167.4	9.7	41.4	89.0

Source: *China Statistical Yearbook,* State Statistical Bureau, China, 1996.

Supply

Power Generation

In 1995, electricity generation in China was 1036 TWh, three quarters of it from coal-fired plants. In the BAU projection, electricity generation grows at 5.4% per annum to reach 3857 TWh in 2020. In 1995, nearly a quarter of the output of electricity and CHP plants was heat. Demand for heat is projected to grow in tandem with electricity demand.

Table 15.10: **Electricity Generation in China (TWh)**

	1995	2010	2020
Solid Fuels	767	1729	2612
Oil	63	168	257
Gas	2	65	123
Nuclear	13	72	127
Hydro	191	457	726
Other Renewables	0	7	11
Total	**1036**	**2497**	**3857**

Installed electricity generating capacity in 1995 was 227 GW. Of this, 70% was coal-fired, 23% hydro, 6% oil-fired and the remaining 1% split among gas-fired and nuclear. During the past 6 years, annual additions to capacity have been on the order of 16 GW. These additions have helped reduce power shortages.

Over the Outlook period, total capacity is projected to increase by 530 GW. By 2020, installed capacity could reach 757 GW with 62% in the form of coal-fired facilities, oil maintaining its current share, nuclear and hydro increasing their shares to 3% and 26% respectively. Non-hydro renewable capacity increases in absolute terms, but its share of total capacity remains small; from 0.1% in 1995 it rises to 0.6% in 2020.

The enormous growth of electricity demand in China is expected to be met by its most abundant domestic resource, coal. The power sector is the second largest consumer of coal, after industry, taking about a third of coal production. The power sector will continue to rely on coal, although coal's share in the electricity generation mix is projected to decline to two-thirds, as some incremental demand for electricity is covered by nuclear and hydro plants. Electricity generation from coal is projected to increase at 5% per annum, from 767 TWh in 1995 to 2612 TWh in 2020. Inputs to power plants increase at a lower pace, due to efficiency improvements, at 4% per annum. By the end of the Outlook period, coal consumption by the power sector could reach 648 Mtoe, or about 45% of primary coal demand.

There are many problems associated with Chinese power plants, such as small unit size, inconsistent coal quality and low load factors due to low plant availabilities or lack of fuel. As a result, the average thermal efficiency of electricity generation in fossil fuel plants ranges between 27% and 29%, compared to around 38% in OECD countries. If heat output is included, then thermal efficiency in China is higher, around 41%.

Most coal plants in China are less than 300 MW in size. In recent years, with demand for electricity increasing rapidly, several units of 300 MW, and even 600 MW are being constructed. The larger units will eventually result in efficiency increases. There are also plans to retrofit or phase out some inefficient small plants. However, acute electricity shortages mean that small and medium size plants are still built, and older plants are kept in service. If this practice persists, efficiency is likely to remain low. If efficiency were to remain at present levels, coal consumption by 2020 would be 25% higher and CO_2 emissions would be 10% higher than projected.

China has extensive hydro-electric resources, about 675 GW, of this amount 290 GW are economically exploitable. In 1996, hydro-power capacity stood at 56 GW and is assumed to reach almost 200 GW by 2020. The most significant hydro project is the Three Gorges, on the Yangtze River. When completed, in about 2010, it will have a capacity of 18200 MW, from 26 generators with 700 MW each. Construction started at the end of 1994. The Yangtze River, the third longest river in the world, was diverted from its natural course in November 1997, to clear the way for the construction of the world's biggest dam - 185 metres high and 1.6 kilometres wide. The project has raised various concerns, both in China and internationally. It could disturb the ecosystem in the region, it would force more than a million people to be relocated and it would submerge archaelogical monuments.

Small increases in gas-fired capacity, particularly in coastal regions and the south, could raise gas-fired generation to 123 TWh by 2020. There are many uncertainties about natural gas use in the power sector, as priority is given to the residential sector and to the petrochemical industry, mainly for fertiliser production. There have been discussions on LNG projects, particularly in southern and eastern China, where natural gas could compete with nuclear. Examples are a 5 GW project in the Yangtze River Delta and a 8x330 MW complex in Shenzen province. China is also developing its own combined cycle gas turbine technology. In general, imported LNG is likely to remain a high-cost form of generation over the Outlook period.

Oil-fired generation is projected to maintain a share of 6% to 7% in the electricity generation mix. In absolute terms, it is projected to increase from 63 TWh in 1995 to 257 TWh by 2020. Oil could be preferred for new power generation in some cases, particularly in coastal areas; an example is the Zhenhai combined-cycle power plant, near Shanghai.

China's first nuclear plant became operational in 1991. This is a 300 MW pressurised water reactor (PWR) of Chinese design with about 70% of its components coming from Chinese sources. The plant is located at Qinshan, south of Shangai, and provides electricity to Shanghai and three eastern provinces. The second nuclear plant is the 2x900 MW Daya Bay complex, near Hong Kong, which absorbs about 70% of the plant's output. Construction began in 1987; the first unit was commissioned in 1993 and the second in 1994. There are four plants under construction. China plans to develop its own advanced nuclear reactors such as the AC-600 PWR. Official plans call for 20 GW of nuclear capacity by the year 2010 and 40 to 50 GW by 2020. The most ambitious of China's nuclear projects is the Yangjiang power complex, 250 km southwest of Hong Kong. The plant, currently under feasibility study, would be the country's largest, with six 1000 MW units. The end of the US ban on trade in nuclear material with China, in Spring 1998, could encourage the development of nuclear power in China.

In the medium term, four new plants are expected to be built, as shown in Table 15.11. Construction of the second phase of Qingshan, with two generators of Chinese design, started in June 1996. Qingshan Phase 3 will have two CANDU-6 pressurised heavy water reactors; construction has started. The third plant is at Lingao, near Daya Bay and will have two PWRs supplied by Framatome. The fourth plant, will have two VVER-1000 reactors, supplied by Russia.

Table 15.11: **Committed Nuclear Projects in China**

Plant Name / Location	Capacity (MW)
Qingshan - Phase 2	2 x 600
Lingao	2 x 1000
Qingshan - Phase 3	2 x 700
Lianyungang	2 x 1000

Given that nuclear is a capital-intensive option - with costs about three times more per kW than a Chinese-manufactured coal plant - and that long lead times are required to build a nuclear plant, it is assumed in the BAU projection that nuclear capacity in China will be 11 GW in 2010 and 20 GW in 2020.

China has abundant renewable energy resources. The development of alternative energy technologies can be economic in some areas, particularly in remote, off-grid locations. Renewable energy development is given priority in many provinces and is often included in rural electrification programmes.

Wind power has the largest potential to contribute to electricity supply, and its development has been given priority by the Chinese government. Small wind turbines are already manufactured domestically. China's wind resource potential exceeds 250 GW; sites where wind speed is high and which therefore are suitable for exploitation, are located in the coastal areas and islands off south-eastern China and in north-west China and inner Mongolia. In the coastal areas, where demand is growing fast, medium- to large-scale generators could be developed that would generate electricity in parallel with diesel engines. In the northwest, where population density is low, the emphasis is more on domestic use of small-scale wind turbines.

Grid-connected capacity in 1994 was 32 MW; in 1997 it had reached 217 MW. At the end of 1994, there were more than 140 000 small-scale wind turbines (50 to 50 000 W) with a capacity of 17 MW. There are two different estimates of how much wind power capacity will be installed in the short to medium term: the State Planning Commission calls for 400 to 500 MW by 2000 and 1000 to 1100 MW by 2010. The Ministry of Power targets 1000 MW by 2000 and 3000 MW by 2010. It is assumed in the BAU projection that wind capacity in China will increase to 2 GW in 2010 and 4 GW in 2020.

Photovoltaic cells are used to provide electricity for isolated areas. Current PV capacity (off-grid) is 5 MW. There are a number of plans for further use of off-grid PV, and the government plans an additional 30MW by 2000. There are areas with high-temperature geothermal potential in Tibet, Yunnan and Sichuan, with a theoretical resource potential of 6.7 GW. However, the majority of this potential is in the sparsely populated area of Tibet, so large expansion of geothermal is unlikely. Geothermal capacity at the end of 1994 was 30 MW. Biomass is used in small-scale applications. There is potential for using bagasse for power generation by the sugar industry in south-coastal regions.

As with other developing countries, there is much uncertainty about funding to finance new power projects. New growth in capacity is expected to be financed both by local and by foreign investment. This can be achieved by introducing wholly-foreign-owned plants, by raising funds through international financial organisations, by foreign government loans and by Chinese and foreign joint ventures. Foreign investment in China's power sector is now about 10% of the total and the government seeks to increase that to 20%. China's first private sector Build-Operate-Transfer (BOT) project was the Guangxi Laibin B Plant. Foreign investment projects, however, are often faced with difficulties, such as difficult bureaucracy or insufficient rates of return.

Coal

China's coal resources are variously estimated at 1-4 trillion tonnes, second in the world to Russian resources. China has 115 billion tonnes of proven reserves, a figure which places China third in the world after the US and Russia, with about 11% of world reserves. While China's overall reserves are large, the proportion of them to a depth of 150 metres is relatively small. The bulk of reserves available over a 20-year time period at present rates of production, are located at depths of 150 to 300 metres, and between 300 and 600 metres beyond that period. Most of these reserves are located in relatively remote areas in the north-central part of eastern China, especially in Shaanxi, Shanxi, Henan and Shandong provinces.

China is the world's largest producer of coal and the percentage contribution of China to world production has been growing steadily. In 1996, total Chinese production reached around 1.4 billion tonnes, and accounted for 37% of total world production. This represents more than a doubling of the 620 million tonnes produced in 1980.

The pattern of coal production in China has altered significantly over the last 40 years. The north and east of the main coal belt were formerly the main production areas, but the focus is now on the coal fields of Shanxi, Shaanxi and Inner Mongolia.

Chinese coal exports were about 29 million tonnes in 1996, representing some 6% of total world coal exports. The north Asian region is the principal market for Chinese coal, with Japan and Korea each receiving about one-quarter of total exports. China and Japan have a long-term trade agreement for the export of steam and coking coal. Chinese coal exports are 2% of total Chinese coal production.

As the world's largest producer and already a significant exporter, China's performance could have implications for the world market, depending on future trends in domestic production, imports and exports. There are many features about the Chinese coal industry which differ from that of any other major player. The level of uncertainty about China's future role in world markets is heightened by the role the government plays in the Chinese industry. It is hard to predict the outcome of policies designed to achieve non-commercial objectives such as self-sufficiency and regional development. China's trade position will depend on the balance between internal demand and supply - the country could turn out to be either a net importer or a net exporter. There may be government pressure to earn foreign exchange from coal exports by encouraging coal production or limiting its domestic consumption. The overriding determinant of the outcome will be the extent to which China embraces market principles in the management of its coal industry and whether the industry remains under state or municipality control or private participation is progressively involved. It is assumed in this Outlook that, while China's export capacity could increase from the current level, the strong domestic pressures on demand and the already overburdened transportation system are unlikely to allow Chinese net exports to rise substantially above present levels.

Oil

China has only recently become a major oil producer, with production increasing from around 0.5 million barrels per day in 1970 to 3.2 million barrels per day in 1997. Almost 90% of China's oil is produced onshore. Nearly one third of it comes from the Daqinq field which currently produces slightly more than 1 million barrels a day. While there are many prospective and unexplored areas in China, the longer-term oil production outlook depends to a large extent on the geologic potential and the timing of development of the remote Tarim basin. The potential of this basin has been recognised for some time, but its exploration and development have been slow. Estimates of potential reserves in the Tarim basin vary from as little as a few billion barrels to upwards of 80 billion barrels. However, the initial experiences of foreign oil companies in the Tarim basin have not been very encouraging.

Chinese reserve estimates are extremely uncertain in general. As discussed in Chapter 7, the oil supply projections in this Outlook are based on remaining discovered reserves of 29.5 billion barrels. This matches a conservative view of the development of Chinese oil production. Production grows till around 2010 and then declines to about 2 million barrels per day by 2020.

Figure 15.7 compares expected oil production and demand. The gap between domestic production and demand widens, especially after 2010. It is projected that China will be importing more than 8 million barrels a day by 2020, making it a major importer in the world oil markets. In comparison, projected net imports of the OECD Pacific region by 2020 are 7.6 million barrels per day.

Figure 15.7: **Domestic Supply and Net Oil Imports in China**

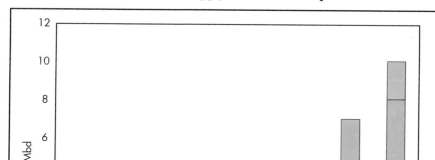

Gas

While natural gas production in China grew strongly throughout the 1960s and 1970s with the discovery of large fields in the Sichuan province, it remains a marginal fuel within the Chinese energy system as it is mostly used as a feedstock for the fertiliser industry. In recent years, gas has suffered from production cutbacks, and current production levels are low relative to the potential reserves base. The current Five Year Plan foresees an annual production target of 25 billion cubic metres of natural gas by 2000 and close to 30 billion cubic metres by 2005.

Biomass

Current Patterns of Biomass Energy Use

Estimates of China's current biomass energy consumption vary greatly, ranging from approximately 170 to 280 Mtoe. For the purposes of this report, an average estimate of 206 Mtoe was calculated as an average of the most reliable sources. This implies that, in 1995, biomass accounted for 19% of China's primary energy consumption, 24% of total final energy consumption, 28% of total energy in stationary uses, and approximately 60 to 70% of rural household energy use.

China's total biomass use (in absolute terms) is the highest in the world, accounting for 20% of the world's biomass primary energy supply and 36% of that of Asia. There are around 800 million people and half a million rural enterprises using biomass energy[11].

Virtually all biomass energy in China is used in rural areas, where approximately 70% of the population lives[12]. The rural sector includes rural households, agricultural activities and town and village enterprises (TVEs). No data are available on the shares of end-uses of biomass, but it can reasonably be assumed that the major portion of biomass is used in households. It is often difficult to separate household uses (cooking, water and space heating) from agricultural uses (like cooking of pig feeds). Data for biomass used in TVEs are

---

11. *Rural Energy Resources: Applications and Consumption in China,* Fang Zhen, China Center for Rural Technology Development, State Science and Technology Commission, Energy Sources, Vol.16, 1994.

12. According to a 1989 study, in 1985, the share of biomass in total energy consumption by urban households was only 1%, while it was 79% in the rural household sector (REDP, *Sectoral Energy Demand in China,* REDP/UNESCAP/UNDP/GOC/GOF, 1989). The major fuel in urban households is coal, which is also the second most used fuel in rural households.

unavailable, but it has been estimated to amount to less than 10% of household biomass fuel use[13].

Regional differences in total rural energy use, and thus in biomass energy use, are significant. In the northern parts of the country, heating requirements are substantial and may involve as much fuel use as cooking. In the southern and central areas, cooking of pig feed in rural homes is a major use of energy, often accounting for a larger share of energy use than the preparation of family meals.

Fuelwood and agricultural residues (straw and stalks) each account for roughly half of total biomass energy use. At present, most biomass is directly burned in low-efficiency energy devices. There is no charcoal production, mainly because of the availability and extensive use of coal briquettes in the household sector.

Past Trends

China's rural areas have undergone substantial change since market reforms were initiated in the late 1970s. In most areas, the 1980s marked a major shift away from subsistence farming towards a more commercialised and industrialised rural economy, which in turn led to significant changes in the rural energy mix. The exact magnitude of these changes is difficult to judge due to the lack of consistent data series. According to figures published by the Ministry of Agriculture, between 1979 and 1989 biomass energy use increased by 24% in absolute terms. However, its share in total rural energy declined from 72% in 1979 to 51% in 1989. Another source indicates that in 1995 this share had further declined to 29%[14].

The major reason for these changes has been the rapid development of town and village enterprises, which use mainly conventional fuels. The share of conventional energy used by households also increased from 14% in 1979 to 20% in 1989, and it can be assumed that this trend has continued in the early 1990s[15]. Surveys indicate that higher rural incomes have meant more sophisticated demands for energy services, with a gradual shift to

13. e.g. for tea and tobacco drying, for pottery firing and heating hothouses. ESMAP, *Energy for Rural Development in China: An Assessment Based on a joint Chinese/ESMAP Study in Six Counties*, Report No. 183/96, World Bank, 1996.
14. Cui Shuhong, *Biomass Energy for Rural Development in China*, in IEA, *Biomass Energy: Data, Analysis and Trends*, Workshop Proceeding, forthcoming.
15. Cui Shuhong gives a figure of 39% in 1995.

higher-quality fuels and more efficient and convenient devices. In most cases, this implies a substitution of biomass fuels by conventional fuels, mainly coal[16].

Projections

It is expected that observed past trends in biomass energy use will continue over the Outlook period. Although there are substantial programmes aimed at promoting the efficient and sustainable use of biomass[17], the ongoing shift to higher-quality fuels resulting from increasing per capita incomes, combined with the adoption of more efficient firewood stoves, will most likely result in a decline of average per capita biomass use, from 170 kgoe per person now to approximately 150 kgoe in 2020. However, due to population growth, the total amount of biomass consumed is expected to increase, from 206 Mtoe in 1995 to 224 Mtoe in 2020. This represents a small annual growth rate of 0.3% on average, compared with 3.6% for conventional primary energy fuels. As a result, the share of biomass in total primary demand is projected to decline from 19% in 1995 to 10% in 2020. Figure 15.8 below summarises the biomass projections for China. The assumptions and methodologies are given in Chapter 10.

Including biomass in the total energy picture has many implications for energy analysis. Not only will the level of energy intensity be affected, but so also will its overall trend. Since biomass is generally used in a very inefficient way, the substitution of biomass by conventional fuels will result in a gain of overall energy efficiency. In the case of China, this is reflected in a more rapidly decreasing energy intensity curve. The inclusion of biomass gives a more realistic picture of actual energy demand and energy mix, allowing more realistic and effective policy decisions.

16. Consumer preferences are complex; in some areas, they prefer to use coal briquettes, instead of firewood or straw, if they can afford them. However, in other relatively wealthy areas, such as in the southern Jiangsu province, farmers still prefer to use straw for cooking, partly because of its relative speed and ease of ignition compared with briquettes.
17. Such as the on-going promotion of biogas digesters, the development of new fuelwood plantations to overcome local fuelwood shortages and the dissemination of more-efficient cooking stoves.

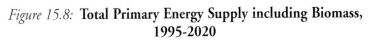

Figure 15.8: **Total Primary Energy Supply including Biomass, 1995-2020**

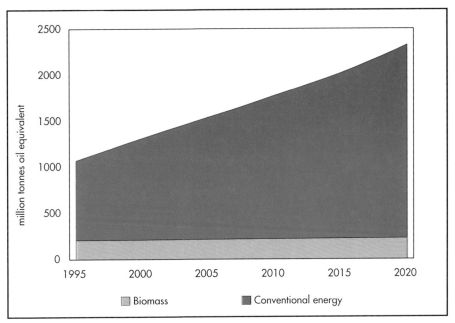

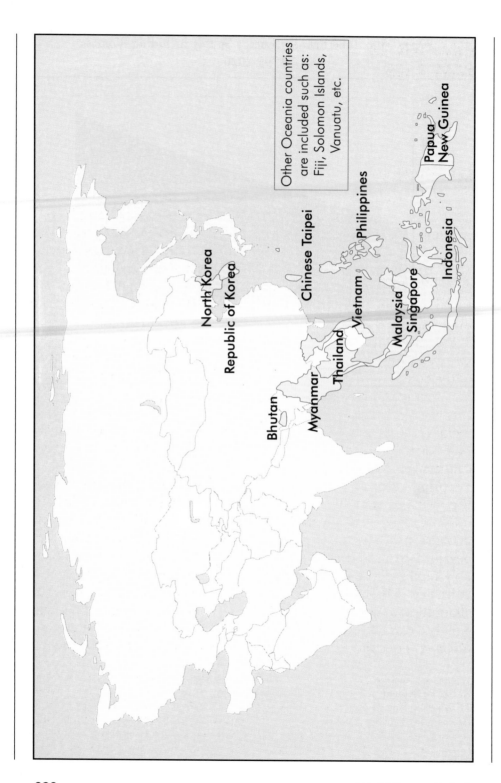

Other Oceania countries are included such as: Fiji, Solomon Islands, Vanuatu, etc.

North Korea

Republic of Korea

Chinese Taipei

Philippines

Vietnam

Thailand

Myanmar

Bhutan

Malaysia

Singapore

Indonesia

Papua New Guinea

CHAPTER 16
EAST ASIA

Introduction

East Asia[1] is of particular importance for the evolution of long-term global energy demand because of the region's rapid economic growth. It includes the maturing industrial economies of the Republic of Korea, Chinese Taipei and Singapore, as well as countries such as Malaysia, Thailand and Indonesia that are continuing a process of economic development and greater integration with the world economy, and countries such as Vietnam that are on the threshold of development. The region's GDP growth rate has averaged 7% over the last three decades, higher than any other region. The average, however, disguises particularly high rates of growth in some of the best performing countries, especially over the last 5 to 10 years. For example, the Republic of Korea's, annual growth exceeded 8% between 1980 and 1995. In Thailand, it was 10% between 1985 and 1995. As a result, per capita incomes in some of the more advanced East Asian economies, such as Singapore and Chinese Taipei, are now comparable with those in some OECD countries.

Most of the countries in the region have taken steps to liberalise their economies, including measures to open foreign trade and improve investment regimes, reduce subsidies and fiscal deficits, privatise state enterprises and control inflation. While some countries began the process more than a decade ago, others have undertaken it only recently. The general result has been increased competition and efficiency, although the recent financial crisis has raised questions about the allocation of capital. Much of the impetus to growth in East Asia has come from the development of a broadly based and export-oriented industrial sector. The share of industry in GDP has increased

---

1. East Asia includes the following countries: Brunei, Indonesia, Malaysia, Myanmar, North Korea, Philippines, Singapore, the Republic of Korea, Chinese Taipei, Thailand, Vietnam, Afghanistan, Bhutan, Fiji, French Polynesia, Kiribati, Maldives, New Caledonia, Papua New Guinea, Samoa, Solomon Islands, and Vanuatu. Please note that the following Asia and Oceania countries have not been considered due to lack of data: American Samoa, Cambodia, Christmas Island, Cook Islands, Laos, Macau, Mongolia, Nauru, Niue, Pacific Islands (US Trust), East Timor, Tonga and Wake Island.

substantially across the region, approaching 40% in some of the more developed economies, while that of agriculture has declined. In those countries where industrialisation commenced earliest and has been deepest - the Republic of Korea, Chinese Taipei, and Singapore - a combination of rising wages and tight labour markets has driven the transition from labour-intensive manufacturing to activities with higher value added and higher levels of capital and technology. In other countries, such as Malaysia and Thailand, the manufacturing sector is still largely based on labour or material resources, but similar pressures will be felt there in time, leading to changes in the composition of the region's production and trade.

Figure 16.1: **Average GDP Growth and 1995 GDP Per Capita**

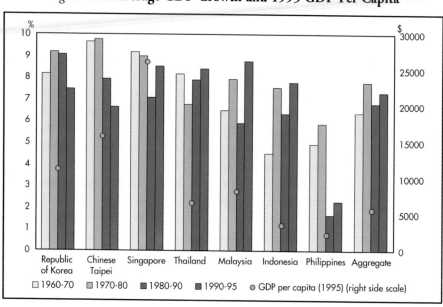

A key uncertainty in the projections presented in this Outlook is the future sustainability of such high economic performance. The recent financial crisis in the region casts shadows over future economic growth, at least in the short- to medium-term.

Table 16.1: **Economic and Population Data for Selected East Asian Countries**

	GDP		Population		GDP per Capita
	1995 ($ Billion 1990 and PPP)	Growth Rates (1985-95) (annual, %)	1995 (millions)	Growth Rates (1985-95) (annual, %)	1995 ($ 1000 1990 and PPP per capita)
Republic of Korea	507	8.8	45	0.9	11.3
Indonesia	677	7.4	193	1.7	3.5
Chinese Taipei	337	7.9	21	1.1	15.8
Thailand	380	9.4	58	1.3	6.5
Malaysia	165	7.7	20	2.5	8.2
Regional Total	**2462**	**7.3**	**583**	**1.8**	**4.2**

Table 16.2: **Energy Demand in Selected East Asian Countries, 1995 (Mtoe)**

	Total Primary Energy Supply				Total Final Consumption	
	Total	Coal	Oil	Gas	Total	Electricity
Republic of Korea	145	28	90	9	114	14
Indonesia	86	6	42	35	48	4
Chinese Taipei	65	17	33	4	44	9
Thailand	52	7	35	10	37	6
Malaysia	33	2	20	11	22	3
Regional Total	**464**	**84**	**264**	**76**	**316**	**42**

Box 16.1: **Asian Financial Crisis**

The severe pressures on foreign exchange markets in many East Asian countries in late 1997 have accentuated internal financial strains and contractionary pressures on economic activity. The crisis has been largely contained, till now, and most of the currencies have regained some of the ground lost during the crisis. But interest rates remain high compared with a year ago and most equity markets are still depressed. Adverse terms of trade, declines in private sector net worth, increases in the cost of capital, and, in the worst cases, major credit limitations are exerting powerful downward pressures on domestic demand. Banks are experiencing financial strains that are likely to worsen as the economic downturns continue.

In the region as a whole, a marked slowdown in economic activity is increasingly evident. The OECD Secretariat projects economic growth of 0.1% in 1998 for the group of Dynamic Asian Economies (Indonesia, Hong Kong, Malaysia, the Philippines, Singapore and Chinese Taipei), compared to the 6.2% in 1996. In the Republic of Korea, the economy is expected to contract in 1998 (-0.2%, compared to a 7.1% in 1996), reflecting a sharp decline in domestic demand and investment.

The repercussions of the financial turmoil on the economies of the East Asian region will continue for some time yet. The economic turndowns are likely to be severest in those countries where currency depreciations have been greatest. In most of these East Asian countries, recovery may not begin before 1999, and it could take longer in the most severe cases.

The impact of the financial difficulties in the East Asian countries began to hit the energy markets, and particularly the oil market, toward the end of 1997 and carried over into the first half of 1998. The impact on global oil demand is estimated to be on the order of 500 thousand barrels per day in 1998[2]. The pace of economic recovery in the region will determine the future pattern of oil demand in these countries.

In line with rapid economic growth, energy demand in the region has grown strongly over the past quarter century. Between 1971 and 1995, total primary commercial energy demand increased at an average annual rate of 6.8%, very close to regional GDP growth. Energy demand more than quadrupled in absolute terms, from 96 Mtoe to 464 Mtoe. This was a faster rate of growth than that experienced in any other region and resulted in East Asia's share of global energy demand increasing from 1.9% to 5.6%. More importantly, the region accounted for about 11% of world incremental energy demand. As shown in Table 16.2, the major energy consumers in the region are the Republic of Korea, Indonesia and Chinese Taipei, where the industrial sector has been the strongest.

2. *Oil Market Report*, IEA, July 1998.

Together, these three countries accounted for over half of East Asian energy demand in 1995. Along with industrialisation, the shift from non-commercial to commercial energy sources, the development of rural electrification and the growing demand for transport services have been the chief motors driving growth in energy consumption.

As shown in Figure 16.2, oil is the dominant fuel in the total primary commercial energy supply of the region. Its share remained broadly constant since 1971. The absolute increase in East Asia's oil consumption accounted for about 24% of world incremental oil demand. Coal's share halved, from 36% in 1971 to 18% in 1995. Natural gas was the fastest-growing source of primary energy over the period, although from a low base. This followed discoveries of large indigenous gas reserves in some countries in the 1970s and the subsequent development of LNG import infrastructure in others, principally the Republic of Korea and Chinese Taipei. The rapid development of the nuclear programme in these two countries also led to an increase in the nuclear share of primary energy demand to 6% by 1995. These figures refer only to commercial energy types. Non-commercial biomass plays an important role in the regional energy supply/demand balance.

Figure 16.2: **Total Primary Energy Supply**

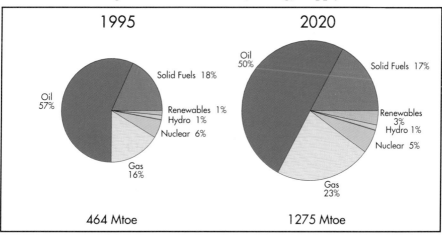

The aggregate commercial energy intensity of the region has declined slightly in the last two decades. This trend is dominated by the two largest economies, the Republic of Korea and Chinese Taipei. In most other countries, intensities have actually increased. This slight fall in energy intensity has been achieved against a background of rapid industrialisation and rising per capita incomes. In the higher income economies, structural change has also favoured the services sector which, except for its transport component, lowers national energy intensities. In the Republic of Korea and Chinese Taipei, there has been a downward trend in the energy intensity in the iron & steel and chemical industries, which together account for almost 60% of industrial energy demand. When non-commercial biomass use is included, the declines in energy intensity experienced over the recent past become more pronounced than those calculated on the basis of commercial energy alone.

In the BAU projection, GDP is assumed to grow significantly slower than over the preceding two decades. As shown in Table 16.3, East Asian economic growth of 4.5% is assumed, compared with 7% in the past three decades. The assumed slowdown reflects the maturing of the larger economies in the region and the impact of the Asian financial crisis. The population growth rate is also assumed to slow from its present level to an average of 1.2% between 1995 and 2020. Together, the population and economic growth assumptions imply that there will continue to be substantial increases in incomes in the region, averaging 3.3% per year to 2020. On this basis, regional per capita income would be about $ 9500 (at 1990 prices and PPP) by the end of the forecast period. As for energy prices, historical series on fuel types in most countries of the region is unavailable or poor. International trends are, therefore, taken as proxies for the growth of end-use prices in the region. Prices for oil products are assumed to follow international crude oil prices. Similary, the coal price follows assumed international prices and the LNG price follows the Japanese LNG import price.

Table 16.3: **Economic Assumptions**

	1971	1995	2010	2020	1995-2020 Annual Growth Rate
Coal Price ($1990 per metric ton)	44	40	42	46	0.5%
Oil Price ($1990 per barrel)	6	15	17	25	2.1%
LNG Price ($1990 per toe)	n.a.	126	141	210	2.1%
GDP ($Billion 1990 and PPP)	499	2462	4879	7404	4.5%
Population (millions)	360	583	710	778	1.2%
GDP per Capita ($1000 1990 and PPP per person)	1.4	4.2	6.9	9.5	3.3%

Energy Demand Outlook

Total primary commercial energy demand in East Asia in the business as usual projection grows at an average annual rate of 4.1% to reach 1275 Mtoe in 2020 (see Table 16.4). This implies that East Asia will account for about 15% of world incremental commercial energy demand over the Outlook period. The trends in primary fuel shares differ from those over the past twenty years and reflect efforts by some countries to reduce dependence on imported oil. As a consequence, coal's share of primary demand, which had declined since 1971, is expected to remain fairly constant to 2020, at about 17%. Although oil is expected to decline in importance, it will remain by far the most important fuel source, accounting for over half of total primary energy demand in 2020. At 375 Mtoe, incremental oil demand in East Asia is expected to be larger than in any other region and is expected to be one of the major forces driving world oil demand. Reflecting the development of the region's resources, natural gas is also expected to play a more important role in the energy balance, increasing its present share of primary energy demand from 16% to 23% in 2020. Gas will be favoured for its ability to substitute for oil in a range of uses, as well as for its environmental characteristics. The shares of nuclear and hydropower are likely to remain constant.

Table 16.4: **Total Primary Energy Supply (Mtoe)**

	1971	1995	2010	2020	1995-2020 Annual Growth Rate
TPES	95	464	890	1275	4.1%
Solid Fuels	34	84	145	219	3.9%
Oil	58	264	472	639	3.6%
Gas	1	76	179	289	5.5%
Nuclear	0	27	53	70	3.9%
Hydro	2	7	11	16	3.5%
Other Renewables	0	7	29	42	7.5%

As shown in Table 16.5, total final consumption is expected to increase at 3.8% per annum. Gas is expected to register substantial growth of 5.4%. Electricity demand is projected to grow at about 5%, higher than the assumed GDP growth rate. Solid fuels are expected to lose significant market share, mainly as a result of inter-fuel substitution in the stationary sectors.

Table 16.5: **Total Final Energy Consumption (Mtoe)**

	1971	1995	2010	2020	1995-2020 Annual Growth Rate
TFC	**79**	**316**	**577**	**813**	**3.8%**
Solid Fuels	30	47	54	57	0.8%
Oil	42	208	388	543	3.9%
Gas	1	19	45	71	5.4%
Electricity	5	42	90	141	4.9%

Energy Related Services

Stationary Sectors

Demand for energy in stationary uses is projected to increase by 2.8% per year. This growth is expected to slow down, as shown in Figure 16.3, mainly due to changes in industrial structure. Although growth in industrial output is expected to continue strongly, its contribution to GDP is likely to decline as the larger economies in the region become increasingly service-oriented. In addition, within the industrial sector, a trend towards less energy-intensive subsectors is expected as the skill and wage base of the region continues to rise, favouring the development of higher-value-added industries. Nevertheless, the iron & steel and chemical industries will remain an important source of growth in industrial energy demand. The increase in energy demand in the residential and commercial sectors will be stronger than that in the industrial sector. Two major factors contributing to this trend are increases in income and substitution of commercial fuels for non-commercial biomass. As for the fuel mix, gas is projected to increase at 5.4% per annum, overtaking solid fuels by the end of the Outlook period. The bulk of the increase in gas demand is projected to come from the industrial sector. In the residential and commercial sectors, gas penetration is likely to remain low in a large part of the region where the demand for space heating and hot water is limited due to a year round mild climate.

Figure 16.3: **Energy Use in Stationary Sectors by Fuel**

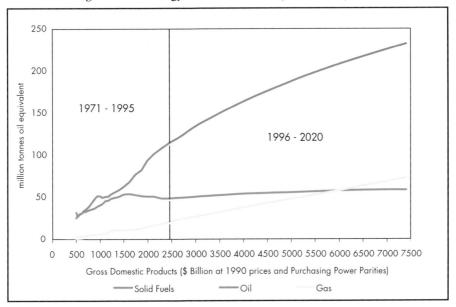

Table 16.6: **Energy Use in Stationary Sectors by Fuel (Mtoe)**

	1971	1995	2010	2020	1995-2020 Annual Growth Rate
Total	55	179	282	359	2.8%
Solid Fuels	30	47	54	57	0.8%
Oil	24	113	183	231	2.9%
Gas	1	19	45	71	5.4%

Mobility

As shown in Figure 16.4, demand for mobility in East Asia is projected to increase in line with rising incomes. With a growth rate of almost 5%, mobility demand is expected to triple over the Outlook period. More importantly, demand for mobility is expected to account for about 65% of the growth in total final oil demand over the period. Its share in total primary oil supply is projected to increase from 36% in 1995 to 50% by 2020.

Figure 16.4: **Energy Use for Mobility**

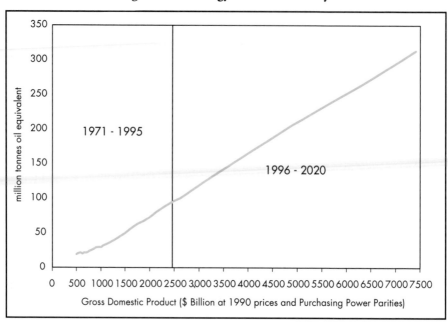

Table 16.7: **Energy Use for Mobility (Mtoe)**

	1971	1995	2010	2020	1995-2020 Annual Growth Rate
Total	19	95	205	313	4.9%

The reasons for growth in mobility demand include increasing economic activity, rising per capita incomes and the continuing process of urbanisation. Reflecting these factors, the growth in the vehicle fleet is expected to remain strong. As Figure 16.5 illustrates, despite growth in the recent past, passenger vehicle ownership is still well below that of Japan. Even allowing for possible impediments to expansion, such as inadequate roads, congestion or government regulation, there remains a vast potential for expansion in vehicle fleets in most countries.

Figure 16.5: **Vehicle Ownership versus GDP per Capita**

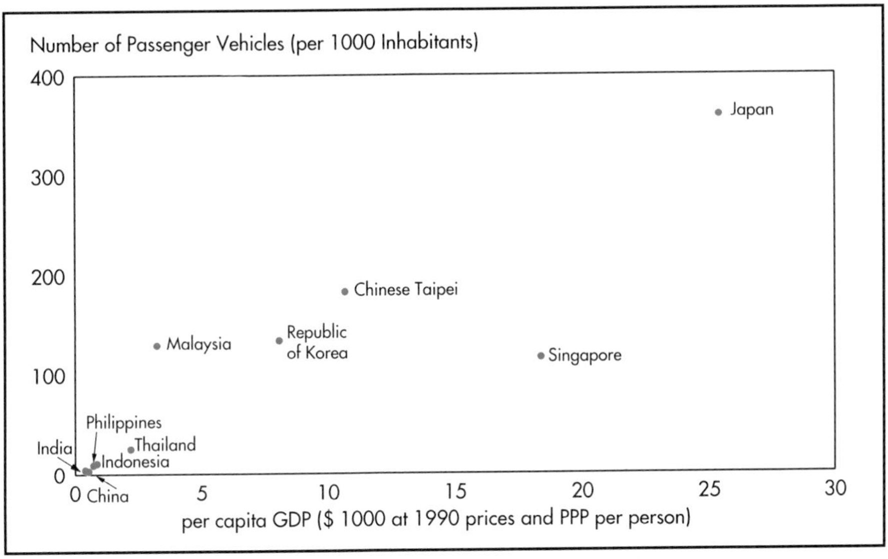

Source: *World Road Statistics '98,* International Road Federation, 1998.

Electricity

Electricity demand in East Asia is projected to grow along with GDP. It is expected to increase by close to 5% per year over the Outlook period, higher than the assumed GDP growth rate. As a result, the current 13% share of electricity in total final commercial energy consumption will reach 17% in 2020.

Table 16.8: **Total Final Electricity Demand (Mtoe)**

	1971	1995	2010	2020	1995-2020 Annual Growth Rate
Electricity	5	42	90	141	4.9%

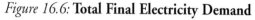

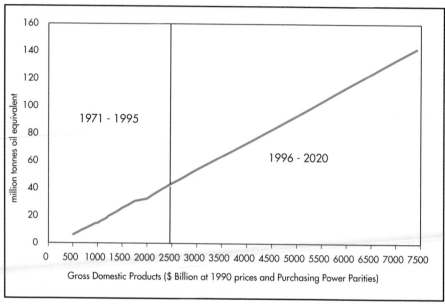

Figure 16.6: **Total Final Electricity Demand**

Although this expected growth appears to be strong, it is well below the 9% annual increase in the 1970s and 1980s. The slowdown reflects, in part, the substantial increase in electrification rates in the industrial, commercial and household sectors, as well as the assumed slower rate of GDP growth.

Table 16.9: **Electricity Sales per Capita and per Customer in Indonesia (kWh)**

	kWh per person	kWh per customer
1975/76	21	2457
1980/81	44	2376
1985/86	76	2124
1990/91	158	2468
1991/92	172	2539
1992/93	188	2593
1993/94	205	2570
1994/95	231	2549
1995/96	261	2536

Source: *Statistik dan Informasi Ketenagalistrikan dan Energi 1995/1996,* Direktorat Jenderal Listrik dan Pengembangan Energi, Jakarta 1996.

As Table 16.9 shows, per capita electricity sales in Indonesia increased rapidly in the period 1975 to 1995, as a result of increasing electrification, but consumption per customer has remained broadly unchanged. Consumption per industrial customer has been increasing, but not consumption per residential customer.

Supply

Power Generation

The region includes a large number of countries with different fuel mixes and significant differences in electricity consumption. Nuclear power is the most significant source of electricity in the Republic of Korea; Singapore's electricity generation is based on oil; Vietnam relies almost exclusively on hydropower; Thailand, Malaysia, Indonesia and Chinese Taipei use a mix of coal, oil, gas and hydropower. Singapore and Chinese Taipei are close to OECD levels of per capita electricity consumption, whereas other countries, like Vietnam and Indonesia, have some of the world's lowest levels. Four countries, the Republic of Korea, Chinese Taipei, Thailand and Indonesia, produce three quarters of electricity generated in the region.

Table 16.10: **Per Capita Income and per Capita Electricity Generation in East Asian Countries, 1995**

Country	$ 1990 and PPP per person	kWh per person
Singapore	26180	7384
Chinese Taipei	15807	5769
Republic of Korea	11298	4117
Malaysia	8168	2257
Thailand	6522	1375
Indonesia	3501	317

Despite the current Asian economic crisis, electricity generation in East Asia is projected to grow substantially over the Outlook period, at 4.9% a year. Most of the growth in electricity generation is expected to come from coal- and gas-fired plants, with coal increasing at 6.7% per annum and gas at 7.3%. Both fuels increase their shares in the electricity generation mix, from 23% for coal and 17% for gas in 1995 to 35% and 30% respectively in 2020. Increased use of gas would require expansion of gas pipelines or LNG infrastructure. These may be delayed because of lack of funding as well as lower demand expectations caused by the recent economic crisis. Coal plants may be preferred if gas is unavailable or if indigenous supplies are reserved for export.

Table 16.11: **Electricity Generation in East Asia (TWh)**

	1995	**2010**	**2020**
Solid Fuels	140	377	705
Oil	175	223	210
Gas	105	324	614
Nuclear	102	205	267
Hydro	78	131	185
Renewables	8	34	49
Total	**608**	**1294**	**2030**

In 1971, oil accounted for more than half of electricity output, followed by hydropower. Since then, other sources have been developed. In 1995, oil-fired generation accounted for 29% of total output and that share is projected to decline further as policies to diversify away from oil continue across the region. By 2020, oil is projected to account for 10% of the generation mix; in absolute terms, electricity generated from oil is projected to increase from 175 TWh in 1995 to 210 TWh in 2020. Use of diesel-fired engines could continue in remote regions. This is, for example, the case in Indonesia where regions outside the interconnected system of Java-Bali rely on diesel engines for their electricity needs. Some customers connected to the grid also rely on their own diesel generators rather than on the unreliable supply from the national utility. Some of the new CCGT plants in East Asian countries are expected to run on oil and gas or, on oil until gas supplies become available. Chinese Taipei is planning to add some orimulsion-fired capacity.

Electricity generation from nuclear power accounted for 17% of total output in 1995. The Republic of Korea started generating electricity from nuclear power in 1978, when the first nuclear reactor became operational, KORI-1, a 564 MW PWR. The Republic of Korea now has 12 reactors (10 PWRs and 2 PHWRs) with an installed capacity of around 10 GW. The most recent unit, Wol Sung 2, started commercial operation in July 1997. Nuclear is the largest single source of electricity in The Republic of Korea; in 1995 it accounted for 36% of electricity generation.

Nuclear power also accounts for about a third of electricity output in Chinese Taipei which had an installed capacity of 5 GW in 1995. The country plans to increase its nuclear capacity, although some opposition exists.

The Philippines built a nuclear plant in 1985, but the fuel for it was never loaded following controversy over the circumstances of its construction and concerns over its safety. The 620 MW Bataan plant is now mothballed. There have been discussions to convert it to a CCGT plant.

Other countries in the region, such as Indonesia, Thailand and Vietnam (and North Korea) have stated their intention to build nuclear plants, but it is assumed in this Outlook that no nuclear plants will be built in countries in the region outside the Republic of Korea and Chinese Taipei. Nuclear capacity in the region increases to 37 GW by 2020. The share of nuclear in the output mix is projected to fall to 9% by the end of the projection period.

Table 16.12: **Nuclear Plants under Construction in the Republic of Korea**

Plant	Unit	Reactor Type	Capacity (MW)
Yonug Gwang	Unit 5	PWR	1000
	Unit 6	PWR	1000
Wol Sung	Unit 3	PHWR	700
	Unit 4	PHWR	700
Ul Chin	Unit 3	PWR	1000
	Unit 4	PWR	1000

Source: KEPCO.

Hydropower accounts for 13% of the region's electricity generation. This share is projected to fall to 9% by the end of the Outlook period. East Asia has significant untapped hydro resources; the Mekong River basin alone could provide 150-180 TWh a year[3]. Many of the sites are located in remote and undeveloped areas that require the construction of long transmission lines.

3. *Thailand Fuel Option Study,* World Bank, Washington, DC, 1993.

A number of hydro projects are being developed in the region, and governments are trying to encourage private sector participation. By 2020, hydropower capacity could increase from 25 GW at present to around 55 GW. Many of the new projects are faced with financial, environmental and social difficulties. The most controversial of these projects is Malaysia's 2400 MW Bakun dam in the remote Sarawak region. The Nam Theun 2 dam project in Laos, along with a number of other hydro projects in Thailand, also faces difficulties.

The most significant non-hydro renewable resources in the region is geothermal energy, concentrated in the Philippines and Indonesia. In 1995, East Asia accounted for 20% of world geothermal electricity generation. The Philippines was the world's second largest producer of geothermal energy, after the US, with an output of 5809 GWh in 1995. Indonesia accounted for 27% of geothermal electricity in East Asia, or 2175 TWh. There are several projects, particularly in Indonesia, to increase geothermal capacity, but they could be delayed as a result of the finacial crisis. Geothermal capacity in the region is assumed to increase from 1.4 GW in 1995 to 8.8 GW by the end of the Outlook. Other renewables are also assumed to increase, but additions are likely to be small.

Co-generation is also encouraged by governments in some of the countries, including The Republic of Korea, Thailand, Chinese Taipei and the Philippines. There is insufficient data on which to estimate present or future co-generation capacity.

Table 16.13: **Fuel Use in Power Stations and as a Share of TPES**

| | 1995 | | 2020 | |
	Mtoe	% of TPES	Mtoe	% of TPES
Solid Fuels	34	7	157	12
Oil	35	8	43	3
Gas	27	6	109	9
Nuclear	27	6	70	5
Hydro	7	1	16	1
Renewables	7	1	42	3
Total	**136**	**29**	**436**	**34**

Fuel consumption for power generation is projected to increase at 4.8% per annum, which is slightly lower than the projected growth in electricity output due to improvements in the efficiency of fossil-fueled power stations. Most improvements will come from the use of efficient combined cycle plants. Several utilities also plan to upgrade their existing plant.

The power generation sector is projected to account for 34% of total primary energy supply in 2020, compared with 29% in 1995. Both coal and gas increase their shares substantially.

To meet rising electricity demand, power-generating capacity in the region would need to increase from 126 GW in 1995 to 432 GW by 2020, requiring substantial investment. Following the financial crisis and the resulting currency depreciations, power plant equipment, most of it imported, and fuel imports have become more expensive. Most of the countries in the region have opened their power sectors to private investors. However, until confidence returns and the new higher prices have been passed to customers, independent power producers may be reluctant to invest in Asian markets. This reluctance could affect capacity construction in the region.

Oil

East Asia includes significant oil exporters, such as Indonesia and Malaysia, and large oil importers like the Republic of Korea, Thailand and Chinese Taipei. In total, the region relies on imported oil to meet rapidly increasing demand.

Indonesia is the largest oil producer in the region. Its existing fields are mature and have complex geology characterised by small, highly porous structures, which results in rapid depletion. Indonesia produced about 1.4 million barrels a day in 1997 and seems to have modest growth potential. However, the increasing use of enhanced oil recovery techniques (EOR) such as steam-flooding and water-flooding is expected to keep Indonesian production stable in the medium term. By 2000, the majority of Indonesian output is expected to be EOR-based; as recently as 1994, the figure was only 30%. However, in the longer term, production seems likely to decline.

The second largest oil producer in East Asia is Malaysia, which produced about 0.75 million barrels of oil a day in 1997, almost all coming from offshore wells. Malaysian production is likely to remain flat in the medium term, as incremental output from new and satellite fields offsets declines from the main mature fields. After 2005, however, decreasing supply from the mature fields may start to pull overall output down. Due to fast growing domestic demand, about 0.5 million barrels a day in 1997, Malaysia's status as an exporter looks likely to be threatened in the near future.

Vietnam, Brunei and Papua New Guinea are three smaller oil producers. With a proven oil reserves level of 600 million barrels, Vietnam currently produces close to 200000 barrels a day of oil, almost exclusively from offshore fields. Brunei supplies about 175 000 barrels a day while output from Papua New Guinea is around 120000 barrels a day. Production in Vietnam and Papua New Guinea is likely to grow modestly in the short to medium term, while Brunei supply is anticipated to remain stable through the medium term.

The sluggish oil supply prospects of the region, compared with rapidly increasing demand, suggests that the projected increase will be met by increasing imports.

Table 16.14: **East Asia Oil Balance (Mbd)**

	1996	2010	2020
Total Demand (incl. bunkers)	6.2	10.1	13.7
All Supply	2.9	2.1	1.7
Imports	3.3	8.0	11.9

Coal

Indonesia is the only large coal producer in the region, its production rising from 0.3 Mt in 1980, to about 45 Mt in 1996. Factors influencing growth have been large reserves of good quality coal, proximity to markets, high labour productivity and low labour cost, and Government policies that encourage foreign investment in the industry.

Indonesian coal production rose by a massive 27% in 1995, and 9.5% in 1996. Exports have continued to rise rapidly (by 26% in 1994, 23% in 1995 and 16% in 1996). Total exports reached 37 Mt in 1996. Japan, Chinese Taipei and the Republic of Korea were the main destinations. Production capacity appears to be sufficient to meet both export demand and expanding domestic demand.

Principal impediments to the expansion of Indonesian coal output arise from infrastructure costs incurred in developing remote sources. Export surpluses may be reduced as domestic demand for electricity rises after 1997. For the rest of this decade, costs are unlikely to increase significantly, because conditions for new production are expected to be favourable and mining equipment and methods should remain much as before. After 2000, supply costs will be influenced by geological mining conditions, mining methods and equipment, labour rates and infrastructure capacities.

Gas

One of the main features of the Outlook for East Asia is the increasing role that natural gas is expected to play in the region, both in final demand and in power generation. The development and increased utilisation of gas require a degree of planning and co-ordination not necessary with other fuel supplies. In East Asia, gas development requires the construction of dedicated transport and distribution facilities, a readily available market and the negotiation of prices for individual markets. Many current gas projects in the region consist of a single supply source (often one field), tied by pipelines to a single demand centre (often a power plant). This pattern will change as the regional market for gas matures and an interconnected pipeline system is developed, linking multiple supply sources with multiple centres of demand. At the current stage of development, large up-front investments in production and distribution infrastructure are required if gas is to increase its share in total energy demand to the extent implied in the projections presented here.

The three largest producers, Malaysia, Indonesia and Vietnam, together account for about 3250 billion cubic metres of proven reserves, with a further 350 billion cubic metres in Brunei and Thailand. Papua New Guinea is also expected to provide increased gas resources over the outlook period. Based on current production trends, East Asia has a reserves-to-production ratio of 66 years[4].

On the demand side, gas is expected to play the most important role in countries with indigenous resources, such as Indonesia, Malaysia and Thailand. These countries have pipeline networks that could form the backbone of a future regional gas transmission system. Total pipelines built so far reach about 5500 km; those currently in progress and planned could add a further 5800 km[5]. However, countries with little or no gas resources, such as the Republic of Korea and Chinese Taipei, also have plans to increase their gas utilisation through imports.

Much of the planned increase in gas utilisation in the region, especially in power generation, is expected to replace oil. So any

4. *Asia Gas Study,* IEA/OECD, 1996.
5. Financial Times - *Asia Gas Report,* August 1997.

under-realisation of the projections presented in the current Outlook will result in even higher demand for oil, and possibly coal. The implications for East Asia will be higher oil import dependence, especially on the Middle East, less potential for fuel diversification and, hence, to strengthen energy security objectives, and increased environmental costs.

Biomass

Current Patterns of Biomass Energy Use

The region's final biomass consumption was estimated at approximately 106 Mtoe in 1995, accounting for about 11% of the world's biomass consumption and 19% of total Asian biomass use. This implies a share of biomass in total final energy consumption of 25% for the whole of East Asia, similar to that of China (24%) but much lower than that of South Asia (56%).

There are wide differences within the region. East Asia includes countries with very different levels of economic development and patterns of energy use. It is therefore not surprising that biomass energy use also varies significantly across the region, as shown in Table 16.15.

Table 16.15: **Final Biomass Energy Use in East Asia, 1995**

	Final biomass (Mtoe)	Share of country in the region	Share of biomass in TFC	Per capita energy use (kgoe)	
				Biomass	Conv. fuels
Indonesia	43.9	42%	48%	227	251
Vietnam	20.3	19%	75%	276	92
Thailand	11.8	11%	24%	203	635
Philippines	10.5	10%	45%	153	186
Myanmar	8.6	8%	80%	191	47
Malaysia	2.8	3%	11%	140	1103
Others	7.8	7%	-	-	-
Total	**105.7**	**100%**	**56%**	**193**	**154**

The major biomass user is Indonesia, which consumes some 42% of the region's supply. Vietnam, Thailand and the Philippines together account for another 40%. Myanmar is the largest consumer in relative terms (share of biomass in total energy use). As expected, the high-income countries of the region, the Republic of Korea, Chinese Taipei, Singapore and Brunei, consume little or no biomass energy. The shares of biomass in total final energy consumption are strongly related to development, modernisation and industrialisation, expressed by per capita levels of GDP and conventional energy use. The level of per capita biomass use is related to these variables and to the availability of biomass resources. Countries with a higher share of forested land or higher production of certain crops have a higher level of per capita biomass consumption.

Past Trends

Most countries of the region do not have satisfactory historical data on biomass energy use. It is therefore difficult to assess past trends in biomass energy use and the pattern and pace of fuel substitution by conventional fuels. Data for the Republic of Korea show a very rapid decline in biomass energy use during the period 1971-95, reflecting the industrialisation and urbanisation of the country in that period. On the other hand, data for Thailand[6] and the Philippines[7] show a steady increase in biomass energy use, both in absolute and per capita terms. In the case of the Philippines, even the share of biomass energy in total residential energy consumption increased between 1977 and 1989. In the case of Thailand, biomass share in total final energy consumption declined from 69% in 1971 to 55% in 1995 in the household and commercial sectors, and from 40% to 26% in the industrial sector.

Projections

Even though per capita biomass energy use is still increasing in some countries, it is expected that for the region, overall average biomass use per capita will gradually decline over the Outlook period, due to further economic development and increasing urbanisation. Combined with expected population growth, this results in total primary biomass consumption increasing from 117 Mtoe in 1995 to 136 Mtoe in 2020 (0.4% per annum). Given that primary

6. *Thailand Energy Situation,* Department of Energy Development and Promotion, Ministry of Science, Technology and Environment, Bangkok, various years.
7. *Sectoral Energy Demand in the Philippines,* Regional Energy Development Programme (REDP), United Nations, Bangkok, 1992.

consumption of conventional energy grows at 4.1% during the same period, the share of biomass in total primary energy demand is projected to decline from 20% in 1995 to 10% in 2020. Figure 16.7 summarises the biomass projections for East Asia. Details regarding methodology and assumptions can be found in chapter 10.

Including biomass in the energy mix has important consequences for energy indicators. As shown in Figure 16.8, it changes significantly the level and inclination of the energy intensity curve, which decreases more rapidly if biomass is included, reflecting the gain in overall efficiency as biomass is pushed out by more efficient fuels.

Figure 16.7: **Total Primary Energy Supply including Biomass, 1995-2020**

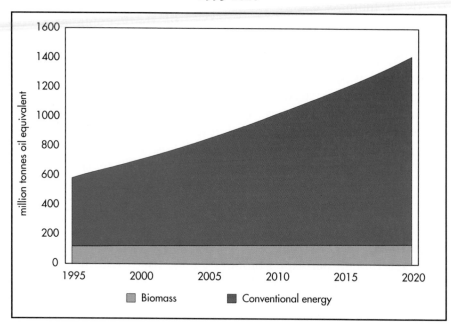

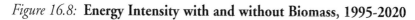

Figure 16.8: **Energy Intensity with and without Biomass, 1995-2020**

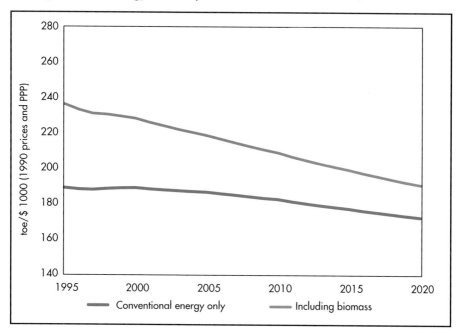

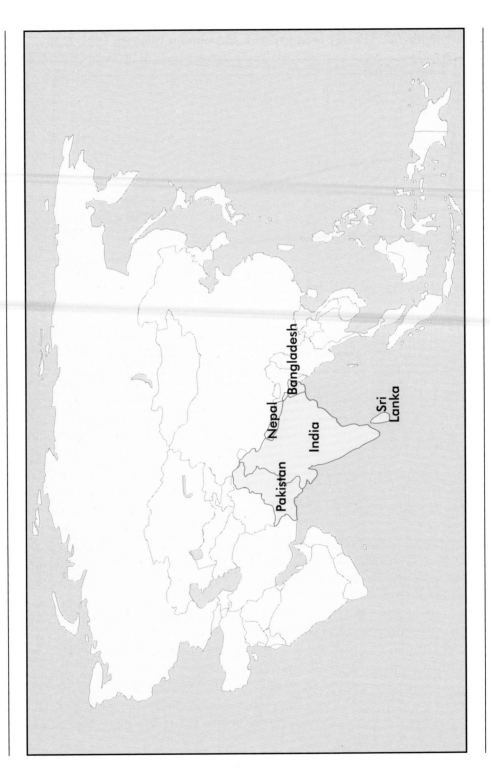

CHAPTER 17
SOUTH ASIA

Introduction

The South Asian region includes India, Pakistan, Bangladesh, Sri Lanka and Nepal. These countries are characterised by large and rapidly growing populations, with per capita incomes amongst the lowest in the world and poor social development indicators. As shown in Table 17.1, the region is dominated by India, which accounted for 71% of GDP and 76% of the region's population in 1995. The next two largest economies are Pakistan and Bangladesh which contributed 16% and 8% respectively of the region's GDP.

In a global context, South Asia is of considerable importance, accounting for about one fifth of the world's population, a share equal to that of China. Measured in purchasing power parities, the region has a 4% share in world GDP and India is the fifth largest economy in the world. In 1995, commercial energy consumption in the region reached 284 Mtoe and has grown 6% per annum in the last two decades. In 1995, South Asia accounted for 3.4% of world commercial energy demand, up from around 1.4% in 1971. As a result of these trends and the dominance of coal in the region's fuel mix, South Asia has also become important in a global environmental context. IEA statistics[1] indicate that India alone contributed 4% of world carbon emissions in 1995 and the region as a whole almost 5%. With continuing growth in economic activity and energy demand, the region will become an increasingly important element in global initiatives to reduce the environmental consequences of growing energy use.

Economic growth in the South Asian region averaged 4.6% in the last two decades. India registered a high economic performance, especially since 1991, when its new economic reform program started. This new programme, which aims to move the country to a more market-driven system, led to average GDP growth of 6.5% in the last 6 years. Other economies in the region are also implementing structural and macroeconomic reforms. However, high population

---

1. *CO$_2$ Emissions from Fuel Combustion: 1972-1995*, IEA/OECD Paris, 1997.

growth has reduced growth in per capita income levels. As Figure 17.1 shows, South Asia's per capita income was $1270 (1990 PPP) in 1995, which is substantially lower than the world average, and is the lowest of the 10 regions discussed in this Outlook. The net annual increase of India's population is more than 20 million persons. Currently, about three-quarters of the population resides in rural areas. Given existing trends, India is expected to overtake China, in terms of population, within the next three decades.

Table 17.1: **South Asian Statistics**

	GDP		Population		TPES (1995)	
	1995 ($ Billion 1990 and PPP)	Growth Rates (1985-1995) (annual, %)	1995 (millions)	Growth Rates (1985-1995) (annual, %)	excl. CRW* (Mtoe)	incl. CRW* (Mtoe)
India	1102	5.4	929	2.0	241	439
Bangladesh	125	4.1	120	2.0	8	28
Nepal	20	4.8	21	2.5	1	7
Pakistan	253	5.2	130	3.1	32	51
Sri Lanka	48	3.9	18	1.4	2	6

* CRW: Combustible Renewables and Waste.

Figure 17.1: **GDP per Capita by Region**

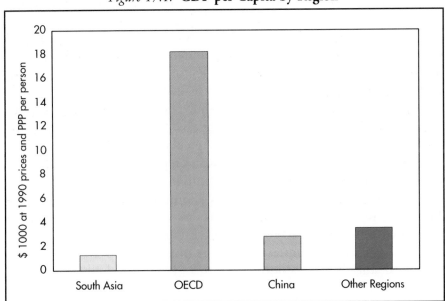

Accompanying the growth in the region's economic activity have been substantial increases in energy consumption. Primary commercial energy demand in South Asia grew at an average annual rate of about 6% between 1971 and 1995, to reach 284 Mtoe. India alone accounted for 241 Mtoe, which ranked this country fifth in the world in terms of primary energy demand. The rate of growth of primary energy demand in the region was well above that in OECD countries and comparable to that of China, but did not match the rates achieved in the dynamic economies of East Asia.

As for the fuel mix, the region's commercial energy supply has remained heavily based on coal. In 1995, coal accounted for 49% of the region's total primary commercial energy demand, and oil contributed a further 35%. The corresponding figures for India were 57% and 33%. In South Asia and in India, these shares remained close to 1971 levels. The only significant development in the fuel mix in recent years has been the growing importance of natural gas; its share of regional energy supplies rose from 5% in 1971 to 12% in 1995. This reflects important gas discoveries made in India, Pakistan and Bangladesh. These resources have been developed largely for use as petrochemical feedstocks and in fertiliser production, but some are also used in the power generation sector. Nuclear and hydropower have remained minor, although not unimportant, sources of energy in the region, together accounting for around 4% of total primary commercial energy demand in 1995. These figures refer only to the demand for commercial energy and exclude the consumption of non-commercial biomass fuels. Biomass continues to meet a substantial proportion of the region's energy demand, particularly in the household sector. Non-commercial energy trends are discussed at the end of the chapter.

The commercial energy intensity (primary energy demand per unit of GDP) in the region has increased consistently at an average rate of 1.2% per annum over the last two decades. This is one of the highest intensity growth rates among the regions analysed in this Outlook. Trends in intensity have been influenced by economic development factors and by the region's fast population growth. Box 17.1 discusses the energy-pricing environment and the issue of subsidies in the Indian energy market.

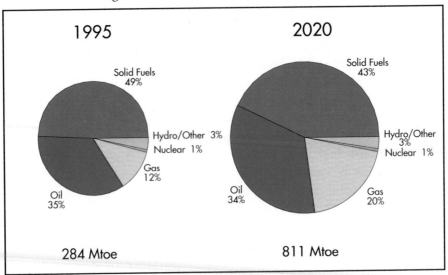

The energy industry in India is heavily regulated and energy prices are controlled by the government. The prices of most energy products are highly subsidised and set well below their economic costs. Direct subsidies are provided to certain fuels (such as kerosene, diesel and LPG), and cross-subsidies exist between consumer categories. Price distortions have accelerated the depletion of domestic resources, discouraged foreign investment in the energy sector and distorted the industrial and infrastructural development of the country.

Retail prices for electricity are determined by the state governments on social and political grounds. The average electricity tariff is currently 80% of the cost of supply. Agricultural and residential electricity users have both been subsidised. Initially, when the subsidy policy was devised, electricity demand in the agricultural sector was very small. Mainly because of the subsidised tariff (13% of average generating cost), electricity demand in the agricultural sector grew rapidly. This sector now uses about 36% of total electricity.

Table 17.2: **Comparison of Average Electricity Retail Price and Supply Cost in India**

Fiscal Year	90/91	91/92	92/93	93/94	94/95	95/96	96/97
Average Price (Paise/kWh)	81.8	89.1	105.4	119.3	129.3	144.4	149.2
Average Cost (Paise/kWh)	108.6	116.8	128.2	144.3	157.7	173.6	186.2
Price/Cost	0.75	0.76	0.82	0.83	0.82	0.83	0.8

Note: 1 rupee (Rs.) = 100 paises.
Source: *Annual Report on the Working of State Electricity Boards and Electricity Departments*, Planning Commission, Government of India, 1997.

Prices for certain oil products, such as kerosene, LPG and fuel oil, are subsidised to accommodate the Government's social policy. A heavy subsidy is set for diesel, because it is mainly used in public transport, road freight and agricultural irrigation. In 1996/97, diesel subsidies alone amounted to close to 83 billion rupees ($2.4 billion).

Not only have subsidies rarely reached their target groups, but persistent oil pricing distortions have created a "dieselisation of the Indian economy".

The outcome of deregulation in India and its impact on energy pricing present major uncertainties for the projections presented here.

One of the notable features of the region's energy profile is the very low level of per capita energy consumption. If only commercial energy is considered, an average of 0.2 tonnes of oil equivalent (toe) was consumed per person in 1995. In Bangladesh, Nepal and Sri Lanka, per capita consumption was well below the regional average. This is the lowest level of per capita energy consumption among all the developing regions. Even in Africa, per capita energy consumption was 0.3 toe in 1995 and, in China, it was 0.7 toe.

As presented in Table 17.3, the GDP of the region is assumed, in our projection, to almost triple over the period to 2020, an annual growth rate of 4.2% per year. The achievement of this growth will depend on the broadening and deepening of the energy sector reform programme, especially in India. The sustainability and success of the reform process remains one of the key uncertainties surrounding the projections presented in this Outlook. It is expected that the slowing of population growth will continue, with an average annual growth rate of 1.5% to 2020. Together, the assumptions for economic and population growth imply an average rise in per capita income of 2.6% per year. This leads to per capita income in 2020 of $2433 (in purchasing power parity terms), around twice its 1995 level, in real terms. Given the various reforms being undertaken in India, it is assumed that energy prices will, over the course of the Outlook period, begin to reflect more closely their economic costs of supply. Hence, it is assumed that the pre-tax price of oil products and of coal will follow international spot market prices. An LNG price similar to that for East Asia has been assumed, even though the proximity to the Middle East could lead to a lower value.

Table 17.3: **Assumptions for South Asia**

	1971	1995	2010	2020	1995-2020 Annual Growth Rate
Coal Price ($1990 per metric ton)	44	40	42	46	0.5%
Oil Price ($1990 per barrel)	6	15	17	25	2.1%
LNG Price ($1990 per toe)	n.a.	126	141	210	2.1%
GDP ($Billion 1990 and PPP)	528	1548	2928	4346	4.2%
Population (millions)	716	1219	1572	1786	1.5%
GDP per Capita ($1000 1990 and PPP per person)	0.7	1.3	1.9	2.4	2.6%

Energy Demand Outlook

Overview

In the business as usual projection, commercial primary energy demand in South Asia is expected to grow at an average annual rate of 4.3% and to reach 811 Mtoe in 2020. This is somewhat higher than projected energy demand in OECD Pacific. Coal and oil continue to dominate the primary fuel structure, supplying more than three-quarters of commercial primary energy demand in 2020. Natural gas has the fastest rate of growth of any fuel. At the level of final energy demand, the share of coal falls relative to increases in demand for gas, oil and electricity. Commercial energy intensity in the region is expected to remain broadly unchanged.

Table 17.4: **Total Primary Energy Supply (Mtoe)**

	1971	1995	2010	2020	1995-2020 Annual Growth Rate
TPES	**72**	**284**	**558**	**811**	**4.3%**
Solid Fuels	39	140	256	348	3.7%
Oil	27	99	191	277	4.2%
Gas	3	34	90	160	6.4%
Nuclear	0	2	4	5	3.7%
Hydro	3	10	17	20	2.9%
Other Renewables	0.0	0.0	0.7	0.8	22.9%

Total final commercial energy demand is expected almost to triple over the Outlook period, with an annual average growth rate of 4.2%. The share of coal falls significantly. Gas is the fastest growing conventional fuel. The transportation sector will be the main driver for the expected increase in oil demand. Despite projected strong growth of electricity, per capita electricity consumption remains extremely low by international comparisons.

Table 17.5: **Total Final Energy Consumption (Mtoe)**

	1971	1995	2010	2020	1995-2020 Annual Growth Rate
TFC	**55**	**188**	**362**	**523**	**4.2%**
Solid Fuels	25	50	70	81	1.9%
Oil	23	87	168	242	4.2%
Gas	2	19	55	92	6.5%
Electricity	5	31	69	107	5.0%

Energy Related Services

Stationary Sectors

Demand for energy in stationary uses is projected to rise in line with GDP in a nearly linear manner at an annual growth rate of 3.7% over the Outlook period. As shown in Figure 17.3, an interesting feature is that coal - which is now the dominant fuel in stationary uses of fossil fuel with a share of about 46% - is expected to be overtaken by oil within a decade, and by gas within about two decades.

In the residential/commercial sector, the consumption of non-commercial biomass energy is by far larger in absolute terms than the consumption of commercial energy. It is estimated that the share of non-commercial biomass use in the final consumption of this sector accounts for about 85%. However, the efficiency of use of non-commercial biomass is low so that the useful energy it provides is also low. Household income is expected to continue to be the major determinant of both the amount of energy consumed and the choice of fuel used in this sector. Demographic trends, such as urbanisation, will also affect future development of the energy use levels in the residential/commercial sector.

Figure 17.3: **Energy Use in Stationary Sectors by Fuel**

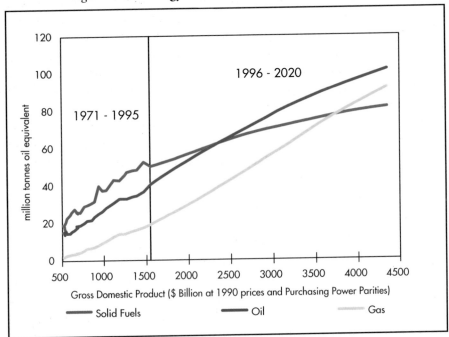

Table 17.6: **Energy Use in Stationary Sectors by Fuel (Mtoe)**

	1971	1995	2010	2020	1995-2020 Annual Growth Rate
Total	**33**	**110**	**200**	**275**	**3.7%**
Solid Fuels	17	50	70	81	1.9%
Oil	14	41	76	102	3.7%
Gas	2	19	55	92	6.5%

Industry is a major consumer of commercial energy in South Asia, accounting for just over half of final energy demand in 1995. India again dominates the region with 86% of industrial energy consumption.

The economic reforms being undertaken in the region are likely to have important consequences for the pace and structure of industrial growth over the Outlook period. The industry sector in India is targeted to lead the economic development process, and its rate of growth will probably be higher than in the recent past. Energy demand growth will be moderated to the extent that structural change favours less energy-intensive activities. This is likely to occur as the region's economies reap the benefits of international trade liberalisation and pursue their comparative advantage in labour-intensive manufacturing. Industrial energy demand has been analysed in three sub-sectors, iron & steel, chemicals-petrochemicals and other industry. Industrial demand is projected to increase by two-and-a-half times between 1995 and 2020. A significant change in fuel mix is also projected: the current 52% share of coal in total industrial demand is projected to decline to 31% and gas is expected to increase its share from 16% now to 31% in 2020. Oil is projected to decrease its market share from 18% to 16%.

Mobility

Figure 17.4 shows energy demand for mobility in South Asia continuing to grow in a linear fashion in relation to GDP. Consumption is projected to triple over the Outlook period, at an average growth rate of 4.5% a year. The main determinant of this growth is the expected increase in disposable income and growth in the industrial sector. Growth from the current low level of passenger vehicle ownership - 4.5 per 1000 people - is expected to contribute significantly to this projection. Another contributing factor is a decline in rail traffic in the region. India, like China, has extensive railways, fuelled by diesel oil. This trend is likely to continue in the future. As the movement of both people and goods by road is considerably more energy-intensive than by rail, this modal shift is expected to be a significant additional factor in the growth of energy consumption for mobility.

Figure 17.4. **Energy Use for Mobility**

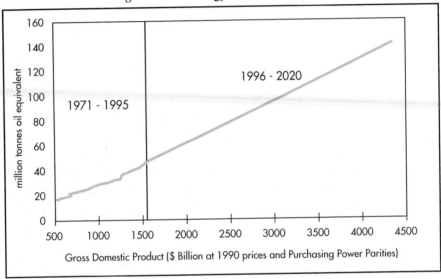

Table 17.7: **Energy Use for Mobility (Mtoe)**

	1971	1995	2010	2020	1995-2020 Annual Growth Rate
Total	17	46	92	141	4.5%

It is expected that more than 60% of the increase in total final energy consumption will come from the transport sector. Rapidly rising oil demand means high import dependence and raises questions about the long-term security of supply. An important issue concerning oil demand is the product mix. Due to recent pricing policies, the share of diesel in road fuels is extremely high. The manner and timetable for phasing out current subsidies and eliminating associated price distortions remain key uncertainties for the trends presented here.

Box 17.2: **"Dieselisation" of the Indian Energy Sector**

About 80% of road vehicles in India run on diesel fuel, compared to 15% in China and 31% in Malaysia. Diesel vehicles are the main source of air pollution in Indian cities. Serious power shortages have forced many institutions to produce their own power or install stand-by electricity generation. In most cases, these are powered by diesel oil. Diesel power generators are used in industrial and commercial establishments (the industrial sector alone had 15 000 MW of diesel-based captive generation capacity in 1995) and in wealthy urban households. Farmers also prefer to use diesel pumps for irrigation. Even electrified rail-lines also use diesel-fired stand-by generators.

As the diesel price is less than half that of gasoline, car owners have an incentive to convert gasoline engines to diesel, and many have done so. Cheap diesel fuel, combined with high rail freight tariffs (which subsidise passenger tariffs) and the railways' inability to meet demand for some types of freight movement, has given rise to greater use of road freight transport, with trucks fuelled by diesel oil. After comparing the higher electricity tariffs (charged to industrial consumers to subsidise agricultural and residential uses) with the low diesel price, industrialists find it cheaper to produce their own electricity using diesel generation than to buy electricity from the unreliable grid.

Primarily as a result of this process, the volume of imported diesel increased by 49% in fiscal year 1995/96 (from 8.64 to 12.85 million tonnes). In the same year, diesel accounted for 46% of oil consumption in India, (up from 40% in fiscal year 1990/91) and the highest in the world.

Table 17.8: **Evolution of India's Diesel Consumption and Imports (1990-1996)**

Year (April-March)		1990/91	91/92	92/93	93/94	94/95	95/96
Total Oil Consumption (TOC), in million tonnes		55.0	57.0	58.9	60.7	65.4	72.5
High Speed Diesel (HSD)	Consump.Vol. (Mt)	21.9	22.7	25.5	26.4	28.2	33.5
	HSD as % of TOC	40	40	43	44	44	46
	% of HSD Import	21%	23%	28%	29%	31%	38%

Source: *India's Energy Sector,* Center for Monitoring Indian Economy, September 1996.

Electricity

Electricity demand in South Asia is expected to increase by 5% per annum over the Outlook period, significantly faster than the region's asssumed GDP growth rate. Its current 17% share of total final consumption will increase to 21% in 2020. In 1995, about 44% of this electricity was used in industry, 54% in the residential/commercial sector and the remaining 2% in other sectors.

Figure 17.5: **Total Final Electicity Demand**

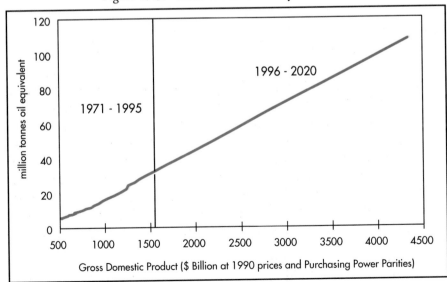

Table 17.9: **Total Final Electricity Demand (Mtoe)**

	1971	1995	2010	2020	1995-2020 Annual Growth Rate
Electricity	5	31	69	107	5.0%

In industry, the share of electricity is expected to grow from 14% to 22%. This rapid expansion is mainly due to a shift toward less energy-intensive activities in other industry and the increased penetration of electric technologies such as arc furnaces in iron and steel production. Electricity demand in the residential/commercial sector is projected almost to triple over the Outlook period. A rapid increase in electrical-appliance ownership and the continuing electrification of rural areas will contribute significantly to the high growth of electricity demand. An uncertainty surrounding this projection is future Government policy on agricultural electricity prices. Currently, agriculture uses more than a quarter of total final electricity in the region and the phasing out of subsidies for agricultural electricity could reduce the trends presented in this Outlook.

Supply

Power Generation

Growth in electricity generation in the region has followed trends in other Asian countries. It averaged 8% growth in the period 1971 to 1995. The region is characterised by chronic electricity shortages, as demand growth has outpaced supply. Shortfalls in building new power plants, poor-quality transmission lines and theft are the main reasons why supply cannot match demand. Plant load factors are often low, due to the age of generating units, lack of the appropriate quality of coal, equipment deficiencies and poor maintenance. In India for example, in 1995, the average generation shortage was around 9% and that of peak demand, 18%[2]. In the country's eighth plan period (1992 to 1997), the capacity of new plants was little more than half the

2. *Energy Data Directory and Yearbook 1997/98*, Tata Energy Research Institute, New Delhi, 1997.

original target. Recent economic sanctions could slow investment projects and future electricity growth. Lack of a national grid accentuates these shortages; at present some of the states have low-cost surplus power during off-peak periods, while other states continue to operate expensive coal-fired units or face power shortages.

India accounts for 85% of the region's electricity generation. Its power system is dominated by coal, the most abundant indigenous resource, the fuel with the most developed infrastructure and the most economic option to meet growth in electricity demand. Pakistan, which accounts for 11% of electricity generation in the region, uses a mix of hydropower, oil and gas. Bangladesh uses its gas resource base, while Nepal and Sri Lanka rely almost exclusively on hydropower.

Table 17.10: **Electricity Generation in South Asia 1995 (TWh)**

	Bangladesh	India	Nepal	Pakistan	Sri Lanka	South Asia
Solid Fuels	0	288	0	0	0	288
Oil	2	12	0	16	0	30
Gas	9	25	0	14	0	48
Nuclear	0	7	0	1	0	8
Hydro	0	83	1	23	4	112
Renewables	0	0	0	0	0	0
Total	**11**	**415**	**1**	**54**	**5**	**485**

In the BAU projection, electricity generation grows faster than GDP, at 5% per annum over the Outlook period, to reach 1657 TWh by 2020. Installed capacity increases at 4.3% per annum, from 106 GW in 1995 to 304 GW in 2020. The growth in capacity is lower than the growth in electricity generation, because of improvements in the performance of power plants, the combined effects of higher utilisation of existing capacity and the introduction of new, more efficient generating plants.

The region is expected to remain dependent on coal-fired generation which is projected to increase at 5.2% per annum and to reach 1026 TWh by 2020. The share of coal-based electricity increases, from 59% in 1995 to 62% by 2020. Coal plant efficiency is very low, at 27% in 1995, and rises to a potential of 34% in 2020. Coal consumption could therefore grow at 4.2% per annum, from 93 Mtoe in 1995 to 262 Mtoe in 2020.

Oil-fired generation is projected to increase from 30 TWh in 1995 to 96 TWh in 2020. A number of projects under construction, or at various stages of planning, will use fuel oil, naphtha or diesel oil. Many CCGT projects under development in India will be naphtha-fired at an initial stage; later on, they will switch to gas when LNG or pipeline gas becomes available.

Several gas-fired projects under development in Bangladesh use indigenous natural gas. In India, where domestic gas production is small, there are some plans to use imported LNG. Pakistan also seeks to reduce its reliance on fuel oil. Electricity generation from gas in the region as a whole is projected to increase from 48 TWh in 1995 to 277 TWh in 2020. Accelerated growth is projected for the second half of the Outlook period, when current plans to expand gas fields, gas pipelines and LNG terminals could materialise.

Table 17.11: **South Asia Electricity Generation (TWh)**

	1995	2010	2020
Solid Fuels	288	661	1026
Oil	30	60	96
Gas	48	126	277
Nuclear	8	15	19
Hydro	112	200	229
Renewables	0	8	10
Total	485	1070	1657

Both Pakistan and India use nuclear power. India's nuclear programme began in 1969, with the commissioning of the Tarapur plant in Maharashtra. The plant has two boiling-water reactors of 150 MW each. Four more nuclear plants use twin PWRs with a total capacity of 1618 MW. A small fast-breeder at Kalpakkam (13 MW) connected to the grid in July 1997. The performance of these plants is poor. In OECD countries, nuclear plants operate in baseload mode and their load factors are 75% to 80%; in India, nuclear plants have load factors of less than 50%. There are four nuclear units under construction: Kaiga 1 and 2, and Rajasthan 3 and 4. Each unit has a capacity of 202 MW. Other plants are at various stages of planning.

Table 17.12: **Indian Nuclear Plant Performance**

Year	Capacity (MW)	Generation (GWh)	Plant Load Factor
1990	1425	6141	49%
1991	1632	5525	39%
1992	1839	6726	42%
1993	1839	5398	34%
1994	1839	5648	35%
1995	2046	7000	39%

Pakistan has had a Canadian-built 128 MW pressurised heavy water reactor at Kanupp, since 1972. The country is building a second 300-MW nuclear plant, using Chinese technology, at Chasma in the Punjab region. There are plans to build a second 300-MW unit at Chasnupp.

We assume nuclear capacity in the region to increase from 2 to 4 GW by 2020, despite some plant retirements. Nuclear power generation is projected to increase from 8 TWh in 1995 to 19 TWh in 2020; this projection assumes that the plant load factor will increase from 47% to 57%.

Hydropower currently accounts for 23% of electricity generation in the region and 24% of installed capacity. With the exception of Bangladesh, all countries in the region rely on hydropower as an abundant indigenous resource. At a 60% load factor, India's hydro potential is estimated at 84 GW. Most of it is located in the north and north-east of the country. Only 15% of the potential resource has been developed and another 7% is under development.

Nepal has large untapped hydroelectric resources, around 83 GW, of which 35 to 44 GW could be economically exploited. Hydro plants could be developed for export of electricity to India. Ten projects of a total capacity of 23 GW have already been identified. Only 12% of the country's 20 million people have access to electricity. Development of hydroelectric power poses some environmental problems.

Sri Lanka relies almost exclusively on hydro-power. A number of small hydro projects are under development, but in the longer term the country will have to increase the use of fossil fuels in the power sector.

Recently, the government of Pakistan announced a three-year ban on new thermal projects, in an effort to promote hydropower.

Hydro-electricity in the region is projected to double over the period 1995 to 2020. As resources are exploited, growth in hydro is slowing down and its share in total generation decreasing. Hydro power in South Asia is assumed to grow at 2.9% per annum, which is significantly lower than average annual growth of 5.3% in the period 1971 to 1995. The share of hydro in electricity generation decreases from 23% in 1995 to 14% by the end of the Outlook.

New hydro plant development in the region is problematic, for environmental, social, and financial reasons. The World Bank withdrew funding from Nepal's 402 MW Arun-3 project in 1995 for environmental reasons. Construction of the 2400 MW Tehri dam in India was suspended following environmental protests. Local populations are opposed to the construction of the 400-MW Maheshwar dam in central India. Completion of the 1450 MW Ghazi Barotha dam in Pakistan will be delayed for lack of financing.

Non-hydro renewable energy for power generation is receiving increased attention. Alternative energy supplies are used in the region to provide electricity in rural areas, particularly where early connection to the grid is not envisaged. In India alone, total renewable capacity at the beginning of 1997 was 1400 MW. The target for renewable capacity in the country's Ninth Plan (1997-2002) is 3000 MW.

Table 17.13: **India's Estimated Renewable Energy Potential (GW)**

Source	Potential
Biomass	6
Wind	20
Small Hydro	10
Ocean	50

Sources: *India Power*, Vol. V. No. 2, April-June 1997, Council of Power Utilities, New Delhi, 1997. *Energy Data Directory and Yearbook 1997/98*, Tata Energy Research Institute, New Delhi, 1997.

Wind power is the most promising of all renewables. Wind capacity in India was 900 MW in March 1997 and is increasing. Solar power is also becoming popular. Bangladesh recently commercialised a 62 kW solar power plant near Dhaka and there are 35 independent systems with a total capacity of 30 MW. In India, there are more than 350000 systems with a total capacity of 25 MW, which could expand to 150 MW by the end of the Ninth Five Year Plan. The country also has larger grid-connected plants of 25-100 MW. Two 50 MW units are planned in Rajasthan.

In India there are 18 projects using biomass, with a total capacity of 69 MW. Another 17 projects totalling 97 MW are planned. Bangladesh plans to build a waste-and-gas plant that will use domestic and industrial waste from the city of Dhaka and domestic natural gas or waste gases from a waste dump.

Coal

India is the only major producer of coal in the region. Output has increased rapidly since the early 1970s. India is now the world's fourth largest coal producer, after China, the United States and the former Soviet Union. Production increased from about 75 million tonnes in 1971 to 333 million tonnes in 1997, of which 310 million tonnes was hard coal and 23 million tonnes brown coal. Some coal is exported to Bangladesh and Nepal but, overall, India is a net importer of coal. In 1997, 15 million tonnes were imported, mostly coking coal.

As shown in Table 17.14, proven reserves in India were estimated at 68.6 billion tonnes at the end of 1995, of which three quarters are found in Bihar, Madhya, Pradesh and West Bengal. While reserves are substantial, Indian coal is generally of poor quality, high in ash and of low calorific value. Domestic coal must be washed to make it suitable for use in coke ovens. Productivity is low by international standards as mechanisation is largely limited to coal cutting. Coal loading is predominantly by hand.

Table 17.14: **Indian Coal Reserves by Type and State, as of January 1995 (billion tonnes)**

Coal Reserves	Proved	Indicated	Inferred	Total
Coking Coal	15.1	13.3	1.5	29.9
Non-Coking Coal	53.5	76.4	40.2	170.1
Total	**68.6**	**89.8**	**41.7**	**200.0**

Source: *GOI Planning Commision, Draft Mid-Term Appraisal of Eighth Five Year Plan,* 1997.

Average coal production costs are low by international standards, and have been kept stable in real terms by lower costs in new developments. The average cost at Coal India's surface mines was $7.12 per tonne (1993), and $20.60 for underground production (1994). Costs are expected to rise as stripping ratios increase.

An additional problem in the coal sector is that reserves are mainly found far from major consuming centres. About three-quarters of coal production is moved by rail, either by the public sector Indian Railways or by dedicated rail transport, to power plants. This places a considerable burden on the Indian rail system. Projections for coal consumption in India mean that substantial investment will be required in transport capacity. The remaining coal output is moved either by truck or by coastal vessels.

In order to meet the projected 250% increase of current coal demand, it will be necessary to increase imports, most of which will be steam coal.

Oil

India's oil fields are located in the Bombay High, Upper Assam, Cambay, Krisha-Godawari and Cauvery basins. In 1997, India produced 760 000 barrels a day of oil.

Output from the offshore Bombay High field, which accounts for roughly half of Indian oil production, has been declining slowly in recent years, and this trend is likely to continue. A gas reinjection and reservoir pressure maintenance programme for the field has been under study for years, but has not progressed beyond that stage. Although production from private sector and joint venture fields has been growing, this is unlikely to reverse continued gradual declines in Indian production. However, improved Bombay High output could potentially stabilise Indian supply for a few years. India is becoming increasingly dependent on imports. In 1997, net imports of about 1 million barrels per day met for more than half of India's oil demand.

Table 17.15: **South Asia Oil Balance (Mbd)**

	1996	2010	2020
Total Demand (incl. bunkers)	2.3	4.1	5.9
All Supply	0.8	0.8	0.7
Imports	1.5	3.3	5.2

Elsewhere in the region, reserves of crude oil are located in Pakistan. Production in 1997 was around 60 000 barrels a day and is likely to remain near that level or decline gradually over the next several years. Demand far outstrips domestic supply, reaching about 350 000 barrels per day. Net imports were about 285 000 barrels per day in 1997.

Imports of both crude and oil products will remain an important source of South Asia's oil supply throughout the Outlook period.

Gas

India's natural gas production reached 0.7 trillion cubic feet in 1997. Indian gas reserves are located mainly in the Bombay High Fields. Further major discoveries are likely. India has been self-sufficient in gas to date but the projected increases in gas demand over the Outlook period will necessitate large imports. Several options are being explored, including building facilities to handle imports of LNG and constructing pipelines from major gas-producing countries.

Both Pakistan and Bangladesh have some natural gas reserves. Pakistan currently produces 0.6 trillion cubic feet of natural gas a year, all of which is used in the domestic market. Projected increases in gas demand will not be met from domestic production, and Pakistan is pursuing options for additional supplies from the Middle East and Central Asia.

Given the projections for gas demand in South Asia over the period to 2020, it is clear that the region will need significant gas imports in the medium term. It will be easy to secure gas supplies from outside the region but this will require substantial investment in infrastructure, either pipelines or LNG facilities. If the required infrastructure development does not keep pace with demand growth, then energy consumption, especially of electricity, will be constrained, or there will be increased reliance on alternative-fuel sources, coal in the case of India and probably oil in the case of Pakistan.

Biomass

Current Patterns of Biomass Energy Use

Despite substantial growth in commercial fuel consumption in the last two decades, South Asia still relies heavily on biomass energy, which accounts for 56% of final energy consumption and 46% of primary energy use. These shares are much higher than those of China and East Asia, and closer to those found in Africa. Of all the developing regions, South Asia has the largest annual biomass primary consumption, estimated at 244 Mtoe. This is about 23% of world biomass energy consumption.

Within the region, India accounts for 80% of biomass energy consumption, although estimates vary greatly. As in China, biomass consumption varies widely among localities, and different methods used for scaling up from local to national biomass consumption can lead to large differences. The figure of 189 Mtoe, used here as a mean estimate for 1995, is an average of the most reliable and complete estimates. The next two largest biomass users in the region are Pakistan, at 9%, and Bangladesh at 7%. Nepal and Sri Lanka jointly account for the remaining 5%.

As shown in Table 17.16, the share of biomass energy in final energy consumption varies significantly across the countries of the regions, as does per capita biomass use. Nepal has the highest share of biomass consumption, at 90%, as well as the highest per capita consumption, reflecting a high availability of biomass fuels combined with very low per capita use of conventional energy.

Table 17.16: **Final Biomass Energy Use in South Asia, 1995**

	Total biomass in TFC (Mtoe)	Share of country in the region	Share of biomass in TFC	Per capita energy use (kgoe)	
				Biomass	Conv. fuels
India	189	80%	55%	203	167
Pakistan	21	9%	47%	162	183
Bangladesh	16	7%	73%	131	49
Nepal	6	3%	90%	293	31
Sri Lanka	4	2%	63%	201	118
South Asia	**235**	**100%**	**56%**	**193**	**154**

A large part of biomass energy is consumed in rural households. However, in South Asia, biomass consumption in urban households and in the industrial sector is quite significant, accounting for 6%-8% and 10%-15% of total biomass consumption. A unique characteristic of South Asia is the large use of animal waste (representing some 20%-30% of the region's biomass use) and the very limited use of charcoal. This is probably due to the relatively low availability of wood as compared with China and East Asia. Another 20%-30% is made up by agricultural residues. Most biomass is burned directly in traditional, low-efficiency devices, although production of biogas from animal waste is increasing in India. Use of biomass for the production of electricity is limited at present, but pilot projects for a number of small plants are underway.

Past Trends

The lack of consistent historical data makes it difficult to assess past trends in biomass energy use and the pattern and pace of fuel substitution by conventional fuels. Data for India show an impressive increase in household consumption of LPG and kerosene in the last 20 years (13% and 6% per annum respectively), but surveys suggest that most of this increase was absorbed by urban households, with little or no effect on rural areas[3]. According to some estimates, in India, the share of biomass energy in rural energy consumption has remained relatively unchanged in the last 15 years, while the total amount of biomass used has increased, due to rural population growth. This is mainly due to the unavailability of alternative fuels. There have been gradual changes in the relative shares of the different biomass fuels, with shifts from dung and agricultural residues to wood, and from collected wood (twigs) to marketed wood (logs)[4].

Projections

It is expected that per capita biomass use in South Asia will slowly decline over the Outlook period. The total amount will continue to increase, from 244 Mtoe now to 308 Mtoe in 2020, due to population growth. This represents an average annual growth rate of less than 1%, compared with 4.3% for conventional primary energy fuels. As a result, the biomass share in total primary demand is projected to decline from 46% in 1995 to 28% in 2020. Figure 17.6 summarises the biomass projections for South Asia.

Given the importance of biomass in South Asia, the inclusion of this energy source in the analysis can greatly affect the messages and inferences that can be drawn. For example, energy intensity including biomass is at a very high level and is declining quite rapidly. This contrasts with the relatively flat path for energy intensity when it is calculated using only conventional energy. This comparison is shown in Figure 17.7. This inconsistency arises because biomass fuels are

3. Demand for LPG in urban areas, National Council of Applied Economic Research, New Delhi, India, 1985 and 1995 (unpublished).
4. Natarajan, *Demand forecast for biofuels in rural households in India,* in IEA, Biomass Energy: Data, Analysis and Trends, Workshop Proceeding, forthcoming.

generally used in a very inefficient way and their substitution by conventional fuels will result in a gain of overall efficiency.

Figure 17.6: **Total Primary Energy Supply including Biomass, 1995-2020**

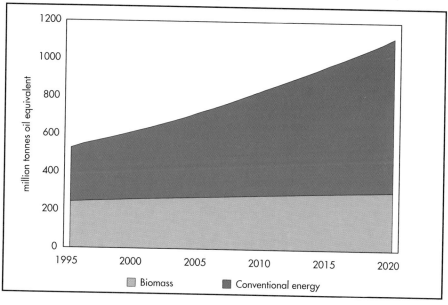

Figure 17.7: **Energy Intensity with and without Biomass, 1995-2020**

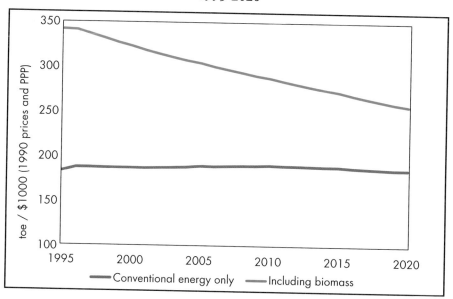

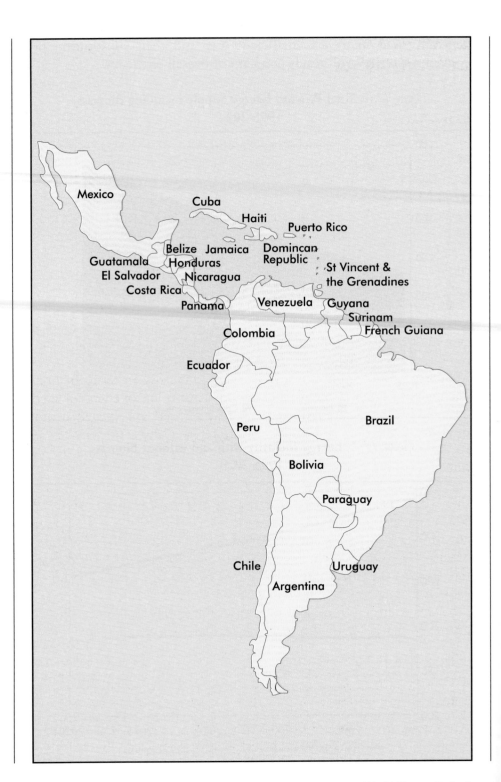

Mexico

Cuba

Haiti

Puerto Rico

Belize Jamaica   Domincan
Republic

Guatamala   Honduras   St Vincent &
El Salvador   Nicaragua   the Grenadines
Costa Rica

Panama   Venezuela   Guyana

Surinam

Colombia   French Guiana

Ecuador

Peru   Brazil

Bolivia

Paraguay

Chile   Uruguay

Argentina

CHAPTER 18
LATIN AMERICA

Introduction

Latin America includes economies with very different characteristics and dynamics[1]. The population of the region in 1995 was estimated to be close to 480 million people and its GDP was $2634 billion (based on purchasing power parity and 1990 prices), equivalent to GDP per capita close to $5500. The region accounted for around 9% of world's GDP.

Latin America is an important exporter of primary commodities, including energy, and its economy is sensitive to changes in commodity prices, although the region is undergoing a structural change to a more industrialised economy. There is vast hydro potential and, despite the dominance of hydropower in the power generation system of most countries in the region, only a fraction of this potential has been utilised. Venezuela and Mexico have important hydrocarbon resources. The region is relatively energy intensive in terms of final energy, but its global environmental impact in terms of energy-related CO_2 emissions is limited, due to its extensive use of hydro and biomass. Part of the reason for the high final energy intensity in the region is its increasing share of the world's production of some energy intensive goods, like steel and aluminium.

Latin America has experienced rather modest economic growth since 1971, slightly over 3% per annum. In 1997, GDP growth averaged 5%, approaching rates recorded before the first oil crisis. Economic growth was especially strong in Argentina, Peru, Chile and Venezuela. Mexico, despite the recent oil price fall, appears to have recovered from the recession triggered by its 1994 financial crisis. The Mexican economy registered growth of 5% in 1996 and 7% in 1997. On the other hand, problems related to fiscal and monetary policies have prevented higher growth in Brazil, which accounts for one third of the region's total GDP.

1. This region includes the following countries: Argentina, Bolivia, Brazil, Chile, Colombia, Costa Rica, Cuba, Dominican Republic, El Salvador, Ecuador, Guatemala, Haiti, Honduras, Jamaica, Mexico, Netherlands Antilles, Nicaragua, Panama, Paraguay, Peru, Trinidad/Tobago, Uruguay, Venezuela, Antigua and Barbuda, Bahamas, Barbados, Belize, Bermuda, Dominica, French Guiana, Grenada, Guadeloupe, Guyana, Martinique, St. Kitts-Nevis-Anguilla, Saint Lucia, St. Vincent-Grenadines, and Surinam. Please note that following countries have not been considered in this Outlook due to lack of data: Aruba, British Virgin Islands, Caymen Islands, Falkland Islands, Montserrat, Saint Pierre-Miquelon and Turks and Caicos Islands.

Table 18.1: **Economic and Population Data for Selected Latin American Countries**

	GDP		Population		GDP per Capita
	1995 ($ Billion 1990 and PPP)	Growth Rates (1985-95) (annual, %)	1995 (millions)	Growth Rates (1985-95) (annual, %)	1995 ($ 1000 1990 and PPP per person)
Mexico	642	1.6	95	2.0	6.8
Brazil	882	2.2	159	1.6	5.5
Argentina	235	2.7	35	1.4	6.8
Venezuela	162	2.8	22	2.4	7.5
Colombia	185	4.5	37	1.8	5.0
Chile	154	7.0	14	1.6	10.9
Regional Total	**2634**	**2.5**	**478**	**1.8**	**5.5**

Table 18.2: **Energy Consumption in Selected Latin American Countries, 1995 (Mtoe)**

	Primary Energy Supply				Final Consumption	
	Total	Coal	Oil	Gas	Total	Electricity
Mexico	125	5	85	26	88	10
Brazil	123	12	82	4	105	22
Argentina	53	1	24	24	38	5
Venezuela	47	0	18	25	34	5
Colombia	24	4	13	4	19	3
Chile	15	2	10	1	12	2
Regional Total	**452**	**25**	**281**	**93**	**342**	**53**

A key feature of the Latin American economy is the process of trade liberalisation. This is expected to have increasingly important effects on economic and energy developments in the region. Many countries are striving to stabilise inflation and to modernise their industries using imported technology and capital. Liberalisation is likely to have a significant impact on energy use, through the upgrading of the technological infrastructure of the region. The energy supply potential is likely to be enhanced and increasing energy trade will lead to greater overall economic efficiency. A major step in this direction is MERCOSUR (Mercado Comun del Sur - the Southern Cone Common Market agreement). The members are Argentina, Brazil, Paraguay and Uruguay, and associate members are Bolivia and Chile. This agreement creates a free trade area of more than 200 million people. MERCOSUR became fully effective in 1995; it provides for common external tariffs in 85% of traded goods. Mexico is also a member of NAFTA (North American Free Trade Agreement), which was implemented in 1994. NAFTA has liberalised Mexico's trade with the United States and Canada. In 1997, Mexico displaced Japan as the second largest importer of US goods. Other regional trade pacts are actively being discussed.

Restructuring and deregulation of the energy sector may also affect future energy trends in Latin America. The future of trade liberalisation and energy sector restructuring create key uncertainties surrounding the projections presented in this Outlook.

Box 18.1: **Restructuring of the Latin American Energy Sector**

The energy sector of Latin America is undergoing substantial change in almost all countries. The main aims of the reforms are to deregulate parts of the energy supply industry and to reduce monopolies.

Private capital is increasingly allowed to play an important role in energy sector development, either through the privatisation of state-owned companies, such as YPF, the former state-owned oil company, in Argentina, or in competition with state utilities. This trend can have a significant impact on the energy sector.

In the hydrocarbon sector, both oil and gas supplies are likely to increase as a result of the introduction of private capital, the more competitive environment and the increasing participation of foreign companies. The region is well endowed with oil and gas resources. A key constraint on capacity expansion in the past has been limited investment.

Almost every country in the region is in the process of reforming the regulatory framework for the power distribution sector, aiming at creating a level playing field which, in turn, will promote competition and attract private investment in the whole electricity system. Competition in generation is expected to lower costs through increased operating efficiency and investment in gas-fired plants with high thermal efficiency.

Total primary commercial energy demand in Latin America increased at an average annual rate of about 4% between 1971 and 1995, to reach over 450 Mtoe. The predominance of oil in overall primary and final energy demand, and the importance of hydro in the generation of electricity, are two striking features of the region as a whole. Energy systems of individual countries, however, are quite distinct, with Argentina being one of the most gas-intensive countries in the world, while the energy systems of the poorest countries are still dominated by biomass.

Figure 18.1: **Total Primary Energy Supply**

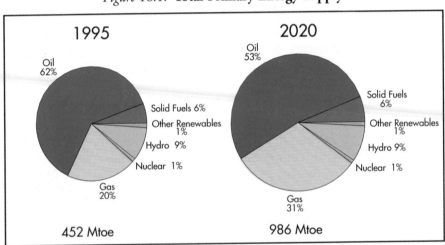

The fuel structure of primary energy demand changed significantly since 1971. As shown in Figure 18.1, oil and gas still account for more than 80% of the region's primary commercial energy demand. While oil has continued to be the dominant fuel, its share fell from 76% in 1971 to just above 62% in 1995. Over the same period, the share of gas increased from 15% to 20%. This shift has been the outcome of changes in relatively few countries. The major impetus has been to conserve oil supplies for export or to reduce dependence on imported oil. As large-scale hydro schemes have been constructed in several countries, hydro's share in electricity generation has increased to about 64%, from 53% in 1971. Over the Outlook period, the share of hydro is projected to decline, partly due to the restructuring of the sector that will favour smaller, less costly schemes based on gas. Coal has always played a small role in the region's energy balance, except in those countries where indigenous resources are available, such as Colombia, or where alternatives such as gas are unavailable. As in other developing regions, non-commercial biomass fuels, mostly wood and sugar cane products, are also used to meet energy demand.

Table 18.3 shows that economic activity in Latin America is assumed to grow at 3.3% over the Outlook period. This is almost the same rate as in the last two decades. The longer-term economic Outlook is expected to be strengthened by the effects of trade liberalisation and consequent productivity improvements. Population growth is assumed to slow down to 1.3% on average over the Outlook period, down from around 1.8% in the last decade. Thus, per capita incomes are likely to increase at about 2% per annum and reach a level of $9000 (in purchasing power parities and 1990 prices) in 2020. It is assumed that domestic energy prices will follow international price trends.

Table 18.3: **Energy Price Assumptions for Latin America**

	1971	1995	2010	2020	1995-2020 Annual Growth Rate
Coal Price ($1990 per metric ton)	44	40	42	46	0.5%
Oil Price ($1990 per barrel)	6	15	17	25	2.1%
Natural Gas Price ($1990 per 1000 cubic feet)	0.6	1.3	1.7	2.5	2.5%
GDP ($Billion 1990 and PPP)	1186	2634	4410	5944	3.3%
Population (millions)	289	478	589	659	1.3%
GDP per Capita ($1000 1990 and PPP per person)	4.1	5.5	7.5	9.0	2.0%

Energy Demand Outlook

Overview

In the business as usual case, commercial energy demand in Latin America is projected to grow at an average annual rate of 3.2% and to reach almost 1000 Mtoe by 2020. This is almost identical to the assumed GDP growth rate over the Outlook period. Oil is expected to remain the dominant fuel, but its share drops to 53% from 62%.

This will be made up mainly by gas, growing at an annual average rate of almost 5%. Hydro will retain its 9% share. No substantial changes in the shares of other fuels are expected.

Table 18.4: **Total Primary Energy Supply (Mtoe)**

	1971	1995	2010	2020	1995-2020 Annual Growth Rate
TPES	**181**	**452**	**738**	**986**	**3.2%**
Solid Fuels	8	25	44	59	3.5%
Oil	137	281	424	520	2.5%
Gas	28	93	185	306	4.9%
Nuclear	0	5	8	8	2.0%
Hydro	8	43	69	84	2.8%
Other Renewables	0	6	8	10	2.1%

Total final commercial energy demand is expected to more than double, at an annual average growth rate of 2.9%. The shares of oil and coal are expected to decline and those of gas and electricity to increase. In 2020, oil is expected to hold a share of close to 60% in total final commercial energy consumption, the second highest share after East Asia, amongst regions analysed in this Outlook. More than 70% of incremental final oil demand is projected to come from the transportation sector.

Table 18.5: **Total Final Energy Consumption (Mtoe)**

	1971	1995	2010	2020	1995-2020 Annual Growth Rate
TFC	**127**	**342**	**540**	**706**	**2.9%**
Solid Fuels	5	16	19	21	1.2%
Oil	98	224	329	407	2.4%
Gas	12	50	94	134	4.0%
Electricity	12	53	98	144	4.1%

Energy Related Services

Stationary Sectors

Energy demand for stationary services is expected to rise broadly in line with GDP, at an annual rate of 2.6%. While oil and coal demand are expected to increase moderately, gas use is projected to rise rapidly, at 4% over the Outlook period.

Future trends in residential/commercial energy demand will depend on per capita income levels, the urbanisation rate and the speed of substitution of non-commercial fuels by commercial energy. Trends in end-use prices will also affect the demand Outlook for the sector. In some Latin American countries, there has already been a restructuring of energy prices in recent years to bring them closer to international levels. In other countries, however, end-use prices (for the household/commercial sector) remain below international levels. In the projections presented here, it has been assumed that all countries in the region gradually adopt a more market-oriented approach to the pricing of energy products.

The industry sector accounts for over a third of final commercial energy consumption and has grown rapidly since 1971, as the region embarked on a programme of industrialisation, often led by the most energy intensive sectors. Given the region's potential for using its resource industries as a base for moving into higher value-added products, it is assumed in this Outlook that industrial production will grow faster than GDP. Energy demand growth in industry, however, is likely to lag behind industrial production, as energy prices continue to approach international levels.

Table 18.6: **Energy Use in Stationary Sectors by Fuel (Mtoe)**

	1971	1995	2010	2020	1995-2020 Annual Growth Rate
Total	**64**	**158**	**238**	**298**	**2.6%**
Solid Fuels	5	16	19	21	1.2%
Oil	47	93	127	146	1.8%
Gas	12	49	92	131	4.0%

Figure 18.2: **Energy Use in Stationary Sectors by Fuel**

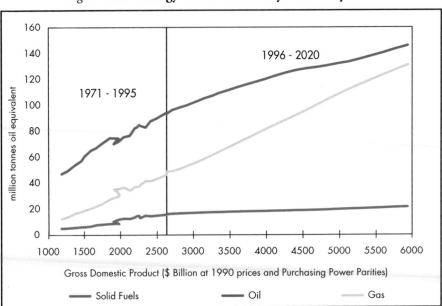

Mobility

Demand for mobility in Latin America is projected to increase in a linear fashion along with GDP. At an average annual growth rate of 2.8%, the current level of consumption is expected to double over the projection period. Compared to other developing regions, Latin America has a relatively high degree of vehicle ownership, reflecting higher per capita incomes, high levels of urbanisation, a history of low, subsidised prices for transport fuels across the region and the large distances between cities. But there are large differences within the region, with the number of passenger vehicles per 1000 people in 1996 about 9 in Guatemala, 130 in Argentina, 84 in Brazil (in 1993) and 95 in Mexico[2]. There is still a substantial potential for increase in vehicle ownership as incomes rise.

There have been many initiatives to encourage the use of alternative fuels in the region. These include an alcohol fuels programme in Brazil and the promotion of compressed natural gas in Argentina, Colombia and Chile. These programmes have affected the fuel mix in these countries in varying degrees, mainly through

2. *World Road Statistics 98*, International Road Federation, 1998.

incentives provided by governments. The deregulation process in the region's energy markets is expected to affect such programmes adversely. We do not foresee a substantial penetration of alternative fuels in the mobility fuel mix over the projection period.

Figure 18.3: **Energy Use for Mobility**

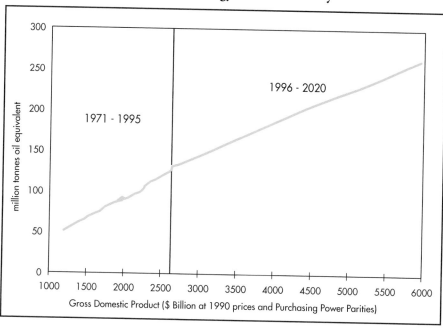

Table 18.7: **Energy Use for Mobility (Mtoe)**

	1971	1995	2010	2020	1995-2020 Annual Growth Rate
Total	51	131	204	263	2.8%

Electricity

Electricity demand in Latin America is projected to grow by 4.1% a year over the Outlook period, significantly faster than the assumed GDP growth rate. This implies almost a tripling of electricity demand. Electricity's current 16% share of total final commercial consumption increases to 20% in 2020, when electricity will be the second most important energy type after oil.

In 1995, about 48% of this electricity was consumed in industry and 52% in the residential/commercial sector. In both sectors, the share of electricity in total final consumption is expected to expand, reflecting rising income levels, urbanisation, structural and technological shifts in the industry sector and the increasing use of electrical appliances in the residential/commercial sectors.

Figure 18.4: **Total Final Electricity Demand**

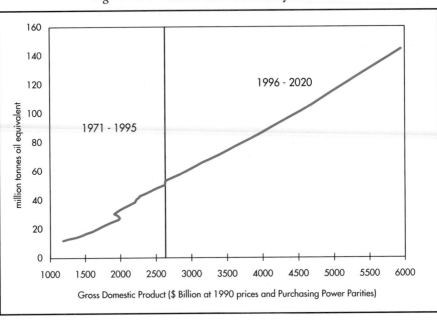

Table 18.8: **Total Final Electricity Demand (Mtoe)**

	1971	1995	2010	2020	1995-2020 Annual Growth Rate
Electricity	12	53	98	144	4.1%

Supply

Power Generation

Latin America's electricity generation is unique among the regions analysed in this Outlook, in that it is highly dependent on the region's abundant hydro resources. In 1995, hydro electricity accounted for 64% of total electricity output in the region.

Oil has been a significant fuel in electricity generation in the past, but its importance has been declining. Its share fell to 17% in 1995, down from one third of total output in 1971. In place of oil, gas-fired generation is becoming increasingly popular, based on increased production of the region's gas reserves, development of infrastructure to deliver the gas across Latin America as well as growing environmental concerns. The most important of these projects is the pipeline that will bring gas from Bolivia to Brazil. Other pipelines are scheduled to deliver Argentinean gas to Chile.

Electricity generation and capacity in Latin America are projected to grow at around 4% a year. Over the Outlook period, the region's electricity generation mix could change significantly and become more dependent on fossil fuels, notably on gas.

Table 18.9: **Electricity Generation Mix (TWh)**

	1995	**2010**	**2020**
Solid Fuels	42	109	163
Oil	134	236	275
Gas	76	222	613
Nuclear	18	30	30
Hydro	495	803	980
Renewables	7	9	11
Total	**772**	**1409**	**2073**

About one third of new capacity in Latin America could come from hydroelectric plants. Hydro electricity generation is assumed to increase at 2.8% a year. The rate of growth will slow as the best sites are developed. Consequently, the share of hydro in the electricity generation mix is expected to decline, from 64% in 1995, to 47% by 2020.

Nearly half of Latin American installed hydro capacity, some 51 GW, is in Brazil, which has a vast hydro potential estimated at 143 GW of firm power per annum[3], equivalent to around 289 GW of installed capacity at a 50% load factor. Existing plants, plants under construction and plants at the feasibility stage account for nearly two

---

3. *Brazilian Energy Balance 1997,* Federative Republic of Brazil, Ministry of Mines and Energy.

thirds of the total potential. Estimates of hydro potential have been increasing, even in recent years. In 1990, estimated hydro potential was 12% less than the most recent estimate of 143 GW. The Amazon basin accounts for about 40% of the potential and there are plans to explore it further in the longer term. Some of the projects in the Amazon area are the 11 GW Monte Belo plant, the 5.7 GW Altamira plant, the 9.5 GW TA-1 plant on the Tapajes river and the 6.9 GW MR-1 plant on the Madeira river[4].

The ELETROBRAS 10-year expansion plan (1996-2006) calls for 22 GW of additional hydro capacity. Under longer term plans, the share of hydro in installed capacity could fall by 2015, but could still account for 80% to 85% of total capacity[5].

There are plans to develop several bi-national projects in Latin America that would lead to an integration of energy supplies in the region. Such plans include: Roncador (2.8 GW), San Pedro (0.8 GW) and Garabi (originally 1.8 GW, but development of 1.5 GW is more likely) on the Uruguay River; Talavera (6 MW) and Paso Centurion (32 MW) on the Jaguarao River and Itati-Itacora (1.7 GW) on the Limay River.

Private participation in hydro schemes is encouraged. An example is the Garabi plant, which could be built on the Argentinian-Brazilian border. ELETROBRAS, which is supervising the project on behalf of the Brazilian and Argentinean governments, is hoping to offer the project to private investors as a "Build, Operate, Transfer" scheme. Other, unfinished hydro projects in the region are also being offered for privatisation.

Gas-fired generation is projected to make spectacular gains, as gas supplies become increasingly available. A large number of CCGT projects are at various stages of development, as are schemes to convert existing oil-fired facilities to burn gas. Gas-based electricity generation is set to increase at 8.7% per annum and to account for nearly a third of electricity output by the end of the Outlook period.

At the same time, oil-fired generation increases in absolute terms, but its share is projected to decline further. Nearly half of Latin America's oil-based electricity output comes from Mexico, where oil-fired capacity accounts for half of the country's total. The liberalisation of Mexico's gas sector is likely to spur gas use in power generation. The deterioration of air quality in urban areas like Mexico City, Monterrey

4. *International Private Power Quarterly,* 1st quarter 1998.
5. *Plan 2015, National Electric Energy Plan,* 1994, Eletrobras, Rio de Janeiro, 1994.

and Guadalajara has sparked increased environmental concerns. In these areas, as well as in Yucatan, existing power stations that currently use fuel oil are planned to change to natural gas. A total of 4.5 GW is scheduled for conversion[6].

Solid fuels accounted for only 5% of the Latin American electricity generation mix in 1995, but its share could increase by 3 percentage points over the Outlook period and coal-fired capacity is likely to expand from 13 to 31 GW.

Nuclear power plants are in operation in Argentina, Brazil and Mexico, with a total capacity of around 2.9 GW, about 2% of the region's installed capacity.

Table 18.10: **Operating Nuclear Power Plants in Latin America**

Plant Name	Size (MW)	Country
Atucha 1	335	Argentina
Embalse	600	Argentina
Angra-1	626	Brazil
Laguna Verde	2 x 654	Mexico

Argentina's Atucha-1 was the region's first nuclear plant. It is a German-built reactor of unique design that uses natural uranium and heavy water in a pressure reactor. The plant started commercial operation in 1974. The second Argentinean plant, Embalse, was built in the mid-1980s by Canada's AECL. The country has a third, unfinished plant, Atucha 2, with a capacity of 692 MW. Construction started in 1980, but the plant was never completed. The Argentine government plans to privatise the country's nuclear sector and to sell the installations as a package, including the completed Atucha 2. This plan is viewed as problematic because the two existing plants are based on different technologies and construction of Atucha 2 has been stalled for several years. It is assumed in this Outlook that Atucha 1 reaches the end of its operational life by 2004 and that Atucha 2 is not completed.

Brazil's only existing nuclear facility began operation in 1982. As part of the Brazil-Germany Nuclear Agreement, the 1975 Brazilian programme called for 8 plants of 1245 MW capacity. Of these, only

6. *Prospectiva del Sector Electrico 1997-2006,* Secretaria de Energia, Mexico, 1997.

Angra 2 is under construction and equipment has been ordered for Angra 3. We assume that Angra 2 is completed as scheduled, i.e., around 2000, and that Angra 3 remains unfinished during the Outlook period.

Mexico's first nuclear reactor was commissioned in September 1990. The second unit was commissioned five years later. The country has no plans to expand its nuclear capacity in the foreseeable future.

Under these assumptions, installed nuclear capacity in Latin America could be around 4.5 GW in 2020. The share of nuclear electricity generation is expected to fall to 1% of total.

In 1995, electricity generation from geothermal energy was 6.7 TWh. Most of it, some 5.7 TWh, was generated in Mexico, which was, in that year, the third largest producer of geothermal energy in the world. The most important geothermal plant is Cerro Prieto, with an installed capacity of 620 MW. Other Latin American countries that use geothermal include Nicaragua and El Salvador. It is assumed that electricity generation from geothermal sources nearly doubles by the end of the outlook.

Wind power is currently in use in some countries, but at a very small scale. Mexico has included a 54 MW project in its 1997-2006 electricity plan[7].

Biomass, particularly bagasse (sugarcane refuse), has found some applications in electricity generation in several Latin American countries. Over the outlook period, this could increase from 9.6 TWh in 1995 to 17 TWh by 2020.

Co-generation is used in several countries but lack of sufficient data makes it difficult to project future levels.

Oil

Major oil producing countries in the region are Mexico, Venezuela, Brazil, Argentina and Colombia. Mexico and Venezuela are large oil-exporting countries. In Mexico, the oil industry provides about 40% of government revenues. Mexico's official reserves were estimated at 40 billion barrels as of end 1997[8] and it produced about 3.4 million barrels of oil per day in 1997, of which half was exported.

---

7. *Prospectiva del Sector Electrico 1997-2006*, Secretaria de Energia, Mexico, 1997.
8. This and the following oil reserve figures are taken from *BP Statistical Review of World Energy 1998*, on-line data; data on production are taken from the IEA's *Oil Market Report*.

More than half of Mexican production is heavy Mayan supply from the offshore Bay of Campeche area. This output is likely to continue to grow in coming years. The key variable in the Mexican outlook is the upstream budget of PEMEX, the state owned oil company, since the country has an ample resource base. PEMEX has responsibility for the entire upstream sector and most of the downstream sector in Mexico. The prospects for PEMEX to continue to have substantial exploration and production budgets are good. In an environment of growing domestic demand, the government is expected to support oil production in order to maintain strong oil export revenues.

Venezuela, a member of OPEC, is one of the most energy-endowed countries in the world. If its extra-heavy oil deposits in the Orinoco belt are included in reserves, then its oil resources are comparable to those of Saudi Arabia. Official oil reserves amounted to 72 billion barrels at the end of 1997, with the bulk of this consisting of heavy or extra-heavy oil. The state-owned oil company PDVSA expects to maintain its official reserves at current levels for the foreseeable future. Venezuela produced about 3.5 million barrels of conventional and unconventional oil per day in 1997. Over the past three years, Venezuela has raised both its oil production capacity and output by more than 200000 barrels a day each year. Future production increases are likely to come from El Furrial Trend and the Orinoco Belt, both located in the eastern part of the country. The participation of foreign joint venture partners is a key element to Venezuela's plan to increase production. The partners will provide both investment capital and technical expertise.

Brazil also has significant oil reserves. Its current official reserves were estimated at about 4.8 billion barrels as of end 1997. The bulk of the current reserves is located in the offshore Campos basin. In 1997, Brazil produced 1.1 million barrels of oil per day, including 260 thousand barrels per day of alcohol fuels. Despite this production level, Brazil needs to meet about 40% of its consumption through imports, mainly from Argentina, Saudi Arabia and Venezuela. Increases in oil production are likely to be driven by deep-water fields in the Campos Basin, such as Marlim, Barracuda, Albacora, and Roncador; however, self-sufficiency appears to be unlikely in the next two decades.

Argentina, with oil production of about 900 thousand barrels a day in 1997, does not appear to have the geological potential for increasing production substantially. Significant volumes of reserves need to be discovered soon if the current level of production is to be maintained in the long term. The drastic restructuring of YPF, the former state-owned oil company, as well as increased private investment, are seen by many as a model for solving problems in the upstream oil sector in the other countries of the region.

Colombia's oil industry got an important boost after the discovery of the giant Cusiana field in 1991. In 1997, Colombia produced about 660 000 barrels of oil per day, of which more than 300 000 were exported. By 1999, full production from Cusiana and the nearby Cupiagua field is likely to be reached. Production from other discovered, but so far undeveloped, fields is likely to augment Colombian production.

Ecuador's potential is limited by export pipeline constraints, the maturity of many existing fields and the need to replace reserves; it is unlikely to be in a position to increase its production capacity significantly. The positions of Peru, Trinidad and Tobago are similar to that of Ecuador. Details of the Outlook's oil supply projections for Latin America can be found in Chapter 7.

Gas

Latin America's gas reserves were estimated to be around 286 trillion cubic feet at the end of 1997 and are located mainly in Venezuela (50%), Mexico (22%) and Argentina (9%). These three countries also account for 80% of the region's gas production, with roughly equal shares in 1996.

Natural gas production in Latin America reached 111 Mtoe in 1996, 9% above 1995 production. Gas production has increased rapidly during the last three years: annual growth averaged 6.6% in 1993-1996, compared to 2.5% in the previous decade. Gas trade among the countries of the region is increasing as infrastructure is developed. The largest exchanges are currently between Bolivia and Argentina. In 1995, Bolivia exported 1.7 Mtoe, or 68% of its production to Argentina.

Mexico produced 30 Mtoe of natural gas in 1996 from reserves of 64 trillion cubic feet. Given rapidly increasing domestic demand, imports from the US have been used as swing supplies. The major problem for Mexico is that most of the gas is produced in the south-eastern part of the country (most gas produced is associated with oil production in the Bay of Campeche), far from main consuming areas in the north. In 1995, Mexico initiated reforms in its natural gas sector aimed at encouraging greater use of gas throughout the country and, more specifically, private sector investments in natural gas storage, transportation and distribution. The private sector response has been favourable.

Venezuela's gas reserves are estimated to be around 143 trillion cubic feet. In 1996, Venezuela produced 29 Mtoe of natural gas. As in Mexico, all of the gas produced in the country is consumed in the domestic markets; about 60% is used in the oil industry for heavy oil recovery with steam injection, 11% in power generation and the rest in petrochemical production and by other industrial/commercial consumers.

Argentina has the third largest proven reserves of natural gas in Latin America after Venezuela and Mexico. Because most of these reserves were discovered in connection with oil exploration, current production is concentrated in the same five basins as oil production (Noroeste in northern Argentina, Cuyana and Neuquen in the center of the country, and Golfo San Jorge and Austral in the south). Argentina's production reached 28.5 Mtoe in 1996. It also imported some 2 Mtoe from neighbouring countries. Supply is roughly equally divided among power generation, industry and residential/commercial users.

Argentina is the most advanced Latin American country in the privatisation of its gas industry. Following the 1992 Gas Law, the former state monopoly Gas del Estado was split into two pipeline companies, Transportadora de Gas del Sur SA (TGS) and Transportadora de Gas del Norte SA (TGN), and eight distributors. A majority of the shares in TGN and most of the distribution operations were sold to private investors in December 1992. TGS, which supplies gas mainly to southern Argentina and greater Buenos Aires, was privatised in early 1994. The state regulatory agency, ENARGAS, is in charge of regulating the industry and setting rates for natural gas carriers operating under a non-discriminatory "open access" system.

Additional pipeline capacity is needed to serve growing domestic and export markets. TGS and TGN are expanding the capacity of existing domestic lines, which are currently almost fully utilised. Export lines are also being developed to serve new markets in neighbouring Chile, Brazil and Uruguay:
  • Chile. Two lines to Chile were commissioned in 1997: the 700 million cubic feet per day (Mcfd) 290-mile GasAndes line from the Neuquen Basin to Santiago, and the 100 Mcfd 30-mile

Methanex line from Tierra Del Fuego to Cabo, which supplies a methanol plant. A 300 Mcfd 590-mile line in Northen Argentina, Gasoducto Atacama, is under construction and is due to enter service in 1999. Two other lines are planned: Nor Andino, a 280 Mcfd 500-mile line which would run from Northern Argentina to Atacama; and Pacifico, a 140 Mcfd 280 mile link from Neuquen to Concepcion.

- Brazil. A 900 Mcfd 2000-mile pipeline project, Mercosur, linking the Noreste with southern Brazil, has been proposed, though there are doubts about the adequacy of reserves to support the $1.5 billion investment.
- Uruguay. A 450 Mcfd link from Buenos Aires to Montevideo is under construction. There are plans to extend the line to Porto Alegre in Brazil to link up with the Bolivia-Brazil line currently being built. The fourth largest gas producer in Latin America is Trinidad and Tobago, where recent gas discoveries have more than doubled reserves in the last five years. The country is experiencing a burst of investment and growth in the gas sector and its initial LNG exports are expected to begin in 1999. Current production of 6.4 Mtoe is consumed domestically, primarily in the petrochemical industry.

Bolivia, although not a large producer, is set to become the natural gas hub of the Southern Cone market. Bolivia currently has one existing gas export pipeline to Argentina (through which it exported 83% of its production in 1996) with a capacity of 212 million cubic feet per day. Bolivia's future pipeline plans include a link to northern Chile, a pipeline to Brazil, and one to Paraguay. The Bolivia-Brazil gas pipeline is by far the most important of the projects. The final deal was signed in September 1996 and the pipeline is tentatively scheduled to begin gas deliveries to the Brazilian cities of Sao Paulo and Porto Alegre in 1998-99. The contract calls for deliveries of up to 7 trillion cubic feet over the next 20 years, while current Bolivian gas reserves are only 4.5 trillion cubic feet.

With the giant Camisea natural gas field (11 trillion cubic feet), Peru could develop into a significant regional producer and exporter of gas. This is the largest gas field in South America, but it is located in remote jungle more than 1200 km south-east of Lima and it remains to be seen whether full-scale project development will occur. Would the project come to fruition, Brazil is expected to be a large potential customer for Peruvian gas. There are talks on building a pipeline to connect the Camisea field to the main Bolivia-Brazil line. The Bolivia/Brazil/Peru pipelines could represent an important link in a future regionally-integrated gas network for the entire southern cone.

Coal

Colombia and Venezuela contain the principal coal deposits in Latin America. The El Cerrejón coalfield of the Eastern Cordillera of Colombia and the coalfields of the neighbouring Zulia region of Venezuela are the largest of these deposits. In Colombia, substantial resources are found close to the surface. In Venezuela, substantial resources are potentially extractable by underground mining, but priority is being given to surface mining. Colombia accounts for about three-quarters of Latin American coal reserves. The El Cerrejón coalfield contains almost two-thirds of Colombia's coal and is the source of nearly all its coal exports.

In 1997, Colombia and Venezuela produced 33 Mt and 6 Mt of coal respectively. As shown in Table 18.11, production grew steadily over the last two decades. Europe is the main export market for Latin American coal, but the southern US is developing as a market and small quantities go to Asia. The expansion potential for exports in both countries depends mainly on improvements in the infrastructure which require considerable amounts of investment.

Table 18.11: **Hard Coal production - Colombia and Venezuela (Mt)**

	1971	1980	1985	1990	1995	1996	1997
Production	2.7	4.1	9.0	22.7	30. 3	33.6	38.4
Percentage of World	0.1	0.2	0.3	0.6	0.8	0.9	1.0

Biomass

Current Patterns of Biomass Energy Use

Latin America is the most economically advanced and urbanised of the five developing regions[9]. It has the highest average per capita income and the lowest share of agriculture in output (11%). It also has the highest level of per capita consumption of conventional fuels and electricity. The share of urban population is by far the highest of all non-OECD regions (74%), very close to the OECD average (76%).

9. Africa, Latin America, China, East Asia and South Asia.

In these circumstances, it is not surprising that Latin America also has the lowest share of biomass of all developing regions: in 1995, primary biomass consumption was 83 Mtoe, or 16% of total primary energy, 18% of total final energy and 32% of stationary energy uses. These numbers are slightly underestimated since, for projection reasons, the sugarcane-derived alcohol used in the transport sector, mainly in Brazil, has been included with gasoline rather than with biomass[10].

Another distinctive aspect of biomass energy use in Latin America is the large proportion used in the industrial sector: 46% of final consumption in 1995.

The largest biomass user in the region is Brazil, with 37% of the region's final biomass consumption[11]. Mexico, Colombia, Cuba, Peru and Chile together account for another 38%.

Firewood accounts for 60% of all biomass use, and for 93% of use in the residential/commercial sector. Bagasse is the next most important biomass fuel, with 25% of total use and 52% of biomass use in industry. There is comparatively large use of charcoal (8% of total biomass), most of it concentrated in Brazil, where charcoal is produced in large, efficient modern kilns and is used mainly in the production of steel.

Past Trends

Unlike the other developing regions, there exist for Latin America relatively consistent and complete time-series for biomass energy use. According to these data, biomass energy use in Latin America increased at an average annual rate of 0.5% between 1971 and 1995, while its share in the region's energy mix has declined steadily from 34% in 1971 to 18% in 1995. This is, however, the result of very different sectoral trends. While biomass energy use has declined in the residential/commercial sector both in absolute and relative terms, dropping from 64% in 1971 to 34% in 1995, the use of biomass in the industrial sector has increased at a sustained rate (2.8% per annum), and its share of total industrial energy use has only slightly declined from 28% to 22%.

10. This amounted in 1995 to 6.8 Mtoe, of which 6.7 Mtoe in Brazil and 0.1 Mtoe in Argentina. If it had been included in biomass, the above shares would be slightly higher, i.e. 17%, 19% and 35% respectively.
11. If alcohol were included, this share would be 43%.

Although these figures are given for the entire region, they are not representative of biomass trends in all countries and sub-regions and are highly influenced by trends in Brazil. As can be observed in Table 18.12, biomass use in Brazil decreased significantly over the period 1971-1995[12], but increased in all other countries.

Table 18.12: **Final Biomass Energy Use in Latin America, 1995**

| | Final biomass energy use* (Mtoe) | of which: in industry | Share of country in the region | Share of biomass in TFC | Biomass energy use (1971-1995) | | |
					Total	Industrial	Resid./ Comm.
Brazil	27.3	69%	37%	21%	-0.8%	3.2%	-4.3%
Mexico	9.4	21%	13%	10%	0.8%	2.2%	0.5%
Colombia	6.8	25%	9%	26%	1.9%	4.2%	1.3%
Cuba	4.6	98%	6%	38%	2.6%	2.6%	1.3%
Peru	3.9	12%	5%	34%	0.7%	1.3%	0.6%
Chile	3.2	24%	4%	21%	3.6%	5.2%	3.2%
Guatemala	2.8	6%	4%	62%	1.9%	-2.8%	2.6%
Paraguay	2.3	53%	3%	62%	3.1%	5.9%	1.4%
Argentina	2.2	82%	3%	6%	1.1%	1.6%	-0.2%
Others	10.5	-	14%	-	-	-	-
Latin America	73.0	46%	100%	18%	0.5%	2.8%	-0.8%

* Excludes alcohol use in transport sector.

Trends in the different biomass fuels have also been very different: during the period 1971-1995, firewood use declined (at 0.7% per annum), and the use of bagasse, charcoal and black liquor grew significantly (2.8% per annum, 3.6% per annum and 11.4% per annum respectively).

Projections

It is expected that current trends will continue during the Outlook period, with decreasing biomass use in the residential/commercial sector (-0.6% per annum) and increasing biomass use in the industrial sector (1.4% per annum), with an overall increasing trend (0.4% per annum) as shown in Figure 18.5. During

12. If alcohol use is included, however, Brazil's biomass consumption remains flat rather than decreases.

the same period, the use of conventional energy increases at much higher rates (3.1% in the industrial sector and 3.0% in the residential/commercial sector[13]). Thus, the share of biomass is projected to further decrease from 22% to 15% in the industrial sector and from 34% to 17% in the residential/commercial sector. Overall, the share of biomass in total final consumption falls from 20% in 1995 to 10% in 2020 (and from 16% to 9% in total primary energy).

Figure 18.5: **Total Primary Energy Supply including Biomass, 1995-2020**

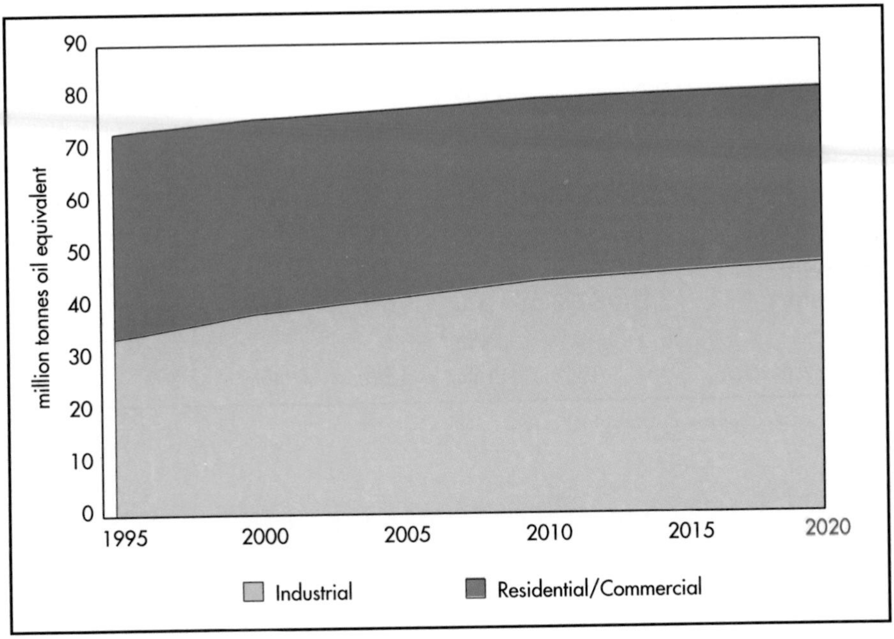

As can be observed in Figure 18.6, including biomass in the energy mix alters significantly the level and inclination of the energy intensity curve, which decreases more rapidly, reflecting the decreasing share of biomass in the energy mix.

13. Including agriculture.

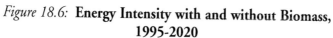

Figure 18.6: **Energy Intensity with and without Biomass, 1995-2020**

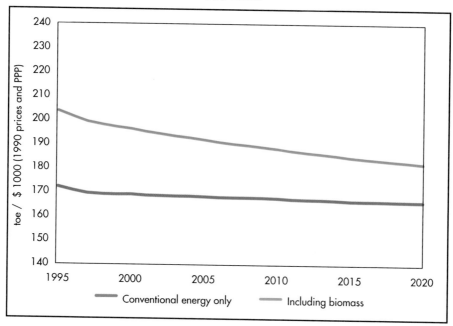

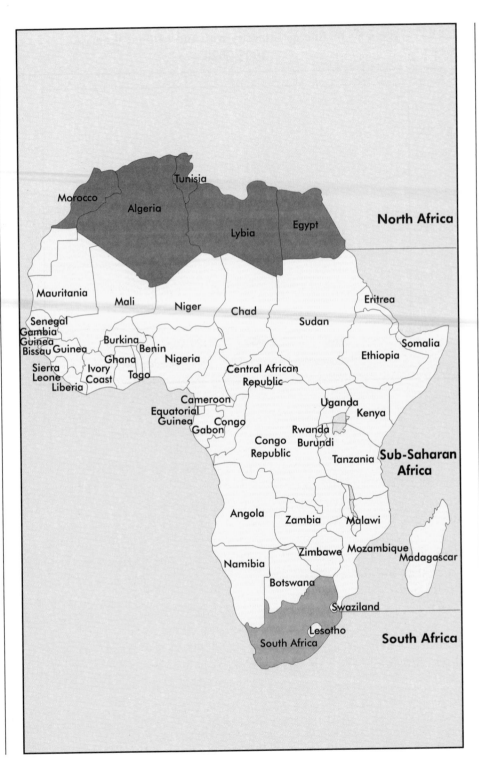

North Africa

Morocco
Tunisia
Algeria
Lybia
Egypt

Mauritania
Mali
Niger
Chad
Eritrea
Senegal
Gambia
Guinea
Bissau
Guinea
Burkina
Benin
Nigeria
Sudan
Somalia
Ghana
Ethiopia
Sierra
Leone
Ivory
Coast
Togo
Liberia
Central African
Republic
Cameroon
Uganda
Equatorial
Guinea
Congo
Gabon
Kenya
Congo
Republic
Rwanda
Burundi
Tanzania
Sub-Saharan
Africa
Angola
Zambia
Malawi
Zimbawe
Mozambique
Madagascar
Namibia
Botswana
Swaziland
Lesotho
South Africa
South Africa

CHAPTER 19
AFRICA

Introduction

Africa is a diverse continent from both economic and energy perspectives. Figure 19.1 shows some differences between the three sub-regions: South Africa, North Africa and Sub-Saharan Africa[1]. There are a number of countries with vast resources of oil, gas and coal. However, the energy sector in the region is largely underdeveloped. Africa includes some of the least developed countries in the world and has the second lowest average income per capita ($1530 per head at 1990 prices and purchasing power parity compared with $1270 for South Asia) among the world regions considered in this Outlook. Population growth is expected to continue to be rapid. In real terms, very limited improvements in the standard of living are expected over the Outlook period. GDP per capita will be one of the major determinants of energy demand in the region and, at the same time, one of the major uncertainties.

Africa's share of total world population exceeds 12% and it consumes less than 3% of the total world commercial energy. By comparison, the United States accounts for less than 5% of population and uses 25% of world energy. As shown in Table 19.1, the current level of commercial primary energy use in the African continent is 226 Mtoe, less than that of France. The per capita energy consumption figure also underlines the extremely low level of energy use: in 1995, it was 0.33 toe per capita in Africa, compared to 4.45 toe per capita for the OECD as a whole.

In 1995, South Africa and North Africa each consumed almost 40% of the region's primary commercial energy. All other countries, which consumed the remaining 20%, account for some 75% of the

1. South Africa is defined here as the Republic of South Africa. North Africa is defined as Morocco, Algeria, Libya, Tunisia and Egypt. Sub-Saharan Africa is defined as the remaining African countries. Please note that the following African countries have not been considered in this Outlook due to lack of data: Comoros, Namibia, Saint Helena, and Western Sahara.

population. More than half a billion people in Sub-Saharan Africa consumed 48 Mtoe of commercial energy, less than that consumed in Belgium.

Figure 19.1: **GDP and Energy Consumption per Capita by Region**

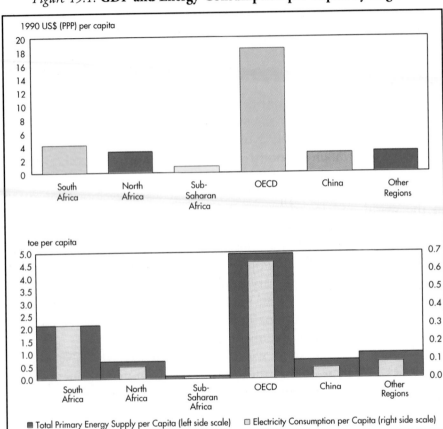

On the supply side, North Africa is an important producer of oil and gas, whereas South Africa is a major supplier of coal. As shown in Figure 19.2, solid fuels accounted for slightly more than one third of Africa's total commercial primary energy demand in 1995. Of this amount, about 90% was used in South Africa, where the energy market relies heavily on indigenous resources. Coal accounts for 83% of South Africa's primary energy demand. Oil is the dominant fuel in the region's fuel mix with a share of 43%. North African countries rely mainly on oil and gas, consuming 53% and 83% of the continent's

World Energy Outlook

total. The relative economic growth rates of these countries have, to a large extent, determined the regional energy mix. Observed substitution across the continent between coal/oil and coal/gas is more apparent than real, resulting more from the relative economic growth rates of different countries than from any actual substitution. On the other hand, the substitution between oil and gas in North Africa, and, at the level of final consumption, the substitution between electricity and other fuels, are of a more substantive nature. Non-commercial biomass meets a large proportion of energy demand in many countries in Sub-Saharan Africa.

Table 19.1: **Economic Performance and Population of Selected African Countries**

	GDP		Population		GDP per Capita
	1995 ($ Billion 1990 and PPP)	Growth Rates (1985-95) (annual, %)	1995 (millions)	Growth Rates (1985-95) (annual, %)	1995 ($ 1000 1990 and PPP per person)
South Africa	172	1.1	41	2.3	4.2
Egypt	156	2.2	58	2.2	2.7
Algeria	84	0.3	28	2.5	3.0
Nigeria	132	3.9	111	3.0	1.2
Libya	25	-1.2	5	3.6	4.6
Regional Total	**1080**	**1.8**	**705**	**2.7**	**1.5**

Table 19.2: **Energy Demand in Selected Africa Countries (Mtoe)**

	Primary Energy Supply				Final Consumption	
	Total	Coal	Oil	Gas	Total	Electricity
South Africa	88.9	73.6	10.8	1.7	46.3	12.3
Egypt	34.7	0.6	22.2	10.9	22.8	4.5
Algeria	24.3	0.5	8.0	15.8	14.1	1.2
Nigeria	18.4	0.0	13.5	4.4	9.3	0.8
Libya	15.8	0.0	11.7	4.0	8.7	1.5
Regional Total	**225.8**	**81.6**	**96.9**	**39.2**	**136.2**	**26.0**

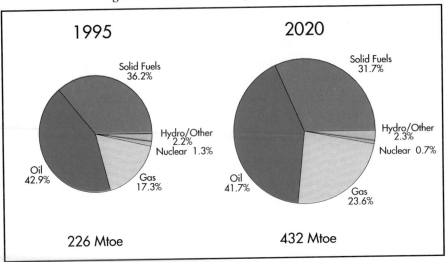

Figure 19.2: **Total Primary Energy Supply**

In order to maintain even the current low standard of living in Africa, GDP will have to grow considerably. In the 1980s, Africa's GDP grew less than population and so Africa had a lower GDP per capita in 1990 than in 1980. Since the early 1990s, economic performance in Sub-Saharan Africa, the poorest sub-region of the continent, has improved. Growth of real GDP across the 49 countries of Sub-Saharan Africa reached 4.3% a year from 1995 to 1997, compared with 1.5% from 1990 to 1994 and 2.5% from 1981 to 1989[2]. The assumption of regional GDP growth over the Outlook period, around 2.5% per annum, is similar to recent history, leading to a marginal rise in GDP per capita over the Outlook period. The evolution of GDP in Africa is the key uncertainty for the projections presented here. The heavy dependence on commodity exports in many African economies makes GDP growth rates sensitive to relatively small shifts in world commodity prices. South Africa is sensitive to movements in the price of coal and precious metals, and North Africa particularly sensitive to the evolution of oil and gas prices. Furthermore, given much of Africa's dependence on agriculture, meteorological conditions are also important. Long-term sustained economic performance in the region will also largely depend on economic factors, such as the success of trade liberalisation, growth of investment and implementation of structural reforms.

2. International Monetary Fund - *World Economic Outlook,* May 1998.

In 1995, Africa had a population of over 700 million. During the last decade, population in Africa grew at an average of 2.7%, or more than 16 million people every year. Clearly, demographics will be a major determinant of future energy demand. It is assumed that African population will grow at 2.4% till 2020. Under this assumption, the population in Africa will exceed 800 million in 2000, will pass the one billion mark shortly before 2010 and reach about 1.3 billion by 2020.

Table 19.3: **Assumptions for the African Region**

	1971	1995	2010	2020	1995-2020 Annual Growth Rate
Coal Price ($1990 per metric ton)	44	40	42	46	0.5%
Oil Price ($1990 per barrel)	6	15	17	25	2.1%
GDP ($Billion 1990 and PPP)	578	1080	1560	1986	2.5%
Population (millions)	366	705	1035	1279	2.4%
GDP per Capita ($1000 1990 and PPP per person)	1.6	1.5	1.5	1.6	0.1%

Energy Demand Outlook

Overview

As shown in Table 19.4, total primary commercial energy demand in Africa is projected to grow by an annual average of 2.6% over the Outlook period. This is slightly higher than the assumed GDP growth rate, and indicates a continuing rise in the energy intensity level. Including non-commercial biomass in the total energy balance changes the intensity trends significantly. This issue is discussed later in this chapter. Oil is expected to continue to dominate the total primary energy demand mix. Coal is likely to lose some market share, which will be made up mainly by gas. No significant changes in the shares of other fuel types are expected.

Table 19.4: **Total Primary Energy Supply (Mtoe)**

	1971	1995	2010	2020	1995-2020 Annual Growth Rate
TPES	76	226	339	432	2.6%
Solid Fuels	37	82	112	137	2.1%
Oil	34	97	145	180	2.5%
Gas	3	39	70	102	3.9%
Nuclear	0	3	3	3	0.3%
Hydro	2	5	6	7	1.6%
Other Renewables	0	0	2	3	8.9%

Total final energy demand is expected to almost double by 2020, at an average annual growth rate of 2.6%. Electricity demand is projected to grow the most rapidly. Its share in total final energy demand is expected to increase from 19% to 23% by 2020. Oil will retain a dominant share of 56% and coal's share is likely to decline over the projection period.

Table 19.5: **Total Final Energy Consumption (Mtoe)**

	1971	1995	2010	2020	1995-2020 Annual Growth Rate
TFC	57	136	202	260	2.6%
Solid Fuels	19	21	26	29	1.4%
Oil	30	78	115	147	2.6%
Gas	1	11	18	23	2.9%
Electricity	7	26	44	60	3.4%

Energy Related Services

Stationary Sectors

Demand for energy in stationary uses is projected to rise in line with GDP at an annual growth rate of 2.6%. Unlike many other regions in this Outlook, the share of oil in total stationary uses is expected to rise significantly. Within the residential/commercial sector, a key question is the long term availability and use of non-commercial biomass energy, in particular in Sub-Saharan Africa. Because commercial fuels are still several times more expensive than traditional fuels, it is still difficult for low-income consumers to switch to commercial energy. Given projected low income levels in the region, the substitution of commercial for non-commercial energy is expected to be slow. In the industrial sector, oil and gas shares are projected to increase at the expense of coal. This is mainly due to expected slower growth in South Africa.

Figure 19.3: **Energy Use in Stationary Sectors by Fuel**

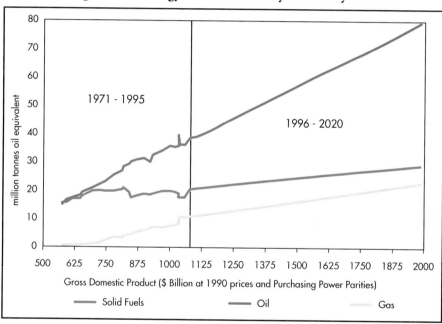

Table 19.6: **Energy Use in Stationary Sectors by Fuel (Mtoe)**

	1971	1995	2010	2020	1995-2020 Annual Growth Rate
Total	**31**	**70**	**102**	**132**	**2.6%**
Solid Fuels	16	21	25	29	1.4%
Oil	15	39	60	80	2.9%
Gas	1	11	17	23	3.1%

Mobility

Table 19.7 shows that demand for mobility is expected to grow at an annual average of slightly over 2% over the Outlook period. This is one of the lowest expected growth rates for this sector in the developing regions. Factors limiting the growth of demand for mobility are both low per capita income and the poor state of transport infrastructure.

Figure 19.4: **Passenger Vehicle Ownership**

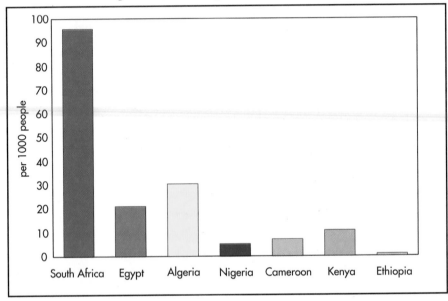

Figure 19.4 shows that passenger vehicle ownership is African countries is extremely low, except for South Africa. Given the limited improvement expected in average real income levels, a substantial increase in the vehicle fleet in most of the countries in the region is unlikely.

Table 19.7: **Energy Use for Mobility (Mtoe)**

	1971	1995	2010	2020	1995-2020 Annual Growth Rate
Total		19	40	56	68	2.1%

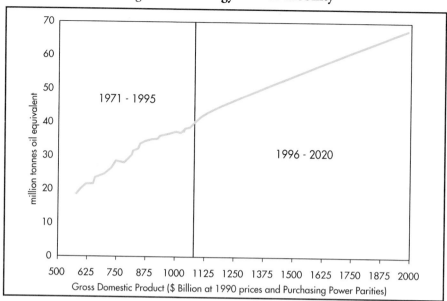

Figure 19.5: **Energy Use for Mobility**

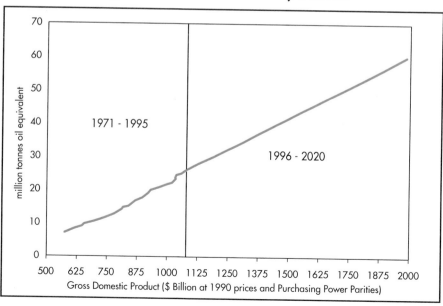

Figure 19.6: **Total Final Electricity Demand**

Electricity

As shown in Figure 19.6, electricity demand in Africa is projected to grow in a linear fashion with GDP. It is expected to double at an average growth rate of 3.4%, significantly faster than assumed for GDP.

Table 19.8: **Total Final Electricity Demand (Mtoe)**

	1971	1995	2010	2020	1995-2020 Annual Growth Rate
Electricity	7	26	44	60	3.4%

A major reason underlying the expectation of strong growth in electricity demand is the current low level of electrification rates in many African countries. Only around one quarter of African households have access to electricity[3]. In South Africa, about 40% of the population had access to electricity in 1995 and used over half the continent's electricity.

Supply

Power Generation

African electricity output amounted to 367 TWh in 1995. South Africa accounted for about half of it; the five countries of North Africa (Algeria, Egypt, Libya, Morocco, Tunisia) produced 30% of total output in the region; all other countries (about 50) produced the remaining 20%.

South Africa accounted for 95% of Africa's coal-fired generation. In the countries of North and Sub-Saharan Africa, oil, gas and hydro plants are the principal sources of electricity supply.

Electricity output in Africa is projected to grow at 3.4% per year in the period to 2020. Coal is expected to lose market share, but will still generate about 43% of all electricity in 2020. Currently, South Africa has about 4.5 GW of excess power generation capacity[4]. Demand growth in the early years of the Outlook period will be met by an increase in the use of existing capacity.

3. Bizuneh Fikru, *African Energy Situation - Challenges and Options,* paper presented at Oil and Gas in Africa Conference, London 27-28 May 1998.
4. *ESKOM 1995 Statistical Yearbook,* South Africa, 1997.

Table 19.9: **African Capacity (GW) and Electricity Generation (TWh)**

	1995		2020	
	Capacity	Generation	Capacity	Generation
Solid Fuels	43	186	70	364
Oil	20	63	32	104
Gas	12	51	73	282
Nuclear	2	11	2	12
Hydro	20	56	30	84
Other Renewables	0	0	2	5
Total	**97**	**367**	**208**	**848**

A few other countries in the region have plans to build coal-fired plants. Egypt is planning to construct two plants: the first at Ayun Musa (2x300 MW) in the Sinai Peninsula, the second at Zaferana (2x600) on the Red Sea coast. Both will also be capable of burning gas.

Natural gas use in power generation is expected to increase rapidly, faster than coal or oil; its share in the electricity output mix is projected to rise from just under 14% in 1995 to 33% in 2020.

Currently, almost all gas-fired generation is concentrated in Algeria, Egypt, Nigeria and Tunisia. Most of the incremental demand for gas is likely to come from North African countries, which will try increasingly to substitute gas for oil in order to free up a greater quantity of oil for export or other uses. Some of the existing oil-fired plants in these countries have already been converted to burn gas. A number of gas-based plants are under development. Examples of such projects include a 50-MW plant in Sebha, south of Tripoli; a 800-MW in Zuwara on the west coast of Libya; a 400 MW plant near Tangiers; a 350-450 MW plant in Kenitra in Morocco and a 2x350 MW plant at Sidi Krier near Alexandria, which could also use fuel oil as a back-up fuel.

The countries in Sub-Saharan Africa are more likely to continue to use oil. Many of these countries currently use oil for power generation in small scale units. Given that Africa has a very poor transport infrastructure, it is unlikely that there will be a substantial shift to coal. Some generators, however, could use more gas. The share of oil is projected to fall from 17% to 12% over the Outlook period.

The share of hydroelectric power is also expected to fall as additions to hydroelectric capacity are made at a slower rate than the growth in electricity demand. Hydro capacity in 1995 was 20 GW and is assumed to grow to 30 GW by 2020. Africa, particularly Sub-Saharan Africa, has a large hydro potential, which could supply about 1300 TWh per year. Current utilisation of hydropower resources is only 4%. Poor integration of the power networks at sub-regional level limits the development of hydro resources. Nevertheless, there are plans to link the electricity supply grids of some countries.

The 520-MW Capanda hydroelectric scheme in Angola is one of the largest projects. Completion is tentatively scheduled for the end of the century. It would double Angola's generating capacity. There are plans to create a national grid by linking the three regional electricity sectors and establishing grid linkages with neighbouring countries.

The Sounda Gorge hydroelectric project, with a final capacity of 1 GW, could make the Congo a significant regional exporter of electricity. Construction of the first phase is underway at the Limpopo River site, which will have a capacity of 10 MW. It will be used to generate cash flow for subsequent phases. The second phase will be the construction of a 130-foot high dam which will boost the plant's generating capacity to 240 MW. A third phase will increase the dam's height to over 300 feet and its generating capacity to 1 GW. Feasibility studies for the third phase are still in progress, and financing remains an issue.

In 1996, twelve members of the South African Development Community signed a co-operation agreement to develop and integrate their hydropower and other water resources. The most important of the projects under this agreement is the 2040 MW Cahora Bassa project in Mozambique. The plant was completed in the 1970s, but has generated little electricity. With the completion of its transmission connections, the plant could sell power to the South African utility ESKOM.

South Africa is the only country in the region which has any nuclear generating capability. The nuclear plant at Koeberg consists of two 965 MW pressurised water reactors which were constructed by Framatome and are owned and operated by ESKOM. The reactors came on line in 1984 and 1985. Given the availability of relatively cheap coal supplies and the end of South African isolation, future expansion of nuclear power is not expected.

Some of the North African countries have expressed interest in building nuclear plants for electricity generation. It is assumed in this study that none of these countries will have nuclear plants operating before 2020.

There is limited use of electricity generation from renewable sources in Africa. Solar energy would seem to be an option for many countries, particularly in rural areas, and a number of small-scale projects are underway, but it is likely that pricing regimes will have to change in order to make large-scale investment and exploitation worthwhile. There is a need to create more commercial operations for maintenance, expansion and new developments.

A number of countries have significant geothermal potential: Kenya, Ethiopia and Uganda. Kenya has a small amount of geothermal generating capacity (45 MW) and has plans to build additional capacity over the next few years.

Wind turbines are already in use in several African countries including Somalia, Kenya, Sudan and Cape Verde. Wind power is also being considered in Egypt and Morocco.

Generation from renewable sources is assumed to grow by 11% per annum over the Outlook period. However, even with such rapid growth, renewable sources will continue to make a very small contribution to the electricity generation mix.

Oil

Africa's official oil reserves at the end of 1997 amounted to 70 billion barrels, or about 7% of the world's official reserves[5]. Three OPEC members are the major oil producers in the region: Libya, Nigeria and Algeria with a share of 42%, 24% and 13% of total reserves. Egypt, Angola and Gabon also have oil reserves. In 1997, total oil production in Africa reached 8.1 Mbd. The top contributors were Nigeria at 2.4 Mbd, Libya at 1.5 Mbd, and Algeria at 1.5 Mbd. The figures include NGLs, which in the case of Algeria, amount to 0.6 Mbd. Total production for these three countries averaged 5.3 Mbd in 1997. Oil revenues are vital for all three countries. In 1996, the share of oil export revenues in total exports from Algeria, Nigeria and Libya were 75%, 97% and 95% respectively[6]. In the case of Algeria, most of the rest of the export revenues come from gas.

In 1997, non-OPEC countries in Africa produced a further 2.8 million barrels per day. One third of this came from Egypt and one quarter from Angola, with small amounts of production in many other countries, including Gabon.

As discussed in more in detail in Chapter 7, future oil production

5. Oil reserve data in this chapter come from the *BP Statistical Review of World Energy 1998*.
6. *OPEC Annual Statistical Bulletin-1996*, 1997.

in Africa looks likely to remain stable up to 2010 and then start to decline. Figure 19.7 shows that, the continent is expected to remain a net oil exporter over the Outlook period. However, the export volume is projected to decrease from 5.5 million barrels per day now to 2.2 million barrels per day in 2020 as a result of a slowdown in production levels and increasing domestic demand.

Figure 19.7: **Oil Supply and Demand**

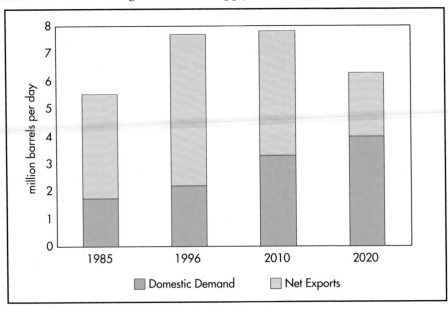

Gas

Gas reserves in Africa are highly concentrated, with over half in North Africa and more than one third in Nigeria. Egypt and Cameroon also have significant gas reserves. Total African gas reserves were 349 trillion cubic feet at the end of 1997, of which 131 is in Algeria, 115 in Nigeria and 46 in Libya. Total production in the region reached 2.2 Mtoe.

Domestic gas demand growth is projected to be around 4% per annum on average. It is driven primarily by the penetration of gas in the power sector. Less than 20% of incremental gas demand is expected to go to final consumption. The lack of infrastructure is the main reason for the limited contribution of gas to industry and to the residential/commercial sectors.

Currently, Algeria and Libya export natural gas to Europe: Algeria via two pipelines and as LNG, Libya using exclusively LNG. Libya currently exports only to Spain from the liquefaction plant at Marsa El Brega. These exports are about 1.5 million tonnes per annum and are unlikely to increase significantly. Algeria has contracted to export about 37 billion cubic meters (bcm) of gas per annum to Europe, around one third via pipeline and two thirds as LNG. The main pipeline connection, jointly owned by SNAM and Sonatrach, is the TransMed pipeline to Italy via Tunisia. This pipeline is tapped in Tunisia. Its capacity is currently 14 bcm per annum, but is due shortly to be expanded to 25 bcm per annum. Additional compressor stations will be installed later in Algeria which will eventually give it a maximum throughput of 30 bcm per annum. The Maghreb-Europe pipeline, which transports gas from Algeria via Morocco to Spain and Portugal, has a capacity of 10 bcm.

Some of the expected growth in European gas demand could be met by supplies from North Africa in general, and Algeria in particular. This would require investment in delivery infrastructure over and above the current de-bottlenecking of the TransMed pipeline. Algeria has embarked upon a substantial project to increase its LNG export capacity from about 22 to 28 bcm per annum. The capacity of the Maghreb-Europe pipeline could be expanded to 20 bcm per annum with additional compressor stations. Total export capacity could rise to 60 or more Gm^3 per year.

Algeria also has a contract to export LNG to the United States, but the volume is relatively minor compared with the exports to Europe. Nigeria and Egypt could also become significant players in the Mediterranean gas market in the long term.

Although primary gas demand in Africa will more than double between now and 2020, this demand-side pressure should not affect the status of North Africa as a significant gas exporter.

Coal

Coal demand in Africa is almost exclusively based in South Africa. Total recoverable reserves in South Africa are estimated to be 42.2 billion tonnes. As shown in Table 19.10, South Africa produced about 220 million tonnes (Mt) of hard coal in 1997, or 97% of African production and 5.8% of the world's total hard coal production.

Table 19.10: **Hard Coal Production - South Africa (Mt)**

	1971	1980	1985	1995	1996	1997
Production	57.7	115.1	173.5	206.2	206.4	220.1
Percentage of World	2.6	4.1	5.4	5.6	5.5	5.8

South Africa is the third largest coal exporter in the world, accounting for 13% of total world coal trade, and the second largest steam coal exporter, accounting for 18.8% of the world steaming coal trade in 1997. Since the completion of deregulation in 1992, no regulations or quotas have applied to coal exports. In 1997, South Africa exported 63.4 Mt of hard coal (steaming coal 57.7 Mt), a rise of 6.7% on the 1996 total of 59.4 Mt. Europe took 54% of exports, a fall from 59.3% in 1996. Asia took 37.1%, a rise from 34.3% in 1996. South African coal is primarily exported through Richards Bay Coal terminal, which has a capacity of about 60 Mt[7]. Further capacity expansion is planned for completion in the near future.

Biomass

Current Patterns of Biomass Energy Use

Biomass energy plays an important role in Africa. The levels of biomass energy use in individual countries are uncertain, but it is estimated that, for the whole region, it accounts for approximately half of total primary energy demand and 60% of total final energy consumption[8].

Africa has the second lowest average per capita GDP and the second lowest per capita level of conventional energy consumption of all world regions (South Asia has the lowest values). The significant differences in economic development, energy endowment and demography between North Africa, South Africa and Sub-Saharan Africa are also reflected in the geographical patterns of biomass energy use, as shown in Table 19.11.

7. *Energy Policies of South Africa,* IEA/OECD, 1996.
8. These figures and all others quoted in this section are IEA figures, obtained from a compilation of data from a large number of sources (see the IEA's *Energy Statistics and Balances of Non-OECD countries, 1995-1996* for sources and coverage). It should be noted that Africa is the region with the most severe problems in terms of biomass data. For example, some neighbouring countries with similar economical and geographical characteristics show unexplained differences in their level of per capita biomass use.

Sub-Saharan Africa accounts for approximately 94% of the continent's total final biomass consumption (205 Mtoe), but it consumes only 25% of the continent's final conventional energy. When biomass is incorporated into the energy mix, the average per capita energy consumption in Sub-Saharan Africa approaches a level comparable to that in North Africa. The level in South Africa remains significantly higher (Figure 19.8). However, because the efficiency of use of biomass is much lower than for conventional energy, the useful energy consumption in Sub-Saharan Africa is much lower than in other parts of Africa.

Figure 19.8: **Average Per Capita Final Energy Use in Africa, 1995**

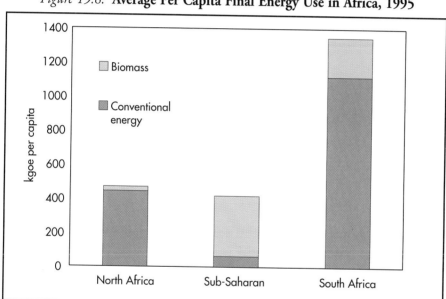

Table 19.11: **Final Biomass Energy Use in Africa, 1995**

	Total biomass in TFC (Mtoe)	Share of the region's biomass use	Share of biomass in TFC	Per capita energy use (kgoe) Biomass	Per capita energy use (kgoe) Conv. fuels
North Africa	3.2	2%	5%	25	443
Sub-Saharan Africa	191.9	94%	86%	354	62
South Africa	9.6	5%	15%	230	1118
Total Africa	**204.6**	**100%**	**60%**	**317**	**318**

Another consequence of including biomass is that the energy intensities of the three sub-regions look significantly different, with Sub-Saharan Africa showing the highest level, instead of the lowest, as it does when only conventional energy is considered (Figure 19.9).

Figure 19.9: **Energy Intensity with and without Biomass, 1995**

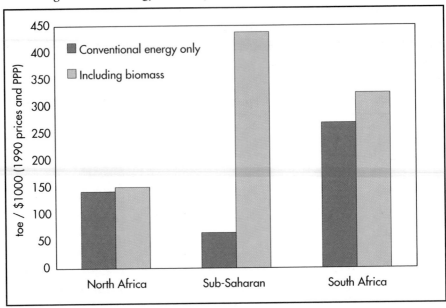

Most biomass energy in Africa is consumed in the household sector. The share of biomass in the residential/commercial and agriculture sector is around 83% for the whole continent (16% in North Africa, 35% in South Africa and 93% in Sub-Saharan Africa).

Many small industrial and commercial businesses use biomass as their main fuel[9]. According to IEA estimates, some 10% of biomass in Sub-Saharan Africa is used in the industrial sector, accounting for 72% of the sector's total energy consumption. In South and North Africa, about 20% of biomass is used in the industrial sector, but, because of the larger use of conventional fuels in these two sub-regions, the shares of biomass in this sector are only 3% and 7%.

Firewood is the most important biomass fuel in Africa, making up about 65% of total final biomass energy consumption. The

9. Biomass is especially important in brick making and agro-industries such as tea curing. The services sector also uses considerable quantities of biomass (see, among others, D.O. Hall and Y.S. Mao (eds), *Biomass Energy and Coal in Africa,* AFREPREN Series, Gaborone, 1994).

remainder includes crop residues, dung and charcoal. There are, however, considerable differences between urban and rural patterns of biomass use. The use of crop residues and dung is largely limited to rural areas, while charcoal use is concentrated in urban areas where it can account for between 40% and 90% of total biomass use. Charcoal tends to be the preferred fuel as it is easier to transport, distribute, store and use.

Much of the biomass used in rural households is collected rather than purchased, but in urban areas, all charcoal and a large part of the firewood is traded. The larger the town, the greater the proportion of firewood that is traded. Fuelwood and charcoal production for the urban areas constitute important sources of employment and income for rural people[10].

Past Trends

Historical biomass data for African countries are scarce. Available information suggests that, over the past 10 to 20 years, final biomass use has increased roughly in line with population, so that per capita final use has remained stable, reflecting a stagnant economic situation and a lack of alternative fuels.[11] There have, however, been changes in the relative shares of the different biomass fuels, notably with shifts from non-commercial to marketed biomass, in the wake of increasing urbanisation. The increasing use of charcoal in urban areas could have far-reaching consequences: surveys carried out in Rwanda, Zambia and Malawi indicate that, because of high charcoal use in urban areas and the poor conversion efficiencies of wood into charcoal[12], urban dwellers use two to three times as much wood-equivalent per capita as do rural people[13].

Projections

Under the business as usual assumptions for population and GDP growth, and given the projected trends for conventional energy fuels,

10. Openshaw, *Malawi: Biomass Energy Strategy Study,* unpublished report, 1997.
11. The 1995 level of GDP per capita was similar to the 1971 level and, apart from North Africa, the level of per capita final consumption of conventional fuels has also remained unchanged.
12. In Africa, traditional methods of charcoal production are estimated to yield as little as 20%-25% in energy terms (see A.C. Hollingdale, R. Krishnan and A.P. Robinson, *Charcoal Production, A Handbook,* Natural Resource Institute, London, 1991).
13. *Biomass Energy and Coal in Africa, D.O. Hall and Y.S. Mao (eds),* AFREPREN Series, Gaborone, 1994, and Openshaw, 1997, op.cit.

it is unlikely that biomass will diminish in importance during the Outlook period. With stagnant per capita incomes, possibly even decreasing in some countries, and with hardly any increase in per capita usage of conventional energy, it is difficult to anticipate a decrease in per capita biomass use. As a result, it is expected that final biomass consumption will increase roughly at the same rate as population (2.4%) between 1995 and 2020. Since final demand of conventional energy is projected to increase at a similar rate (2.5% per annum), the share of biomass in total final energy consumption drops only slightly, from 60% in 1995 to 59% in 2020.

Figure 19.10: **Total Primary Energy Supply including Biomass, 1995-2020**

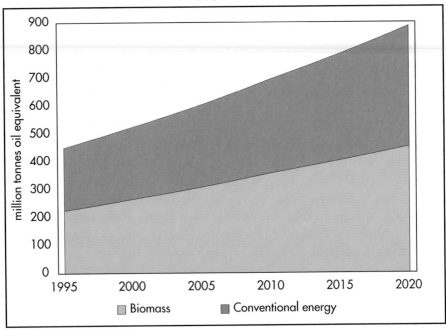

It is expected that the share of charcoal will continue to increase. Since the conversion efficiencies for charcoal production in Africa are expected to improve only slightly, primary biomass energy will rise only slightly faster (2.8%) than final biomass consumption. Consumption of primary conventional fuels is expected to grow at 2.6%, so that the share of biomass in total final energy demand will actually increase slightly, from 50% in 1995 to 51% in 2020.

It is not sure that continuing high levels of biomass energy can be produced in a sustainable way, given available resources and especially increasing deforestation. Much has been written on fuelwood scarcity in Africa, but data on biomass resources and potential supply are even more inadequate than data on biomass consumption. Recent work[14] suggests that previous assessments based on remote sensing, which were not accompanied by large-scale ground surveys, may have grossly underestimated actual and potential biomass resources. It has been noted that many supply surveys concentrated on fuelwood, ignoring the extensive supply of crop residues, forest residues and dung in many countries, which can amount to as much as 30% to 40% of total biomass supply. Moreover, many surveys only accounted for fuelwood from cut trees and branches, whereas in many countries a large part of the fuelwood supply consists of twigs and small branches harvested without serious damage to trees.

At an aggregate level, it would appear that biomass availability in Africa is two to four times larger than current consumption. However there are significant imbalances in the geographical distribution of the resources, both at national and sub-national level. These imbalances and the contrast with population distribution have resulted in localised fuel scarcity and resource degradation, especially around large towns. With continuing urbanisation, these problems are likely to increase.

14. Op. cit. in footnote 9.

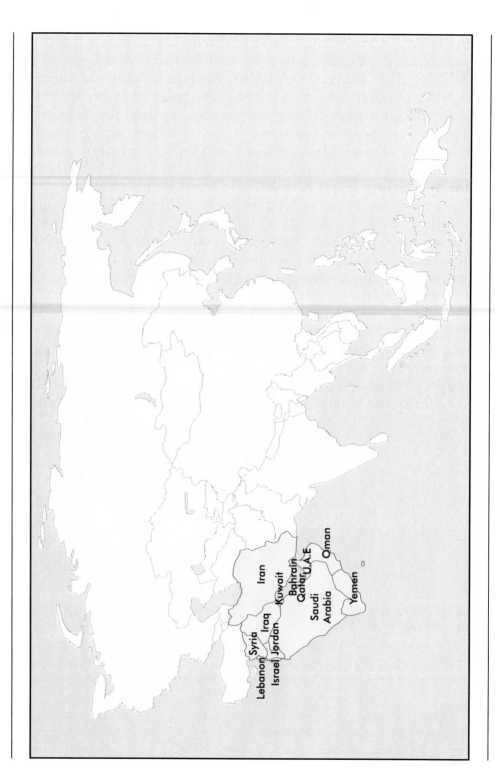

CHAPTER 20
MIDDLE EAST[1]

Introduction

This chapter presents the business as usual (BAU) projection for the Middle East region[2]. The energy projections described in this chapter have been prepared using a simulation, rather than an econometric approach, as the energy data for this region is not sufficiently robust for econometric equations to be estimated.

Background

The Middle East is usually considered an energy supplier, rather than an energy consumer. This traditional approach obscures the fact that the region's energy demand has grown quickly in recent years and is likely to continue to do so. A rapidly growing population (the most rapid of the ten regions considered in this Outlook) and a large projected increase in conventional oil production are expected to result in energy demand expanding rapidly during the projection period. The principle assumptions used in preparing the energy demand projections for the Middle East are shown in Table 20.1.

Table 20.1: **Middle East Assumptions**

	1995	2010	2020	1995-2020 Annual Growth Rate
GDP ($Billion 1990 and PPP)	551	768	1075	2.7%
Population (millions)	154	245	283	2.5%
GDP per Capita ($1990 and PPP per person)	3578	3134	3792	0.2%

1. The Middle East region is defined as Bahrain, Iran, Iraq, Israel, Jordan, Kuwait, Lebanon, Oman, Qatar, Saudi Arabia, Syria, United Arab Emirates and Yemen.
2. Background information on the structure of energy demand in the region is available in the *1996 World Energy Outlook* and in the IEA's 1995 publication *Middle East Oil and Gas.*

An interesting feature of these assumptions is that the region's GDP and population are assumed to grow at similar rates, resulting in average per capita income growing by only 0.2% per annum. An inequitable distribution of increases in GDP between the richest and poorest sections of the population may result in energy demand increasing less rapidly than would otherwise be the case.

The large projected increase in the region's oil production (see Chapter 7) may produce a mixed impact on the Middle East's economy. Higher oil exports are likely to result in large balance of payments surpluses for many countries in the region, and the resulting appreciation in exchange rates could harm their non-oil industries. The United Arab Emirates is an example of an oil-exporting country diversifying its economy away from oil via the establishment of free trade zones. How successful the countries in the region will be in taking this course depends, amongst other things, on how well they deploy the large increase in oil revenues.

In many countries in the region, an informal social contract exists, whereby the general population benefits from the fact that their country is a large net oil exporter. Much of the benefit comes in the form of low energy prices. The subsidies reduce the profitability of the energy distribution companies. The situation is made worse by the fact that many publicly-owned enterprises do not pay their energy bills. Subsidies not only reduce the energy prices paid by consumers, but also result in large public sector deficits when oil prices or production are low.

Some progress in reducing energy subsidies has occurred in recent years. During the mid-1990s, Iran and Saudi Arabia, the two largest economies in the region, doubled some of their internal oil product prices in order to reduce the size of their public deficits and release additional oil for export. Iran's action followed warnings that if it did not take action to restrain domestic oil consumption, it could cease to be a net oil exporter by the year 2000[3]. It has been estimated that doubling gasoline and diesel prices in March 1995 earned Iran an additional $300 million in export revenues. Constraining domestic consumption of oil products to increase oil product exports increases the governments' hard currency revenue both because the volume of exports increases and because the export price is higher than the internal price.

---

3. *Middle East Oil and Gas*, IEA/OECD, page 106.

Another way for the region's governments to earn additional oil export revenues is to substitute gas for oil consumption in the internal market. Sectors in which this policy has been applied include households, industry and power generation. During the projection period, this policy is assumed to continue. The increasing use of gas in power stations will not only diversify the region's fuel mix away from oil but also promote the development of a gas network, which will, in turn, increase the possibility for gas consumption in other sectors. This substitution may release heavy fuel oil, requiring an upgrade of refinery conversion capacity to convert into saleable products.

One of the main benefits of the region's low energy prices has been the development of a thriving chemicals industry. Converting the region's substantial energy reserves into chemicals not only helps to diversify the region's economy away from energy, and oil in particular, but also provides well-paid employment and stimulates economic development. High transport costs to the industrialised countries and tariffs, aimed at protecting the European chemicals industry, have so far limited the chemical industry's growth. The European Union (EU) and Gulf Cooperation Council (GCC) have discussed the possibility of a free trade area. Were such a free trade area to come about, then exports of chemicals from the region to the EU could increase dramatically. Such a change could significantly alter the energy demand projections and GDP assumptions presented in this chapter.

Energy Demand Outlook

Overview

In 1995, oil accounted for 62% of total primary energy demand and gas made up the majority of the remaining 38%. The Middle East's coal consumption is insignificant and is concentrated in power station use in Israel and Iran's iron & steel industry. During the projection period, gas demand is expected to expand rapidly at 3.7% per annum. Total gas demand will increase by around 160 Mtoe, of which some 60 Mtoe will go to consuming sectors and the remainder to the secondary energy producers, primarily power generators.

Table 20.2: Total Primary Energy Supply (Mtoe)

	1995	2010	2020	1995-2020 Annual Growth Rate
TPES	**294**	**399**	**564**	**2.6%**
Solid Fuels	5	13	18	5.0%
Oil	183	219	281	1.7%
Gas	104	164	261	3.7%
Hydro	1	3	3	2.9%
Other Renewables	0	1	1	2.7%

Oil is likely to retain its role as the dominant fuel in TPES. Nevertheless, it is projected to account for less than 50% of TPES in 2020. Oil demand will grow more slowly than the demand for any other fuel, at just 1.7%. The current low level of non-oil demand means that oil only loses significant market share in the latter half of the projection period. Demands for coal, hydro and other renewables are all projected to grow rapidly, but the current low levels of consumption of these fuels means that even by 2020 they will still account for less than 1% of TPES. The general Outlook for the Middle East is dominated by oil and gas, but with the split between these two fuels becoming more evenly balanced.

Table 20.3: Total Final Energy Consumption (Mtoe)

	1995	2010	2020	1995-2020 Annual Growth Rate
TFC	**197**	**264**	**373**	**2.6%**
Coal	1	2	2	2.7%
Oil	132	160	204	1.7%
Gas	39	65	104	3.9%
Electricity	23	37	63	4.0%
Heat	0	1	1	2.7%

Total final energy consumption is projected to grow at a rate similar to GDP during the projection period (2.6% and 2.7%). Electricity and gas demand are both projected to grow at an annual average rate of around 4%. Electricity and gas infrastructures must first be developed before these projected increases in demand can be realised. Finance for these developments must come either from the region's governments, or from private direct investment. Consumers will have to pay market prices for these fuels that fully reflect the huge infrastructure investment charges required to deliver them.

Figure 20.1: **Total Final Energy Consumption versus GDP (1971 - 2020)**

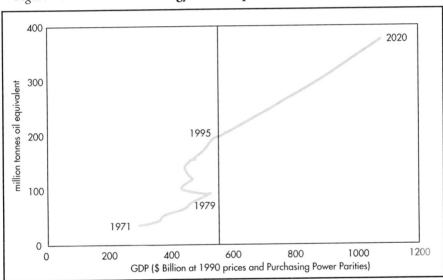

The relatively low growth rate in final oil consumption reflects the desire of the oil exporting countries to minimise domestic oil consumption in order to maximise oil export revenues.

Stationary Sectors[4]

Energy consumption in the stationary sectors remained robust during the decline in Middle East GDP that occurred during the 1980s. In 1993, when GDP recovered to its 1979 level, total fossil fuel demand in the stationary sectors was almost twice the level in 1979. A return to favourable economic conditions is likely to result in

4. The Stationary Sectors cover all total final energy consumption except electricity and all fuels consumed in the transport sector.

continued expansion of energy demand in the stationary sectors. The potential for growth is large given the existing low level of energy appliance ownership.

Table 20.4: **Energy Use in Stationary Sectors (Mtoe)**

	1995	2010	2020	1995-2020 Annual Growth Rate
Total	**117**	**159**	**227**	**2.7%**
Solid Fuel	1	2	2	2.7%
Oil	76	92	120	1.9%
Gas	39	65	104	3.9%
Heat	0	1	1	2.7%

Figure 20.2: **Energy Use in Stationary Sectors versus GDP (1971 - 2020)**

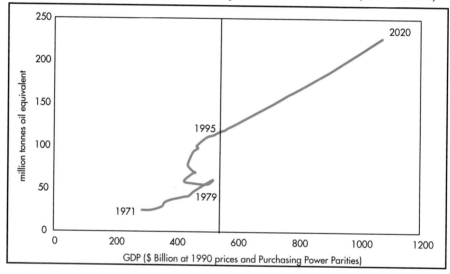

Mobility

Table 20.5: **Energy Demand for Mobility (Mtoe)**

	1995	2010	2020	1995-2020 Annual Growth Rate
Total	56	67	84	1.6%

Total vehicle ownership in the Middle East has remained largely unchanged in recent years, at around 100 vehicles per thousand people. Slowly rising per capita incomes will produce some increase in this level during the projection period, but it is unlikely that car ownership will reach, for example, OECD Europe's level of 400 - 500 cars per thousand people. There are two reasons for this assumption. First, car ownership levels are highly dependent on income distribution. Second, women are actively discouraged from driving in some countries and this policy will inevitably limit the proportion of the population that owns cars.

Aviation fuel demand was influenced in the past by the large number of expatriate flights to and from the region. In many countries, a policy of reducing the number of expatriate workers has reduced aviation fuel consumption. Increasing levels of GDP are likely to increase the number of internal and external flights, but uncertainties exist as to the extent of this factor's impact on total transport energy demand. Some modest year-on-year growth in aviation fuel demand is likely to take place.

As with other total final consumption sectors, energy demand continued to grow on average in the 1980s, despite substantial reductions in GDP. As Figure 20.3 indicates, in the years leading up to 1995, energy demand in the transport sector grew rapidly, at an annual average rate of 9.7%. Such high demand growth is considered unsustainable and may indeed reflect data inadequacies. The region's demand is less than that of Germany, suggesting that a large potential for energy demand growth exists in the region.

Figure 20.3: **Energy Demand for Mobility**

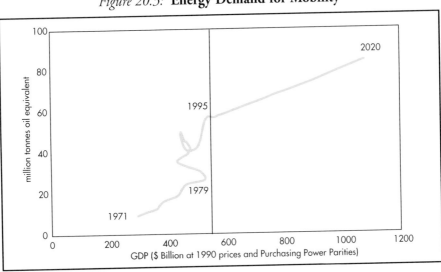

Given the uncertainties of energy demand in the transport sector and possible data problems, a cautious approach has been adopted here. Energy demand (excluding electricity) is projected to grow at a rate of just 1.6% during the projection period. This modest growth rate also reflects the desire of many governments in the region to minimise domestic oil consumption, in order to maximise oil exports. By contrast with other sectors, such as stationary uses and power generation, it is not easy to switch consumption from oil to gas. It is therefore likely that a policy of promoting oil exports will result in measures designed to discourage excessive consumption in the region's transport sector. A further factor likely to constrain consumption is the gradual removal of gasoline and diesel price subsidies for budgetary reasons.

Electricity

Table 20.6: **Total Final Electricity Consumption (Mtoe)**

	1995	2010	2020	1995-2020 Annual Growth Rate
Electricity	23	37	63	4.0%

Figure 20.4: **Total Final Electricity Consumption**

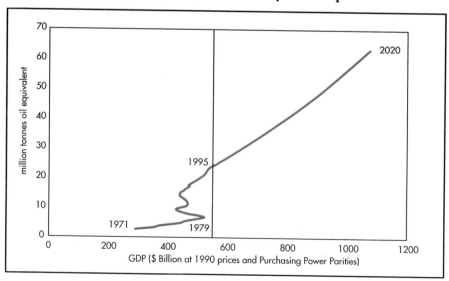

Total final electricity consumption has been growing at over 7% in recent years, and would have gone even higher had not supply constraints interfered. During the projection period, electricity demand growth is projected to moderate and grow at 4% a year.

Final consumption of electricity is projected to grow more rapidly than for any other fuel in total final consumption.

Supply

Power Generation

Electricity generation in the Middle East grew at an average rate of 10.8% during the period 1971 to 1995, a rate even higher than in Asian regions. During the Outlook period, electricity generation is projected to grow at a substantially lower rate of 4%, as the rate of electrification is expected to slow down.

The region's electricity mix is dominated by oil and gas, which in 1995 accounted for 90% of total generation. The most interesting feature has been the switch from oil to gas-fired generation, as countries in the region seek to free oil for export. In 1971, oil accounted for 71% of electricity output and gas only 15%. Gas-fired power generation grew quickly, at 16% a year between 1971 and 1995, while oil-fired generation increased by 9%. In 1995, gas-fired output had reached about the same level as for oil. This trend is likely to continue over the projection period and electricity generated from gas is expected to increase its share of output from 44% in 1995 to 60%. The share of oil-fired generation could fall to 28% by 2020.

Most of the existing power plants are steam boilers and burn heavy fuel oil, gas and crude oil, primarily for baseload use. Gas turbines and diesel engines are used for medium and peaking duty. In total, these plants account for about 90% of capacity. The majority of the Middle East's new capacity is likely to be gas-fired. Combined-cycle gas turbines can meet the region's increase in baseload needs but an increase in single-cycle gas turbine capacity is expected. The penetration of highly efficient gas turbines could boost average natural gas generating efficiency to about 45% in 2020. Natural gas consumption for electricity generation is projected to grow at 4.3%. By 2020, gas used in power generation could meet some 37% of total Middle Eastern gas demand.

Apart from building new capacity, there is a need for upgrading or conversion of a number of existing stations, by adding a steam cycle to gas turbines or converting fuel oil to gas capacity.

Some countries in the region do not have gas reserves and will need to import gas for use in power generation plants. Israel is considering importing natural gas via pipeline from Egypt or Russia. Prospects for importing LNG from Qatar have also been discussed. And there have been discussions on linking the electricity networks of Syria, Turkey, Jordan and Egypt.

Table 20.7: **Electricity Generation (TWh) and Capacity (GW)**

| | 1995 | | 2020 | |
	Capacity	Generation	Capacity	Generation
Solid Fuels	3	19	11	73
Oil	44	149	87	235
Gas	37	144	97	499
Hydro & Other Renewables	5	16	10	32
Total	**89**	**327**	**206**	**839**

Israel is the only country in the region to use coal-fired power stations. Coal-based capacity in 1995 was 3125 MW[5]. The country's coal power plants are Maor David (4x350 MW), Maor David B (575 MW) and Rutenberg (2x575 MW). These are dual-fired plants which can burn fuel oil as well as coal, but coal is cheaper. In addition, Israel is seeking to reduce its dependence on imported oil. Coal-fired capacity is projected to reach 11 GW by 2020.

Hydroelectric capacity in the region was about 5 GW in 1995, most of it in Iran and Syria. These two countries accounted for 93% of hydroelectricity generation in 1993. It is assumed that another 5 GW of new hydro will be added to existing capacity by the end of the Outlook. Most of this new capacity will come from hydroelectric dams currently under construction in Iran, including 2000 MW at Godar-e-Landar; 2000 MW at Karun-3; and 400 MW at Karkheh. Iran has the largest untapped hydropower potential in the Middle East, estimated at 14.7 GW conventional hydropower and 3.75 GW pumped storage. Almost all of this potential is located in the country's mountainous south and southwestern regions.

In the 1970s, Iran began constructing a number of nuclear plants, with a combined capacity of 9.7 GW. Following the Iranian revolution, all these projects were abandoned. Currently, Iran has plans to complete

5. *Statistical Report 1995,* The Israel Electric Corporation Ltd.

a 1000 MW nuclear plant at Bushehr. It is assumed that escalating costs and political difficulties will impede completion of this plant.

Some of the countries in the region are exploring the possibility of using renewable sources in electricity generation. Jordan has a 40 kW photovoltaic plant and 1 MW of wind power. Wind power is also being explored in Iran, where many wind turbines are already in operation, providing electricity to 2000 homes in Manjiil and Rudbar. The Israel Electric Corporation is involved in a number of wind and solar demonstration projects. The overall contribution of these is, however, expected to be very small over the Outlook period.

From 1971 to 1995, electricity generating capacity increased from 7.6 GW to 89 GW, equivalent to an average annual growth rate of 11%. Total power generation capacity in the Middle East is projected to reach 206 GW by the end of the Outlook.

In recent years, a lack of power generation capacity has resulted in electricity shortages in some countries in the region. The summer peak load for air conditioning places a heavy strain on available capacity, and power shortages usually occur in the summer.

Many of the countries in the region have experienced financial difficulties in their power generation sectors because of rapid growth in electricity demand and past pricing structures. In 1996, the Syrian Ministry of Electricity calculated that every kWh produced cost the government S£3.72 (8 US cents) while consumers paid S£1.20 per kWh[6].

In Saudi Arabia, power generation capacity grew at an annual rate of 14.5% from 1975 to 1996 and was largely funded by the high oil prices that continued until 1985. Lower oil prices toward the end of the 1980s meant the end of subsidised funds for power generation. Electricity prices are currently controlled by the government and are far below production costs. To reduce the resulting financing difficulties, the Saudi government introduced a surcharge of 5 Halalas (approximately 1.3 US cents) per kWh in January 1995 for monthly consumption in excess of 2000 kWh[7]. The revenue from this surcharge is deposited into a special electricity fund to help finance the construction of new power generation capacity.

The United Arab Emirates has also attempted to reduce its subsidies for electricity. In 1994 electricity tariffs for expatriates (70%

6. *Country Profile Syria,* 1996-97, Economist Intelligence Unit, London, 1997.
7. *Electricity Growth & Development in the Kingdom of Saudi Arabia up to the year 1416 H (1995/1996 G), Electrical Affairs Agency,* Kingdom of Saudi Arabia, 1996.

to 80% of the population) were doubled, but they were still less than production costs.

Given that the power budget for many Middle East countries is often a significant proportion of annual government expenditure, the pricing difficulties described above present electricity utilities with major problems. As a result, governments are increasingly forced to examine full-cost pricing and private sector involvement. This is currently hindered by a number of obstacles, including:

- delays in payment for power generation schemes;
- lack of market rates for electricity, which forces companies to accept government promises on subsidies;
- the need to enter into complex negotiations with the state supplier of fossil fuels;
- the possible non-purchase of electricity and the non-supply of input fuels after the power station has been built, because of the above contractual difficulties.

Oil

In 1996, the Middle East's total oil production[8] amounted to 20.4 million barrels per day (Mbd). Of this total, about 80% was exported. As Table 20.8 shows, the percentage of Middle East oil exports is projected to increase. By 2020, it will be about 87% of total oil production.

Table 20.8: **Middle East Oil Balance (Mbd)**

	Demand	Supply	Net Imports
1996	4.1	20.4	-16.3
2010	4.9	44.7	-39.7
2020	6.3	49.2	-42.9

Note: This table includes all types of oil - conventional, unconventional, NGLs, etc.

Total production from the region is projected to peak at around 51.8 Mbd in 2018. Unlike many other energy projections, this Outlook does not treat the Middle East as the world's residual oil producer, capable of producing ever larger quantities of oil to balance demand and supply. Instead, we project that the region's total oil

8. This total includes both OPEC and non-OPEC production and covers all types of liquids, e.g. conventional oil, unconventional oil, NGLs, etc.

production will reach a plateau around 2014 at 51.7 Mbd and then go into decline towards the end of the Outlook. The following chart shows how the region's oil production is projected to be allocated between domestic oil demand and exports.

Figure 20.5: **Middle East Oil Balance**

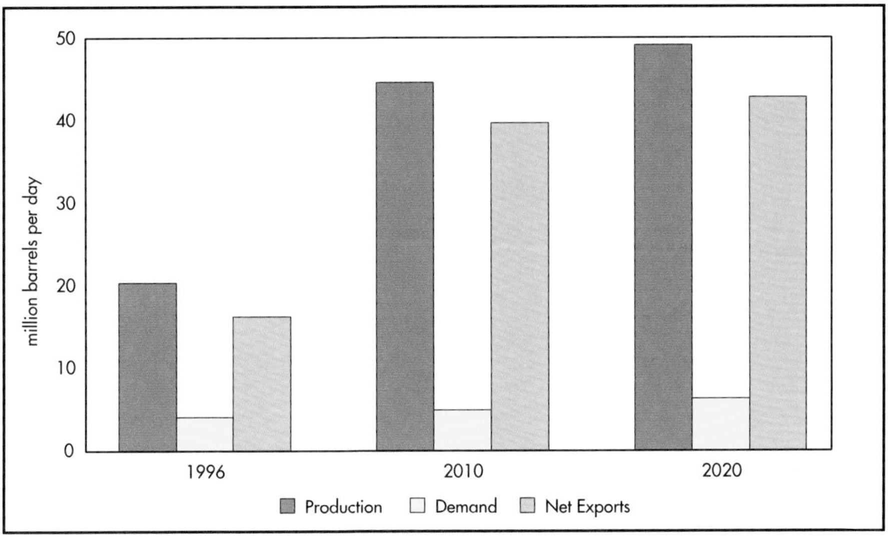

Note: This chart includes all types of oil - conventional, unconventional, NGLs, etc.

Gas

Table 20.9: **Middle East Gas Balance (Mtoe)**

	1995	2010	2020	1995-2020 Annual Growth Rate
Demand	104	164	261	3.7%
Supply	110	214	376	5.1%
Net Imports	-6	-50	-116	12.9%

Note: 1 Mtoe = 0.0429 tcf.

The region's gas supply is projected to grow even more rapidly than oil, at an annual average rate of 5.1%. Rising European and Asian gas demand will provide a ready market for the region's huge gas reserves. By 2020, the percentage of the Middle East's gas production being exported will have increased from 5% in 1995 to 31%. Gas exports from the region are projected to grow at an annual average rate of 12.9% per annum, and will earn substantial foreign exchange revenues for the region.

Whereas oil exports are projected to be 2116 Mtoe in 2020, gas exports will be just 116 Mtoe, or 5% of oil exports. Thus, while gas exports will provide important additional revenues for the region, they will continue to be dwarfed by the revenue earned from oil exports. The dramatic increase in the Middle East's gas production expected during the projection period is shown in Figure 20.6.

Figure 20.6: **Middle East Gas Production (tcf)**

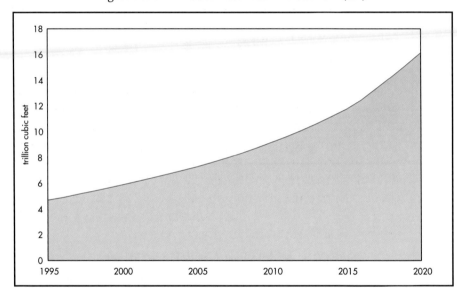

Comparison with Other Projections

Apart from the IEA, two other organisations have recently produced energy projections for the Middle East, the United States Department of Energy (USDOE)[9] and the European Union (EU)[10].

As is evident from Table 20.10, all three organisation project the Middle East's energy demand to grow at an annual average rate of

9. *International Energy Outlook 1998 - With Projections Throughs 2020,* USDOE/EIA-0484(98), Washington, DC, April 1998.
10. *European Energy to 2020 - A Scenario Approach, Energy in Europe,* Special Issue - Spring 1996, Directorate General for Energy DG XVII, European Commission.

around 2.5%. Little difference exists in terms of the TPES fuel mix as indicated in Table 20.10.

Table 20.10: **TPES by Fuel (Annual Growth Rates, 1995-2020)**

	IEA	EU	USDOE
Solids	5.0%	4.4%	2.6%
Oil	1.7%	1.3%	2.2%
Gas	3.7%	3.7%	2.6%
Nuclear	0.0%	0.0%	-
Other	2.9%	0.0%	6.7%
Total	**2.6%**	**2.3%**	**2.5%**

*Note: The EU's energy projections are actually for 1990 - 2020 and not 1995 - 2020. The USDOE projects 10 TWh of nuclear electricity in the region by 2005.

The main difference among the projections is in the rate at which gas demand grows vis-à-vis oil demand. In both the IEA and EU energy projections, regional gas demand grows more than twice as quickly as regional oil demand. In the USDOE projections, a greater role is projected for oil in the fuel mix. Some differences exist in the other fuels, but these are insignificant given the small quantities of energy involved. In summary, while the IEA and EU expect the share of gas to rise rapidly during the projection period, the USDOE anticipates the share of gas to increase more modestly.

PART IV

TABLES
BUSINESS AS USUAL PROJECTION

STATISTICAL NOTE

The analysis of commercial energy is based on data up to 1995, published in mid-1997. The biomass analysis used data available at end May 1998. Subsequent revisions to both commercial and biomass data give rise to differences between energy consumption and supply figures for 1995 in this Outlook and those in IEA statistical publications of mid-1998. The IEA published for the first time in 19981 historical data from 1971 to 1996 for combustible renewables and waste for non-OECD countries. Where historical series are incomplete or unavailable, data have been estimated. The methods used for estimation are consistent with those used for biomass in this Outlook although, for a number of reasons, minor numerical discrepancies occur. The reasons include the revisions referred to above and the level of country disaggregation employed.

Business as Usual Projection: World

ENERGY BALANCE	million tonnes oil equivalent				percentage shares				average annual growth rates		
	1971	1995	2010	2020	1971	1995	2010	2020	1971-1995	1995-2010	1995-2020
Demand for Energy Related Services (ERS)											
Electricity (final demand)	377	932	1477	1938					3.8%	3.1%	3.0%
Mobility	836	1520	2223	2698					2.5%	2.6%	2.3%
Fossil fuel & heat in Stationary Uses											
(Industry,Services,Agriculture,Households)	2475	3341	4222	4824	100	100	100	100	1.3%	1.6%	1.5%
Solid Fuels	757	889	1133	1305	31	27	27	27	0.7%	1.6%	1.5%
Oil	1102	1202	1476	1666	45	36	35	35	0.4%	1.4%	1.3%
Gas	549	982	1295	1489	22	29	31	31	2.5%	1.9%	1.7%
Heat	67	268	318	364	3	8	8	8	6.0%	1.1%	1.2%
Total Final Consumption	3687	5794	7922	9461	100	100	100	100	1.9%	2.1%	2.0%
Solid Fuels	783	897	1141	1314	21	15	14	14	0.6%	1.6%	1.5%
Oil	1893	2678	3637	4285	51	46	46	45	1.5%	2.1%	1.9%
Gas	567	1019	1349	1560	15	18	17	16	2.5%	1.9%	1.7%
Electricity	377	932	1477	1938	10	16	19	20	3.8%	3.1%	3.0%
Heat	67	268	318	364	2	5	4	4	6.0%	1.1%	1.2%
Electricity Generation (incl. CHP Plants)	1269	3091	4470	5482	100	100	100	100	3.8%	2.5%	2.3%
Solid Fuels	618	1362	2023	2521	49	44	45	46	3.3%	2.7%	2.5%
Oil	268	308	367	418	21	10	8	8	0.6%	1.2%	1.2%
Gas	246	565	1034	1477	19	18	23	27	3.5%	4.1%	3.9%
Nuclear	29	608	670	604	2	20	15	11	13.5%	0.6%	0.0%
Hydro	104	215	296	352	8	7	7	6	3.1%	2.2%	2.0%
Other Renewables	4	34	80	110	0	1	2	2	9.8%	6.0%	4.9%

ENERGY BALANCE	million tonnes oil equivalent				percentage shares				average annual growth rates		
	1971	1995	2010	2020	1971	1995	2010	2020	1971-1995	1995-2010	1995-2020
Other Transformation	419	612	942	1207					1.6%	2.9%	2.8%
Solid Fuels	102	88	105	112							
Oil	168	210	290	352							
Gas	86	227	338	431							
Electricity	68	202	316	411							
Renewables	0	0	0	0							
Heat	-4	-116	-108	-100							
Less Output from Electricity + CHP plants											
Electricity	-444	-1135	-1793	-2349							
Heat	-62	-150	-208	-261							
Total Primary Energy Supply	4988	8341	11508	13749	100	100	100	100	2.2%	2.2%	2.0%
Solid Fuels	1503	2347	3269	3947	30	28	28	29	1.9%	2.2%	2.1%
Oil	2448	3324	4468	5264	49	40	39	38	1.3%	2.0%	1.9%
of which International Marine Bunkers:	119	129	175	209	-	-	-	-	0.3%	2.0%	1.9%
Gas	899	1810	2721	3468	18	22	24	25	3.0%	2.8%	2.6%
Nuclear	29	608	670	604	1	7	6	4	13.5%	0.6%	0.0%
Hydro	104	215	296	352	2	3	3	3	3.1%	2.2%	2.0%
Other Renewables	4	36	83	113	0	0	1	1	9.8%	5.7%	4.7%
Other Primary	0	0	0	0	0	0	0	0	-	-	-

	1971	1995	2010	2020	1971	1995	2010	2020	1971-1995	1995-2010	1995-2020
OECD Combustible Renewables and Waste (included above)	-	142	159	172	-	2	1	1	-	0.7%	0.8%
Non-OECD CRW (not included above)	-	904	1108	1246	-	10	9	8	-	1.4%	1.3%
Total Primary Energy Supply (including CRW)	-	9245	12616	14995	-	100	100	100	-	2.1%	2.0%

Business as Usual Projection: World

CARBON DIOXIDE EMISSIONS	1971	1990	1995	2010	2020	1971	1990	1995	2010	2020	1971-1995	1995-2010	1995-2020	1990-2010
	million tonnes CO_2					percentage shares					average annual growth rate			total growth
Mobility	**2465**	**4136**	**4467**	**6536**	**7937**						**2.5%**	**2.6%**	**2.3%**	**58%**
Fossil fuel in Stationary Uses (Industry,Services,Agriculture,Households)	**7428**	**8883**	**8615**	**11015**	**12638**	**100**	**100**	**100**	**100**	**100**	**0.6%**	**1.7%**	**1.5%**	**24%**
Solid Fuels	3132	3590	3447	4450	5142	42	40	40	40	41	0.4%	1.7%	1.6%	24%
Oil	2966	3049	2946	3673	4195	40	34	34	33	33	0.0%	1.5%	1.4%	20%
Gas	1330	2244	2223	2891	3301	18	25	26	26	26	2.2%	1.8%	1.6%	29%
Total Final Consumption	**9892**	**13019**	**13082**	**17551**	**20575**	**100**	**100**	**100**	**100**	**100**	**1.2%**	**2.0%**	**1.8%**	**35%**
Solid Fuels	3233	3659	3477	4482	5176	33	28	27	26	25	0.3%	1.7%	1.6%	23%
Oil	5288	7058	7297	10050	11933	53	54	56	57	58	1.4%	2.2%	2.0%	42%
Gas	1372	2302	2308	3018	3467	14	18	18	17	17	2.2%	1.8%	1.6%	31%
Electricity Generation (incl. CHP Plants)	**3649**	**6672**	**7498**	**11363**	**14478**	**100**	**100**	**100**	**100**	**100**	**3.0%**	**2.8%**	**2.7%**	**70%**
Solid Fuels	2313	4598	5199	7776	9694	63	69	69	68	67	3.4%	2.7%	2.5%	69%
Oil	855	1024	978	1167	1325	23	15	13	10	9	0.6%	1.2%	1.2%	14%
Gas	481	1050	1322	2420	3458	13	16	18	21	24	4.3%	4.1%	3.9%	130%
Other Transformation	**810**	**1331**	**1159**	**1721**	**2133**						**1.5%**	**2.7%**	**2.5%**	**29%**
Solid Fuels	76	153	-100	-92	-115									
Oil	485	627	658	903	1092									
Gas	250	551	601	910	1156									
Total Emissions	**14732**	**21400**	**22150**	**31189**	**37848**	**100**	**100**	**100**	**100**	**100**	**1.7%**	**2.3%**	**2.2%**	**46%**
Solid Fuels	5621	8410	8576	12166	14755	38	39	39	39	39	1.8%	2.4%	2.2%	45%
Oil	7007	9087	9343	12675	15012	48	42	42	41	40	1.2%	2.1%	1.9%	39%
of which International Marine Bunkers:	*380*	*378*	*410*	*555*	*663*						*0.3%*	*2.0%*	*1.9%*	*47%*
Gas	2103	3903	4231	6348	8081	14	18	19	20	21	3.0%	2.7%	2.6%	63%

Business as Usual Projection: World

POWER GENERATION	1971	1995	2010	2020	1971	1995	2010	2020	1971-1995	1995-2010	1995-2020
						percentage shares				average annual growth rates	
Electricity Generation (TWh)	**5248**	**13204**	**20852**	**27326**	**100**	**100**	**100**	**100**	**3.9%**	**3.1%**	**3.0%**
Solid Fuels	2131	5077	7960	10490	41	38	38	38	3.7%	3.0%	2.9%
of which Combustible Renewables and Waste:	*31*	*128*	*165*	*194*	*1*	*1*	*1*	*1*	*6.1%*	*1.7%*	*1.7%*
Oil	1100	1315	1663	1941	21	10	8	7	0.7%	1.6%	1.6%
Gas	691	1932	5063	8243	13	15	24	30	4.4%	6.6%	6.0%
Nuclear	111	2332	2568	2317	2	18	12	8	13.5%	0.6%	0.0%
Hydro	1209	2498	3445	4096	23	19	17	15	3.1%	2.2%	2.0%
Other Renewables	5	49	154	239	0	0	1	1	10.0%	7.9%	6.5%
Capacity (GW)	-	**3079**	**4556**	**5915**	-	**100**	**100**	**100**	-	**2.6%**	**2.6%**
Solid Fuels	-	1032	1362	1760	-	34	30	30	-	1.9%	2.2%
of which Combustible Renewables and Waste:	-	*25*	*32*	*38*	-	*1*	*1*	*1*	-	*1.7%*	*1.7%*
Oil	-	404	527	604	-	13	12	10	-	1.8%	1.6%
Gas	-	571	1309	2035	-	19	29	34	-	5.7%	5.2%
Nuclear	-	347	375	334	-	11	8	6	-	0.5%	-0.2%
Hydro	-	713	940	1109	-	23	21	19	-	1.9%	1.8%
Other Renewables	-	13	43	73	-	0	1	1	-	8.5%	7.2%

Business as Usual Projection: OECD

ENERGY BALANCE	1971	1995	2010	2020	1971	1995	2010	2020	1971-1995	1995-2010	1995-2020
	million tonnes oil equivalent				percentage shares				average annual growth rates		
Demand for Energy Related Services (ERS)											
Electricity (final demand)	269	585	803	934					3.3%	2.1%	1.9%
Mobility	616	1015	1349	1479					2.1%	1.9%	1.5%
Fossil fuel & heat in Stationary Uses											
(Industry,Services,Agriculture,Households)	**1548**	**1525**	**1602**	**1555**	**100**	**100**	**100**	**100**	**-0.1%**	**0.3%**	**0.1%**
Solid Fuels	336	236	235	246	22	15	15	16	-1.5%	0.0%	0.2%
Oil	809	643	639	610	52	42	40	39	-1.0%	-0.1%	-0.2%
Gas	401	613	674	623	26	40	42	40	1.8%	0.6%	0.1%
Heat	3	32	55	75	0	2	3	5	11.0%	3.6%	3.5%
Total Final Consumption	**2433**	**3125**	**3754**	**3968**	**100**	**100**	**100**	**100**	**1.0%**	**1.2%**	**1.0%**
Solid Fuels	341	236	235	246	14	8	6	6	-1.5%	0.0%	0.2%
Oil	1402	1636	1956	2051	58	52	52	52	0.6%	1.2%	0.9%
Gas	418	635	705	661	17	20	19	17	1.8%	0.7%	0.2%
Electricity	269	585	803	934	11	19	21	24	3.3%	2.1%	1.9%
Heat	3	32	55	75	0	1	1	2	11.0%	3.6%	3.5%
Electricity Generation (incl. CHP Plants)	**849**	**1751**	**2290**	**2514**	**100**	**100**	**100**	**100**	**3.1%**	**1.8%**	**1.5%**
Solid Fuels	412	775	984	1108	49	44	43	44	2.7%	1.6%	1.4%
Oil	179	107	104	111	21	6	5	4	-2.1%	-0.2%	0.1%
Gas	153	227	525	678	18	13	23	27	1.7%	5.7%	4.5%
Nuclear	27	512	516	438	3	29	23	17	13.0%	0.0%	-0.6%
Hydro	74	108	121	128	9	6	5	5	1.6%	0.8%	0.7%
Other Renewables	4	21	39	52	0	1	2	2	7.6%	4.4%	3.8%

ENERGY BALANCE	1971	1995	2010	2020	1971	1995	2010	2020	1971-1995	1995-2010	1995-2020
	million tonnes oil equivalent				percentage shares				average annual growth rates		
Other Transformation											
Solid Fuels	242	308	369	388					1.0%	1.2%	0.9%
Oil	37	35	36	38							
Gas	89	89	98	100							
Electricity	68	88	100	94							
Renewables	49	101	139	160							
Heat	0	0	0	0							
	0	-5	-5	-5							
Less Output from Electricity + CHP plants											
Electricity	-318	-686	-942	-1094							
Heat	-2	-25	-48	-68							
Total Primary Energy Supply	3204	4473	5423	5707	100	100	100	100	1.4%	1.3%	1.0%
Solid Fuels	790	1047	1256	1391	25	23	23	24	1.2%	1.2%	1.1%
Oil	1670	1832	2159	2262	52	41	40	40	0.4%	1.1%	0.8%
Gas	639	950	1329	1433	20	21	25	25	1.7%	2.3%	1.7%
Nuclear	27	512	516	438	1	11	10	8	13.0%	0.0%	-0.6%
Hydro	74	108	121	128	2	2	2	2	1.6%	0.8%	0.7%
Other Renewables	4	23	41	54	0	1	1	1	7.7%	4.1%	3.5%
Other Primary	0	1	1	1	0	0	0	0	-	-	-

	1971	1995	2010	2020	1971	1995	2010	2020	1971-1995	1995-2010	1995-2020
Combustible Renewables and Waste (included above)	62	142	159	172	2	3	3	3	3.5%	0.7%	0.8%
Total Primary Energy Supply (including CRW)	3204	4473	5423	5707	100	100	100	100	1.4%	1.3%	1.0%

Business as Usual Projection: OECD

CARBON DIOXIDE EMISSIONS	1971	1990	1995	2010	2020	1971	1990	1995	2010	2020	1971-1995	1995-2010	1995-2020	1990-2010
	million tonnes CO$_2$					percentage shares					average annual growth rate			total growth
Mobility	1794	2706	2969	3946	4325						2.1%	1.9%	1.5%	46%
Fossil fuel in Stationary Uses (Industry,Services,Agriculture,Households)	4546	3818	3611	3727	3575	100	100	100	100	100	-1.0%	0.2%	0.0%	-2%
Solid Fuels	1458	1058	730	721	750	32	28	20	19	21	-2.8%	-0.1%	0.1%	-32%
Oil	2096	1453	1467	1453	1389	46	38	41	39	39	-1.5%	-0.1%	-0.2%	0%
Gas	992	1306	1414	1553	1436	22	34	39	42	40	1.5%	0.6%	0.1%	19%
Total Final Consumption	6340	6524	6580	7673	7900	100	100	100	100	100	0.2%	1.0%	0.7%	18%
Solid Fuels	1477	1059	730	722	751	23	16	11	9	10	-2.9%	-0.1%	0.1%	-32%
Oil	3830	4115	4384	5327	5625	60	63	67	69	71	0.6%	1.3%	1.0%	29%
Gas	1033	1350	1466	1625	1524	16	21	22	21	19	1.5%	0.7%	0.2%	20%
Electricity Generation (incl. CHP Plants)	2327	3417	3762	5257	6088	100	100	100	100	100	2.0%	2.3%	1.9%	54%
Solid Fuels	1490	2697	2891	3698	4151	64	79	77	70	68	2.8%	1.7%	1.5%	37%
Oil	571	395	340	331	352	25	12	9	6	6	-2.1%	-0.2%	0.1%	-16%
Gas	265	326	531	1227	1585	11	10	14	23	26	2.9%	5.7%	4.5%	277%
Other Transformation	346	412	421	496	488						0.8%	1.1%	0.6%	20%
Solid Fuels	-135	-91	-131	-134	-138									
Oil	277	294	298	332	337									
Gas	204	209	253	298	288									
Total Emissions	9013	10353	10763	13427	14476	100	100	100	100	100	0.7%	1.5%	1.2%	30%
Solid Fuels	2832	3664	3490	4286	4764	31	35	32	32	33	0.9%	1.4%	1.3%	17%
Oil	4678	4804	5022	5990	6315	52	46	47	45	44	0.3%	1.2%	0.9%	25%
Gas	1503	1885	2251	3150	3397	17	18	21	23	23	1.7%	2.3%	1.7%	67%

Business as Usual Projection: OECD

POWER GENERATION	1971	1995	2010	2020	1971	1995	2010	2020	1971-1995	1995-2010	1995-2020
					percentage shares				average annual growth rates		
Electricity Generation (TWh)	**3698**	**7978**	**10957**	**12721**	**100**	**100**	**100**	**100**	**3.3%**	**2.1%**	**1.9%**
Solid Fuels	1446	3138	4053	4777	39	39	37	38	3.3%	1.7%	1.7%
of which Combustible Renewables and Waste:	*6*	*115*	*143*	*164*	*0*	*1*	*1*	*1*	*13.0%*	*1.5%*	*1.4%*
Oil	800	562	551	585	22	7	5	5	-1.5%	-0.1%	0.2%
Gas	488	1020	2872	4041	13	13	26	32	3.1%	7.1%	5.7%
Nuclear	104	1964	1978	1681	3	25	18	13	13.0%	0.0%	-0.6%
Hydro	855	1260	1410	1483	23	16	13	12	1.6%	0.8%	0.7%
Other Renewables	5	34	93	153	0	0	1	1	8.3%	6.9%	6.2%
Capacity (GW)	-	**1814**	**2378**	**2752**	-	**100**	**100**	**100**	-	**1.8%**	**1.7%**
Solid Fuels	-	602	642	764	-	33	27	28	-	0.4%	1.0%
of which Combustible Renewables and Waste:	-	*22*	*27*	*31*	-	*1*	*1*	*1*	-	*1.4%*	*1.4%*
Oil	-	189	203	210	-	10	9	8	-	0.5%	0.4%
Gas	-	342	795	1037	-	19	33	38	-	5.8%	4.5%
Nuclear	-	283	282	239	-	16	12	9	-	0.0%	-0.7%
Hydro	-	387	428	451	-	21	18	16	-	0.7%	0.6%
of which Pumped Storage Hydro:	-	*75*	*85*	*88*	-	*4*	*4*	*3*	-	*0.8%*	*0.7%*
Other Renewables	-	10	29	52	-	1	1	2	-	7.3%	6.9%

Business as Usual Projection: OECD Europe

ENERGY BALANCE	1971	1995	2010	2020	1971	1995	2010	2020	1971-1995	1995-2010	1995-2020
	million tonnes oil equivalent				percentage shares				average annual growth rates		
Demand for Energy Related Services (ERS)											
Electricity (final demand)	**95**	**195**	**280**	**329**					**3.1%**	**2.4%**	**2.1%**
Mobility	**157**	**308**	**462**	**546**					**2.8%**	**2.7%**	**2.3%**
Fossil fuel & heat in Stationary Uses											
(Industry,Services,Agriculture,Households)	**636**	**617**	**661**	**655**	**100**	**100**	**100**	**100**	**-0.1%**	**0.5%**	**0.2%**
Solid Fuels	192	109	106	109	30	18	16	17	-2.3%	-0.2%	0.0%
Oil	370	260	239	223	58	42	36	34	-1.5%	-0.5%	-0.6%
Gas	71	225	280	274	11	36	42	42	4.9%	1.5%	0.8%
Heat	3	23	36	48	0	4	5	7	9.5%	2.9%	2.9%
Total Final Consumption	**887**	**1120**	**1403**	**1529**	**100**	**100**	**100**	**100**	**1.0%**	**1.5%**	**1.3%**
Solid Fuels	196	109	106	109	22	10	8	7	-2.4%	-0.2%	0.0%
Oil	523	567	701	768	59	51	50	50	0.3%	1.4%	1.2%
Gas	71	225	280	274	8	20	20	18	4.9%	1.5%	0.8%
Electricity	95	195	280	329	11	17	20	22	3.1%	2.4%	2.1%
Heat	3	23	36	48	0	2	3	3	9.5%	2.9%	2.9%
Electricity Generation (incl. CHP Plants)	**283**	**579**	**771**	**807**	**100**	**100**	**100**	**100**	**3.0%**	**1.9%**	**1.3%**
Solid Fuels	153	208	250	184	54	36	32	23	1.3%	1.2%	-0.5%
Oil	71	47	42	46	25	8	5	6	-1.7%	-0.7%	-0.1%
Gas	17	55	194	319	6	9	25	40	5.1%	8.8%	7.3%
Nuclear	13	225	225	190	5	39	29	24	12.5%	0.0%	-0.7%
Hydro	28	42	50	54	10	7	7	7	1.8%	1.2%	1.0%
Other Renewables	2	3	10	14	1	1	1	2	2.1%	7.7%	6.1%

ENERGY BALANCE	1971	1995	2010	2020	1971	1995	2010	2020	1971-1995	1995-2010	1995-2020
	million tonnes oil equivalent				percentage shares				average annual growth rates		
Other Transformation	96	103	130	138					0.3%	1.5%	1.2%
Solid Fuels	22	15	16	16							
Oil	57	36	36	36							
Gas	-2	21	31	32							
Electricity	20	36	50	58							
Renewables	0	0	0	0							
Heat	0	-5	-5	-5							
Less Output from Electricity + CHP plants											
Electricity	-114	-230	-330	-386							
Heat	-2	-17	-30	-42							
Total Primary Energy Supply	1151	1554	1944	2046	100	100	100	100	1.3%	1.5%	1.1%
Solid Fuels	370	331	371	310	32	21	19	15	-0.5%	0.8%	-0.3%
Oil	652	650	779	850	57	42	40	42	0.0%	1.2%	1.1%
Gas	86	301	506	625	7	19	26	31	5.4%	3.5%	3.0%
Nuclear	13	225	225	190	1	14	12	9	12.5%	0.0%	-0.7%
Hydro	28	42	50	54	2	3	3	3	1.8%	1.2%	1.0%
Other Renewables	2	4	11	16	0	0	1	1	2.9%	6.3%	5.1%
Other Primary	0	1	1	1	0	0	0	0	-	-	-
Combustible Renewables and Waste (included above)	16	49	57	65	1	3	3	3	4.8%	1.1%	1.1%
Total Primary Energy Supply (including CRW)	1151	1554	1944	2046	100	100	100	100	1.3%	1.5%	1.1%

Business as Usual Projection: OECD Europe

CARBON DIOXIDE EMISSIONS	1971	1990	1995	2010	2020	1971	1990	1995	2010	2020	1971-1995	1995-2010	1995-2020	1990-2010
	million tonnes CO_2					percentage shares					average annual growth rate			total growth
Mobility	**466**	**832**	**911**	**1368**	**1617**						**2.8%**	**2.7%**	**2.3%**	**64%**
Fossil fuel in Stationary Uses (Industry,Services,Agriculture,Households)	**1969**	**1586**	**1469**	**1536**	**1495**	**100**	**100**	**100**	**100**	**100**	**-1.2%**	**0.3%**	**0.1%**	**-3%**
Solid Fuels	815	546	336	327	339	41	34	23	21	23	-3.6%	-0.2%	0.0%	-40%
Oil	1023	610	620	571	533	52	38	42	37	36	-2.1%	-0.5%	-0.6%	-6%
Gas	131	430	513	638	624	7	27	35	42	42	5.8%	1.5%	0.8%	48%
Total Final Consumption	**2434**	**2418**	**2381**	**2905**	**3112**	**100**	**100**	**100**	**100**	**100**	**-0.1%**	**1.3%**	**1.1%**	**20%**
Solid Fuels	832	546	337	327	339	34	23	14	11	11	-3.7%	-0.2%	0.0%	-40%
Oil	1472	1442	1531	1938	2149	60	60	64	67	69	0.2%	1.6%	1.4%	34%
Gas	131	430	513	639	624	5	18	22	22	20	5.8%	1.5%	0.8%	48%
Electricity Generation (incl. CHP Plants)	**890**	**1083**	**1091**	**1558**	**1576**	**100**	**100**	**100**	**100**	**100**	**0.9%**	**2.4%**	**1.5%**	**44%**
Solid Fuels	623	858	813	969	686	70	79	75	62	44	1.1%	1.2%	-0.7%	13%
Oil	228	142	149	134	145	26	13	14	9	9	-1.7%	-0.7%	-0.1%	-5%
Gas	39	84	129	454	745	4	8	12	29	47	5.1%	8.8%	7.3%	442%
Other Transformation	**111**	**158**	**126**	**149**	**150**						**0.5%**	**1.1%**	**0.7%**	**-6%**
Solid Fuels	-64	-7	-37	-40	-41									
Oil	145	120	110	110	110									
Gas	29	45	53	79	81									
Total Emissions	**3435**	**3659**	**3597**	**4612**	**4839**	**100**	**100**	**100**	**100**	**100**	**0.2%**	**1.7%**	**1.2%**	**26%**
Solid Fuels	1391	1398	1113	1257	984	40	38	31	27	20	-0.9%	0.8%	-0.5%	-10%
Oil	1845	1703	1790	2183	2404	54	47	50	47	50	-0.1%	1.3%	1.2%	28%
Gas	199	559	695	1172	1451	6	15	19	25	30	5.3%	3.5%	3.0%	110%

Business as Usual Projection: OECD Europe

POWER GENERATION	1971	1995	2010	2020	1971	1995	2010	2020	1971-1995	1995-2010	1995-2020
						percentage shares				average annual growth rates	
Electricity Generation (TWh)	1322	2678	3836	4492	100	100	100	100	3.0%	2.4%	2.1%
Solid Fuels	557	828	997	801	42	31	26	18	1.7%	1.2%	-0.1%
of which Combustible Renewables and Waste:	6	30	43	53	0	1	1	1	7.3%	2.3%	2.3%
Oil	316	237	214	230	24	9	6	5	-1.2%	-0.7%	-0.1%
Gas	74	255	1131	2021	6	10	29	45	5.3%	10.4%	8.6%
Nuclear	51	861	863	729	4	32	22	16	12.5%	0.0%	-0.7%
Hydro	320	486	585	629	24	18	15	14	1.8%	1.2%	1.0%
Other Renewables	3	10	46	82	0	0	1	2	4.9%	10.7%	8.8%
Capacity (GW)	-	628	853	1009	-	100	100	100	-	2.1%	1.9%
Solid Fuels	-	173	160	129	-	27	19	13	-	-0.5%	-1.1%
of which Combustible Renewables and Waste:	-	6	8	10	-	1	1	1	-	2.3%	2.3%
Oil	-	84	82	80	-	13	10	8	-	-0.2%	-0.2%
Gas	-	75	279	459	-	12	33	45	-	9.2%	7.5%
Nuclear	-	126	127	107	-	20	15	11	-	0.0%	-0.7%
Hydro	-	167	188	201	-	27	22	20	-	0.8%	0.8%
of which Pumped Storage Hydro:	-	30	32	34	-	5	4	3	-	0.5%	0.5%
Other Renewables	-	4	18	34	-	1	2	3	-	10.8%	9.1%

Tables for the Business as Usual Projection

Business as Usual Projection: OECD North America

ENERGY BALANCE	1971	1995	2010	2020	1971	1995	2010	2020	1971-1995	1995-2010	1995-2020
	million tonnes oil equivalent				percentage shares				average annual growth rates		
Demand for Energy Related Services (ERS)											
Electricity (final demand)	140	300	402	464					3.2%	2.0%	1.8%
Mobility	409	593	739	777					1.6%	1.5%	1.1%
Fossil fuel & heat in Stationary Uses											
(Industry,Services,Agriculture,Households)	739	688	695	650	100	100	100	100	-0.3%	0.1%	-0.2%
Solid Fuels	100	76	80	87	14	11	11	13	-1.2%	0.3%	0.6%
Oil	317	247	249	239	43	36	36	37	-1.0%	0.1%	-0.1%
Gas	322	358	354	308	44	52	51	47	0.4%	-0.1%	-0.6%
Heat	0	8	12	16	0	1	2	2	-	3.0%	3.0%
Total Final Consumption	1289	1581	1836	1891	100	100	100	100	0.9%	1.0%	0.7%
Solid Fuels	100	76	80	87	8	5	4	5	-1.2%	0.3%	0.6%
Oil	709	819	958	978	55	52	52	52	0.6%	1.1%	0.7%
Gas	339	379	385	346	26	24	21	18	0.5%	0.1%	-0.4%
Electricity	140	300	402	464	11	19	22	25	3.2%	2.0%	1.8%
Heat	0	8	12	16	0	0	1	1	-	3.0%	3.0%
Electricity Generation (incl. CHP Plants)	476	927	1183	1320	100	100	100	100	2.8%	1.6%	1.4%
Solid Fuels	233	498	648	830	49	54	55	63	3.2%	1.8%	2.1%
Oil	58	17	24	27	12	2	2	2	-5.0%	2.1%	1.8%
Gas	135	132	254	271	28	14	21	21	-0.1%	4.5%	2.9%
Nuclear	12	212	182	114	2	23	15	9	12.8%	-1.0%	-2.4%
Hydro	37	56	58	60	8	6	5	5	1.8%	0.3%	0.3%
Other Renewables	1	13	18	18	0	1	1	1	14.6%	2.0%	1.4%

ENERGY BALANCE	1971	1995	2010	2020	1971	1995	2010	2020	1971-1995	1995-2010	1995-2020
	million tonnes oil equivalent				percentage shares				average annual growth rates		
Other Transformation	126	165	192	198					1.1%	1.0%	0.7%
Solid Fuels	5	8	9	10							
Oil	22	37	44	45							
Gas	74	65	66	60							
Electricity	25	53	72	83							
Renewables	0	0	0	0							
Heat	0	1	1	1							
Less Output from Electricity + CHP plants											
Electricity	-166	-353	-474	-547							
Heat	0	-8	-12	-16							
Total Primary Energy Supply	1724	2312	2724	2846	100	100	100	100	**1.2%**	**1.1%**	**0.8%**
Solid Fuels	338	582	737	927	20	25	27	33	2.3%	1.6%	1.9%
Oil	789	873	1025	1050	46	38	38	37	0.4%	1.1%	0.7%
Gas	548	576	705	676	32	25	26	24	0.2%	1.4%	0.6%
Nuclear	12	212	182	114	1	9	7	4	12.8%	-1.0%	-2.4%
Hydro	37	56	58	60	2	2	2	2	1.8%	0.3%	0.3%
Other Renewables	1	13	18	18	0	1	1	1	14.6%	2.0%	1.4%
Other Primary	0	0	0	0	0	0	0	0	-	-	-
Combustible Renewables and Waste *(included above)*	43	81	87	92	2	4	3	3	2.7%	0.5%	0.5%
Total Primary Energy Supply (including CRW)	1724	2312	2724	2846	100	100	100	100	**1.2%**	**1.1%**	**0.8%**

Business as Usual Projection: OECD North America

CARBON DIOXIDE EMISSIONS	1971	1990	1995	2010	2020	1971	1990	1995	2010	2020	1971-1995	1995-2010	1995-2020	1990-2010
	million tonnes CO_2					percentage shares					average annual growth rate			total growth
Mobility	1181	1583	1720	2142	2250		100	100	100	100	1.6%	1.5%	1.1%	35%
Fossil fuel in Stationary Uses														
(Industry,Services,Agriculture,Households)	2069	1673	1558	1564	1453	100	100	100	100	100	-1.2%	0.0%	-0.3%	-6%
Solid Fuels	449	305	191	202	221	22	18	12	13	15	-3.5%	0.3%	0.6%	-34%
Oil	776	547	534	538	515	37	33	34	34	35	-1.5%	0.1%	-0.1%	-2%
Gas	845	821	833	825	717	41	49	53	53	49	-0.1%	-0.1%	-0.6%	0%
Total Final Consumption	3250	3255	3278	3706	3703	100	100	100	100	100	0.0%	0.8%	0.5%	14%
Solid Fuels	449	305	191	202	221	14	9	6	5	6	-3.5%	0.3%	0.6%	-34%
Oil	1915	2087	2203	2608	2677	59	64	67	70	72	0.6%	1.1%	0.8%	25%
Gas	885	864	883	896	805	27	27	27	24	22	0.0%	0.1%	-0.4%	4%
Electricity Generation (incl. CHP Plants)	1154	1852	2154	3042	3800	100	100	100	100	100	2.6%	2.3%	2.3%	64%
Solid Fuels	744	1596	1791	2373	3082	64	86	83	78	81	3.7%	1.9%	2.2%	49%
Oil	187	99	55	76	86	16	5	3	3	2	-4.9%	2.1%	1.8%	-23%
Gas	223	157	308	593	633	19	8	14	19	17	1.3%	4.5%	2.9%	277%
Other Transformation	239	232	267	292	278						0.5%	0.6%	0.2%	26%
Solid Fuels	-46	-23	-28	-29	-32									
Oil	113	124	140	164	168									
Gas	173	131	154	157	142									
Total Emissions	4643	5339	5699	7041	7781	100	100	100	100	100	0.9%	1.4%	1.3%	32%
Solid Fuels	1147	1878	1955	2546	3271	25	35	34	36	42	2.2%	1.8%	2.1%	36%
Oil	2215	2310	2399	2849	2931	48	43	42	40	38	0.3%	1.2%	0.8%	23%
Gas	1281	1151	1345	1646	1580	28	22	24	23	20	0.2%	1.4%	0.6%	43%

Business as Usual Projection: OECD North America

POWER GENERATION	1971	1995	2010	2020	1971	1995	2010	2020	1971-1995	1995-2010	1995-2020
					percentage shares				average annual growth rates		
Electricity Generation (TWh)	**1925**	**4110**	**5508**	**6363**	**100**	**100**	**100**	**100**	**3.2%**	**2.0%**	**1.8%**
Solid Fuels	805	1983	2650	3536	42	48	48	56	3.8%	2.0%	2.3%
of which Combustible Renewables and Waste:	*0*	*67*	*80*	*88*	*0*	*2*	*1*	*1*	*26.1%*	*1.2%*	*1.1%*
Oil	242	98	134	151	13	2	2	2	-3.7%	2.1%	1.8%
Gas	407	551	1319	1500	21	13	24	24	1.3%	6.0%	4.1%
Nuclear	45	812	697	437	2	20	13	7	12.8%	-1.0%	-2.4%
Hydro	426	648	680	703	22	16	12	11	1.8%	0.3%	0.3%
Other Renewables	1	19	29	36	0	0	1	1	15.6%	2.9%	2.6%
Capacity (GW)	**-**	**912**	**1159**	**1317**	**-**	**100**	**100**	**100**	**-**	**1.6%**	**1.5%**
Solid Fuels	-	372	418	564	-	41	36	43	-	0.8%	1.7%
of which Combustible Renewables and Waste:	*-*	*12*	*15*	*16*	*-*	*1*	*1*	*1*	*-*	*1.2%*	*1.1%*
Oil	-	45	51	58	-	5	4	4	-	0.9%	1.0%
Gas	-	209	415	450	-	23	36	34	-	4.7%	3.1%
Nuclear	-	116	96	59	-	13	8	4	-	-1.2%	-2.7%
Hydro	-	165	172	177	-	18	15	13	-	0.3%	0.3%
of which Pumped Storage Hydro:	*-*	*22*	*22*	*22*	*-*	*2*	*2*	*2*	*-*	*0.0%*	*0.0%*
Other Renewables	-	5	7	10	-	1	1	1	-	2.1%	2.4%

Business as Usual Projection: OECD Pacific

ENERGY BALANCE	1971	1995	2010	2020	1971	1995	2010	2020	1971-1995	1995-2010	1995-2020
	million tonnes oil equivalent				percentage shares				average annual growth rates		
Demand for Energy Related Services (ERS)											
Electricity (final demand)	34	90	122	141					**4.1%**	**2.0%**	**1.8%**
Mobility	50	114	148	155					**3.5%**	**1.7%**	**1.2%**
Fossil fuel & heat in Stationary Uses											
(Industry,Services,Agriculture,Households)	173	220	246	251	100	100	100	100	**1.0%**	**0.8%**	**0.5%**
Solid Fuels	44	52	49	49	25	24	20	20	0.7%	-0.3%	-0.2%
Oil	121	136	150	149	70	62	61	59	0.5%	0.6%	0.4%
Gas	8	30	39	41	4	14	16	16	5.9%	1.8%	1.3%
Heat	0	1	8	12	0	1	3	5	-	12.0%	8.9%
Total Final Consumption	257	424	516	547	100	100	100	100	**2.1%**	**1.3%**	**1.0%**
Solid Fuels	45	52	49	49	17	12	10	9	0.6%	-0.3%	-0.2%
Oil	171	250	298	304	66	59	58	56	1.6%	1.2%	0.8%
Gas	8	30	39	41	3	7	8	8	5.9%	1.8%	1.2%
Electricity	34	90	122	141	13	21	24	26	4.1%	2.0%	1.8%
Heat	0	1	8	12	0	0	1	2	-	12.0%	8.9%
Electricity Generation (incl. CHP Plants)	90	245	336	387	100	100	100	100	**4.3%**	**2.1%**	**1.8%**
Solid Fuels	27	70	87	94	30	29	26	24	4.1%	1.4%	1.2%
Oil	49	43	38	39	55	18	11	10	-0.6%	-0.8%	-0.4%
Gas	2	41	77	89	2	17	23	23	14.4%	4.3%	3.1%
Nuclear	2	76	109	134	2	31	32	35	16.2%	2.4%	2.3%
Hydro	9	11	12	13	10	4	4	3	0.6%	1.0%	0.8%
Other Renewables	1	4	12	19	1	2	3	5	5.8%	7.1%	6.3%

ENERGY BALANCE	1971	1995	2010	2020	1971	1995	2010	2020	1971-1995	1995-2010	1995-2020
	million tonnes oil equivalent				percentage shares				average annual growth rates		
Other Transformation	**20**	**40**	**48**	**51**					**2.9%**	**1.2%**	**1.0%**
Solid Fuels	11	12	11	11							
Oil	9	15	18	19							
Gas	-4	2	2	2							
Electricity	5	12	17	19							
Renewables	0	0	0	0							
Heat	0	0	-1	-1							
Less Output from Electricity + CHP plants											
Electricity	-39	-102	-139	-160							
Heat	0	0	-6	-10							
Total Primary Energy Supply	**329**	**607**	**755**	**815**	**100**	**100**	**100**	**100**	**2.6%**	**1.5%**	**1.2%**
Solid Fuels	82	134	148	154	25	22	20	19	2.1%	0.7%	0.6%
Oil	229	309	354	361	70	51	47	44	1.2%	0.9%	0.6%
Gas	5	73	119	132	2	12	16	16	11.6%	3.3%	2.4%
Nuclear	2	76	109	134	1	13	14	16	16.2%	2.4%	2.3%
Hydro	9	11	12	13	3	2	2	2	0.6%	1.0%	0.8%
Other Renewables	1	5	13	20	0	1	2	2	6.7%	6.2%	5.6%
Other Primary	0	0	0	0	0	0	0	0	-	-	-
Combustible Renewables and Waste (included above)	4	12	14	16	1	2	2	2	5.3%	1.0%	1.0%
Total Primary Energy Supply (including CRW)	**329**	**607**	**755**	**815**	**100**	**100**	**100**	**100**	**2.6%**	**1.5%**	**1.2%**

Business as Usual Projection: OECD Pacific

CARBON DIOXIDE EMISSIONS	1971	1990	1995	2010	2020	1971	1990	1995	2010	2020	1971-1995	1995-2010	1995-2020	1990-2010
	million tonnes CO$_2$					percentage shares					average annual growth rate			total growth
Mobility	148	291	338	436	459						3.5%	1.7%	1.2%	50%
Fossil fuel in Stationary Uses (Industry,Services,Agriculture,Households)	508	560	583	627	627	100	100	100	100	100	0.6%	0.5%	0.3%	12%
Solid Fuels	194	207	202	192	191	38	37	35	31	30	0.2%	-0.3%	-0.2%	-7%
Oil	298	296	313	344	341	59	53	54	55	54	0.2%	0.6%	0.4%	16%
Gas	17	56	69	90	94	3	10	12	14	15	6.1%	1.8%	1.3%	61%
Total Final Consumption	656	850	921	1062	1085	100	100	100	100	100	1.4%	1.0%	0.7%	25%
Solid Fuels	197	208	202	192	191	30	24	22	18	18	0.1%	-0.3%	-0.2%	-7%
Oil	443	586	650	780	799	67	69	71	73	74	1.6%	1.2%	0.8%	33%
Gas	17	56	69	90	95	3	7	8	8	9	6.1%	1.8%	1.2%	60%
Electricity Generation (incl. CHP Plants)	283	482	517	657	711	100	100	100	100	100	2.5%	1.6%	1.3%	36%
Solid Fuels	122	243	286	356	383	43	50	55	54	54	3.6%	1.5%	1.2%	47%
Oil	156	154	135	121	121	55	32	26	18	17	-0.6%	-0.8%	-0.4%	-22%
Gas	4	85	95	181	207	1	18	18	27	29	14.4%	4.3%	3.1%	112%
Other Transformation	-4	23	28	55	60						-	4.5%	3.1%	140%
Solid Fuels	-25	-61	-66	-64	-65									
Oil	19	50	48	57	59									
Gas	2	34	46	62	66									
Total Emissions	935	1355	1466	1774	1856	100	100	100	100	100	1.9%	1.3%	0.9%	31%
Solid Fuels	294	389	423	484	510	31	29	29	27	27	1.5%	0.9%	0.8%	24%
Oil	618	791	833	958	979	66	58	57	54	53	1.2%	0.9%	0.7%	21%
Gas	22	175	211	333	367	2	13	14	19	20	9.8%	3.1%	2.2%	90%

Business as Usual Projection: OECD Pacific

POWER GENERATION	1971	1995	2010	2020	1971	1995	2010	2020	1971-1995	1995-2010	1995-2020
						percentage shares			average annual growth rates		
Electricity Generation (TWh)	**451**	**1190**	**1613**	**1865**	**100%**	**100**	**100**	**100**	**4.1%**	**2.0%**	**1.8%**
Solid Fuels	84	327	406	441	19	27	25	24	5.8%	1.5%	1.2%
of which Combustible Renewables and Waste:	*0*	*18*	*21*	*23*	*0*	*1*	*1*	*1*	*19.2%*	*1.0%*	*1.0%*
Oil	242	227	203	204	54	19	13	11	-0.3%	-0.8%	-0.4%
Gas	7	214	422	519	2	18	26	28	15.1%	4.6%	3.6%
Nuclear	8	291	418	515	2	24	26	28	16.2%	2.4%	2.3%
Hydro	109	126	145	152	24	11	9	8	0.6%	1.0%	0.8%
Other Renewables	1	5	18	35	0	0	1	2	6.2%	8.5%	7.8%
Capacity (GW)	-	**274**	**366**	**426**		**100**	**100**	**100**	-	**2.0%**	**1.8%**
Solid Fuels	-	57	65	71		21	18	17	-	0.8%	0.9%
of which Combustible Renewables and Waste:	-	*4*	*5*	*5*		*1*	*1*	*1*	-	*1.0%*	*1.0%*
Oil	-	60	69	73		22	19	17	-	1.0%	0.8%
Gas	-	58	101	128		21	28	30	-	3.7%	3.2%
Nuclear	-	41	59	73		15	16	17	-	2.4%	2.3%
Hydro	-	56	69	73		21	19	17	-	1.4%	1.1%
of which Pumped Storage Hydro:	-	*23*	*30*	*33*		*8*	*8*	*8*	-	*1.9%*	*1.4%*
Other Renewables	-	1	4	9		0	1	2	-	10.7%	10.2%

Business as Usual Projection: Transition Economies

ENERGY BALANCE	1971	1995	2010	2020	1971	1995	2010	2020	1971-1995	1995-2010	1995-2020
	million tonnes oil equivalent				percentage shares				average annual growth rates		
Demand for Energy Related Services (ERS)											
Electricity (final demand)	66	102	169	233	100			100	**1.8%**	**3.4%**	**3.4%**
Mobility	100	77	120	162					**-1.1%**	**3.0%**	**3.0%**
Fossil fuel & heat in Stationary Uses											
(Industry,Services,Agriculture,Households)	**540**	**661**	**787**	**900**	**100**	**100**	**100**	**100**	**0.8%**	**1.2%**	**1.2%**
Solid Fuels	206	109	119	120	38	16	15	13	-2.6%	0.6%	0.4%
Oil	150	117	142	165	28	18	18	18	-1.0%	1.3%	1.4%
Gas	120	219	311	399	22	33	39	44	2.6%	2.4%	2.4%
Heat	64	216	216	216	12	33	27	24	5.2%	0.0%	0.0%
Total Final Consumption	**706**	**840**	**1077**	**1295**	**100**	**100**	**100**	**100**	**0.7%**	**1.7%**	**1.7%**
Solid Fuels	216	109	119	121	31	13	11	9	-2.8%	0.6%	0.4%
Oil	240	181	240	296	34	22	22	23	-1.2%	1.9%	2.0%
Gas	120	232	332	428	17	28	31	33	2.8%	2.4%	2.5%
Electricity	66	102	169	233	9	12	16	18	1.8%	3.4%	3.4%
Heat	64	216	216	216	9	26	20	17	5.2%	0.0%	0.0%
Electricity Generation (incl. CHP Plants)	**289**	**536**	**625**	**693**	**100**	**100**	**100**	**100**	**2.6%**	**1.0%**	**1.0%**
Solid Fuels	143	164	210	212	50	31	34	31	0.6%	1.7%	1.0%
Oil	48	63	50	50	17	12	8	7	1.1%	-1.4%	-0.9%
Gas	83	228	267	351	29	43	43	51	4.3%	1.1%	1.7%
Nuclear	2	57	67	48	1	11	11	7	16.1%	1.2%	-0.7%
Hydro	13	25	29	32	5	5	5	5	2.7%	1.1%	1.0%
Other Renewables	0	0	0	0	0	0	0	0	-	0.0%	0.0%

ENERGY BALANCE	1971	1995	2010	2020	1971	1995	2010	2020	1971-1995	1995-2010	1995-2020
	million tonnes oil equivalent				percentage shares				average annual growth rates		
Other Transformation	**88**	**16**	**40**	**59**	**100**				**-6.8%**	**6.1%**	**5.2%**
Solid Fuels	46	27	27	26	43						
Oil	33	31	38	44	34						
Gas	4	38	48	56	22						
Electricity	10	37	44	50	0						
Renewables	0	0	0	0	1						
Heat	-4	-117	-117	-117	0						
Less Output from Electricity + CHP plants											
Electricity	-77	-140	-214	-284					2.5%	2.9%	2.9%
Heat	-60	-99	-99	-99					2.1%	0.0%	0.0%
Total Primary Energy Supply	**946**	**1154**	**1429**	**1664**	**100**	**100**	**100**	**100**	**0.8%**	**1.4%**	**1.5%**
Solid Fuels	405	300	357	360	43	26	25	22	-1.2%	1.2%	0.7%
Oil	321	275	329	390	34	24	23	23	-0.6%	1.2%	1.4%
Gas	206	498	647	835	22	43	45	50	3.7%	1.8%	2.1%
Nuclear	2	57	67	48	0	5	5	3	16.1%	1.2%	-0.7%
Hydro	13	25	29	32	1	2	2	2	2.7%	1.1%	1.0%
Other Renewables	0	0	0	0	0	0	0	0	-	-2.5%	-1.5%
Other Primary	-1	-1	-1	-1	0	0	0	0	-	-	-

	1971	1995	2010	2020	1971	1995	2010	2020	1971-1995	1995-2010	1995-2020
Combustible Renewables and Waste (not included above)	-	27	28	29	-	2	2	2	-	0.3%	0.3%
Total Primary Energy Supply (including CRW)	-	**1181**	**1457**	**1693**	-	**100**	**100**	**100**	-	**1.4%**	**1.5%**

Business as Usual Projection: Transition Economies

CARBON DIOXIDE EMISSIONS	million tonnes CO$_2$					percentage shares					average annual growth rate			total growth
	1971	1990	1995	2010	2020	1971	1990	1995	2010	2020	1971-1995	1995-2010	1995-2020	1990-2010
Mobility	307	456	221	344	464						-1.4%	3.0%	3.0%	-25%
Fossil fuel Stationary Uses (Industry,Services,Agriculture,Households)	1540	1999	1278	1592	1856	100	100	100	100	100	-0.8%	1.5%	1.5%	-20%
Solid Fuels	818	680	473	517	525	53	34	37	32	28	-2.3%	0.6%	0.4%	-24%
Oil	450	615	307	370	429	29	31	24	23	23	-1.6%	1.3%	1.3%	-40%
Gas	272	704	498	704	902	18	35	39	44	49	2.6%	2.3%	2.4%	0%
Total Final Consumption	1847	2455	1499	1936	2320	100	100	100	100	100	-0.9%	1.7%	1.8%	-21%
Solid Fuels	854	696	475	520	529	46	28	32	27	23	-2.4%	0.6%	0.4%	-25%
Oil	719	1041	497	663	820	39	42	33	34	35	-1.5%	1.9%	2.0%	-36%
Gas	273	718	528	753	971	15	29	35	39	42	2.8%	2.4%	2.5%	5%
Electricity Generation (incl. CHP Plants)	924	1668	1395	1637	1838	100	100	100	100	100	1.7%	1.1%	1.1%	-2%
Solid Fuels	577	847	658	847	853	62	51	47	52	46	0.5%	1.7%	1.0%	0%
Oil	154	259	202	161	158	17	16	14	10	9	1.1%	-1.5%	-1.0%	-38%
Gas	193	562	535	629	828	21	34	38	38	45	4.3%	1.1%	1.8%	12%
Other Transformation	258	303	241	279	307						-0.3%	1.0%	1.0%	-8%
Solid Fuels	158	72	71	68	61									
Oil	91	101	83	101	118									
Gas	10	131	87	109	128									
Total CO$_2$ Emissions	3029	4426	3135	3852	4465	100	100	100	100	100	0.1%	1.4%	1.4%	-13%
Solid Fuels	1589	1614	1204	1435	1443	52	36	38	37	32	-1.2%	1.2%	0.7%	-11%
Oil	964	1401	781	926	1095	32	32	25	24	25	-0.9%	1.1%	1.4%	-34%
Gas	476	1411	1150	1491	1927	16	32	37	39	43	3.7%	1.7%	2.1%	6%

Business as Usual Projection: Transition Economies

POWER GENERATION	1971	1995	2010	2020	1971	1995	2010	2020	1971-1995	1995-2010	1995-2020
					percentage shares				average annual growth rates		
Electricity Generation (TWh)	**973**	**1631**	**2491**	**3298**	**100**	**100**	**100**	**100**	**2.2%**	**2.9%**	**2.9%**
Solid Fuels	481	498	703	770	49	31	28	23	0.1%	2.3%	1.8%
of which Combustible Renewables and Waste:	23	3	3	3	2	0	0	0	-8.4%	0.0%	0.0%
Oil	158	140	156	179	16	9	6	5	-0.5%	0.7%	1.0%
Gas	176	487	1036	1793	18	30	42	54	4.3%	5.2%	5.4%
Nuclear	6	216	257	181	1	13	10	5	16.0%	1.2%	-0.7%
Hydro	152	290	340	375	16	18	14	11	2.7%	1.1%	1.0%
Other Renewables	0	0	0	0	0	0	0	0	-	0.0%	0.0%
Capacity (GW)	-	**434**	**586**	**776**	-	**100**	**100**	**100**	-	**2.0%**	**2.3%**
Solid Fuels	-	137	150	145	-	32	26	19	-	0.6%	0.2%
of which Combustible Renewables and Waste:	-	1	1	1	-	0	0	0	-	0.0%	0.0%
Oil	-	49	60	66	-	11	10	8	-	1.4%	1.2%
Gas	-	120	237	431	-	28	40	56	-	4.6%	5.3%
Nuclear	-	41	44	29	-	9	8	4	-	0.5%	-1.4%
Hydro	-	88	95	104	-	20	16	13	-	0.6%	0.7%
Other Renewables	-	0	0	0	-	0	0	0	-	0.0%	0.0%

Business as Usual Projection: China

ENERGY BALANCE	million tonnes oil equivalent				percentage shares				average annual growth rates		
	1971	1995	2010	2020	1971	1995	2010	2020	1971-1995	1995-2010	1995-2020
Demand for Energy Related Services (ERS)											
Electricity (final demand)	10	68	165	255					8.2%	6.0%	5.4%
Mobility	6	59	130	190					10.3%	5.4%	4.8%
Fossil fuel & heat in Stationary Uses											
(Industry,Services,Agriculture,Households)	179	521	850	1079	100	100	100	100	4.5%	3.3%	3.0%
Solid Fuels	147	409	610	748	82	78	72	69	4.4%	2.7%	2.4%
Oil	31	80	157	213	17	15	19	20	4.0%	4.6%	4.0%
Gas	1	13	36	47	1	2	4	4	9.6%	7.0%	5.2%
Heat	0	19	46	71	0	4	5	7	-	5.9%	5.3%
Total Final Consumption	**195**	**649**	**1145**	**1524**	**100**	**100**	**100**	**100**	**5.1%**	**3.9%**	**3.5%**
Solid Fuels	147	416	617	755	75	64	54	50	4.4%	2.7%	2.4%
Oil	37	132	280	395	19	20	24	26	5.5%	5.1%	4.5%
Gas	1	13	36	47	1	2	3	3	9.6%	7.0%	5.2%
Electricity	10	68	165	255	5	11	14	17	8.2%	6.0%	5.4%
Heat	0	19	46	71	0	3	4	5	-	5.9%	5.3%
Electricity Generation (incl. CHP Plants)	**37**	**275**	**567**	**825**	**100**	**100**	**100**	**100**	**8.7%**	**5.0%**	**4.5%**
Solid Fuels	30	241	459	648	82	88	81	79	9.0%	4.4%	4.0%
Oil	4	13	36	55	11	5	6	7	5.0%	6.8%	5.8%
Gas	0	1	12	24	0	0	2	3	-	20.7%	14.9%
Nuclear	0	3	19	33	0	1	3	4	-	12.2%	9.6%
Hydro	3	16	39	62	7	6	7	8	8.0%	6.0%	5.5%
Other Renewables	0	0	2	3	0	0	0	0	-	-	-

ENERGY BALANCE	1971	1995	2010	2020	1971	1995	2010	2020	1971-1995	1995-2010	1995-2020
	million tonnes oil equivalent				percentage shares				average annual growth rates		
Other Transformation	19	55	122	178					4.5%	5.4%	4.8%
Solid Fuels	13	7	11	13							
Oil	2	18	39	55							
Gas	2	3	8	10							
Electricity	2	21	50	77							
Renewables	0	0	0	0							
Heat	0	6	14	22							
Less Output from Electricity + CHP plants											
Electricity	-12	-89	-215	-332							
Heat	0	-26	-61	-94							
Total Primary Energy Supply	239	864	1559	2101	100	100	100	100	5.5%	4.0%	3.6%
Solid Fuels	190	664	1087	1416	80	77	70	67	5.3%	3.3%	3.1%
Oil	43	164	355	506	18	19	23	24	5.7%	5.3%	4.6%
Gas	3	17	57	81	1	2	4	4	7.2%	8.5%	6.5%
Nuclear	0	3	19	33	0	0	1	2	-	12.2%	9.6%
Hydro	3	16	39	62	1	2	3	3	8.0%	6.0%	5.5%
Other Renewables	0	0	2	3	0	0	0	0	-	-	-
Other Primary	0	0	0	0	0	0	0	0	-	-	-
Combustible Renewables and Waste (not included above)	-	206	216	224	-	19	12	10	-	0.3%	0.3%
Total Primary Energy Supply (including CRW)	-	1070	1775	2325	-	100	100	100	-	3.4%	3.2%

Business as Usual Projection: China

CARBON DIOXIDE EMISSIONS	1971	1990	1995	2010	2020	1971	1990	1995	2010	2020	1971-1995	1995-2010	1995-2020	1990-2010
	million tonnes CO_2					percentage shares					average annual growth rate			total growth
Mobility	16	142	180	389	564						10.5%	5.3%	4.7%	174%
Fossil fuel in Stationary Uses (Industry,Services,Agriculture,Households)	675	1506	1893	2955	3682	100	100	100	100	100	4.4%	3.0%	2.7%	96%
Solid Fuels	578	1318	1682	2508	3072	86	88	89	85	83	4.5%	2.7%	2.4%	90%
Oil	93	168	190	391	538	14	11	10	13	15	3.0%	4.9%	4.2%	133%
Gas	3	20	21	56	72	0	1	1	2	2	7.9%	6.9%	5.1%	180%
Total Final Consumption	692	1648	2073	3344	4246	100	100	100	100	100	4.7%	3.2%	2.9%	103%
Solid Fuels	578	1359	1709	2536	3099	84	82	82	76	73	4.6%	2.7%	2.4%	87%
Oil	110	268	344	752	1074	16	16	17	22	25	4.9%	5.4%	4.7%	181%
Gas	3	20	21	56	72	0	1	1	2	2	8.0%	6.8%	5.1%	176%
Electricity Generation (incl. CHP Plants)	132	607	982	1930	2753	100	100	100	100	100	8.7%	4.6%	4.2%	218%
Solid Fuels	118	556	938	1787	2523	90	92	95	93	92	9.0%	4.4%	4.0%	221%
Oil	13	49	43	114	175	10	8	4	6	6	4.9%	6.8%	5.8%	135%
Gas	0	2	2	29	55	0	0	0	1	2	-	20.7%	14.9%	395%
Other Transformation	52	156	-4	48	83						-	-	-	-70%
Solid Fuels	42	106	-75	-111	-136									
Oil	5	43	57	120	169									
Gas	4	8	14	38	50									
Total Emissions	875	2411	3051	5322	7081	100	100	100	100	100	5.3%	3.8%	3.4%	121%
Solid Fuels	739	2021	2572	4212	5486	84	84	84	79	77	5.3%	3.3%	3.1%	108%
Oil	128	360	443	987	1418	15	15	15	19	20	5.3%	5.5%	4.8%	174%
Gas	7	30	36	123	177	1	1	1	2	3	6.9%	8.5%	6.5%	312%

Business as Usual Projection: China

POWER GENERATION	1971	1995	2010	2020	1971	1995	2010	2020	1971-1995	1995-2010	1995-2020
					percentage shares				average annual growth rates		
Electricity Generation (TWh)	**144**	**1036**	**2497**	**3857**	**100**	**100**	**100**	**100**	**8.6%**	**6.0%**	**5.4%**
Solid Fuels	99	767	1729	2612	69	74	69	68	8.9%	5.6%	5.0%
of which Combustible Renewables and Waste:	0	0	0	1	0	0	0	0	-	-	-
Oil	15	63	168	257	10	6	7	7	6.2%	6.8%	5.8%
Gas	0	2	65	123	0	0	3	3	-	24.6%	17.1%
Nuclear	0	13	72	127	0	1	3	3	-	12.2%	9.6%
Hydro	30	191	457	726	21	18	18	19	8.0%	6.0%	5.5%
Other Renewables	0	0	7	11	0	0	0	0	-	-	-
Capacity (GW)	-	**227**	**501**	**757**	-	**100**	**100**	**100**	-	**5.4%**	**4.9%**
Solid Fuels	-	158	323	472	-	70	64	62	-	4.9%	4.5%
of which Combustible Renewables and Waste:	-	0	0	0	-	0	0	0	-	21.7%	14.7%
Oil	-	13	30	45	-	6	6	6	-	5.7%	5.1%
Gas	-	1	10	18	-	0	2	2	-	17.5%	12.8%
Nuclear	-	2	11	20	-	1	2	3	-	11.6%	9.3%
Hydro	-	52	125	199	-	23	25	26	-	6.0%	5.5%
Other Renewables	-	0	3	4	-	0	1	1	-	16.7%	11.9%

Business as Usual Projection: Rest of the World*

ENERGY BALANCE	1971	1995	2010	2020	1971	1995	2010	2020	1971-1995	1995-2010	1995-2020
	million tonnes oil equivalent				percentage shares				average annual growth rates		
Demand for Energy Related Services (ERS)											
Electricity (final demand)	31	176	339	516					7.5%	4.4%	4.4%
Mobility	114	369	625	868					5.0%	3.6%	3.5%
Fossil fuel & heat in Stationary Uses											
(Industry,Services,Agriculture,Households)	207	634	982	1290	100	100	100	100	4.8%	3.0%	2.9%
Solid Fuels	68	135	169	191	33	21	17	15	2.9%	1.5%	1.4%
Oil	112	362	538	678	54	57	55	53	5.0%	2.7%	2.5%
Gas	28	137	274	421	13	22	28	33	6.9%	4.7%	4.6%
Heat	0	0	1	1	0	0	0	0	-	2.1%	2.7%
Total Final Consumption	352	1179	1945	2675	100	100	100	100	5.2%	3.4%	3.3%
Solid Fuels	80	135	169	191	23	11	9	7	2.2%	1.5%	1.4%
Oil	214	729	1160	1543	61	62	60	58	5.2%	3.1%	3.0%
Gas	28	139	276	424	8	12	14	16	7.0%	4.7%	4.6%
Electricity	31	176	339	516	9	15	17	19	7.5%	4.4%	4.4%
Heat	0	0	1	1	0	0	0	0	-	2.1%	2.7%
Electricity Generation (incl. CHP Plants)	94	530	989	1451	100	100	100	100	7.5%	4.3%	4.1%
Solid Fuels	33	182	369	554	35	34	37	38	7.4%	4.8%	4.5%
Oil	37	124	177	202	39	23	18	14	5.2%	2.4%	2.0%
Gas	10	108	229	424	10	20	23	29	10.5%	5.1%	5.6%
Nuclear	0	36	68	86	0	7	7	6	21.5%	4.3%	3.5%
Hydro	15	65	106	130	16	12	11	9	6.4%	3.3%	2.8%
Other Renewables	0	13	39	55	0	2	4	4	27.9%	7.7%	6.0%

ENERGY BALANCE	1971	1995	2010	2020	1971	1995	2010	2020	1971-1995	1995-2010	1995-2020
	million tonnes oil equivalent				percentage shares				average annual growth rates		
Other Transformation	**69**	**232**	**411**	**583**					**5.2%**	**3.9%**	**3.8%**
Solid Fuels	6	19	31	36							
Oil	44	71	114	153							
Gas	13	98	183	271							
Electricity	6	43	83	124							
Renewables	0	0	0	0							
Heat	0	0	0	0							
Less Output from Electricity + CHP plants											
Electricity	-37	-219	-422	-640							
Heat	0	0	0	0							
Total Primary Energy Supply	**479**	**1721**	**2923**	**4068**	**100**	**100**	**100**	**100**	**5.5%**	**3.6%**	**3.5%**
Solid Fuels	119	337	570	781	25	20	19	19	4.4%	3.6%	3.4%
Oil	295	924	1451	1897	61	54	50	47	4.9%	3.0%	2.9%
Gas	51	346	688	1119	11	20	24	28	8.3%	4.7%	4.8%
Nuclear	0	36	68	86	0	2	2	2	21.5%	4.3%	3.5%
Hydro	15	65	106	130	3	4	4	3	6.4%	3.3%	2.8%
Other Renewables	0	13	40	56	0	1	1	1	28.1%	7.6%	5.9%
Other Primary	0	0	0	0	0	0	0	0	-	-	-
Combustible Renewables and Waste (not included above)	-	671	863	993	-	28	23	20	-	1.7%	1.6%
Total Primary Energy Supply (including CRW)	**-**	**2392**	**3787**	**5061**	**-**	**100**	**100**	**100**	**-**	**3.1%**	**3.0%**

* South Asia, East Asia, Latin America, Africa and Middle East.

Business as Usual Projection: Rest of the World*

CARBON DIOXIDE EMISSIONS	1971	1990	1995	2010	2020	1971	1990	1995	2010	2020	1971-1995	1995-2010	1995-2020	1990-2010 total growth
	million tonnes CO_2					percentage shares					average annual growth rate			
Mobility	347	832	1096	1857	2584						4.9%	3.6%	3.5%	123%
Fossil fuel in Stationary Uses (Industry,Services,Agriculture,Households)	667	1561	1834	2740	3525	100	100	100	100	100	4.3%	2.7%	2.6%	76%
Solid Fuels	278	534	562	704	795	42	34	31	26	23	3.0%	1.5%	1.4%	32%
Oil	327	813	982	1458	1839	49	52	54	53	52	4.7%	2.7%	2.5%	79%
Gas	62	214	290	579	892	9	14	16	21	25	6.6%	4.7%	4.6%	171%
Total Final Consumption	1014	2393	2930	4597	6109	100	100	100	100	100	4.5%	3.0%	3.0%	92%
Solid Fuels	323	545	563	705	796	32	23	19	15	13	2.3%	1.5%	1.4%	29%
Oil	629	1634	2073	3308	4414	62	68	71	72	72	5.1%	3.2%	3.1%	102%
Gas	62	214	294	584	899	6	9	10	13	15	6.7%	4.7%	4.6%	173%
Electricity Generation (incl. CHP Plants)	267	980	1359	2539	3799	100	100	100	100	100	7.0%	4.3%	4.2%	161%
Solid Fuels	127	499	712	1444	2167	48	51	52	57	57	7.4%	4.8%	4.6%	190%
Oil	117	321	394	560	641	44	33	29	22	17	5.2%	2.4%	2.0%	74%
Gas	23	160	253	535	991	9	16	19	22	27	10.5%	5.1%	5.6%	244%
Other Transformation	155	460	502	898	1255						5.0%	4.0%	3.7%	95%
Solid Fuels	11	67	35	84	98									
Oil	111	190	220	350	467									
Gas	32	203	247	464	690									
Total Emissions	1436	3833	4791	8034	11163	100	100	100	100	100	5.1%	3.5%	3.4%	110%
Solid Fuels	461	1110	1310	2233	3062	32	29	27	28	27	4.4%	3.6%	3.5%	101%
Oil	857	2146	2687	4218	5522	60	56	56	52	49	4.9%	3.1%	2.9%	97%
Gas	117	577	794	1583	2580	8	15	17	20	23	8.3%	4.7%	4.8%	174%

* South Asia, East Asia, Latin America, Africa and Middle East.

Business as Usual Projection: Rest of the World*

POWER GENERATION	1971	1995	2010	2020	1971	1995	2010	2020	1971-1995	1995-2010	1995-2020
					percentage shares				average annual growth rates		
Electricity Generation (TWh)	**432**	**2559**	**4908**	**7450**	**100**	**100**	**100**	**100**	**7.7%**	**4.4%**	**4.4%**
Solid Fuels	104	674	1475	2331	24	26	30	31	8.1%	5.4%	5.1%
of which Combustible Renewables and Waste:	2	10	19	26	1	0	0	0	6.3%	4.2%	3.9%
Oil	128	550	788	920	30	21	16	12	6.3%	2.4%	2.1%
Gas	27	423	1090	2286	6	17	22	31	12.1%	6.5%	7.0%
Nuclear	1	139	262	328	0	5	5	4	21.5%	4.3%	3.5%
Hydro	171	758	1238	1511	40	30	25	20	6.4%	3.3%	2.8%
Other Renewables	0	15	54	75	0	1	1	1	-	8.9%	6.6%
Capacity (GW)	**-**	**605**	**1091**	**1630**	**-**	**100**	**100**	**100**	**-**	**4.0%**	**4.0%**
Solid Fuels	-	135	248	379	-	22	23	23	-	4.2%	4.2%
of which Combustible Renewables and Waste:	-	2	4	6	-	0	0	0	-	4.2%	3.9%
Oil	-	154	235	283	-	25	22	17	-	2.9%	2.5%
Gas	-	108	267	549	-	18	24	34	-	6.2%	6.7%
Nuclear	-	21	38	47	-	3	3	3	-	4.1%	3.3%
Hydro	-	185	292	355	-	31	27	22	-	3.1%	2.6%
Other Renewables	-	3	12	16	-	0	1	1	-	10.9%	7.8%

* South Asia, East Asia, Latin America, Africa and Middle East.

Business as Usual Projection: East Asia

ENERGY BALANCE	1971	1995	2010	2020	1971	1995	2010	2020	1971-1995	1995-2010	1995-2020
	million tonnes oil equivalent				percentage shares				average annual growth rates		
Demand for Energy Related Services (ERS)											
Electricity (final demand)	5	42	90	141					9.1%	5.2%	4.9%
Mobility	19	95	205	313					7.0%	5.3%	4.9%
Fossil fuel & heat in Stationary Uses											
(Industry,Services,Agriculture,Households)	55	179	282	359	100	100	100	100	5.1%	3.1%	2.8%
Solid Fuels	30	47	54	57	55	26	19	16	1.8%	0.9%	0.8%
Oil	24	113	183	231	43	63	65	64	6.8%	3.3%	2.9%
Gas	1	19	45	71	2	11	16	20	13.0%	5.8%	5.4%
Heat	0	0	0	0	0	0	0	0	-	-	-
Total Final Consumption	79	316	577	813	100	100	100	100	6.0%	4.1%	3.8%
Solid Fuels	30	47	54	57	39	15	9	7	1.8%	0.9%	0.8%
Oil	42	208	388	543	53	66	67	67	6.9%	4.2%	3.9%
Gas	1	19	45	71	1	6	8	9	13.0%	5.8%	5.4%
Electricity	5	42	90	141	7	13	16	17	9.1%	5.2%	4.9%
Heat	0	0	0	0	0	0	0	0	-	-	-
Electricity Generation (incl. CHP Plants)	15	136	291	436	100	100	100	100	9.7%	5.2%	4.8%
Solid Fuels	3	34	87	157	18	25	30	36	11.0%	6.6%	6.4%
Oil	10	35	45	43	65	26	16	10	5.6%	1.6%	0.7%
Gas	0	27	65	109	2	20	22	25	21.2%	6.0%	5.7%
Nuclear	0	27	53	70	0	20	18	16	-	4.7%	3.9%
Hydro	2	7	11	16	14	5	4	4	5.0%	3.5%	3.5%
Other Renewables	0	7	29	42	0	5	10	10	-	10.1%	7.5%

ENERGY BALANCE	1971	1995	2010	2020	1971	1995	2010	2020	1971-1995	1995-2010	1995-2020
	million tonnes oil equivalent				percentage shares				average annual growth rates		
Other Transformation	8	64	133	201					9.0%	5.0%	4.7%
Solid Fuels	1	4	5	5							
Oil	6	20	38	53							
Gas	0	29	69	109							
Electricity	1	10	21	33							
Renewables	0	0	0	0							
Heat	0	0	0	0							
Less Output from Electricity + CHP plants											
Electricity	-6	-52	-111	-175							
Heat	0	0	0	0							
Total Primary Energy Supply	95	464	890	1275	100	100	100	100	**6.8%**	**4.4%**	**4.1%**
Solid Fuels	34	84	145	219	36	18	16	17	3.8%	3.7%	3.9%
Oil	58	264	472	639	60	57	53	50	6.5%	3.9%	3.6%
Gas	1	76	179	289	1	16	20	23	18.5%	5.9%	5.5%
Nuclear	0	27	53	70	0	6	6	5	-	4.7%	3.9%
Hydro	2	7	11	16	2	1	1	1	5.0%	3.5%	3.5%
Other Renewables	0	7	29	42	0	1	3	3	-	10.1%	7.5%
Other Primary	0	0	0	0	0	0	0	0	-	-	-
Combustible Renewables and Waste (not included above)	-	117	129	136	-	20	13	10	-	0.7%	0.6%
Total Primary Energy Supply (including CRW)	-	**581**	**1018**	**1411**	-	**100**	**100**	**100**	-	**3.8%**	**3.6%**

Business as Usual Projection: East Asia

CARBON DIOXIDE EMISSIONS	1971	1990	1995	2010	2020	1971	1990	1995	2010	2020	1971-1995	1995-2010	1995-2020	1990-2010
	million tonnes CO$_2$					percentage shares					average annual growth rate			total growth
Mobility	**55**	**185**	**282**	**611**	**931**						**7.0%**	**5.3%**	**4.9%**	**230%**
Fossil fuel Stationary Uses (Industry,Services,Agriculture,Households)	**191**	**421**	**509**	**755**	**936**	**100**	**100**	**100**	**100**	**100**	**4.2%**	**2.7%**	**2.5%**	**79%**
Solid Fuels	119	209	205	236	251	62	50	40	31	27	2.3%	1.0%	0.8%	13%
Oil	70	195	278	453	576	37	46	55	60	62	5.9%	3.3%	3.0%	133%
Gas	2	17	26	66	108	1	4	5	9	12	11.0%	6.3%	5.8%	281%
Total Final Consumption	**246**	**607**	**792**	**1366**	**1867**	**100**	**100**	**100**	**100**	**100**	**5.0%**	**3.7%**	**3.5%**	**125%**
Solid Fuels	120	209	205	236	251	49	34	26	17	13	2.3%	1.0%	0.8%	13%
Oil	125	380	561	1064	1508	51	63	71	78	81	6.5%	4.4%	4.0%	180%
Gas	2	17	26	66	108	1	3	3	5	6	11.0%	6.3%	5.8%	282%
Electricity Generation (incl. CHP Plants)	**42**	**205**	**308**	**638**	**1007**	**100**	**100**	**100**	**100**	**100**	**8.6%**	**5.0%**	**4.9%**	**210%**
Solid Fuels	11	95	132	343	618	25	46	43	54	61	11.1%	6.6%	6.4%	260%
Oil	31	86	113	144	135	73	42	37	23	13	5.6%	1.6%	0.7%	67%
Gas	1	24	63	151	254	1	12	21	24	25	21.2%	6.0%	5.7%	533%
Other Transformation	**19**	**87**	**134**	**294**	**450**						**8.4%**	**5.4%**	**5.0%**	**240%**
Solid Fuels	4	2	-7	-8	-9									
Oil	15	32	58	108	151									
Gas	1	52	83	194	308									
Total Emissions	**308**	**899**	**1233**	**2298**	**3325**	**100**	**100**	**100**	**100**	**100**	**6.0%**	**4.2%**	**4.0%**	**156%**
Solid Fuels	134	307	330	571	860	44	34	27	25	26	3.8%	3.7%	3.9%	86%
Oil	170	498	731	1316	1794	55	55	59	57	54	6.3%	4.0%	3.7%	164%
Gas	3	94	173	412	670	1	10	14	18	20	17.9%	6.0%	5.6%	339%

Business as Usual Projection: East Asia

POWER GENERATION	1971	1995	2010	2020	1971	1995	2010	2020	1971-1995	1995-2010	1995-2020
					percentage shares				average annual growth rates		
Electricity Generation (TWh)	**72**	**608**	**1294**	**2030**	**100**	**100**	**100**	**100**	**9.3%**	**5.2%**	**4.9%**
Solid Fuels	9	140	377	705	13	23	29	35	12.1%	6.8%	6.7%
of which Combustible Renewables and Waste:	0	0	1	2	0	0	0	0	-	5.5%	7.1%
Oil	38	175	223	210	52	29	17	10	6.6%	1.6%	0.7%
Gas	1	105	324	614	2	17	25	30	20.9%	7.8%	7.3%
Nuclear	0	102	205	267	0	17	16	13	-	4.7%	3.9%
Hydro	24	78	131	185	34	13	10	9	5.0%	3.5%	3.5%
Other Renewables	0	8	34	49	0	1	3	2	-	10.1%	7.5%
Capacity (GW)	**-**	**126**	**275**	**432**		**100**	**100**	**100**		**5.3%**	**5.1%**
Solid Fuels	-	23	57	106		18	21	25		6.4%	6.4%
of which Combustible Renewables and Waste:	-	0	0	1		0	0	0		5.5%	7.1%
Oil	-	41	64	66		33	23	15		2.9%	1.9%
Gas	-	21	79	160		17	29	37		9.2%	8.5%
Nuclear	-	14	28	37		11	10	8		4.7%	3.9%
Hydro	-	25	40	55		20	15	13		3.1%	3.2%
Other Renewables	-	1	6	9		1	2	2		10.1%	7.5%

Business as Usual Projection: South Asia

ENERGY BALANCE	1971	1995	2010	2020	1971	1995	2010	2020	1971-1995	1995-2010	1995-2020
	million tonnes oil equivalent				percentage shares				average annual growth rates		
Demand for Energy Related Services (ERS)											
Electricity (final demand)	5	31	69	107					8.0%	5.4%	5.0%
Mobility	17	46	92	141					4.3%	4.7%	4.5%
Fossil fuel & heat in Stationary Uses											
(Industry,Services,Agriculture,Households)	33	110	200	275	100	100	100	100	5.2%	4.1%	3.7%
Solid Fuels	17	50	70	81	52	46	35	30	4.6%	2.2%	1.9%
Oil	14	41	76	102	42	37	38	37	4.6%	4.3%	3.7%
Gas	2	19	55	92	6	17	27	33	10.1%	7.3%	6.5%
Heat	0	0	0	0	0	0	0	0	-	-	-
Total Final Consumption	**55**	**188**	**362**	**523**	**100**	**100**	**100**	**100**	**5.3%**	**4.5%**	**4.2%**
Solid Fuels	25	50	70	81	46	27	19	16	3.0%	2.2%	1.9%
Oil	23	87	168	242	42	46	46	46	5.7%	4.5%	4.2%
Gas	2	19	55	92	3	10	15	18	10.1%	7.3%	6.5%
Electricity	5	31	69	107	9	17	19	21	8.0%	5.4%	5.0%
Heat	0	0	0	0	0	0	0	0	-	-	-
Electricity Generation (incl. CHP Plants)	**17**	**123**	**244**	**363**	**100**	**100**	**100**	**100**	**8.7%**	**4.7%**	**4.4%**
Solid Fuels	10	93	182	262	62	75	75	72	9.6%	4.6%	4.2%
Oil	2	7	14	22	11	6	6	6	5.8%	4.7%	4.7%
Gas	1	12	26	54	8	10	11	15	9.7%	5.5%	6.3%
Nuclear	0	2	4	5	2	2	2	1	7.6%	4.6%	3.7%
Hydro	3	10	17	20	17	8	7	5	5.3%	3.9%	2.9%
Other Renewables	0	0	1	1	0	0	0	0	-	38.8%	22.9%

ENERGY BALANCE	1971	1995	2010	2020	1971	1995	2010	2020	1971-1995	1995-2010	1995-2020
	million tonnes oil equivalent				percentage shares				average annual growth rates		
Other Transformation											
Solid Fuels	8	15	45	68					2.9%	7.5%	6.2%
Oil	3	-3	4	5							
Gas	3	5	9	14							
Electricity	0	3	9	14							
Renewables	2	10	23	35							
Heat	0	0	0	0							
Less Output from Electricity + CHP plants											
Electricity	-7	-42	-92	-142							
Heat	0	0	0	0							
Total Primary Energy Supply	72	284	558	811	100	100	100	100	5.9%	4.6%	4.3%
Solid Fuels	39	140	256	348	53	49	46	43	5.5%	4.1%	3.7%
Oil	27	99	191	277	38	35	34	34	5.5%	4.5%	4.2%
Gas	3	34	90	160	5	12	16	20	10.2%	6.7%	6.4%
Nuclear	0	2	4	5	0	1	1	1	7.6%	4.6%	3.7%
Hydro	3	10	17	20	4	3	3	2	5.3%	3.9%	2.9%
Other Renewables	0	0	1	1	0	0	0	0	-	38.8%	22.9%
Other Primary	0	0	0	0	0	0	0	0	-	-	-
Combustible Renewables and Waste *(not included above)*	-	244	285	308	-	46	34	28	-	1.0%	0.9%
Total Primary Energy Supply (including CRW)	-	528	844	1119	-	100	100	100	-	3.2%	3.0%

Business as Usual Projection: South Asia

CARBON DIOXIDE EMISSIONS	1971	1990	1995	2010	2020	1971	1990	1995	2010	2020	1971-1995	1995-2010	1995-2020	total growth 1990-2010
	million tonnes CO$_2$					percentage shares					average annual growth rate			
Mobility	57	101	141	280	427						3.8%	4.7%	4.5%	177%
Fossil fuel in Stationary Uses (Industry,Services,Agriculture,Households)	109	297	358	617	820	100	100	100	100	100	5.1%	3.7%	3.4%	108%
Solid Fuels	68	182	200	277	323	63	61	56	45	39	4.6%	2.2%	1.9%	52%
Oil	37	84	115	218	291	34	28	32	35	35	4.9%	4.3%	3.8%	158%
Gas	4	31	43	123	206	4	10	12	20	25	10.3%	7.3%	6.5%	302%
Total Final Consumption	**167**	**398**	**499**	**897**	**1247**	**100**	**100**	**100**	**100**	**100**	**4.7%**	**4.0%**	**3.7%**	**125%**
Solid Fuels	99	192	200	277	323	60	48	40	31	26	3.0%	2.2%	1.9%	45%
Oil	63	176	256	497	718	38	44	51	55	58	6.0%	4.5%	4.2%	183%
Gas	4	31	43	123	206	2	8	9	14	17	10.3%	7.3%	6.5%	302%
Electricity Generation (incl. CHP Plants)	**49**	**257**	**410**	**813**	**1213**	**100**	**100**	**100**	**100**	**100**	**9.2%**	**4.7%**	**4.4%**	**216%**
Solid Fuels	40	220	360	707	1018	82	86	88	87	84	9.5%	4.6%	4.2%	221%
Oil	6	16	22	44	69	12	6	5	5	6	5.8%	4.7%	4.7%	169%
Gas	3	20	28	62	126	6	8	7	8	10	9.7%	5.5%	6.3%	202%
Other Transformation	**18**	**30**	**4**	**68**	**96**						**-5.8%**	**20.3%**	**13.3%**	**127%**
Solid Fuels	10	9	-17	21	24									
Oil	7	18	14	27	39									
Gas	0	3	7	20	34									
Total Emissions	**233**	**685**	**913**	**1777**	**2556**	**100**	**100**	**100**	**100**	**100**	**5.8%**	**4.5%**	**4.2%**	**160%**
Solid Fuels	150	421	544	1005	1365	64	61	60	57	53	5.5%	4.2%	3.8%	139%
Oil	76	210	292	567	825	33	31	32	32	32	5.8%	4.5%	4.2%	171%
Gas	7	54	77	205	366	3	8	8	12	14	10.3%	6.7%	6.4%	278%

Business as Usual Projection: South Asia

POWER GENERATION	1971	1995	2010	2020	1971	1995	2010	2020	1971-1995	1995-2010	1995-2020
						percentage shares				average annual growth rates	
Electricity Generation (TWh)	**76**	**485**	**1070**	**1657**	**100**	**100**	**100**	**100**	**8.0%**	**5.4%**	**5.0%**
Solid Fuels	32	288	661	1026	42	59	62	62	9.5%	5.7%	5.2%
of which Combustible Renewables and Waste:	0	0	5	7	0	0	0	0	-	-	-
Oil	6	30	60	96	7	6	6	6	7.3%	4.7%	4.8%
Gas	4	48	126	277	5	10	12	17	10.8%	6.7%	7.3%
Nuclear	1	8	15	19	2	2	1	1	7.6%	4.6%	3.7%
Hydro	33	112	200	229	43	23	19	14	5.3%	3.9%	2.9%
Other Renewables	0	0	8	10	0	0	1	1	-	-	-
Capacity (GW)	-	**106**	**212**	**304**	-	**100**	**100**	**100**	-	**4.7%**	**4.3%**
Solid Fuels	-	53	109	161	-	50	51	53	-	5.0%	4.6%
of which Combustible Renewables and Waste:	-	0	1	2	-	0	0	1	-	14.6%	10.5%
Oil	-	11	15	20	-	10	7	6	-	2.2%	2.4%
Gas	-	15	35	63	-	14	17	21	-	5.9%	5.9%
Nuclear	-	2	3	4	-	2	2	1	-	3.5%	2.7%
Hydro	-	26	46	53	-	24	22	17	-	3.9%	2.9%
Other Renewables	-	0	4	5	-	0	2	1	-	-	-

Business as Usual Projection: Latin America

ENERGY BALANCE	1971	1995	2010	2020	1971	1995	2010	2020	1971-1995	1995-2010	1995-2020
	million tonnes oil equivalent				percentage shares				average annual growth rates		
Demand for Energy Related Services (ERS)											
Electricity (final demand)	12	53	98	144					6.4%	4.2%	4.1%
Mobility	51	131	204	263					4.0%	3.0%	2.8%
Fossil fuel & heat in Stationary Uses											
(Industry,Services,Agriculture,Households)	64	158	238	298	100	100	100	100	3.8%	2.8%	2.6%
Solid Fuels	5	16	19	21	8	10	8	7	5.0%	1.1%	1.2%
Oil	47	93	127	146	73	59	53	49	2.9%	2.1%	1.8%
Gas	12	49	92	131	19	31	39	44	5.9%	4.3%	4.0%
Heat	0	0	0	0	0	0	0	0	-	-	-
Total Final Consumption	127	342	540	706	100	100	100	100	4.2%	3.1%	2.9%
Solid Fuels	5	16	19	21	4	5	3	3	4.8%	1.1%	1.2%
Oil	98	224	329	407	77	65	61	58	3.5%	2.6%	2.4%
Gas	12	50	94	134	10	15	17	19	6.0%	4.4%	4.0%
Electricity	12	53	98	144	9	16	18	20	6.4%	4.2%	4.1%
Heat	0	0	0	0	0	0	0	0	-	-	-
Electricity Generation (incl. CHP Plants)	32	114	215	317	100	100	100	100	5.5%	4.3%	4.2%
Solid Fuels	2	8	24	36	5	7	11	11	6.9%	7.4%	6.1%
Oil	16	32	57	67	51	28	27	21	2.9%	3.9%	2.9%
Gas	6	21	49	112	20	18	23	35	5.0%	5.9%	7.0%
Nuclear	0	5	8	8	0	4	4	2	-	3.4%	2.0%
Hydro	8	43	69	84	24	37	32	27	7.5%	3.3%	2.8%
Other Renewables	0	6	8	10	0	5	4	3	23.6%	2.1%	2.1%

ENERGY BALANCE	1971	1995	2010	2020	1971	1995	2010	2020	1971-1995	1995-2010	1995-2020
	million tonnes oil equivalent				percentage shares				average annual growth rates		
Other Transformation	35	61	104	141					2.3%	3.6%	3.4%
Solid Fuels	1	1	1	1							
Oil	23	26	38	46							
Gas	9	22	42	60							
Electricity	2	12	23	34							
Renewables	0	0	0	0							
Heat	0	0	0	0							
Less Output from Electricity + CHP plants											
Electricity	-14	-66	-121	-178							
Heat	0	0	0	0							
Total Primary Energy Supply	181	452	738	986	100	100	100	100	3.9%	3.3%	3.2%
Solid Fuels	8	25	44	59	5	6	6	6	4.8%	3.8%	3.5%
Oil	137	281	424	520	76	62	57	53	3.0%	2.8%	2.5%
Gas	28	93	185	306	15	20	25	31	5.2%	4.7%	4.9%
Nuclear	0	5	8	8	0	1	1	1	-	3.4%	2.0%
Hydro	8	43	69	84	4	9	9	9	7.5%	3.3%	2.8%
Other Renewables	0	6	8	10	0	1	1	1	23.6%	2.1%	2.1%
Other Primary	0	0	0	0	0	0	0	0	-	-	-

	1971	1995	2010	2020	1971	1995	2010	2020	1971-1995	1995-2010	1995-2020
Combustible Renewables and Waste *(not included above)*	-	83	91	95	-	16	11	9	-	0.6%	0.5%
Total Primary Energy Supply (including CRW)	-	535	829	1081	-	100	100	100	-	3.0%	2.8%

Business as Usual Projection: Latin America

CARBON DIOXIDE EMISSIONS	1971	1990	1995	2010	2020	1971	1990	1995	2010	2020	1971-1995	1995-2010	1995-2020	1990-2010
	million tonnes CO_2					percentage shares					average annual growth rate			total growth
Mobility	151	316	388	603	778						4.0%	3.0%	2.8%	91%
Fossil fuel in Stationary Uses (Industry,Services,Agriculture,Households)	189	369	428	628	777	100	100	100	100	100	3.5%	2.6%	2.4%	70%
Solid Fuels	22	55	66	78	90	12	15	16	12	12	4.7%	1.1%	1.2%	43%
Oil	139	229	252	343	394	74	62	59	55	51	2.5%	2.1%	1.8%	50%
Gas	28	85	109	207	294	15	23	26	33	38	5.9%	4.3%	4.0%	143%
Total Final Consumption	339	685	816	1231	1555	100	100	100	100	100	3.7%	2.8%	2.6%	80%
Solid Fuels	23	55	66	78	90	7	8	8	6	6	4.6%	1.1%	1.2%	43%
Oil	289	545	638	942	1166	85	80	78	77	75	3.4%	2.6%	2.4%	73%
Gas	28	85	111	211	300	8	12	14	17	19	6.0%	4.4%	4.0%	147%
Electricity Generation (incl. CHP Plants)	74	155	185	394	621	100	100	100	100	100	3.9%	5.2%	5.0%	154%
Solid Fuels	7	22	34	99	148	9	15	18	25	24	6.9%	7.4%	6.1%	341%
Oil	52	94	103	181	212	71	60	56	46	34	2.9%	3.9%	2.9%	94%
Gas	15	39	48	113	262	20	25	26	29	42	5.0%	5.9%	7.0%	193%
Other Transformation	82	135	134	220	291						2.1%	3.4%	3.1%	64%
Solid Fuels	2	2	-1	-2	-2									
Oil	58	86	83	122	151									
Gas	22	47	53	100	142									
Total Emissions	495	974	1135	1845	2467	100	100	100	100	100	3.5%	3.3%	3.2%	89%
Solid Fuels	32	79	99	176	235	6	8	9	10	10	4.8%	3.9%	3.5%	123%
Oil	400	725	824	1245	1528	81	74	73	67	62	3.1%	2.8%	2.5%	72%
Gas	64	171	212	425	704	13	18	19	23	29	5.1%	4.7%	4.9%	149%

Business as Usual Projection: Latin America

POWER GENERATION	1971	1995	2010	2020	1971	1995	2010	2020	1971-1995	1995-2010	1995-2020
						percentage shares			average annual growth rates		
Electricity Generation (TWh)	166	772	1409	2073	100	100	100	100	**6.6%**	**4.1%**	**4.0%**
Solid Fuels	7	42	109	163	4	5	8	8	7.6%	6.5%	5.6%
of which Combustible Renewables and Waste:	2	10	13	17	1	1	1	1	6.2%	2.1%	2.3%
Oil	54	134	236	275	33	17	17	13	3.8%	3.9%	2.9%
Gas	17	76	222	613	10	10	16	30	6.5%	7.4%	8.7%
Nuclear	0	18	30	30	0	2	2	1	-	3.4%	2.1%
Hydro	87	495	803	980	53	64	57	47	7.5%	3.3%	2.8%
Other Renewables	0	7	9	11	0	1	1	1	23.6%	2.3%	2.2%
Capacity (GW)	-	187	326	480	-	100	100	100	-	**3.8%**	**3.8%**
Solid Fuels	-	13	21	31	-	7	6	6	-	3.1%	3.5%
of which Combustible Renewables and Waste:	-	2	3	4	-	1	1	1	-	2.7%	2.7%
Oil	-	38	67	78	-	20	21	16	-	3.9%	2.9%
Gas	-	23	63	157	-	12	19	33	-	6.9%	8.0%
Nuclear	-	3	4	4	-	2	1	1	-	3.0%	1.8%
Hydro	-	109	170	207	-	58	52	43	-	3.0%	2.6%
Other Renewables	-	1	2	2	-	1	1	0	-	3.8%	3.1%

Business as Usual Projection: Africa

ENERGY BALANCE	1971	1995	2010	2020	1971	1995	2010	2020	1971-1995	1995-2010	1995-2020
	million tonnes oil equivalent				percentage shares				average annual growth rates		
Demand for Energy Related Services (ERS)											
Electricity (final demand)	7	26	44	60					5.6%	3.6%	3.4%
Mobility	19	40	56	68					3.2%	2.2%	2.1%
Fossil fuel & heat in Stationary Uses											
(Industry,Services,Agriculture,Households)	31	70	102	132	100	100	100	100	3.4%	2.6%	2.6%
Solid Fuels	16	21	25	29	50	29	25	22	1.1%	1.4%	1.4%
Oil	15	39	60	80	48	55	59	60	4.0%	3.0%	2.9%
Gas	1	11	17	23	2	15	17	17	13.0%	3.1%	3.1%
Heat	0	0	0	0	0	0	0	0	-	-	-
Total Final Consumption	57	136	202	260	100	100	100	100	3.7%	2.7%	2.6%
Solid Fuels	19	21	26	29	33	15	13	11	0.4%	1.4%	1.4%
Oil	30	78	115	147	53	57	57	56	4.0%	2.6%	2.6%
Gas	1	11	18	23	1	8	9	9	13.3%	2.9%	2.9%
Electricity	7	26	44	60	12	19	22	23	5.6%	3.6%	3.4%
Heat	0	0	0	0	0	0	0	0	-	-	-
Electricity Generation (incl. CHP Plants)	23	80	131	171	100	100	100	100	5.3%	3.3%	3.1%
Solid Fuels	18	44	65	83	78	55	50	49	3.8%	2.7%	2.6%
Oil	3	13	21	22	12	16	16	13	6.6%	3.4%	2.2%
Gas	0	15	34	53	2	19	26	31	16.6%	5.4%	5.1%
Nuclear	0	3	3	2	0	4	2	2	-	0.5%	0.3%
Hydro	2	5	6	7	9	6	5	4	3.8%	1.6%	1.6%
Other Renewables	0	0	2	3	0	0	1	2	-	12.6%	8.9%

ENERGY BALANCE	1971	1995	2010	2020	1971	1995	2010	2020	1971-1995	1995-2010	1995-2020
	million tonnes oil equivalent				percentage shares				average annual growth rates		
Other Transformation											
Solid Fuels	4	41	59	74	100	100	100	100	10.3%	2.4%	2.4%
Oil	0	17	21	24							
Gas	1	6	9	11							
Electricity	2	12	19	26							
Renewables	1	5	9	13							
Heat	0	0	0	0							
Less Output from Electricity + CHP plants											
Electricity	-8	-32	-53	-73							
Heat	0	0	0	0							
Total Primary Energy Supply	76	226	339	432	100	100	100	100	4.6%	2.7%	2.6%
Solid Fuels	37	82	112	137	49	36	33	32	3.4%	2.1%	2.1%
Oil	34	97	145	180	45	43	43	42	4.4%	2.7%	2.5%
Gas	3	39	70	102	3	17	21	24	12.1%	4.0%	3.9%
Nuclear	0	3	3	3	0	1	1	1	-	0.5%	0.3%
Hydro	2	5	6	7	3	2	2	2	3.8%	1.6%	1.6%
Other Renewables	0	0	2	3	0	0	1	1	-	12.6%	8.9%
Other Primary	0	0	0	0	0	0	0	0	-	-	-

Combustible Renewables and Waste (not included above)	-	225	357	453	-	50	51	51	-	3.1%	2.8%
Total Primary Energy Supply (including CRW)	-	451	696	886	-	100	100	100	-	2.9%	2.7%

Business as Usual Projection: Africa

CARBON DIOXIDE EMISSIONS	1971	1990	1995	2010	2020	1971	1990	1995	2010	2020	1971-1995	1995-2010	1995-2020	1990-2010 total growth
	million tonnes CO$_2$					percentage shares					average annual growth rate			
Mobility	58	109	118	164	199						3.0%	2.2%	2.1%	50%
Fossil fuel & heat in Stationary Uses (Industry,Services,Agriculture,Households)	113	202	218	309	388	100	100	100	100	100	2.8%	2.4%	2.3%	53%
Solid Fuels	67	84	87	106	122	59	42	40	34	31	1.1%	1.4%	1.4%	27%
Oil	45	102	110	168	219	40	50	50	54	56	3.8%	2.9%	2.8%	65%
Gas	1	16	22	35	47	1	8	10	11	12	14.0%	3.1%	3.1%	112%
Total Final Consumption	171	312	336	473	587	100	100	100	100	100	2.9%	2.3%	2.3%	52%
Solid Fuels	79	85	87	107	122	46	27	26	23	21	0.4%	1.4%	1.4%	26%
Oil	91	211	226	330	416	53	68	67	70	71	3.9%	2.6%	2.5%	57%
Gas	1	16	23	36	48	1	5	7	8	8	14.3%	2.9%	2.9%	119%
Electricity Generation (incl. CHP Plants)	79	213	246	398	517	100	100	100	100	100	4.8%	3.3%	3.0%	87%
Solid Fuels	70	151	170	253	323	88	71	69	63	62	3.8%	2.7%	2.6%	67%
Oil	9	38	41	67	70	11	18	16	17	14	6.6%	3.4%	2.2%	79%
Gas	1	24	36	79	124	1	11	15	20	24	16.6%	5.4%	5.1%	232%
Other Transformation	1	99	110	150	185						22.0%	2.1%	2.1%	51%
Solid Fuels	-6	54	60	74	85									
Oil	2	12	20	29	37									
Gas	4	34	31	47	63									
Total Emissions	251	624	693	1022	1290	100	100	100	100	100	4.3%	2.6%	2.5%	64%
Solid Fuels	143	290	317	433	531	57	47	46	42	41	3.4%	2.1%	2.1%	49%
Oil	102	260	286	427	524	41	42	41	42	41	4.4%	2.7%	2.5%	64%
Gas	6	74	90	162	235	2	12	13	16	18	12.0%	4.0%	3.9%	119%

Business as Usual Projection: Africa

POWER GENERATION	1971	1995	2010	2020	1971	1995	2010	2020	1971-1995	1995-2010	1995-2020
					percentage shares				average annual growth rates		
Electricity Generation (TWh)	**91**	**367**	**622**	**851**	**100**	**100**	**100**	**100**	**6.0%**	**3.6%**	**3.4%**
Solid Fuels	56	186	278	364	62	51	45	43	5.1%	2.7%	2.7%
of which Combustible Renewables and Waste is	*0*	*0*	*1*	*1*	*0*	*0*	*0*	*0*	*6.0%*	*5.7%*	*3.4%*
Oil	11	63	99	104	12	17	16	12	7.7%	3.1%	2.0%
Gas	1	51	158	282	1	14	25	33	17.7%	7.9%	7.1%
Nuclear	0	11	12	12	0	3	2	1	-	0.5%	0.3%
Hydro	23	56	72	84	25	15	12	10	3.8%	1.6%	1.6%
Other Renewables	0	0	3	5	0	0	1	1	-	15.5%	10.8%
Capacity (GW)	**-**	**97**	**152**	**208**	**-**	**100**	**100**	**100**	**-**	**3.0%**	**3.1%**
Solid Fuels	-	43	53	70	-	44	35	33	-	1.4%	1.9%
of which Combustible Renewables and Waste is	*-*	*0*	*0*	*0*	*-*	*0*	*0*	*0*	*-*	*0.0%*	*0.0%*
Oil	-	20	30	32	-	20	20	16	-	2.9%	2.0%
Gas	-	12	40	73	-	12	27	35	-	8.4%	7.5%
Nuclear	-	2	2	2	-	2	1	1	-	0.0%	0.0%
Hydro	-	20	26	30	-	21	17	15	-	1.6%	1.6%
Other Renewables	-	0	1	1	-	0	1	1	-	21.1%	14.2%

Business as Usual Projection: Middle East

ENERGY BALANCE	1971	1995	2010	2020	1971	1995	2010	2020	1971-1995	1995-2010	1995-2020
	million tonnes oil equivalent				percentage shares				average annual growth rates		
Demand for Energy Related Services (ERS)											
Electricity (final demand)	2	23	37	63					10.7%	3.2%	4.0%
Mobility	9	56	67	84					8.1%	1.2%	1.6%
Fossil fuel & heat in Stationary Uses											
(Industry,Services,Agriculture,Households)	24	117	159	227	100	100	100	100	6.8%	2.1%	2.7%
Solid Fuels	0	1	2	2	2	1	1	1	4.8%	2.1%	2.7%
Oil	12	76	92	120	50	65	58	53	7.9%	1.3%	1.9%
Gas	12	39	65	104	48	34	41	46	5.2%	3.4%	3.9%
Heat	0	0	1	1	0	0	0	0	-	2.1%	2.7%
Total Final Consumption	35	197	264	373	100	100	100	100	7.5%	2.0%	2.6%
Solid Fuels	0	1	2	2	1	1	1	1	4.8%	2.1%	2.7%
Oil	21	132	160	204	60	67	60	55	8.0%	1.3%	1.7%
Gas	12	39	65	104	34	20	25	28	5.2%	3.4%	3.9%
Electricity	2	23	37	63	6	12	14	17	10.7%	3.2%	4.0%
Heat	0	0	1	1	0	0	0	0	-	2.1%	2.7%
Electricity Generation (incl. CHP Plants)	8	76	109	164	100	100	100	100	9.9%	2.4%	3.1%
Solid Fuels	0	4	11	16	0	5	10	10	-	6.7%	5.5%
Oil	6	37	39	49	76	49	36	30	7.9%	0.4%	1.2%
Gas	2	34	56	96	20	44	51	59	13.5%	3.4%	4.3%
Nuclear	0	0	0	0	0	0	0	0	-	-	-
Hydro	0	1	3	3	4	2	3	2	6.1%	4.9%	2.9%
Other Renewables	0	0	0	0	0	0	0	0	-	6.5%	5.5%

ENERGY BALANCE	1971	1995	2010	2020	1971	1995	2010	2020	1971-1995	1995-2010	1995-2020
	million tonnes oil equivalent				percentage shares				average annual growth rates		
Other Transformation	14	50	70	98					5.4%	2.2%	2.7%
Solid Fuels	0	0	0	0							
Oil	12	14	20	28							
Gas	2	31	44	61							
Electricity	0	5	7	9							
Renewables	0	0	0	0							
Heat	0	0	0	0							
Less Output from Electricity + CHP plants											
Electricity	-2	-28	-44	-72							
Heat	0	0	0	0							
Total Primary Energy Supply	55	295	399	564	100	100	100	100	7.3%	2.0%	2.6%
Solid Fuels	0	5	13	18	1	2	3	3	11.7%	5.9%	5.0%
Oil	38	183	219	281	70	62	55	50	6.7%	1.2%	1.7%
Gas	16	104	164	261	29	35	41	46	8.2%	3.1%	3.7%
Nuclear	0	0	0	0	0	0	0	0	-	-	-
Hydro	0	1	3	3	1	0	1	0	6.1%	4.9%	2.9%
Other Renewables	0	0	1	0	0	0	0	0	-	2.1%	2.7%
Other Primary	0	0	0	0	0	0	0	0	-	-	-

	1971	1995	2010	2020	1971	1995	2010	2020	1971-1995	1995-2010	1995-2020
Combustible Renewables and Waste (not included above)	-	1	1	1	-	0	0	0	-	1.0%	1.0%
Total Primary Energy Supply (including CRW)	-	296	400	565	-	100	100	100	-	2.0%	2.6%

Business as Usual Projection: Middle East

CARBON DIOXIDE EMISSIONS	million tonnes CO$_2$					percentage shares					average annual growth rate			total growth
	1971	1990	1995	2010	2020	1971	1990	1995	2010	2020	1971-1995	1995-2010	1995-2020	1990-2010
Mobility	25	121	166	199	247						8.1%	1.2%	1.6%	65%
Fossil fuel Stationary Uses (Industry,Services,Agriculture,Households)	65	271	322	431	605	100	100	100	100	100	6.9%	2.0%	2.6%	59%
Solid Fuels	2	4	5	7	9	2	2	2	2	2	5.0%	2.1%	2.7%	58%
Oil	36	203	227	276	359	56	75	70	64	59	7.9%	1.3%	1.9%	36%
Gas	27	65	90	148	237	42	24	28	34	39	5.1%	3.4%	3.9%	130%
Total Final Consumption	90	392	488	629	853	100	100	100	100	100	7.3%	1.7%	2.3%	61%
Solid Fuels	2	4	5	7	9	2	1	1	1	1	5.0%	2.1%	2.7%	58%
Oil	62	323	393	474	606	68	82	81	75	71	8.0%	1.3%	1.7%	47%
Gas	27	65	90	148	237	30	16	18	24	28	5.1%	3.4%	3.9%	130%
Electricity Generation (incl. CHP Plants)	23	150	210	296	441	100	100	100	100	100	9.7%	2.3%	3.0%	97%
Solid Fuels	0	9	16	43	61	0	6	8	14	14	-	6.7%	5.5%	360%
Oil	19	88	116	123	154	84	58	55	42	35	7.8%	0.4%	1.2%	41%
Gas	4	53	78	130	225	16	36	37	44	51	13.5%	3.4%	4.3%	143%
Other Transformation	35	109	119	166	232						5.3%	2.2%	2.7%	52%
Solid Fuels	0	0	0	0	0									
Oil	29	42	46	64	89									
Gas	6	67	73	102	143									
Total Emissions	148	651	817	1091	1526	100	100	100	100	100	7.4%	1.9%	2.5%	68%
Solid Fuels	1	13	21	49	71	1	2	3	5	5	11.7%	5.9%	5.0%	267%
Oil	110	453	555	662	850	74	70	68	61	56	7.0%	1.2%	1.7%	46%
Gas	37	185	242	381	605	25	28	30	35	40	8.2%	3.1%	3.7%	106%

Business as Usual Projection: Middle East

POWER GENERATION	1971	1995	2010	2020	1971	1995	2010	2020	1971-1995	1995-2010	1995-2020
					percentage shares				average annual growth rates		
Electricity Generation (TWh)	**28**	**327**	**513**	**839**	**100**	**100**	**100**	**100**	**10.8%**	**3.0%**	**3.8%**
Solid Fuels	0	19	50	73	-	6	10	9	-	6.8%	5.6%
of which Combustible Renewables and Waste:	0	0	0	0	-	0	0	0	-	-	-
Oil	20	149	171	235	71	46	33	28	8.8%	0.9%	1.8%
Gas	4	144	260	499	15	44	51	60	16.0%	4.0%	5.1%
Nuclear	0	0	0	0	0	0	0	0	-	-	-
Hydro	4	16	32	32	14	5	6	4	6.1%	4.9%	2.9%
Other Renewables	0	0	0	0	0	0	0	0	-	6.8%	5.7%
Capacity (GW)	-	**89**	**126**	**206**	-	**100**	**100**	**100**	-	**2.4%**	**3.4%**
Solid Fuels	-	3	8	11	-	4	6	6	-	6.6%	5.3%
of which Combustible Renewables and Waste:	-	0	0	0	-	0	0	0	-	-	-
Oil	-	44	59	87	-	49	46	42	-	2.0%	2.8%
Gas	-	37	49	97	-	41	39	47	-	2.0%	4.0%
Nuclear	-	0	0	0	-	0	0	0	-	-	-
Hydro	-	5	10	10	-	6	8	5	-	4.9%	2.9%
Other Renewables	-	0	0	0	-	0	0	0	-	6.8%	5.7%

DEFINITIONS AND CONVERSION FACTORS ANNEX

This section of the 1998 WEO provides general information on the fuel and sectoral definitions used throughout the Outlook, along with some approximate conversion factors. Readers interested in obtaining more detailed information should consult the IEA publications Energy Statistics of OECD Countries 1995-1996 (the 'red book'), Energy Balances of OECD Countries 1995 - 1996 (the 'blue book') and Energy Statistics and Balances of Non-OECD Countries 1994-1995 (the 'green book').

Energy Definitions [1]

Solid Fuels

For the purposes of this Outlook the following definition of solid fuels has been adopted. In the OECD countries solid fuels is equal to the sum of coal and combustible renewables and waste (see below). In the non-OECD countries solid fuels only includes coal and therefore excludes combustible renewables and waste. When comparing the solid fuels projections presented in this Outlook with data shown in recent IEA statistical publications the reader should therefore pay close attention to the definition of solid fuels being used in each publication.

Coal

Coal includes all coal, both primary (including hard coal and lignite) and derived fuels (including patent fuel, coke oven coke, gas coke, BKB, coke oven gas and blast furnace gas). Peat is also included in this category.

Combustible Renewables & Waste

Combustible Renewables & Waste comprises solid biomass and animal products, gas/liquids from biomass, industrial waste and

---

1. The precise individual energy definitions used by the IEA can be found on pages I.5 and I.6 of Energy Balances of OECD Countries 1995-1996 (the 'blue book'). Note that the Outlook's regional definition of Solid Fuels differs from that used in recent IEA statistical publications.

municipal waste. Biomass is defined as any plant matter used directly as fuel or converted into fuels or electricity and/or heat. Included here are: wood, vegetal waste (including wood waste and crops used for energy production), ethanol, animal materials/wastes and sulphite lyes. (Sulphite lyes are also known as "black liquor" and are an alkaline spent liquor from the digesters in the production of sulphate or soda pulp during the manufacture of paper. The energy is derived from the lignin removed from the wood pulp). Municipal waste comprises wastes produced by the residential, commercial and public service sectors that are collected by local authorities for disposal in a central location for the production of heat and/or power). Hospital waste is included in this category.

Oil

Oil comprises the small quantity of crude oil (crude oil, natural gas liquids, refinery feedstocks and additives as well as other hydrocarbons) directly consumed and petroleum products (refinery gas, ethane, LPG, aviation gasoline, motor gasoline, jet fuels, kerosene, gas/diesel oil, heavy fuel oil, naphtha, white spirit, lubricants, bitumen, paraffin waxes, petroleum coke and other petroleum products). Note that oil includes refineries own use of oil.

Gas

Gas includes natural gas (both associated and non-associated gas, but excluding natural gas liquids) and gas works gas.

Nuclear

The nuclear data shown in the Total Primary Energy Supply (TPES) tables refers to the primary heat equivalent of the electricity produced by a nuclear plant with an average thermal efficiency of 33%.

Hydro

The hydro data shown in the TPES tables refers to the energy content of the electricity produced in hydro power plants assuming 100% efficiency. Hydro output excludes output from pumped storage plants.

Other Renewables

Other renewables includes geothermal, solar, wind, tide, wave energy and the use of these energy forms for electricity generation. Unless the actual efficiency of the geothermal process is known, the quantity of geothermal energy entering electricity generation is inferred from the electricity production at geothermal plants assuming an average thermal efficiency of 10 per cent. For solar, wind, tide and wave energy, the quantities entering electricity generation are equal to the electrical energy generated (i.e. 100% efficiencies). Direct use of geothermal and solar heat is also included in this category (when referring to TPES).

Heat

Heat shows the disposition of heat produced for sale. The large majority of the heat included in this category results from the combustion of fuels, although some small amounts are produced from electrically powered heat pumps and boilers. Any heat extracted from ambient air by heat pumps is shown as indigenous production.

Other Primary

Other Primary covers the small quantities of heat and electricity entering directly into the Total Primary Energy Supply (TPES) balance.

Energy Related Service Sector Definitions

Electricity

Electricity includes all electricity consumed in final consumption, it therefore excludes own uses and losses, etc. Note that it also excludes heat consumption.

Mobility

Mobility includes all energy consumed in the transport sector except electricity.

Stationary

The Stationary sector is equal to total final consumption of energy minus total final consumption of electricity and all non-electricity fuels in the Mobility sector. An equivalent definition of the Stationary sector is that it is the sum of non-electricity energy consumption in the industry, residential, commercial, public service, agricultural, other sectors, non-specified and non-energy sectors.

Power Generation

Power Generation covers all inputs into electricity and CHP plants. It includes both fossil and non-fossil inputs such as nuclear and renewables.

Energy Balance Definitions

Indigenous Production

Indigenous production is the production of primary energy, i.e. hard coal, lignite, peat, crude oil, NGLs, natural gas, combustible renewables & waste, nuclear, hydro, geothermal, solar and the heat from heat pumps that is extracted from the ambient environment. Production is calculated after the removal of impurities.

Imports and Exports

Imports and exports comprise amounts having crossed the national territorial boundaries of the country, whether or not customs clearance has taken place.

International Marine Bunkers

International marine bunkers cover those quantities delivered to sea-going ships of all flags, including warships. Consumption by ships engaged in transport in inland and coastal waters is not included.

Stock Changes

Stock changes reflect the difference between opening stock levels on the first day of the year and closing levels on the last day of the year of stocks on national territory held by producers, importers, energy transformation industries and large consumers. A stock build is shown as a negative number, and a stock draw as a positive number.

Tables for the Business as Usual Projection

Total Primary Energy Supply (TPES)

Total primary energy supply (TPES) is formally defined as indigenous production + imports - exports - international marine bunkers ± stock changes. In the Outlook, however, the regional TPES exclude marine bunkers, whereas the world TPES includes international marine bunkers.

Statistical Differences

Statistical differences is a category which includes the sum of the unexplained statistical differences for individual fuels, as they appear in the basic energy statistics. It also includes the statistical differences that arise because of the variety of coal conversion factors.

Electricity Plants

Electricity plants refers to plants which are designed to produce electricity only. If one or more units of the plant is a CHP unit (and the inputs and outputs can not be distinguished on a unit basis) then the whole plant is designated as a CHP plant. Both public and electricity plants are included.

Combined Heat and Power Plants

Combined heat and power plants (also known as autoproducer plants), refers to plants which are designed to produce both heat and electricity. Both public and autoproducer plants are included.

Total Final Consumption (TFC)

Total final consumption (TFC) is the sum of consumption by the different end-use sectors. In final consumption, petrochemical feedstocks are shown under industry, while non-energy use of such oil products as white spirit, lubricants, bitumen, paraffin waxes and other products are shown under non-energy use, and are included in total final consumption only. Backflows from the petrochemical industry are not included in total final consumption.

Industry

Consumption in the Industry sector includes the following sub-sectors (energy used for transport by industry is not included here but reported under transport):

Iron and Steel Industry
[ISIC Group 271 and Class 2731];
Chemical industry [ISIC Division 24];
of which: petrochemical feedstocks. The petrochemical industry includes cracking and reforming processes for the purpose of producing ethylene, propylene, butylene, synthesis gas, aromatics, butadene and other hydrocarbon-based raw materials in processes such as steam cracking, aromatics plants and steam reforming.

- Non-ferrous metals basic industries [ISIC Group 272 and Class 2732];
- Non-metallic mineral products such as glass, ceramic, cement, etc. [ISIC Division 26];
- Transport equipment [ISIC Divisions 34 and 35];
- Machinery. Fabricated metal products, machinery and equipment other than transport equipment [ISIC Divisions 28, 29, 30, 31 and 32];
- Mining (excluding fuels) and quarrying [ISIC Divisions 13 and 14];
- Food and tobacco [ISIC Divisions 15 and 16];
- Paper, pulp and print [ISIC Divisions 21 and 22];
- Wood and wood products (other than pulp and paper) [ISIC Division 20];
- Construction [ISIC Division 45];
- Textile and leather [ISIC Divisions 17, 18 and 19];
- Non-specified (any manufacturing industry not included above) [ISIC Divisions 25, 33, 36 and 37].

Transport Sector
The transport sector includes all fuels for transport except international marine bunkers [ISIC Divisions 60, 61 and 62]. It includes transport in the industry sector and covers road, railway, air, internal navigation (including small craft and coastal shipping not included under marine bunkers), fuels used for transport of materials by pipeline and non-specified transport. Fuel used for ocean, coastal and inland fishing is included in agriculture (other sectors).

Other Sectors
Other sectors cover agriculture (including ocean, coastal and inland fishing) [ISIC Divisions 01, 02 and 05], residential, commercial

and public services [ISIC Divisions 41, 50, 51, 52, 55, 63, 64, 65, 66, 70, 71, 72, 73, 74, 75, 80, 85, 90, 91, 92, 93, 95 and 99], and non-specified consumption.

Non-Energy

Non-Energy covers all use of fuels for non-energy purposes. Non-energy is included in total final consumption. It is assumed that the use of these products is exclusively non-energy use. For example, petroleum products such as white spirit, paraffin waxes, lubricants and bitumen are consumed for non-energy reasons. Non-energy use of coal includes carbon blacks, graphite electrodes, etc.

Other Transformation

Other transformation is a diverse category and essentially covers the energy consumed in converting primary energy into a form that can be consumed in the final consuming sectors. Examples of the energy products produced by the other transformation sector include petroleum products from crude oil and heat from fossil fuels via heat plants. Note that the other transformation sector excludes energy consumption in electricity and CHP plants which are treated separately. Other transformation therefore includes transfers, statistical differences, heat plants, gas works, petroleum refineries, coal transformation, liquefaction, other transformation, own use and distribution losses.

Approximate Energy Conversion Factors

This section provides approximate Mtoe (million tonnes of oil equivalent) conversion factors for each of the major energy types considered in this Outlook. Note that the standard unit used throughout this Outlook is tonne of oil equivalent (toe), where tonne refers to a metric ton, i.e. 1000 kilograms. In order to convert to long and short tons use the following conversion factors; 1 tonne = 0.984 long tons and 1 tonne = 1.1023 short tons.

Oil

The following table is reproduced from Chapter 7 and shows the regional and world conversion factors that existed in 1995 between million barrels of oil and million tonnes of oil equivalent (Mtoe). Note that the relationship between barrels of oil and Mtoe is not exact but changes over time for a variety of reasons, such as changes in the petroleum product mix. For simplicity, it has been assumed that the 1995 conversion factors continue to apply throughout the projection period 1995-2020.

1995 World Oil Demand - Oil Market Report Basis

	Inland Demand Mtoe	Bunkers Mtoe	Total Mtoe	Total Mbd	Aggregate Barrels per toe
OECD	1832.2	70.99	1903.2	40.6	7.79
North America**	873.3	27.7	901.1	19.8	8.02
Europe**	650.2	36.0	686.2	14.1	7.50
Pacific**	308.7	7.3	316.0	6.7	7.74*
Non-OECD	1362.9	58.2	1421.1	29.5	7.58
Transition Economies**	274.6	1.5	276.1	6.0	7.93
Africa	96.9	8.3	105.2	2.2	7.63
China	163.9	2.6	166.5	3.3	7.23*
Other Asia**	362.6	22.4	385.0	7.9	7.49
Latin America**	281.5	8.6	290.1	6.0	7.55
Middle East	183.4	14.7	198.1	4.1	7.55
World	3195.1	129.2	3324.3	70.1	7.70

* The figure for China appears to be too low and that for OECD Pacific appears to be too high. These figures need further investigation.

** Pending submission of the detailed historical data needed to incorporate them into the OECD, the following OECD countries are shown in the IEA Oil Market Report (until August 1998) in the relevant non-OECD regions: the Czech Republic and Poland in Non-OECD Europe, Korea in Other Asia and Mexico in Latin America. Note also that, whereas the OMR mbd includes marine bunkers, the IEA mtoe does not.

Sources: Mtoe data are taken from the IEA statistical databases and the Mbd (million barrels per day) are taken from the Oil Market Report (OMR) dated 11 May 1998.

Gas

The general conversion factor used throughout the Outlook for gas is

1 trillion cubic feet of gas (tcf) = 23.31 million tonnes of oil equivalent (Mtoe)

or equivalently
1 Mtoe = 0.0429 tcf

In each of the three OECD regions gas has historically been measured using different units, a general guide to these different regional gas units vis-à-vis a tonne of oil equivalent is shown below.

Natural Gas

	Net Tonne of Oil Conversion Factor*
United States	42.9 thousand cubic feet ($103ft^3$)
OECD Europe	1270 cubic metres (m^3)
Japan	0.855 tonnes of LNG

* e.g. 1 toe = 42.9 thousand cubic feet of gas.

Coal

Trying to estimate conversion factors for coal is particularly difficult as they depend on the precise definition of coal used and the mix of different coals within the total. Details of how the IEA defines coal are shown above in the above Energy Definitions section. Comparing the Domestic Supply data for 1995 in original units, as shown in Energy Statistics of OECD Countries 1995-1996 (the 'red book'), with the Total Primary Energy Supply Mtoe data for 1995 shown in Energy Balances of OECD Countries 1995-1996 (the 'blue book') produces the following approximate conversion factors.

Coal	Tonnes of Coal per Tonne of Oil Equivalent*
OECD North America	1.9
OECD Pacific	2.3
OECD Europe	2.7
OECD	2.2

* e.g. 1.9 tonnes of coal = 1 tonne of oil equivalent in the case of OECD North America

Electricity

Electricity is generally measured in TWh (Terawatt hours). The conversion factor used by the IEA to convert from TWh to Mtoe is shown below:

1 TWh = 0.086 Mtoe

Regional Definitions

OECD Europe

OECD Europe comprises the following 21 countries: Austria, Belgium, Czech Republic, Denmark, Finland, France, Germany, Greece, Hungary, Iceland, Ireland, Italy, Luxembourg, Netherlands, Norway, Portugal, Spain, Sweden, Switzerland, Turkey and the United Kingdom. Although Poland joined the OECD in November 1996, at the time of writing Polish energy data had not yet been incorporated into the IEA's OECD Europe statistics. For the purpose of this Outlook, Poland is therefore included in the Transition Economies region.

OECD North America

OECD North America consists of the United States of America (US) and Canada. Although Mexico joined the OECD in 1994, it has been included in the Latin American region for modelling purposes.

OECD Pacific

The region includes Japan, Australia and New Zealand. Although the Republic of Korea joined the OECD in 1996, it has been included amongst other East Asian countries for modelling purposes. At the time of writing the Republic of Korea's energy data had not yet been incorporated into the IEA's OECD Pacific statistics.

Transition Economies

This region covers the countries of non-OECD Europe (Albania, Bulgaria, Romania, Slovak Republic and Former Yugoslavia) and the Former Soviet Union (Armenia, Azerbaijan, Belarus, Estonia, Georgia, Kazakhstan, Kyrgyzstan, Latvia, Lithuania, Moldova, Russia, Tajikistan, Turkmenistan, Ukraine and Uzbekistan). Although an OECD country since November 1996, Poland is also included here because at the time of writing Polish energy data had not yet been incorporated into the IEA's OECD Europe statistics. For statistical reasons, this region also includes Cyprus, Gibraltar and Malta.

China

This region comprises the whole of the People's Republic of China, including Hong Kong, which became a Special Administrative region of China in 1997. China excludes Chinese Taipei.

East Asia

East Asia includes the following countries: Brunei, Democratic People's Republic of Korea, Indonesia, Malaysia, Myanmar, Philippines, Singapore, Republic of Korea, Chinese Taipei, Thailand, Vietnam, Fiji, French Polynesia, Kiribati, Maldives, New Caledonia, Papua New Guinea, Samoa, Solomon Islands, and Vanuatsu. In the IEA statistics, many small countries of Asia and Oceania are merged together under the category of Other Asia. Since Afghanistan and Bhutan are included in the Other Asia aggregate, it was not possible to separate them out from the rest of Other Asia. Afghanistan and Bhutan have therefore been excluded from the South Asia region. The following Asia and Oceania countries have not been considered due to lack of data: American Samoa, Cambodia, Christmas Island, Cook Islands, Laos, Macau, Mongolia, Nauru, Niue, Pacific Islands (US Trust), East Timor, Tonga and Wake Island.

South Asia

The South Asian region includes India, Pakistan, Bangladesh, Sri Lanka and Nepal. For statistical reasons, Afghanistan and Bhutan are included in East Asia rather then South Asia (see the above definition of East Asia for further details).

Latin America

This region includes the following countries: Argentina, Bolivia, Brazil, Chile, Colombia, Costa Rica, Cuba, Dominican Republic, El Salvador, Ecuador, Guatemala, Haiti, Honduras, Jamaica, Mexico, Netherlands Antilles, Nicaragua, Panama, Paraguay, Peru, Trinidad/Tobago, Uruguay, Venezuela, Antigua and Barbuda, Bahamas, Barbados, Belize, Bermuda, Dominica, French Guiana, Grenada, Guadeloupe, Guyana, Martinique, St. Kitts-Nevis-Anguilla, Saint Lucia, St. Vincent-Grenadines, and Surinam. The following countries have not been considered in this Outlook due to lack of data: Aruba, British Virgin Islands, Caymen Islands, Falkland Islands, Montserrat, Saint Pierre-Miquelon and Turks, and Caicos Islands.

Africa

Africa comprises the countries of North Africa (Morocco, Algeria, Libya, Tunisia and Egypt), the Republic of South Africa, and all countries of Sub-Saharan Africa, except Comoros, Namibia, Saint Helena, and Western Sahara, which have not been considered due to lack of data.

Middle East

The Middle East region is defined as Bahrain, Iran, Iraq, Israel, Jordan, Kuwait, Lebanon, Oman, Qatar, Saudi Arabia, Syria, United Arab Emirates and Yemen. It includes the neutral zone.

MAIN SALES OUTLETS OF OECD PUBLICATIONS
PRINCIPAUX POINTS DE VENTE DES PUBLICATIONS DE L'OCDE

AUSTRALIA – AUSTRALIE
D.A. Information Services
648 Whitehorse Road, P.O.B 163
Mitcham, Victoria 3132 Tel. (03) 9210.7777
Fax: (03) 9210.7788

AUSTRIA – AUTRICHE
Gerold & Co.
Graben 31
Wien I Tel. (0222) 533.50.14
Fax: (0222) 512.47.31.29

BELGIUM – BELGIQUE
Jean De Lannoy
Avenue du Roi, Koningslaan 202
B-1060 Bruxelles Tel. (02) 538.51.69/538.08.41
Fax: (02) 538.08.41

CANADA
Renouf Publishing Company Ltd.
5369 Canotek Road
Unit 1
Ottawa, Ont. K1J 9J3 Tel. (613) 745.2665
Fax: (613) 745.7660

Stores:
71 1/2 Sparks Street
Ottawa, Ont. K1P 5R1 Tel. (613) 238.8985
Fax: (613) 238.6041

12 Adelaide Street West
Toronto, QN M5H 1L6 Tel. (416) 363.3171
Fax: (416) 363.5963

Les Éditions La Liberté Inc.
3020 Chemin Sainte-Foy
Sainte-Foy, PQ G1X 3V6 Tel. (418) 658.3763
Fax: (418) 658.3763

Federal Publications Inc.
165 University Avenue, Suite 701
Toronto, ON M5H 3B8 Tel. (416) 860.1611
Fax: (416) 860.1608

Les Publications Fédérales
1185 Université
Montréal, QC H3B 3A7 Tel. (514) 954.1633
Fax: (514) 954.1635

CHINA – CHINE
Book Dept., China Natinal Publiations
Import and Export Corporation (CNPIEC)
16 Gongti E. Road, Chaoyang District
Beijing 100020 Tel. (10) 6506-6688 Ext. 8402
(10) 6506-3101

CHINESE TAIPEI – TAIPEI CHINOIS
Good Faith Worldwide Int'l. Co. Ltd.
9th Floor, No. 118, Sec. 2
Chung Hsiao E. Road
Taipei Tel. (02) 391.7396/391.7397
Fax: (02) 394.9176

**CZECH REPUBLIC –
RÉPUBLIQUE TCHÈQUE**
National Information Centre
NIS – prodejna
Konviktská 5
Praha 1 – 113 57 Tel. (02) 24.23.09.07
Fax: (02) 24.22.94.33
E-mail: nkposp@dec.niz.cz
Internet: http://www.nis.cz

DENMARK – DANEMARK
Munksgaard Book and Subscription Service
35, Nørre Søgade, P.O. Box 2148
DK-1016 København K Tel. (33) 12.85.70
Fax: (33) 12.93.87

J. H. Schultz Information A/S,
Herstedvang 12,
DK – 2620 Albertslung Tel. 43 63 23 00
Fax: 43 63 19 69
Internet: s-info@inet.uni-c.dk

EGYPT – ÉGYPTE
The Middle East Observer
41 Sherif Street
Cairo Tel. (2) 392.6919
Fax: (2) 360.6804

FINLAND – FINLANDE
Akateeminen Kirjakauppa
Keskuskatu 1, P.O. Box 128
00100 Helsinki

Subscription Services/Agence d'abonnements :
P.O. Box 23
00100 Helsinki Tel. (358) 9.121.4403
Fax: (358) 9.121.4450

*FRANCE
OECD/OCDE
Mail Orders/Commandes par correspondance :
2, rue André-Pascal
75775 Paris Cedex 16 Tel. 33 (0)1.45.24.82.00
Fax: 33 (0)1.49.10.42.76
Telex: 640048 OCDE
Internet: Compte.PUBSINQ@oecd.org

Orders via Minitel, France only/
Commandes par Minitel, France exclusivement :
36 15 OCDE

OECD Bookshop/Librairie de l'OCDE :
33, rue Octave-Feuillet
75016 Paris Tel. 33 (0)1.45.24.81.81
33 (0)1.45.24.81.67

Dawson
B.P. 40
91121 Palaiseau Cedex Tel. 01.89.10.47.00
Fax: 01.64.54.83.26

Documentation Française
29, quai Voltaire
75007 Paris Tel. 01.40.15.70.00

Economica
49, rue Héricart
75015 Paris Tel. 01.45.78.12.92
Fax: 01.45.75.05.67

Gibert Jeune (Droit-Économie)
6, place Saint-Michel
75006 Paris Tel. 01.43.25.91.19

Librairie du Commerce International
10, avenue d'Iéna
75016 Paris Tel. 01.40.73.34.60

Librairie Dunod
Université Paris-Dauphine
Place du Maréchal-de-Lattre-de-Tassigny
75016 Paris Tel. 01.44.05.40.13

Librairie Lavoisier
11, rue Lavoisier
75008 Paris Tel. 01.42.65.39.95

Librairie des Sciences Politiques
30, rue Saint-Guillaume
75007 Paris Tel. 01.45.48.36.02

P.U.F.
49, boulevard Saint-Michel
75005 Paris Tel. 01.43.25.83.40

Librairie de l'Université
12a, rue Nazareth
13100 Aix-en-Provence Tel. 04.42.26.18.08

Documentation Française
165, rue Garibaldi
69003 Lyon Tel. 04.78.63.32.23

Librairie Decitre
29, place Bellecour
69002 Lyon Tel. 04.72.40.54.54

Librairie Sauramps
Le Triangle
34967 Montpellier Cedex 2 Tel. 04.67.58.85.15
Fax: 04.67.58.27.36

A la Sorbonne Actual
23, rue de l'Hôtel-des-Postes
06000 Nice Tel. 04.93.13.77.75
Fax: 04.93.80.75.69

GERMANY – ALLEMAGNE
OECD Bonn Centre
August-Bebel-Allee 6
D-53175 Bonn Tel. (0228) 959.120
Fax: (0228) 959.12.17

GREECE – GRÈCE
Librairie Kauffmann
Stadiou 28
10564 Athens Tel. (01) 32.55.321
Fax: (01) 32.30.320

HONG-KONG
Swindon Book Co. Ltd.
Astoria Bldg. 3F
34 Ashley Road, Tsimshatsui
Kowloon, Hong Kong Tel. 2376.2062
Fax: 2376.0685

HUNGARY – HONGRIE
Euro Info Service
Margitsziget, Európa Ház
1138 Budapest Tel. (1) 111.60.61
Fax: (1) 302.50.35
E-mail: euroinfo@mail.matav.hu
Internet: http://www.euroinfo.hu/index.html

ICELAND – ISLANDE
Mál og Menning
Laugavegi 18, Pósthólf 392
121 Reykjavik Tel. (1) 552.4240
Fax: (1) 562.3523

INDIA – INDE
Oxford Book and Stationery Co.
Scindia House
New Delhi 110001 Tel. (11) 331.5896/5308
Fax: (11) 332.2639
E-mail: oxford.publ@axcess.net.in

17 Park Street
Calcutta 700016 Tel. 240832

INDONESIA – INDONÉSIE
Pdii-Lipi
P.O. Box 4298
Jakarta 12042 Tel. (21) 573.34.67
Fax: (21) 573.34.67

IRELAND – IRLANDE
Government Supplies Agency
Publications Section
4/5 Harcourt Road
Dublin 2 Tel. 661.31.11
Fax: 475.27.60

ISRAEL – ISRAËL
Praedicta
5 Shatner Street
P.O. Box 34030
Jerusalem 91430 Tel. (2) 652.84.90/1/2
Fax: (2) 652.84.93

R.O.Y. International
P.O. Box 13056
Tel Aviv 61130 Tel. (3) 546 1423
Fax: (3) 546 1442
E-mail: royil@netvision.net.il

Palestinian Authority/Middle East:
INDEX Information Services
P.O.B. 19502
Jerusalem Tel. (2) 627.16.34
Fax: (2) 627.12.19

ITALY – ITALIE
Libreria Commissionaria Sansoni
Via Duca di Calabria, 1/1
50125 Firenze Tel. (055) 64.54.15
Fax: (055) 64.12.57
E-mail: licosa@ftbcc.it

Via Bartolini 29
20155 Milano Tel. (02) 36.50.83

Editrice e Libreria Herder
Piazza Montecitorio 120
00186 Roma Tel. 679.46.28
Fax: 678.47.51

Libreria Hoepli
Via Hoepli 5
20121 Milano Tel. (02) 86.54.46
Fax: (02) 805.28.86

Libreria Scientifica
Dott. Lucio de Biasio 'Aeiou'
Via Coronelli, 6
20146 Milano Tel. (02) 48.95.45.52
Fax: (02) 48.95.45.48

JAPAN – JAPON
OECD Tokyo Centre
Landic Akasaka Building
2-3-4 Akasaka, Minato-ku
Tokyo 107 Tel. (81.3) 3586.2016
Fax: (81.3) 3584.7929

KOREA – CORÉE
Kyobo Book Centre Co. Ltd.
P.O. Box 1658, Kwang Hwa Moon
Seoul Tel. 730.78.91
Fax: 735.00.30

MALAYSIA – MALAISIE
University of Malaya Bookshop
University of Malaya
P.O. Box 1127, Jalan Pantai Baru
59700 Kuala Lumpur
Malaysia Tel. 756.5000/756.5425
Fax: 756.3246

MEXICO – MEXIQUE
OECD Mexico Centre
Edificio INFOTEC
Av. San Fernando no. 37
Col. Toriello Guerra
Tlalpan C.P. 14050
Mexico D.F. Tel. (525) 528.10.38
Fax: (525) 606.13.07
E-mail: ocde@rtn.net.mx

NETHERLANDS – PAYS-BAS
SDU Uitgeverij Plantijnstraat
Externe Fondsen
Postbus 20014
2500 EA's-Gravenhage Tel. (070) 37.89.880
Voor bestellingen: Fax: (070) 34.75.778

Subscription Agency/ Agence d'abonnements :
SWETS & ZEITLINGER BV
Heereweg 347B
P.O. Box 830
2160 SZ Lisse Tel. 252.435.111
Fax: 252.415.888

NEW ZEALAND – NOUVELLE-ZÉLANDE
GPLegislation Services
P.O. Box 12418
Thorndon, Wellington Tel. (04) 496.5655
Fax: (04) 496.5698

NORWAY – NORVÈGE
NIC INFO A/S
Ostensjoveien 18
P.O. Box 6512 Etterstad
0606 Oslo Tel. (22) 97.45.00
Fax: (22) 97.45.45

PAKISTAN
Mirza Book Agency
65 Shahrah Quaid-E-Azam
Lahore 54000 Tel. (42) 735.36.01
Fax: (42) 576.37.14

PHILIPPINE – PHILIPPINES
International Booksource Center Inc.
Rm 179/920 Cityland 10 Condo Tower 2
HV dela Costa Ext cor Valero St.
Makati Metro Manila Tel. (632) 817 9676
Fax: (632) 817 1741

POLAND – POLOGNE
Ars Polona
00-950 Warszawa
Krakowskie Prezdmiescie 7 Tel. (22) 264760
Fax: (22) 265334

PORTUGAL
Livraria Portugal
Rua do Carmo 70-74
Apart. 2681
1200 Lisboa Tel. (01) 347.49.82/5
Fax: (01) 347.02.64

SINGAPORE – SINGAPOUR
Ashgate Publishing
Asia Pacific Pte. Ltd
Golden Wheel Building, 04-03
41, Kallang Pudding Road
Singapore 349316 Tel. 741.5166
Fax: 742.9356

SPAIN – ESPAGNE
Mundi-Prensa Libros S.A.
Castelló 37, Apartado 1223
Madrid 28001 Tel. (91) 431.33.99
Fax: (91) 575.39.98
E-mail: mundiprensa@tsai.es
Internet: http://www.mundiprensa.es

Mundi-Prensa Barcelona
Consell de Cent No. 391
08009 – Barcelona Tel. (93) 488.34.92
Fax: (93) 487.76.59

Libreria de la Generalitat
Palau Moja
Rambla dels Estudis, 118
08002 – Barcelona
(Suscripciones) Tel. (93) 318.80.12
(Publicaciones) Tel. (93) 302.67.23
Fax: (93) 412.18.54

SRI LANKA
Centre for Policy Research
c/o Colombo Agencies Ltd.
No. 300-304, Galle Road
Colombo 3 Tel. (1) 574240, 573551-2
Fax: (1) 575394, 510711

SWEDEN – SUÈDE
CE Fritzes AB
S–106 47 Stockholm Tel. (08) 690.90.90
Fax: (08) 20.50.21

For electronic publications only/
Publications électroniques seulement
STATISTICS SWEDEN
Informationsservice
S-115 81 Stockholm Tel. 8 783 5066
Fax: 8 783 4045

Subscription Agency/Agence d'abonnements :
Wennergren-Williams Info AB
P.O. Box 1305
171 25 Solna Tel. (08) 705.97.50
Fax: (08) 27.00.71

Liber distribution
Internatinal organizations
Fagerstagatan 21
S-163 52 Spanga

SWITZERLAND – SUISSE
Maditec S.A. (Books and Periodicals/Livres
et périodiques)
Chemin des Palettes 4
Case postale 266
1020 Renens VD 1 Tel. (021) 635.08.65
Fax: (021) 635.07.80

Librairie Payot S.A.
4, place Pépinet
CP 3212
1002 Lausanne Tel. (021) 320.25.11
Fax: (021) 320.25.14

Librairie Unilivres
6, rue de Candolle
1205 Genève Tel. (022) 320.26.23
Fax: (022) 329.73.18

Subscription Agency/Agence d'abonnements :
Dynapresse Marketing S.A.
38, avenue Vibert
1227 Carouge Tel. (022) 308.08.70
Fax: (022) 308.07.99

See also – Voir aussi :
OECD Bonn Centre
August-Bebel-Allee 6
D-53175 Bonn (Germany) Tel. (0228) 959.120
Fax: (0228) 959.12.17

THAILAND – THAÏLANDE
Suksit Siam Co. Ltd.
113, 115 Fuang Nakhon Rd.
Opp. Wat Rajbopith
Bangkok 10200 Tel. (662) 225.9531/2
Fax: (662) 222.5188

TRINIDAD & TOBAGO, CARIBBEAN TRINITÉ-ET-TOBAGO, CARAÏBES
Systematics Studies Limited
9 Watts Street
Curepe
Trinadad & Tobago, W.I. Tel. (1809) 645.3475
Fax: (1809) 662.5654
E-mail: tobe@trinidad.net

TUNISIA – TUNISIE
Grande Librairie Spécialisée
Fendri Ali
Avenue Haffouz Imm El-Intilaka
Bloc B 1 Sfax 3000 Tel. (216-4) 296 855
Fax: (216-4) 298.270

TURKEY – TURQUIE
Kültür Yayinlari Is-Türk Ltd.
Atatürk Bulvari No. 191/Kat 13
06684 Kavaklidere/Ankara
Tel. (312) 428.11.40 Ext. 2458
Fax : (312) 417.24.90

Dolmabahce Cad. No. 29
Besiktas/Istanbul Tel. (212) 260 7188

UNITED KINGDOM – ROYAUME-UNI
The Stationery Office Ltd.
Postal orders only:
P.O. Box 276, London SW8 5DT
Gen. enquiries Tel. (171) 873 0011
Fax: (171) 873 8463

The Stationery Office Ltd.
Postal orders only:
49 High Holborn, London WC1V 6HB
Branches at: Belfast, Birmingham, Bristol,
Edinburgh, Manchester

UNITED STATES – ÉTATS-UNIS
OECD Washington Center
2001 L Street N.W., Suite 650
Washington, D.C. 20036-4922 Tel. (202) 785.6323
Fax: (202) 785.0350
Internet: washcont@oecd.org

Subscriptions to OECD periodicals may also be
placed through main subscription agencies.

Les abonnements aux publications périodiques de
l'OCDE peuvent être souscrits auprès des
principales agences d'abonnement.

Orders and inquiries from countries where Distribu-
tors have not yet been appointed should be sent to:
OECD Publications, 2, rue André-Pascal, 75775
Paris Cedex 16, France.

Les commandes provenant de pays où l'OCDE n'a
pas encore désigné de distributeur peuvent être
adressées aux Éditions de l'OCDE, 2, rue André-
Pascal, 75775 Paris Cedex 16, France.

12-1996

IEA PUBLICATIONS - 9, rue de la Fédération - 75739 PARIS CEDEX 15
PRINTED IN FRANCE BY JARACH-LA RUCHE
(61 98 22 1P) ISBN 92-64-16185-6 – 1998